RED WAVE

An American in the Soviet Music Underground

JOANNA STINGRAY & MADISON STINGRAY

DoppelHouse Press | Los Angeles, California

RED WAVE
An American in the Soviet Music Underground
By Joanna Stingray & Madison Stingray

FIRST ENGLISH EDITION

All photographs taken by Joanna Stingray and Judy Fields,
unless otherwise noted.

Book and cover design: Kourosh Biegpour
Typesetting and photo editing: Carrie Paterson

Publisher's Cataloging-in-Publication Data

Names: Stingray, Joanna, 1960-, author. | Stingray, Madison, 1996-, author.
Title: Red wave : an American in the Soviet music underground / Joanna
    Stingray and Madison Stingray.
Description: Los Angeles, CA: DoppelHouse Press, 2020.
Identifiers: LCCN: 2020936483 | ISBN: 9781733957922 (pbk.) |
    9781733957946 (ebook)
Subjects: LCSH Stingray, Joanna, 1960-. | Rock musicians--Biography. |
    Sound recording executives and producers--Biography. | Subculture-
    -Russia (Federation) | Subculture--Soviet Union. | Music and
    youth--Soviet Union. | Punk rock music--Russia (Federation) |
    Punk rock music--Soviet Union. | Popular music--Political aspects-
    -Soviet Union. | Popular music--Social aspects--Soviet Union.
    | Rock music--1981-1990. | Rock music--1991-2000. | BISAC
    BIOGRAPHY & AUTOBIOGRAPHY / Music | BIOGRAPHY
    & AUTOBIOGRAPHY / Personal Memoirs
Classification: LCC ML420.S8474 2020 | DDC 780.2/092--dc23

◆ DEDICATIONS ◆

I am forever grateful to Boris Grebenshchikov, for helping to make me who I am and for giving me a purpose at a very naive, young age. I was blessed to be taken under his wing and to have his warmth fuel my own work and love.

Viktor Tsoi, one of the truest friends one could hope to have in life. His honesty, his laughter, his kindness are always within me. His wings will forever hug the sun over St. Petersburg.

Sergey Kuryokhin, my "Capitán," my "papa," who inspired me to live life with a fire in my bones and to push boundaries. He taught me to not be afraid of the universe and the big dreams that come out of it.

All my cultural *tovarishees*, thank you for showing me true freedom and filling my heart and soul with the most magnificent colors. You surrounded me with fun, creativity and love that overwhelmed and inspired me. *MIR and Rock 'n Roll!!*

Contents

◆ INTRODUCTION ◆

I still remember the day I fell down the rabbit hole. It was April 1984, and I had just landed at Sheremetyevo airport in Moscow. Everywhere I looked, it was dark, cold, and lifeless, and walking through the concrete halls I felt empty and tense. It seemed like I was walking forever, farther and farther from home and the palm trees that had been the bookmarks to my life.

I arrived at the customs area with long lines of grim people waiting their turn silently. Everywhere I looked there were motionless soldiers, more like mannequins or stuffed bears than real people. Were they even breathing? Was I? I inhaled. On my tongue, the cigarette smoke mixed with the warm odor of a hundred bodies packed together.

The next three days that followed, I was still falling. Moscow out of the bus window was a grey and sullen ghost, yet full of life. People in black or dark blue raced through the city streets. I remember thinking that this was a place to which I would never come back, an evil empire of despair behind the Iron Curtain. My father, for what felt like the first time, was right.

On the fourth day, I arrived in Leningrad to more monotonous views of a drab country. The dirty glass of the bus made it feel like a moving prison, the rote history from the watchful guide like the morning prayers for a flock of fallen angels. During an afternoon break back at the 'tourist' hotel I decided I had had enough, and through a maze of maneuvers I landed at the feet of the father of 'underground' Russian rock 'n roll, the magical Boris Grebenshchikov. I remember being in his apartment, and he was this real person in front of me with color in his eyes and his cheeks. I was listening to Russian rock, this crazy soundtrack to life and love and loss, and I felt it – I had finally arrived in my Wonderland.

From that moment, my whole life changed. I found myself in Leningrad's underground rock music and art scene, a chaotic, captivating world – a piece of the Soviet Union tucked away like a heart beneath the ribs. From the moment I met Boris and all the other creative pirates, I was hooked on this place that turned misery into music and suffering into song. The next four years of my life I spent continent-hopping across the Atlantic, alternating one week in that enchanted land of contradictions and fairy tales with three months in Los Angeles trying to claw my way back.

All that creative energy and powerful emotion drove me to want to share Leningrad's beautiful music and art with the West. I smuggled out my friends' music and released a double album titled *Red Wave – Four Underground Bands from the U.S.S.R.* "Music has no borders" became my mantra.

As I fell head over heels into the crazy tea party, in love with the guys, the city, and the country as well, I found a way to warm the coldness on the streets of communist Russia, to peel back the masks to see expressions of individuality and life. It was clear to me that the reason these musicians could be so creative and artistic was because they had nothing else to do to distract them. The American dream had been abandoned for sitting in front of the television like a vegetable in a microwavable dinner, but in the Soviet Union these guys still had to make up their own dreams to entertain themselves.

By 1987, the U.S.S.R. was in the thick of *glasnost* and *perestroika*, and it was unclear what the final destination culturally would be. By that time, I had become a hero to the Russian youth and an enemy of the Russian state, had my visa blocked and my wedding missed, been questioned by both the FBI and the KGB. But by the end of that year, I had somehow managed to marry Yuri Kasparyan, and Gorbachev had managed to divorce himself from the chains of the old guard. The dramatic changes left everything and everyone, including me, waiting to see what would happen next.

What scared me was that in Mother Russia, the one thing that never changes is the unpredictability of what's to come.

For a dozen years, from April 1984 through April 1996, I was obsessed with Wonderland and its people, who infused the city with an electricity even when the power would inadvertently cut out. I tried to spend as much time as I could soaking it all in, until the rabbit hole would spit me out and close, seemingly forever. The following story is my own recollection of those experiences in Russia, occasionally supported by press articles and some of the many taped interviews I conducted during those times, and my memories of all the adventures that I got to share with the most wonderful cast of characters.

◆ **1984–1987** ◆

♦ The Truth About Communism

I was six or seven years old when my dad turned to me and said, "Don't ever, ever go behind the Iron Curtain."

I have vivid memories from the mid-'60s of him sitting in his warm, woodsy office making a movie, a documentary called *The Truth About Communism* that he wrote, directed, and produced. It consumed his life for three or four years – splicing and dicing reels and reels of film, cutting, taping, and throwing remnants on the floor like empty bags of potato chips. He was extremely passionate about the U.S.S.R., with Ronald Reagan at his back narrating the film and making one of his first public statements against the Evil Empire as then-Governor of California. *The Truth About Communism* became a well-known anti-communist propaganda piece in the late 1970s, shown at high schools around the country, including mine. I believed my dad, his voice sticking in the back of my mind for years like a little alarm clock hidden under a pile of pillows.

Yet at that time, Russia still wasn't a real part of my life. I spent my early years in Topanga Canyon in the Santa Monica Mountains, traipsing through the hills and biking to school or following my mom as she dragged me and my sisters to every musical that came through Los Angeles. She divorced my father when I was twelve years old, moving us to a rented duplex in Beverly Hills on the wrong side of the nicest theoretical railroad tracks in the world, where palm fronds littered the overgrown yard and the hum of Wilshire Boulevard came down from the north. It was a block from Beverly Hills High School, the center of my thoughts in those days. Government corruption, impossibly long food lines, and KGB intimidation? I was more concerned with my big feathery hair, ditching classes, and stealing as many frozen brownies from my best friend's fridge as I could fit in my stomach.

Besides my father, my only exposure to Russia came from a class I loved on Russian history. In the late 1970s, the State Department endorsed educational exchanges with the U.S.S.R., and one incredible teacher of mine took it upon himself to plan a week-long trip there over winter break. My best friend Diana was going, and I was desperate to join her, in part because I knew how much it would piss off my Communist-hating father and in part because I didn't want to be left out of any adventure. My mom worked a ton of extra hours like always to try to send me on the field trip, but in the end I was back in the duplex while everyone else boarded a plane and was swept away, leaving me with my bike and such a severe disappointment that I wouldn't forget that feeling for years.

I was lucky enough that I didn't have to wait to go to Russia to get my first exposure to rock 'n roll. My high school boyfriend, Paul, introduced me to the music that David Bowie called "dangerous" and "darker than ourselves." It was the only thing that could eclipse all of my egocentric problems and teenage angst and make me feel like there was power in the world that could sway even the tallest of giants. Paul was a ticket scalper – a tall, street-smart guy paying a bunch of strange characters to camp out in line for days to buy the best seats. I sat in the front row for David Bowie, The Rolling Stones, Alice Cooper, Elton John, and Paul McCartney & Wings, to name a few. I loved every hot and heavy night pressed against the stage, feeling the music shake the hoops in my ears, and I was absolutely crazy about Bowie. There was something about his charisma, his side-eye glances and sultry shrugs, and the way he shone in metallic like some sort of fallen angel. He made me want to perform, made me believe that it was something worth living.

The first band I joined was managed by my friend Jeff Smith, who'd collected a group of decent musicians with dirty hair and cheerful eyes. Standing at the front with an oversized microphone and silly curly hair, I was a typical high school singer who could belt like a caribou and couldn't stay in tune; I had the look, I had tons of energy, but I also had no idea what I was doing.

Jeff's father, Joe, ran Capitol Records. Back then it was the big time, a dizzying thirteen-story tower on Hollywood Boulevard and Vine that loomed over the tourists and wannabee sweethearts with its big sign and disinterested attitude. Jeff lived in a big house on Roxbury Drive in Beverly Hills, and we'd go over there to practice inside the ivy and brick. His father came into the 'smoking room' to hear us bang around and jump up and down like we were the big hits on tour already – talk about putting your father into

■ My father Sidney Fields and Alexander Kerensky filming *The Truth about Communism*, early 1960s.

an awkward position! We were barely good enough to play at our high school talent show, but Jeff dragged his father in as if his dad was supposed to sign us right then and there.

Joe, to his credit, sat through whatever terrible song we had decided to play and just kept nodding along in time. At the end he looked up and said, "You know what kids? You just have to keep practicing. If you want it badly enough, you'll keep at it and you'll get better and better."

It was the first time I'd ever received constructive criticism as an artist, if you could call me that. I really took it to heart, holding it with me as I bounced around college and sang in the tiny moldy shower stalls that plagued the quintessential American dorm buildings. I went to USC on a diving scholarship, then to Boston University for a change of pace, where the cold stoked a fire under me to transfer back to UCLA and finish out my degree in the land of perpetual summer and smog. If you'd have told me then I'd spend over a decade of my life bundled up against the Siberian cold, I would have told you that you couldn't pay me enough money.

In the summer of 1981, during my stint at UCLA, I went to work at a clothing store. Admittedly, that was not remotely close to what Joe had in mind when he'd encouraged me to practice singing. Within days I was bored out of my mind, locked into a monotonous routine of work: eat, sleep…work, eat, sleep. I decided then and there that I would never ever have a regular 9-to-5 job. However hard I needed to practice, however many notes I had to crack and sharps I had to sing, I would do it.

Within weeks, my best friend and I decided that we should try to start another band.

The Go-Go's were an all-girl group from Los Angeles who had become famous, so we figured, in that typical La-La-Land daydream, that we could be too. We decided that she'd learn the guitar and I'd sing. I also wanted to write music, like Bowie, which is no small feat if you can't play an instrument very well. I struggled through it, crumpled copious amounts of paper, but I did manage a couple of brainless, youthful songs called "Beverly Hills Brat" and "Boys, They're My Toys."

In my mind, this was it. I wanted to quit college and be a rock 'n roll star. My mom was remarried to an incredible self-made lawyer, real estate developer, art collector, and well-known philanthropist. Both of them saw my plans as at the very least, idiotic and at the very worst, self-destructive. My mom's face went sheet-white as she stared at me and asked, "Do you have any idea how lucky you are that your stepfather is paying for you to get an education?" She threatened to cut me off if I didn't finish my degree, so with no better option I stuck with it. In the back of my mind, though, I was going to be a rockstar.

I slogged through class and procrastinated by writing songs. By the time I graduated in 1983, I had a handful that I thought could put me under the neon lights on the Sunset Strip. I recorded an EP with my old high school friends, and with my demo in hand I shopped around to get a record deal like a woman out of the seventeen-hundreds trying to barter silver for gold. Through my old boyfriend, Paul, I met Marshall Berle, comedian Milton Berle's nephew. With his long, thin face and oversized sunglasses, he became my manager and released my EP on his small independent label, Time Coast Records. Marshall was pretty well connected and before long we'd talked a few people into investing in my career. I re-recorded "Beverly Hills Brat" as my first single, and we shot a video between the palm trees and gated mansions, rolling down the wide streets in a Rolls Royce and me with wild hair. The record came out and was available for purchase in Tower Records, a store I consequently frequented daily as I stood in front of my EP, welling with pride and smiling happily and hopefully at every punk, hipster, and businessman that walked by.

I went on a small promotional tour and played a few intimate shows here and there, but my biggest splash was at Studio 54. It was 1983, when New York was bursting out of its glossy reputation and full of soul, grit, and artistic expression that manifested itself in sequins, bright colors, and twisted feral faces.

Years prior, my mom and stepdad had hosted a party at their house for Andy Warhol, where I asked him to sign the Rolling Stones' *Sticky Fingers* album cover that he'd designed, and he drew a vagina instead. Somehow, I managed to reconnect with him inside Studio 54's white paneled walls, and he eventually connected me with the club's

■ At my Studio 54 performance, October 4, 1983, with my former boyfriend, Paul Gomberg.

■ Flyer for my Studio 54 performance.

management. At midnight on October 4, 1983, with the city that never sleeps dancing outside, Studio 54 played the video to "Beverly Hills Brat" as I lip-synched on a high bridge that moved out over the twinkling crowd. I felt like I had made it, like I was stardust falling in everyone's eyes.

Unfortunately, my American rock career would only last a few months. My manager Marshall had taken the money we raised together, from *my* friends and contacts, and invested in Ratt, a heavy metal band with tattoos, long hair, and eyeliner. My high-flying stardust days were over.

I had put everything into those few songs, positive I'd succeed with Joe Smith's mantra in my head that if I tried hard enough, I could get there. It was the first time in my life that everything had fallen apart, like some half-baked pie that crumbled before you could get it on the plate. I was devastated and depressed, holed up in my dark room screaming at my mom and hating the world because I had no idea what to do next. Eventually, with my manager gone, my mother fed up, and my friends on their own professional paths, I picked up the phone and called my sister Judy who was studying abroad in London. Across a continent and an ocean, she hadn't had the chance to get sick of me yet.

"I need a change of scenery," I told her. "I'm going crazy stuck over here. Can I come visit?"

"I don't know," she replied, her voice far away. "I'm going on a school tour to Russia, Moscow and Leningrad. It's only three hundred dollars with all expenses paid."

It was the beginning of 1984 at that point. With Ronald Reagan in the White House, the State Department had started aggressively pushing for more educational and cultural exchanges as an almost subversive way to show Soviet citizens that Americans were freer, richer, and happier. Memories of my missed high school opportunity to go to the U.S.S.R. flooded back, mingling with the anxiety over my rockstar career that stung so strongly it was like a frying pan to the face.

"I want to go."

She checked if there was space, which there was. When I was confirmed on the trip, I had no idea what a pivotal moment in my life this would become – I was just so relieved to avoid another dull department store job for at least a few months. I picked up the phone again and called my best friend from high school to tell her that I was finally off to see the Soviet Union.

"Um *hello*, my sister married a Russian emigrant!" She reminded me. She gave me his name, Andrei Falalayev, whom I invited to lunch to talk about my trip.

"You have to meet my buddy," were the first words out of his mouth as he slid into a plastic red booth at the deli. "He's amazing. Are you going to Leningrad?"

"That's the plan," I said. "I'm not sure if we'll be able to leave the tour though."

"He's the most famous underground rockstar in Russia. Everyone loves him."

"I didn't know rock existed in Russia," I laughed, wondering what could compare to the American stars I'd heard. "How would I get a hold of him?"

As you would maybe expect of an underground, grit-and-grin type of guy, Andrei's buddy didn't have a phone, but his friend did. I took a name and number, saying I'd try to track him down.

"You've got to be careful, Joanna," Andrei said. "These guys aren't *supposed* to hang out with foreigners. It's considered illegal activity." He leaned forward across his plate of pancakes and the sticky table, as if sharing a secret. "But Boris Grebenshchikov doesn't care."

◆ Down the Rabbit Hole

We walked off the flight, through passport control, and into an arrival hall flanked by a line-up of grizzled, stone-faced guards with rifles. I had a flashback of walking into a diving competition, the chill of the large enclosed space and the feeling that everyone, their heads ducked down and their bodies flexing, is against you. Without even thinking, I began rolling my shoulders, my athletic ritual I thought I'd long forgotten. I had never enjoyed those competitions, and I didn't enjoy it now.

The guards took our bags under the floor-to-ceiling fluorescent lights and left to go through everything, pawing clothes aside until all that was left were the suitcases' bones. Judy and I stood there, side by side, shifting from one foot to the other as time became yet another foreign concept. I hated the thorny feeling of being powerless, much like I imagine it feels to visit a place like North Korea today.

After they handed us back our bags, we boarded the bus and drove to the Cosmos Hotel, which was still about twenty minutes from the center of Moscow. It was a gloomy, deserted, and desolate place, stuck on an ugly street corner. I asked a woman for directions to the elevator to get to my room, and she just stared at me like she was watching paint dry and peel away from a wall. Tapping into my survival mode, I found the elevator myself.

When I unpacked, I realized just how much my suitcases had been absolutely raided. The airport luggage handlers had taken my hairdryer, tampons, toothpaste, lipstick, and everything else that they couldn't easily get. Oddly enough, they didn't touch my album

■ Touring Moscow, April 1984.

cover or press photos I'd brought to show Boris how a real rockstar plays the game. In hindsight I should have taken it as a sign that the Moscow airport customs agents preferred my tampons over my album!

The tour group reconvened downstairs, where they drilled into our heads that we had to stick with the tour at all times. If we didn't, our little denim butts could be kicked out on the next overnight flight. I could tell the rules were very, very important to our Communist ringmasters, a hard pill to swallow for someone who had been driving since fourteen and sneaking out of high school weekly.

We spent three days in Moscow, which might as well have been three days on a different planet, surrounded by Moscow's bold communist-era murals and statues that glorified hard work and community. They were captivating and colorful like some sickening delusional drug. There were no advertisements, no billboards, no big street signs, just generic words in Russian on the buildings that said things like "*apteka*" (pharmacy) or "*bulochnaya*" (bakery) in block letters. The people wore blues and grays like bruises on their bodies, few smiled, and no one waved back at me. Everyone seemed unhappy to be there, waiting in the long public lines for their medicine and bread. The whole city felt cold, unwelcoming, and rigid.

Soon, though, I began to notice an artistic side to Moscow too, the sparkling eyes of an otherwise scowling and disinterested city. We saw historical landmarks, museums, buildings, and city parks, many of which were designed before the Communist revolution and still retained that flirty nostalgia of a previous time. The onion domes of St. Basil's

Cathedral were psychedelic in a stormy sea of dormant colors. Little by little, I could sense that somewhere deep down, the underbelly of the Soviet Union was warm and vibrant, hidden under all the metal armor. The country had obviously conditioned itself throughout the Communist era to accept a characterless chill, but there was still a rich culture underneath the unnerving facade. I found myself wishing the Russian people could celebrate their colorful side, wishing that someone could crack a smile or spill a laugh. It made me angry to see how people bought into this official Communist Moscow mentality. I remember thinking then that my father was basically right, that the Soviet Union was an awful place overrun by gargoyles and that I'd never want to visit again.

On the fourth day, we went on to Leningrad. Right away, it was obvious that the city had an energy and excitement that was much easier to find than Moscow. There was more color, soft yellows and pale blues and deep greens reflecting off the silvery canal waters and brightening the more Baroque and neoclassical architecture and onion-domed churches. My discontent was suddenly replaced by wonder, the dark blanket of the city more enchanting than sinister, like something out of a Siberian fairy tale.

As soon as we checked into the hotel, I told my sister that I was going to try to find this rocker guy Boris. I was sick of the official tour, locked into a glacial itinerary of statues and parks. This new city felt inspiring, and looking for Boris sounded like a challenge to spice things up. If they caught me away from the tour, would I really get sent home? I felt pretty confident I'd be fine, a born-and-bred American, with exceptionalism running through my veins.

I learned very quickly that nothing is easy in the Soviet Union. My sister Judy and I walked up to the old Russian *babushka* stationed on our floor, a government minder and local viceroy in charge of everything that went on in her domain, including full jurisdiction over whether or not two wide-eyed American girls could place a phone call or not.

"Hi, I'm Joanna." I gave her a huge bubbly smile. She didn't budge.

Hmm. "I. Would. Like. To. Make. A. Phone. Call." I said more seriously, trying to annunciate every word.

She watched me as I got out the piece of paper with the number.

"Please. Call. This. Number. Thanks." I placed it in front of her and waited for what seemed like hours, chewing the inside of my lip.

Finally, she grunted, which I counted as success. Boris didn't have a phone, but his cello player, Seva Gakkel did. After a few rings, a woman answered with a simple hello: "*Dobre dan.*"

"Hi, I'm Joanna from California! Is Seva there?"

Click.

I looked back at Miss Congeniality, shrugged my shoulders, and slid the phone number back across the desk to her. Heaving a sigh, she dialed again.

"Hello?" It was a male voice this time, and in English.

"Hi!" I practically shouted, rushing to catch him before I heard the ugly click of the line. "My name is Joanna, and I'm from America, and my friend Andrei told me to call you to get in touch with his friend Boris. I'm a musician too!"

"Ah yes, where are you staying?" He asked. He was not a native speaker but spoke fluently and quickly with a soft Russian accent that made every word he said seem considered and significant. I tried to pronounce the name of the hotel, the Moskva.

"Come to the big metro station around the corner by your hotel at five p.m.," he said, and hung up. That was that. We had our invitation.

My sister and I looked at each other. Judy didn't wait for me to say anything before asking, "Wait, we're going to leave the tour?"

"Why not?"

"We can't, we'll get in so much trouble," she said, proving that the tour operators' message had been well received by at least some of us.

"I don't know what to tell you," I said. "I really want to go. We've just got to bite the bullet."

"There are real bullets here, Joanna…"

I cut her off. "We'll just say we're not feeling well and that we have to stay in and go to bed early tonight."

Little did anyone suspect that after the group had gone out, Judy and I were sneaking downstairs and out the back door of the brutish building, leaving our beds made and empty. Without knowing a word of Russian, we found our way to the metro station. I had no idea what to do next, waiting as hundreds of people pushed past us on their way home at rush hour. They were a sea of dark, brooding ships dragging along the concrete. We stood as still as possible next to the main exit, my hands in my pockets, wrapped around my passport and wallet. For the first time since I'd gotten there, I felt the tingling sensation in my body that reminded me I was a real human and capable of anything.

"Did he say what he looked like?" Judy asked me.

"He hung up before I could ask."

"Well it's a good thing you stand out." She glanced at my bleach blonde bangs and shaved sides. I looked like I fronted a punk band with some obscure name and angsty setlist.

And then, there he was. I knew it was Boris immediately. At first glance he was practically indistinguishable from every other Russian, buried in a typical winter fur hat and long tweed coat. But we locked eyes, and I just *knew* in that moment that a very special person, a magical person, was entering my life. I didn't know how or why, but I could just feel that I would never be the same ever again.

"Hello, nice to meet you," Seva said from behind Boris. I looked at him long enough to notice his long face and thoughtful blue eyes. But once my eyes met Boris' again, they never left. It was like looking into the sun long enough that you always see it directly in front of you.

Seva and Boris grabbed Judy and me by our arms and kept moving.

"We're going to my place," said Seva as he pulled me along through the crowd. His long legs took one stride for every two I took. "We can talk there. We aren't supposed to meet with foreigners. You never know who's an informant."

I glanced at him in disbelief. Did he really think anyone would assume I was a threat with my dangling budget earrings and mismatched layers?

He lowered his voice. "I'm serious." He pulled Judy and me aside into a covered doorway. Boris leaned casually against it, nodding along as Seva instructed us, "Don't speak English in public, and never tell anyone you're an American." He pulled at his short beard with his thumb and pointer finger. "Come on, we have to get out of the street."

We started walking briskly again. "You're here on a tour, yes?" he asked. Judy nodded.

"If anyone ever catches you out in public alone, tell them you were separated from your tour, yes? Best to avoid trouble."

It was hard at that first meeting to understand the gravity of what he was saying. In that moment I was blinded and enamored; there was something about the way Boris walked and the soft hidden smile always resting on his face that made me feel powerful and passionate in Lenin's City, that turned the grey clouds to silver.

Seva's apartment was in the center of Leningrad in a Stalinist neoclassical building that was slumped and dull. The main entrance and stairs were all plain grey concrete, everything leaning slightly to one side as if the building itself were exhausted. Seva's apartment felt lived in, full of antique trinkets on the walls that reminded me of my grandparents' house. An acoustic guitar hung on the wall. Just inside the main door sat a bench filled with a bunch of *tapki*, or slippers. No one ever walked around their apartment in shoes. As I looked through the bench to find a suitable pair, I noticed that much like the building, most of the *tapki* looked old, worn, and lived in.

The kitchen door swung open and a woman rushed past us to leave.

"Who was that?" I asked Seva.

"My mom."

"Can I meet her?" Without even realizing it, meeting Seva and Boris had started me on a quest to get under the impassive exterior of the Soviets.

"Not now. Maybe next time."

Judy and I settled around a small, fabric-covered table with Boris while Seva brought out pickles, cookies, and cups of umber tea. The ceilings stretched up three meters above him while he moved around the space backlit by the tall windows. There were two main rooms that I could see, a large gathering room with a smaller lumpy bed and a proper bedroom, with a small bathroom and an even smaller kitchen shoved at odd angles into the apartment. I felt warm and happy; the whole thing was somehow festive with the heavy clouds and cold air pressing up against the windows. Russian hospitality was something that would always feel as welcoming and wholehearted as it did on that first visit, every single time. The contrast between Russians in public and in private could not have been more striking, like jumping between an ice bath and a hot tub.

The bedroom was covered in Seva's posters, several of which were of The Beatles and John Lennon, as well as several deep and faded religious icons hung over the white walls or a faded tapestry. They were surrounded by necklaces and other beaded wall decorations, like something out of a sepia '70s photograph. There's a great photo of Seva in his bed beneath the potpourri of pictures, draped in a patterned blanket with a bandanna wrapped around his forehead.

Seva himself looked like a cross between George Harrison and Jesus Christ, complete with long shadowy hair and a dark mustache and beard. He had a low-key vibe and a casual cadence to his posture. His words were direct in a way that made me feel I had his full attention and consideration, the same with the small smile that reached his eyes. Sitting across from him and Boris that first time, I saw the two could really not be more different. Unlike Seva's subtle seriousness, Boris had an unguarded, spontaneous attitude. He was gorgeous in a way that made me stop and stare, reminding me perpetually of David Bowie with his flowing blonde hair that framed his angular chin and bright blue eyes. He had an exceptional spirit that overwhelmed his chiseled physical stature and made him appear ten feet tall even just lounging next to me.

To my surprise, Boris' English was as good as Seva's. As we talked, Boris pulled out a piece of white paper and an old plastic film can. He poured grass from the can on the paper, licked it, rolled it, lit it, and smoked. I thought he was smoking a joint, but when I asked, he said it was called a papirosi cigarette. The smoke was sweet and transparent, and it framed his face in this angelic way that made him seem even more supernatural.

■ Me, Boris Grebenshchikov, and Seva Gakkel at Seva's apartment, Leningrad, April 1984.

"How in the world is your English so good?" Judy asked.

"We had four of the best teachers in the world: Elvis, Dylan, Lennon, and McCartney," said Boris, trying to curtail his witty smile. He went on, "When you listen to their records every day, you start to wonder what they're saying. Then you get a bilingual dictionary and just start looking up words. It's not that hard really."

"How do you get their records?" Judy asked.

"First we listened on short wave radio from London. But the black market has almost everything," said Seva.

"We don't just listen," Boris said. "We sing the songs too. Anyone who plays music will probably speak at least basic English. After I found The Beatles, I started reading American poets like Jack Kerouac and Allen Ginsberg."

I widened my eyes and nodded like I was also a big fan, but in reality, I had only the faintest idea of the sultry spirited figures who wore those names. All I remembered from university was the semester at sea I'd taken across the world, dipping my toes into the Mediterranean but never into *On the Road* or *Dharma Bums*. These guys knew more about my culture than I did.

"Every once in a while," Boris continued, "someone gets their hands on an American movie, and we all gather around to watch it."

"But tell us about your music, Joanna," said Seva. "We'd love to hear it."

I played "Beverly Hills Brat" and "Boys They're My Toys" on my Walkman. Boris listened on the headphones, leaning back on the worn sofa with one leg tossed carelessly across his other and his eyes closed.

"This is really good," he said. "But what is a brat?"

I explained that they were the rich kids with whom I'd grown up, the posers and the players with their shiny cars and upturned noses.

"Ha! We don't have that problem here," Seva said. He took the plastic headphones. "I agree, I like it."

"Do you have any of your music?" I asked, happy with the feedback and wanting to offer some of my own.

"Yes, but only on cassette, not on a record like yours," Boris said. "We don't have access to a studio. We need someone who works at a real studio to borrow a tape machine for the weekend. If someone gets hold of a tape recorder for a couple of days, everyone shows up to record. The tapes are copied and distributed all throughout the country. Sometimes we even make artistic covers, just like in America."

"Why can't you record in a real studio?" I asked.

"We're not an 'official' band," Seva said.

"Some groups have signed government contracts. They can play in public and get paid," Boris said. "They have access to studios and high-quality instruments, and they can release music on Melodiya, the only record label in Russia."

"Why don't you do that?" I asked.

Boris paused and leaned forward, like he was simultaneously teaching a lesson to a child and sharing a secret with me, as if he'd known me our whole lives. "Because 'official' bands have to turn over their lyrics first to the government. They're censored. That makes them dull. But everyone has to have a government job here, so for some, being in an 'official' band is a job like any other. I used to be a night watchman. It was great – if I worked twenty-four hours straight, I could take the next five days off. It gives me time to play. Now I am a music tutor, and I work when I want. I might play my own music illegally underground, but I'm more free this way. It's really not so bad." With everything he said, there was always that slight smile tugging at his lips or some deeply contained laughter lighting up his eyes, like he was slightly amused by everything and never took the world too seriously.

I put on my headphones as Boris slid the cassette into my Walkman and pressed play. From the first chord that filled my head, the music was haunting and spiritual, and when Boris sang his voice was piercingly distraught and absolutely consuming. The music was driving and frenetic, a wolf howling or a waterfall blasting over boulders and down an eighty-foot drop, and even though I didn't understand a word I felt enlightened and magnified. It felt deep, grand, and intense, conveying simultaneous alternate realities of despair and hope, sadness and joy, darkness and ecstasy. It was pure. It was Boris.

I blushed and sank back in my chair, hit by a hard combination of embarrassment and panic as a warm and almost nauseous feeling came over me. Here I was, thinking I was some big-shot American rocker from Studio 54 over whom all these repressed Russian musicians would drool, but I could not have been more wrong. In that moment, I realized that I was not an artist, but instead just some silly kid with sugary dreams, writing dumb songs about my high school classmates. Boris had more talent in one song than I could ever hope to have in my entire body. It was like a strike of lightning illuminating the world of music for me, and I finally understood the power, resonance, and backbone of what an incredible song should be.

As we began to wrap up, Boris leaned into me and said, "I'm going to play at an underground concert tomorrow night if you can sneak out again. I'd love to have you there. It is not our rock band, but a crazy experimental evening led by Sergey Kuryokhin, or 'Capitán' as he's better known." He pronounced it Cap-ee-TAN, that glimmer still in his eyes.

"It will be incredibly unpredictable," Seva said excitedly.

◆

Of course, I wanted to go. I felt that nothing would be meaningful until I could hear more of this music and see more of these guys who seemed to experience life on a deeper, esoteric level. The next day, Judy and I again told our tour guide that I wasn't feeling well and Judy would have to stay and take care of me. We snuck out around eight in the evening and met one of Boris and Seva's friends around the corner from the hotel with the sun still bright above us. She nodded at me, which I took as a signal to follow her. We were as discreet as possible, never speaking a word of English and doing our best to look as cold and indifferent as we could. I caught Judy's eye out of the corner of my eyes, and we shared a quick-lived smile.

The friend led us to what looked like an abandoned old house, cracked and sighing with a slanted roof and covered windows. We entered into a room where the exposed rusted pipes looked ready to burst in the white brick and the windows were covered with oversized black fabric. If this building had been anywhere back in Los Angeles, there would have been a giant "condemned" sign on the front door.

The room's key attribute was its large size. The hosts had set up about forty mismatched wooden chairs that were all filled. Boris wrapped his strong hand around the neck of a cello and attempted to play it, awkwardly holding the bow like a fork. A few other musicians hit drumsticks and dug their heels into the ground to keep time with him. One guy played

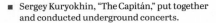

■ Sergey Kuryokhin, "The Capitán," put together and conducted underground concerts.

■ Boris playing cello at the first underground concert I went to in Leningrad, April 1984.

the electric bass guitar without electricity while Sergey conducted with a saxophone in his mouth, all behind a contraption of hanging weights and irons that sounded like a synthesizer. Unlike Seva and Boris' quieter demeanor, Sergey Kuryokhin was a rambunctious, childlike, and mischievous streak of movement and light. He had a young angular face but was already a master at his craft and in complete control of utter madness. It was such an eclectic sound that I wondered for a moment if it could be called music, but somehow all this jumbled chaos transformed into something palpable and vibrant that filled up my entire being. This art, this transformational experimentalism, was the purest form of creation and existence I had ever felt in my life.

The 1980s in Leningrad was similar to what I heard about the hippy '60s in America, a time all would come to reminisce about decades later with a sparkle in their eyes and the taste of euphoria still on their tongues. It was one of the best nights of my life, and looking back, it was the moment I realized I was witnessing something extremely special and surreal. My new friends were incredible musicians, but they were artists as well and capable of forging these intense and intimate experiences through paintings, dancing, poetry, and so on. They found ways to fill the long empty days of communistic enterprises by this type of indirect protest, producing imagery, lyrics, and movements that bonded participants and shaped solidarity. My sister Judy and I looked at each other and knew we had to capture this momentum and perception of the world, subsequently taking film, pictures, and interviews of our new friends as much as possible in the time that followed. This damp underground

■ Kolya Vasin told us that he sent a telex every year for John Lennon's birthday and one year Yoko and John sent him back a signed album. It was one of his prized possessions.

scene off a side street in Leningrad was the eye of a storm, surrounding us with an electric and overpowering energy that was inescapable.

After the show, Boris and Sergey took me to meet their friend Kolya Vasin, better known as "The Beatles Guy." His room in a communal flat was filled with what had to be over a thousand Beatles items: oversized posters, colorful records that were still only available from the Russian black market over twenty years after release in the West, portraits and buttons and magnets with those four iconic faces bright and open and ready to start singing in the very language Judy and I were generally forbidden to speak. I'd never seen anything like it, nor met anyone as dedicated and devoted as Kolya. With flushed cheeks he told us that he had been sending a telex to John Lennon every year for his birthday and one year he received a signed album back from John and Yoko.

Kolya was nothing like I expected when I had been told about "The Beatles Guy." He was big and burly with a dark tousled beard and mustache that concealed a large reoccurring grin. He couldn't have been more jovial. He didn't know English except for what he learned from Beatles song lyrics, so that's what guided our conversations as he served us warm food and drinks that spilled over the rims of the glasses.

"Thank you so much for dinner, Kolya," I said.

"Johnny!" he responded, pronouncing my name as so many Russians perceived it. "All you need is love!"

"True, all you need is love, Kolya." I responded. "I loved the dinner."

"Johnny! I am the walrus!" was his reply.

He pointed towards an overstuffed harlequin scrapbook he'd made of John Lennon's life and gestured like he was writing a signature in midair. As I looked through it, I realized that he'd had all his guests sign the name "John Lennon" across the wide white pages. He smiled at me as I signed my own version.

Sergey Kuryokhin was there too. In these early days, Sergey would end up hanging around with Boris and me most nights I was in Leningrad. It didn't hurt that, like me, he didn't smoke or do drugs, a rarity among the Russians. He drank – he wouldn't be Russian if he didn't – but that was the extent of his vices. I was first drawn to him because of his endless energy and expressive enthusiasm.

"Jo," he'd say, working against the language barrier, then he'd make a funny face, yelp, or grunt to convey his thoughts. He was just about the most evocative person I'd ever met.

Sergey was a genius, and he knew it. Everyone did. He constantly had musical ideas floating through his head like shiny jellyfish on an open endless ocean. His foot was always tapping or his fingers moving and jumping as if they were playing some imaginary piano. I don't know when he slept. He was transcendent – whether it was official rock artists, underground bands, classical musicians, jazz performers, the intelligentsia, or music critics, everyone respected and loved Sergey Kuryokhin.

That first night I met him is still one of my favorite experiences, full of dazzling strangers and indelible memories. As Judy and I were wrapping up to sneak back to the hotel, The Beatles Guy looked at me beaming and shouted, "Strawberry fields forever, Johnny!"

We were scheduled to leave the next day, but I couldn't get on the plane without saying one more goodbye to Boris. We arranged to meet again in the street, camouflaged between the grim barreling bodies of the working world, and he led me to his place. He lived on the top floor of an old smirking building that had flights and flights of stairs. He floated up like the angel he was as I desperately tried to keep up, huffing and puffing my platinum hair out of my face. There were hundreds of drawings and writings on the stair walls, yellow and red and black portraits and poetry offered to the guru of rock 'n roll where fans would sometimes even stand and serenade. As the apartment door swung open, a bunch of people scattered out of the kitchen to their bedrooms. The only one left was the one face I knew: Seva.

"It's a communal flat," Boris said. "It's difficult to get an apartment, especially in the city center, so most people live bunched together like this."

"Why are they running away?"

"You can get in trouble for talking to foreigners, but if people go into the bedrooms, they technically didn't see you. It's an alibi. I can almost guarantee that the KGB will stop

■ Me and Boris, sitting on the rooftop of his apartment building, Leningrad, 1984.

by after you leave."

I tried to ignore that thought as we sat down to the sweet cookies and bitter tea Boris put out. Boris again rolled a papirosi. I normally hated cigarette smoke, but Boris' didn't bother me. I found myself inhaling deeply, trying to imprint the savory scent in my brain as I listened to Boris' voice.

"There was a banker guy here a few months ago who said he worked with David Bowie. He took some of my recordings and supposedly Bowie heard them and liked them. He asked if Bowie could buy me something I needed. Could you find him again? He could help me."

"I'll try. Do you have his number?" Boris gave it to me.

"I want to come back." I said. "I think you have an incredible gift. People in America should hear your music, and I want to help you. If I can come back, what could I bring?"

"Many have said they'll come back," Seva said. "They never do." He gave a small shrug and held up his hands.

"I'm coming back." I could think of nothing else. I hadn't even left, and already I was planning when, not if, I'd return. The brief encounters I had with these musicians, the unpolished silver heart of the city, had already clued me in to what I never knew I was missing back home. Up until that point I'd been content to float through life without ever really grounding myself. These guys, Herculean in spirit and mind, were my saving grace. For the first time, I felt the novelty of purpose: both the inspirational purpose these men had for their music, and the motivational purpose for me to get back to this place, where I was learning what it was to be human and consequently what it was to be myself.

That morning before leaving the hotel to find Boris, I thought of giving him a present from America as a way for him to remember me while I was gone. I thought of the Western alcohol bottles he collected along his bedroom shelf, drained and shiny, or the Bob Dylan poster on the wall. What could I give him that he hadn't already started collecting? I remembered him mentioning that he had never seen red sneakers like my red Converse All Stars and my big, baggy jeans with enough pockets to store an entire orchestra. I knew the shoes would be too small, but I brought them with me and gave them to him. I watched him squeeze and twist and turn his feet until he forced them in and tied up the tight white laces, then doing the same dance with my jeans.

"It's perfect," he said. He didn't know that years later I would be taking fashion queues from him, loading cool silver rings with big colored stones onto my fingers and falling in love with the striped t-shirts he used to wear. His style was so Bohemian, reminding me of the freedom of the open seas which I would cross to come back to Russia and Boris again.

"You still didn't answer me," I said, returning to the moment. "If I can come back, what else do you want? And what do you want me to tell Bowie you need?"

"A Fender Stratocaster guitar." He said it as if he had known his whole life that's what he wanted, and when I promised I'd ask, his cheeks pushed into his eyes as he smiled.

I asked Boris then if I could interview him on my Walkman. It would be the first of many interviews over the years, an excerpt of which is printed here.

Before we said the final goodbye on that first trip, Boris said he wanted to take me to church. It was Orthodox Easter, and Boris was on paper a Christian and in spirit, a sage of acceptance, tolerance, and knowledge. I'd grown up in a household with a mother who had been raised Catholic and a father who had been raised Jewish, resulting in a religious impasse that had left me suspicious of and unresponsive to its ability to heal or incentivize. I agreed to go with Boris anyway. Religion was technically illegal in Russia, but like many things in Russia it had become unofficially tolerated. Standing outside the soft orange building I could tell his eyes, like Seva's, doubted me as we hugged goodbye. He had no way of understanding that as I walked away, watching him in my jeans, red shoes, and bandanna tied casually over his golden hair, I finally felt like I had faith in something. He was the light, and like any sane, instinctual creature, I wanted to follow the light.

That's how it started. For the next twelve years, Russia became my life as I made good on my promise and returned again and again. It was the first time I think an American had proved Boris and Seva wrong.

◆ Interview with Boris Grebenshchikov

Joanna – How did the band get started?

Boris – The band started around 1972 with one of my childhood friends. We had no amplification and didn't care about it. We just began to write our own songs, and we got an idea of forming a band. The people just began to drift around us, and some good musicians began to appear – so it happened. Nobody ever tried to do something to request somebody – just friends and friends of friends happened to be good musicians, and right now we have very good players.

Who writes the songs?

I write 99% of them, but we arrange the music together. I just put out an idea – play something. I think I'll go that way and that way, and then we begin to rehearse when we rehearse. We don't usually rehearse.

Would you leave the country now if you could?

I think what I'm doing here is very needed. The people need what we are doing, and if we won't do it, nobody will do it. We are just beginning, right now, to create a place for ourselves in this social structure. It is a shame that previously there was no place for people like us. Before it was – you either just conform to what everybody's doing and to the way of doing things or you just stay in your ethical place, do what you want but nobody hears about it. Right now, with what we are doing we are getting bigger and bigger and instead of stopping us – um, well – they can stop us at any given time…

How?

They could put us in jail or something, but we are talking about right now and to do this kind of thing would be out of hand. They would like to have some reason to do this, but they have no reason. Still, we are trying not what everybody in official arts is doing but quite opposite things. Maybe fifteen years ago it was impossible.

Why is it possible now?

Because nobody quite understands what is going on. Nobody knows for sure what will be the next official line in art, so just to be on the safe side they have a little bit of everything, and we are trying not to be a little bit but a really bigger and bigger bit.

How do you get your music heard?

We are one of the first bands in Russia who began to do our own music and put it out on tape. Everybody in this country has a ¼-inch tape player. When we started it in 1980, we made our own covers, and every tape which I give to somebody or sell, or something gets copied and the copies begin to circulate wider and wider all around the country. Right now, I get letters from all over Russia, even from the most eastern cities like Vladivostok and Khabarovsk in Siberia near Japan and the people - they are listening to what we are doing, especially lots of young people. We are getting bigger and bigger, and I'm interested to see where this gamble will lead us because really it is a gamble. We do our own thing, and the government tries from one side to hush us and from to the other to cooperate. The government is not centralized enough to have one opinion on anything. Some people are for us and others are against us. At this point we've managed to survive somehow, and it's a very funny thing – now when we're beginning to be real rockstars, in terms of popularity and autographs and all this stuff, we are not getting any money.

Is this a problem?

No, not really because when you worry about money you do nothing, and we've carved a place for ourselves in this wall – this stone wall where we manage to live.

What about concerts – where do you play and how is it all arranged?

You see we have a very funny kind of organization right here for the last two years. It's called the Rock Club, and the members are just all the amateur (underground) bands. It is sponsored by the KGB.

It's sponsored by the KGB?

Yes, but it is unofficial of course. It is something like a trade union of non-professional rockers because all the professionals are playing pure shit – one hundred percent shit, and the non-professionals are trying to experiment.

What does the Rock Club do?

They give out permission to play. For every concert we play we take out a lot of papers and we go there and there and put stamps and signatures on it. But, at last we receive permission to play. The Rock Club also lends us instruments and sound equipment, although they make it very difficult to get anything decent.

Do you have to show them the lyrics to your songs?

Of course. They go through them – but again the system is very funny because they pay attention only to the lyrics. You can play any kind of music.

What happens if they check your lyrics, say they're okay and then while performing you change them?

I've done this a lot of times.

What happened?

It depends – but usually nobody pays any attention.

Do they have KGB watching in the audience?

Uh huh, of course.

Are the kids afraid of this? Can they dance and get excited?

They can get excited but only sitting in their seats, or else some administrator or cop or somebody comes and stops them or throws them out.

How many people are usually at the shows?

It depends but usually three or four hundred. Sometimes it's bigger.

How do the kids find out about the concerts?

Word of mouth.

Is it free?

No. You see the organization which lends the place sells tickets and they take all the profits. We receive nothing because we are not official.

Do you have to organize it through the Rock Club?

Yes, you're supposed to but sometimes you play underground and it's even better.

Where is underground?

Not an auditorium but at someone's house or something.

Can you play outside Leningrad?

In principle we can play anywhere.

So ... they are going to clamp down on you or...

They will try to buy us.

Try to buy you with money?

Uh huh.

To stop playing?

No – to just start playing what they think is good. Many of our friends who were underground bands got offers from official organizations to become official musicians and play the music the government wants.

Do they check your mail?

Uh huh – sometimes. They do everything sometimes. Sometimes they don't look, sometimes they do, and sometimes letters just don't get to me. It all happens totally spontaneously. They're very unpredictable.

Is your phone tapped?

I don't have one anymore, but my mother's phone is.

Are more kids forming bands?

Yes and while ten years ago everybody was content just listening to Western rock and trying to copy it, recently people began to realize that they could do stuff in Russian and they could record their own music. And even though the quality would be poor – still it would be recorded. Ten years ago, nobody thought about it or dreamed it could be done. Now in every city throughout Russia the people are beginning to record their own music and to circulate it. I've heard some bands from unimaginable towns of Siberia and everywhere. They are playing not always different music, but still it's their own thing and some people are beginning to get better. Ten years ago, it was a question of whether ten bands from Leningrad and Moscow could get in the system and become professionals – to

■ Me interviewing Boris, Leningrad, November 1984.

have professional status and money.

Right now, nobody gives a shit about all these things. Everybody's playing and recording. It looks a little like the situation was in England around 1976–77. Everybody's discovering they can do what they want. Actually it's quite funny, because much good can come of it – the person first begins to listen to the music, then begins to try and imitate something that he can do in his own material and he'll begin to play for larger audiences – more and more people are hearing about him, and when he's confronted with all that energy which a performer gets from the audience, he begins to think what is this image and he begins to think for himself. Usually, people do not think – they do what they're supposed to do, and I hope that all this music which is being created will change the way of thinking. Previously, they just tried to imitate what's going on. You had hippies, then we had hippies; you had punks, now we have punks; and I think that maybe it will change and the young people here will try and discover what they are, who they are, and they will do what they want to do and do it how they want it to be done, and they will discover themselves – to begin to live! That is what I am hoping for – to awaken them, to make them free in their own lives.

You said earlier that the KGB offers money to some underground bands to get them to play "good" music...

You see really the KGB are the best organization right now in this country in terms of they know that all that's happening will be happening anyhow – so at least right now when it's semi-official they can control it a little and they can know what's happening and when it's underground they can't control it and it's really in the interest of that country that all this young music and young energy will come out because this country is stifled because nobody wants to do anything – not the workers, not the government, nobody. Nobody wants nothing and the young people are beginning to discover that they want something, they want to be someone, they don't want to live in slumber all their lives – get drunk every evening, go to work every morning, and that's it, day after day. And the reason for this situation is that nobody wants any changes right now high up. They're content with finishing their lives because theirs is very good – every one of them at the top. They want to live their lives as it always was. They don't want any changes. Some other persons in the KGB and other commissions are beginning to understand that maybe it's not the best way to run it – maybe there can be a better way. When you edit this better not mention KGB too much.

Because they're being okay? They're trying to be helpful?

Really, they're not okay, of course, 'cause it's the same shit everywhere.

I guess if they act like they're trying to help you, then they can suppress you.

Yes because it's all a question of the wing – of the person who is in charge right now. The KGB is just not thinking about all this stuff – they're just letting it be – to help us. Mind control – that's all they want. To know what's happening – who is saying what, who is thinking what and who is doing what.

But what happens when it gets too big?

They can just put a person out – somehow if they don't want somebody to do it.

What about Aquarium? You guys are the biggest – what's going to happen?

You see I don't know what can happen because it's always unpredictable. But right now, they are trying to integrate us. They're trying to live with us because if they just put us out, the young people will be discouraged, and they will try to do something not in the way the government wants. So, they're trying through us to somehow control the youth 'cause they just want that we want what they want from us. They want it so we won't touch all this governmental sacred stuff. So we won't sing about politics and sing offensive words – so we will just go quietly. You do what you want, we won't touch you – just do this and this.

Is it easy for you to do this and this?

You see it's quite easy for us right now because I won't touch these things with a hot iron, 'cause I don't want to get entangled in all this political shit again like many people have done before, and they didn't get no satisfaction out of it because it's very easy to become popular when you flirt with politics and west and east and all this. You become instantly popular overnight – people listen to you for one week exactly, and then they forget about you because nobody is interested – they know nothing will change. Anyhow, we won't sing about politics because the less you think about it, the less it concerns you. I want young people to live outside all of this.

So for you, the #1 thing is music not politics?

It's not exactly even the music – the music is just a way of expressing it. It's a too overused word, but I'm trying to put forward some spiritual abilities – "feeling" – the heart, the sincerity, and I'm interested in only to get through to people this feeling that you can feel and be sincere and you can be spiritual and can have god.

The one thing I noticed before I came to Leningrad was how the people who I saw in the streets looked like machines... Is there emotion between family members?

What's really going on behind closed doors is absolutely the same as everywhere. The people do everything that's possible and everything that's not possible. Only in the streets when all young people know that if you are doing something he may be arrested or frisked.

Are you allowed in our hotel? When we enter, we must show a card.

If you dress like you're from the West, look sure of yourself and just walk right in they don't check.

For your night watchman job, they just said – you need a job, and this is what we are going to give you?

At the time I was working as a mathematician in a sociology institute, and the band went to a music festival for the weekend and we were christened the first punk band in Russia. We were then thrown out of the festival, and when I got back to Leningrad I was fired from my job.

Did they say it was because of the band?

Yes, a letter was sent out to everyone saying that the band Aquarium plays anti-Soviet works and behaves like no Soviet citizen can behave, and they are the black sheep of all the music and public enemy #1. After I was fired from my job, I became a free person, and I was very happy.

We were told not to socialize with Russians because people around them or their neighbors will tell authorities and get them in trouble. Is this true?

Yes. My neighbors half the time tell the police Americans were here, and the other half of the time they ask to borrow my tapes to listen to my music.

Can you get anything from the black market?

If you have the money to pay you can get anything: jeans, video equipment, anything.

Is there any way for you to come visit America?

Definitely not, because right now these two countries aren't getting on well, and I think even in good times they won't let me out.

I heard every man is obligated to be in the army for two years. Were you in the army?

I was studying in the university at the time, so I was eligible to be an officer. For three or four years now they've been trying to draft me somehow. I think many of our friends never went into the army because they had brain damage or something - some excuse.

So you can get around not going quite easily?

It's not easy, because you have to go through lots of investigation – go to a crazy house or something.

You don't seem to care too much about material things. Is this because you can't get much here, or because you don't have much money?

No, you see you can get everything here if you have money, but using energy for the purpose of getting money drains everything else. If you're after money, then you have nothing except money, and if you want to do something with this money you can't because you are already drained. I needn't worry about money, and it just happens sometimes that something I need someone ends up giving to me.

Are there any girl rock singers or musicians?

No, but I would like that. Things here are still very old fashioned.

Maybe you'll be the first famous Russian rock singers in America?

I don't care about being famous, I just want to remove the borders of the world – I just want to be a man.

◆ Back in the U.S.S.R.

Before the plane touched down at LAX, I was already dreaming and scheming about how to return to the Soviet Union. I became like a crazed missionary running around the sandy beaches and Hollywood hills telling anyone who'd listen about these incredible musicians who'd changed my life. I was confident that I would return but wasn't quite sure how. In mid-1984, Gorbachev, *glasnost*, and *perestroika* were still at least a couple years away, so I had little opportunity to just hop on the next British Airways Boeing 737. I needed another sponsored educational tour, and to also raise the money to get there.

I took a job at a travel agency, thinking I could solve both problems at once by earning money while having resources to learn about every tour scheduled to head to the U.S.S.R. Finally, I found one and booked myself onto it. While I sat at my small metal desk, hiding behind a mammoth old computer and stacks of plastic, dirty travel binders, I dreamed about the looks on Boris and Seva's faces when I would show up again. They'd said no one comes back, but they'd never met someone like me.

I tried to call Seva to tell him to send word to Boris that I was coming back. After a few brief words, I heard the phone go dead and then hit a continuously busy line. Several days went by before the phone rang again for me.

"Hello. I am calling from New York," said a girl with a thick Russian accent.

"Who are you?" I asked.

"I have just come from Russia."

"Okay, great," I said. "But what's your name?"

"Boris will be waiting for you to return." She spoke as if she didn't even hear my questions. "Get pen. I will give you address."

It was that easy. She was short on answers, but I was already beginning to understand that specifics often didn't matter in the Soviet Union. If I took my hands off the driver's wheel, a plan would miraculously come together.

I dug up the contact information for Luther Gribble, the banker from David Bowie's team who had met Boris. He connected me to Bowie's management office in New York, and after sharing my photos and more of Boris' music, Bowie offered to pay for the Fender Stratocaster guitar Boris wanted! It almost didn't feel real. Bowie signed a poster to Boris as well, his classic big B and flourished scribble across his uncanny, phantasmagorical face.

My educational tour again started in London, where I met up with Judy. With her big sweet eyes and sensitive deference to the world, Judy was always searching, enamored by psychics, astrologers, self-helpers, and meditation. She got her chart done by a horoscope reader who told her that all her planets were in water and earth, and it would serve her to be around people with planets in fire. She brought them my photo, and they told her I was one of those people with my planets in flames, a strong energy that would be a good influence on her.

"I didn't have a path or purpose or anything like that," she told me recently when I asked her about why she kept letting me drag her around with me all of those years. "You had such a clear focus and passion to do something, so I thought I might as well just support you." She wanted nothing more than to help me with whatever I was doing, even if that meant squeezing into a middle seat for three hours with cheap snacks on our way to our destination.

Cold fluorescent lights and scowling customs guards in dark blue suits and flat hats again met us in the arrival hall. This time, I wasn't worried about them taking my lipstick or tampons, but I was paranoid about the Stratocaster. They went through my bag, and I could see them take interest in the guitar.

"It's my guitar, and after I go on this tour of Moscow and Leningrad I'm going to Paris because I have to play a show there, and if you take this guitar away I'm not going to be able to play and a lot of people are going to be furious," I rambled, feeling the nerves hitting my hands and spine.

The guards ignored me and called over a few other inspectors.

"Seriously, I really need that thing, please don't take it away – it's my most important possession and necessary for me to make a living, because like I just said I have this really,

really, really important concert in Paris next week after I tour here. Did you hear me?"

Five or six customs inspectors ignored me while they pointed at the instrument and muttered to each other. Finally, they motioned for the customs form I'd received on the flight. I handed it over. They began to write details of my guitar on the back of the form. They described it down to the serial number.

"When leave," the lead guard said, "bring guitar. Or not leave." What goes in must come out.

I nodded vigorously, the wheels in my head already spinning into overdrive. How was I supposed to leave the country without the guitar? The thought haunted me all the way to the hotel, where Judy and I told the guide that we were tired and would skip the afternoon touring. An hour later, we scurried out of the hotel as inconspicuously as possible, lugging the large black guitar case between us. We walked for a few blocks before we dared ask someone for directions. Having the guitar along made me feel incredible conspicuous, and every time someone so much as glanced at us sideways Judy and I were sure they were KGB and would scramble to the other side of the street or around a different corner. By the time we found Boris' building and wrestled ourselves and Bowie's gift up the daunting stairs, the only thought I had left about the guitar was that I refused to carry such a heavy and cumbersome item back through any airport with me.

Somehow, I'd find a way to leave it.

Boris opened the door smiling, like he had been casually waiting there for four months in his farmer jeans that I'd given him from the first time and a beige sweater. "Jo, Judy, welcome back, come on in." We hugged, and the two of us changed our shoes for *tapki*, following Boris into his room where Sergey Kuryokhin, Seva, and three new faces, whom I soon learned to call Afrika, Timur, and Alex, met us.

We sat down to tea and sweet biscuits as I handed Boris the guitar case. He opened it, and I saw his face freeze in that angelic expression of his, unable to comprehend what was happening.

"It's for you," I said. "A shiny Fender Stratocaster, just like you asked. David Bowie paid for it."

"What? Really?"

"I told you I was coming back…"

"Yes, but I didn't think you would. And I wasn't serious that you had to bring me this."

"Boris, I wanted to. I love that I get to help you make music."

"Thank you," he said quietly.

News of my return spread quickly through Boris' friends, so as we sat and talked, several more people I'd never met filtered into the small, dim kitchen and fogged up the windows. They surrounded us, or more accurately, they surrounded the guitar. Even though I couldn't understand them, I could understand their awe and fascination as they pointed to the pick-ups, the bridge, and the tuners.

"And here's a signed David Bowie poster," I said as I unrolled it on the small, leaning table.

"Aaaaaaall right," Boris nodded his head in ecstasy as he took it in his hands. "It is fantastic."

"I can keep bringing things you can't get here," I said excitedly. My eyes drifted to the guitar, and I stopped. "I have a problem though. The customs guards wrote down the guitar's details on the back of my customs form. Look, they noted every detail, even the serial number."

"Assa ye, ye, I wouldn't worry about that," the young kid I came to know as Afrika said.

He couldn't have been older than eighteen, with blond hair, bold eyes, and a smile that reached both his ears and overshadowed his entire, rail-thin body. He came from the south near the Black Sea, his entire being infused with the bright and sunny spirit of those lower altitudes. He spoke English well but would always greet us with "Assa, ye, ye," followed by a Young Pioneers Salute.[1] Despite his perfunctory confidence and the conviction in his voice, I doubted his ability to outsmart Soviet customs control.

"Afrika and Timur will take care of it," Boris said as he put his cigarette to his pink lips. Timur nodded, his dark hair and angular face framing his intense, active eyes. I'd find out later that he was in an underground artistic collective called the "New Artists," known now also as the avant-garde movement Neoacademism for the New Academy of Fine Arts that Timur founded.

"The important thing is that you've come at a good time," Boris continued. "Tomorrow, there's a festival at the Rock Club. A lot of bands are playing, including mine. You should come."

"It sounds amazing," I said, forcing myself to stop worrying about the guitar for the moment. "What's the Rock Club again?"

"It's what they call an official music venue that hosts unofficial bands." I could hear

---

1   Used during ceremonies to commemorate Soviet heroes, the Young Pioneers Salute is a bent right arm, right hand directly above the head, the palm flat and facing downwards, and the fingers together. It symbolizes that the interests of the People supersede all.

■ Afrika, me, and Boris, Moscow, 1984.

the mockery in Boris' voice when he said official and unofficial. "It's owned by the state, and the bands who don't sign state contracts play there. We don't get paid because the ticket money goes to the hall, and the equipment is shit." He cracked a slow, easy smile. "But we get to play live.

"The Rock Club is our home in a way. It's officially called 'The Theater of People's Creativity' and is part of the trade union system. It's an amateur theater where regular people can perform, and the KGB can keep their sharp eyes on everyone. It's run by a guy named Kolya Mikhailov. Everyone loves him, except the KGB. He has to walk a fine line."

"That's so interesting," Judy finally spoke up. I could see her listening to everything and picking at her jeans with her short nails. "But all this sneaking around is going to get us in trouble at some point."

"I know, but this is exactly why we came," I told her. "We want to see these guys live. Just think how incredible it will be! This is a once in a lifetime opportunity. Almost no one else in America knows this exists."

"Except David Bowie," Seva said with his gentle laugh.

I didn't care about getting in trouble. Making it to Boris' with the guitar had made me confident that the KGB weren't paying attention to me, and somehow that made me assume that because I had an American passport my government would swoop in to save the day the minute there was any possibility I could be sent off to a seedy Siberian gulag. In hindsight, I should have been more careful, but I'm lucky enough that I can say if I was more careful, I wouldn't be writing this story.

◆

The next day, Boris again sent one of his friends to meet Judy and me before the concert and to lead us to the Rock Club. We were used to the drill by then – no English in public, move quickly, keep your head down and your eyes glued to the dirty pavement that lined the wide roads. This time, Boris warned, the KGB agents would very likely be at the concert. Judy and I had to be inconspicuous, he'd said, staring at my platinum hair. I barely heard him. I was so crazy about these guys that Stalin himself could have airdropped into the venue, and I still wouldn't have left.

After twisting through a few long streets, we arrived at the front entrance of the Rock Club. From the outside it didn't look like anything special, with store facades on the street level and shadowy apartment windows up above. What made it stand out were the hundreds of people standing waiting to get inside. There were rocker types with wild haircuts and silver rings, students linking arms, guys in suits that I immediately presumed were the KGB, and ladies in office attire with glasses and kitten heels. Everyone was jostling and pushing like at a metro stop. As Judy and I tried to elbow our way forward, I locked eyes with a guy about my age with bleached blonde bangs the same color as my hair. We both paused long enough to recognize the similar peroxide highlights, and for the moment I stared at him, I felt the entire crowd disappear around me. My heart started ringing in my ears like a dinner bell that reminds you how hungry you are. A moment later, the crowd rushed back into my senses, and he was gone.

As I stood scanning the sea of round, indistinct faces, one of Boris' friends found us to take us backstage. Boris, his band, and various wives and girlfriends were getting ready. Clothes lay in piles tossed over metal chairs, makeup falling to the ground in black and pink clumps. For a moment I felt like I had left the U.S.S.R. behind – I could have been anywhere in the world, backstage at any concert, and no one would have guessed the difference. Boris' friend showed us a door at the end of the hall and said we should leave from there when the concert was over, a secret passage directly out to the street that would avoid the fans and the undercover authorities.

We left Boris and the rest, all half-dressed and passing around bottles, to find our seats. The hall had a beautiful neoclassical interior with a tight stage and bodies cozied up to strangers. People were absolutely everywhere, seated and standing and folded into little alcoves around the sides. There must have been some three hundred in total. I suddenly realized what a star Boris and the other performers were. His band was technically illegal, but it had evidently become very popular underground since they started recording and clandestinely distributing their music to the culturally underfed public. Somehow, they'd climbed high enough to command an audience of hundreds of people at a club that the government was forced to acknowledge as quasi-legal. I felt a thrill in my chest, knowing that out of all those rock'n roll pilgrims I had had the chance to make a connection to their messiah.

The first band was a group called Zoopark, fronted by Mike Naumenko, and the crowd immediately surged forward with an intensity for which I was not prepared. Judy and I braced against each other as people leapt from their seats, threw their hands in the air, and started dancing. To my ears, Zoopark sounded like the rock'n roll I recognized, just with Russian lyrics. Mike looked like any American rocker from the 1970s, down to his mirrored aviator sunglasses. I found out later he was one of the first rockers to write lyrics in Russian, along with Boris. I never saw much of him playing after that night; people told me he had a severe drinking problem. To be honest, there were very few Russians I met who didn't seem to have a drinking problem.

I noticed the same surge of euphoria in the crowd when the band Strannye Igry (Strange Games) followed, a new-wave, ska-type band with trumpets, trombones, and saxophones, probably six or eight members all in a line facing the audience with choreographed movements as they played. As I watched them, I was reminded of a marching band at an American football game, minus the padded shoulders and sparkling buttons. Their sound was undeniably rock though, a cross-cultural phenomenon I realized everyone came to love regardless of geography.

After the set finished, I noticed a man in a suit a few rows ahead of us. He was dressed in a boxy gray combination with thick-rimmed glasses, standing casually while the hoard of red-faced Russians jumped around him and repeatedly turning around to look at Judy and me. He had to be with the KGB, I thought. He turned around again.

"Are you Joanna?"

I didn't answer.

"Boris told me all about you."

I turned away as if I didn't hear him as paranoia set in. Was he actually Boris' friend? How did he know me? Who else around here worked for the KGB? Did Judy and I need to leave? There was a sick, strange excitement that came with knowing the KGB were curious about me, because it validated how important Boris and the other undergrounders were and how lucky I was to get to be so close to that greatness.

I was suddenly distracted again as the lights went down and the next band rushed onto the stage, their tall silhouettes already sending the crowd into an even bigger frenzy.

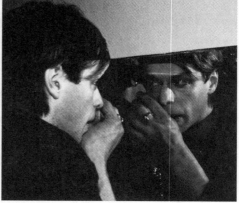

■ Viktor Tsoi, lead singer of Kino.

■ Boris Grebenshchikov, leader of Aquarium.

I made out a tall, romantic, Asian-looking singer with an angular face and a beautiful animated voice. His name was Viktor Tsoi, and his band was called Kino. He stood still, long arms by his side, and tapped his heel to the beat while looking straight into the moving belly of the audience. His undemanding posture gave him a firm command of the stage; there was no wild running or convulsing like some singers did. In standing still, he forced people to pay attention to him, to listen to the music and get carried away themselves by it all. Every note he sang was strong, steady, and textured with the shared experiences of humanity. On a slow, pulsating song called "Tranquilizer," I felt hypnotized. On another song, I couldn't understand the lyrics, but the melodies were addictive, and by the time the third chorus hit I found myself singing along. *Vedeli noche, guliali fsiu noche do ootra – Saw the night, walked all night 'til morning* – I had no idea what it meant at the time, but I couldn't stop singing.

It took me a while before I noticed Kino's drummer, a tall stunning guy who played dramatically standing up, and then the guitar player. I realized with a start it was the blonde man I'd stared at in the street before the show. I could feel that movie-magic happening again as the rest of the room disappeared and my pounding heart replaced the drumbeat. He was gorgeous. I couldn't resist watching him through the set, later discovering his name was Yuri. To me, he was Michelangelo's David: lean, muscular, and powerful.

After Kino, Judy and I cheered as Boris and his band Aquarium finally pushed onto the stage. He told me he'd stolen the band's name from a beer joint on Kupchino Street. This was the first time I heard him with the full Aquarium line-up, a drummer, guitar player, keys, violinist and bass player, and Seva the cellist. I had seen the keyboard player Sergey Kuryokhin, The Capitán, perform live in the basement show during my first trip, and I soon learned that in addition to playing in Aquarium he was also a producer for many of these underground groups and a highly respected jazz and classical pianist in his own right. In almost every video I took of the bands over the next few years, Sergey would be there in the back, his frantic magical hands and his roguish smile filling up the corners of the frame.

As always, it was Boris who caught my eye. He sauntered onto the stage with the white Fender Stratocaster hanging off his body like a piece of shining armor. All night, he traded off using it with his guitar player Sasha Liapin, and seeing it onstage made me feel proud, as if I made a very small contribution to this subtle revolution happening before my eyes.

Aquarium's set had me in chills for the entire hour. The crowd was insane over Boris, their biggest hero. The way the guitar hung from his shoulder was like watching Atlas carry the whole damn world: he looked miraculous. Aquarium played a hard driving rock song followed by a more bluesy folksong and then a stripped-down lyrical ballad. The entire crowd sang along in unison to an anthem called "*Rock 'n roll Myortv*," meaning "Rock 'n Roll's Dead." At several moments, I had to pinch myself that I was in the Soviet Union – the alleged inhospitable and melancholy archenemy – and that I had fallen in love with its rock bands.

When the final ovation died down and the crowd began slowly shuffling to the exits, Judy and I ran backstage to congratulate Boris. In the middle of our conversation, someone interrupted and pulled Boris aside with nervous eyes.

"The KGB are backstage," Boris whispered as he came back to us. I felt a sudden anxiety, not for myself but for Boris and the rest of the musicians. Had we jeopardized them by being there? "You need to leave right away."

♦

We raced down the hall towards the door that Boris' friend had showed us earlier, two deer trying to avoid the headlights of the KGB. At least we had a sure way to escape. Judy and I looked at each other as we ran side by side, giggling nervously at the close call, reaching out our arms and coming face to face with what felt like a brick wall. We pushed harder. Oh my god, I thought frantically, the door's locked. Without saying a word, Judy and I turned back around, slowing down as a man came out from one of the other dressing rooms. Taking the lead, I quickly turned right down another hall, searching for some way to get us out of there. We ended up in the main auditorium again, so we scurried down some steps and tried to blend in with the last concertgoers heading to the main exits. Moving through the tail-end of the crowd I realized I had lost Judy. I kept moving towards the exit, searching every elated face in hopes of seeing my sister's familiar button nose and blunt bangs. In a couple of seconds, I reached the doors, thinking, "At least, I'm home free."

Like two phantoms, these guys in suits rose out of the cigarette smoke and grabbed me on each arm, dragging me left away from the open doors and warm night air. Hundreds of people were moving around us, not daring to stop or say a word. These guys wore no uniform or special insignia, and they looked like they could be gangsters for all I knew. In a state of disbelief, I watched the shadows pass by as not a soul stopped to intervene or acknowledge me.

The three of us hurried down a stairwell, their long thick fingers still wrapped around my arms. They took me to a dim room with no windows and two chairs staring wretchedly at a hard metal table. It reminded me of a movie. They pointed to one of the chairs, and I sat down, shaking. Immediately they started firing questions at me, no introductions or explanations or English.

I kept repeating, "I don't speak Russian, I don't speak Russian, I don't speak Russian." They raised their voices, faces pulled tight into disturbing, bitter scowls.

"I don't speak Russian, I don't speak Russian, I don't speak Russian."

I tried to tuck a piece of platinum behind my ear and out of the way, praying they would think I was just a student with crazy hair on a long-term study abroad semester who happened to have fallen in with the Rock Club scene.

"What. Is. Name?" one asked in halting English. I clammed up.

"Your name?" His voice got louder. "Your name?" Nothing.

"What is name?!"

I knew if I gave them my name, there was a good chance I'd never be allowed back in the U.S.S.R. I kept seeing Boris' face in my mind and knew that if I said the words "Joanna Fields" that then and there everything would vanish into the thin, clammy air. In my desperation I opened my mouth and boldly blurted, "Tell me who you are, and I will tell you my name."

"Who bring you?" One of the guys lit a cigarette, his eyes cold as the hot smoke filled his mouth and nostrils.

"Why here?" The other added. I stayed silent.

"Do you know Viktor Tsoi? … Mike Naumenko? … Boris Grebenshchikov?"

"No." I said. "I don't know those names."

"Who are you?"

I didn't know what to tell them. My mind was so twisted, and my heart was running up my spine and into my throat. Practically choking on it, I heard myself spit out, "I am an American citizen. You can call the Embassy if you want to know my name."

The two guys looked at each other. They didn't seem to know what to do with me, with my scared eyes and angry, bold attitude. They said a few words to each other and then looked at me again.

"Go." One of them said, dropping his cigarette to the floor and pointing at the door.

I left quickly, following the empty hall back to the main door and rushed out into the street. I could feel the adrenaline shoving my heart against my ribs, but I was so happy to be around other people again as people drifted from the club. Not knowing what to do, I began walking up the street to burn off the energy that was making my hands tingle with nerves. A young woman fell into step with me and whispered, "You're being followed by the KGB. Walk around the city and lose them. Then come join us at the party." She recited the address quickly, then vanished like some grumpy fairy godmother before I could ask her about my sister.

With the adrenaline still sparking at my heels and the address repeating over and over in my mind, I walked a few more blocks before turning and noticing another agent in a gray suit. He put his head down, and I almost laughed at his overt method of stalking. I was just a dumb twenty-four-year-old, and even I could spot the rat on my tail. I ducked around a corner and walked a few more blocks. When I checked again, he was still there, pretending to be fascinated with the cement under his shoes. It was turning back into a bad movie – he was very obviously following me, and I was very obviously trying to outmaneuver the man. I put my hair up in a hat I'd had stuffed into my coat pocket and wandered dizzyingly around a few more blocks. When I checked again, he finally seemed to be gone. In hindsight, I think that they were trying to scare me more than anything else.

I finally showed up to the party out of breath, on edge, and exhilarated. As I pushed my way into the room, the first person I saw was Judy, listening happily to a group of musicians as they laughed over something, and acting like an only child. After the harsh reality of the night, I was more amused than anything else. I told the packed room what had happened, realizing by their entertained expressions that this was a common occurrence more than a traumatic event. It was part of Russians' lives, particularly those in the arts scene, and they had long since grown accustomed to it. In the back of my mind

■ The Sologub brothers, Grysha and Vitia, from Strannye Igry (Strange Games), Leningrad, 1984.

■ My sister Judy Fields documented many musicians and *tusofkas*, Leningrad, 1984.

though, I was starting to change my care-free attitude about security and surveillance, not to protect myself but to protect these people who stood welcoming me into the party with warm, open arms. This was the first obstacle of many that I would encounter that would threaten my time in the Soviet Union.

Boris and Sergey both hugged me tightly. "All fine?" Boris asked. Sergey's eyes were angry, unable to conceal his distaste for the KGB.

"Yeah," I told them. "I mean, it was terrifying, but all fine."

At that party I met Viktor Sologub, who went by Vitia, and his brother Grygori, or Grysha, who played the bass and guitar respectively in the band Strange Games I'd thought was so cool. Vitia's English was pretty good, making up for the few words his brother could speak with me. Vitia was a rare Russian who neither drank nor smoked, a tolerant and protective soul who watched over his brother and looked out for his friends. He talked very quickly with a certain urgency and nervousness about him, his eyes always watching the corners and back walls and all his energy thrown into checking and double-checking everything.

"That Strat you brought Boris was *krutoi*!"

"Thanks," I laughed. "What would you want if I could get it?"

"Wow," Vitia said. "A Fender P Bass. Gray."

"Okay, I can try."

"You got that, really?" He went on. "A gray Fender P Bass."

"I got it."

"Maybe write it down so you don't forget? Fender P Bass. Gray."

As the party continued, I lost the nervousness of my KGB incident and found myself face to face with one amazing person after another. There was Sasha Titov, the bass player in Aquarium with his sharp nose and curly hair, and jazz critic Alex Kan with his low voice and focused eyes. Nearly everyone spoke some level of English, or if not, Alex or Boris would help translate. Most of the time it was Alex at my arm facilitating the translations, as Boris was surrounded by all the Aquarium wives and other women lounging at his feet and laughing at his measured, easy talk. I'd come to see this at every *tusofka* – "spending time doing nothing" – in the future, with Boris on the couch and the women around him on the floor looking up and smiling with adulation and flirty devotion. It was so obvious they had crushes on him, and I remember thinking it couldn't be fun to be an Aquarium band member.

At one point in the party, Boris introduced me to a guy in a gray suit and glasses who looked strangely familiar.

"This is Arkady, one of our best poets," Boris said proudly.

I blushed; it was the guy from the concert whom I'd ignored after he said hello. "Oh my gosh, I was so rude at the concert. I thought you were KGB. I'm am so sorry." He and Boris laughed.

Off in the corner I noticed Viktor and Yuri – the guitarist with the blonde bangs who'd slipped a time bomb into my heart – of Kino. Beside them was Igor Tikhomirov, the smiley, curly-haired bass player that I would nickname Mickey Mouse as I got to know his happy, amiable attitude in my future visits. After a few minutes I tried to casually work my way over to them, interrupting the conversation to repeatedly tell them how incredible they were. They responded by repeatedly telling me how incredible Boris' guitar was. As we spoke, I noticed Viktor was the exact opposite of how he appeared on stage. Gone was the stoicism, the coldness, the dark, passionate energy that radiated off of him, replaced by a warm and personable joviality. Even with his talent and fame, he exuded a mellow vibe that made it so easy to talk with him.

Viktor's English was more than passable, and he helped translate for Yuri in our conversation. They said they'd heard I was an American rocker and asked about my music. In turn, I asked about their band, who wrote the songs, and how long they'd been together. It was a fairly predictable, languid conversation, but I felt like a cartoon character with my heart beating out of my chest. Yuri captivated my attention, his chiseled jaw and clear eyes convincing me that I was in love with a man with whom I couldn't even communicate alone. In my mind, the language barrier only added to the romance. He would laugh at my compliments, gently touch my arm, and stare at me for long stretches even as Viktor continued to talk between us.

"Joanna, what are you doing tomorrow?" Viktor asked.

I felt a pit appear in my stomach. "Unfortunately, I have to go home, back to America." After a long pause, I told them, "But I'll be back."

The next morning, I went to Boris' apartment before heading to the airport. He took me up to the building's roof, the safest place to avoid unwanted eavesdroppers.

"Careful of the rail," he said as I held onto the edge's barrier. "It is rotten."

"Is that safe?" I asked nervously.

"I don't believe so," he said with a smile. He knew that to put his head in the clouds required a little risk.

"Boris, I hate to ask you this, but what about the Stratocaster? The customs guards really wrote everything down and told me to be sure I left the country with it."

"Don't worry," he said in his leisurely way. "Let's have tea, and everything will be fine."

Back in Boris' apartment, I kept making a show of glancing at my watch. "Boris, the guit-"

Just as I opened my mouth, the apartment door swung open and Afrika and Timur bounded in, carrying a guitar case.

"Oh my god, thank you," I said. "I'm so sorry I have to take it back."

Afrika saluted me. "Assa ye, ye!" He handed me the case and I popped it open.

Inside was a guitar with a handmade wooden body, painted a shiny white. The neck, electric pick-ups, nobs, and whammy bar were all about the same size and color as the one I'd brought in. The serial number was in the same spot as the original, and as I grabbed my customs form and checked the original number, I saw it matched it digit for digit.

"You made a knock-off?" I asked, shocked.

"Assa ye, ye," Afrika said nobly. "Everything is the same as what it says on your customs form, except for quality. And how are the customs guards going to figure that out?" He made an exaggerated shrug. "They won't!"

"This is amazing." I didn't know what to say next. The guitar sat in front of me like the Stratocaster's younger, awkward brother, a bunch of funny materials making up its gangly, bright body. For the first time, I realized how consequential innovation was in the Soviet Union. As an American, I'd never known true hardship or censorship and had figured I always had to play by the rules. Not these guys. When they wanted something, they figured it out. I looked up at them standing around me with amused smiles and an animal glint in their eyes.

"So, what do you want me to bring back next?"

◆ A Rebel Without a Clue

"And this one," I said, flipping over the next photo, "is Boris and me in his kitchen just after we met."

"Now who's Boris again?" The music equipment executive asked, his eyebrows knotted together as he tried to place the round, charismatic face in the photo.

"He's basically the Bob Dylan of the Soviet Union. He's the one whose song I just played."

"It's incredible that these guys exist," the executive said, more to himself. He then looked back at me. "I had no idea there was rock 'n roll music in the Soviet Union."

Seeing Boris' reaction to the Fender Stratocaster, the disbelief in his shocked, sparkling eyes, and the toothy smile that erupted on his face, I was determined to do more. I hit the ground running. Desperate to set up my next trip, I went back to work at the travel agency while trying to build connections to music equipment companies in the States to orchestrate the next instrument shipment. David Weiderman, the smiling blonde manager of the Hollywood Guitar Center where I'd purchased Boris' first gift, introduced me to several companies and to Doug Buttleman, the coolest guy at Yamaha, and Dan Smith at Fender.

I had many conversations following that second trip of August 1984. Judy and I had collected piles of photos as well as a few tapes of Aquarium's music that we hid in our suitcases and prayed wouldn't be confiscated. So many Americans shared my initial preconceived ideas about the sinister and gelid Soviet Union that no one, including these

■ Boris in concert, 1984. Photos by Igor Petruchenko.

top executives, thought people like Boris Grebenshchikov or Viktor Tsoi could exist. I was ready to pull back the curtain and show them a snippet of Wonderland.

After the first few meetings, I realized I barely had to say please; everyone agreed I was on to something special. They wanted to help, to see more of this magical, twisted world, and so I asked for more and more musical instruments. Within weeks, I had secured a synthesizer for Sergey Kuryokhin, a Strat for Yuri that shone like the winter sun, and a four-track mixer. I even got a shiny gold Beatles record for Kolya, The Beatles Guy, from Capitol Records, with his name on the plaque.

"From Me to You," I told him when I handed it over.

"Hey Jude," he said to me, his face a red wash of rapture and amazement as he held up the shiny yellow disc, "Here Comes the Sun."

◆

Arriving back in the Soviet Union that third time in November 1984, the cold, fluorescent arrival hall was just as intimidating as it had been before. This time, though, I had gotten word to Boris saying that my travel tour would spend the first three and a half days in Moscow before going to Leningrad. He replied that he would meet me in

Moscow, and as I hurried off the plane to beat the rest of the tired, sleep-deprived bodies to customs, I could imagine his warmth soaking through the walls.

Boris took me to an "official" concert. In exchange for submitting their lyrics to government censors and agreeing to play when and where the government decreed, "official" bands could earn a real living and maybe even become "officially" famous.

"Sell-outs," Sergey Kuryokhin would sneer about them in conversation. To prize fame over artistic control and freedom was, in his eyes, depravity and profanity.

The show to which Boris and I headed was by the most well-known official rock band, Mashina Vremeni (Time Machine). Andrei Makarevich, one of Boris' best friends, led the band.

"Andrei loves The Beatles," Boris said as we walked into the concert hall.

"How did you meet him?"

"He started singing Western rock songs in Moscow in the '70s, like I was doing in Leningrad. But because it was more difficult to get away with these underground things in the capital, Andrei moved to Leningrad for a while and we both wrote our own lyrics in Russian. We became great friends."

"Then why did he end up signing an official contract?" I asked.

"We were both offered contracts. I turned it down, but he just wanted to play music and he could make a living on a government contract, so he said yes."

"And you don't mind?"

"He's a great musician, and I respect his talent. And he's my friend. We all make compromises in this country."

Time Machine's concert was in a huge concert hall with what seemed like ten thousand people, politely applauding as the band strode out in their stiff suits. Gone was the rough-and-tumble energy of the basement concert, exchanged for a more subdued performance, where no one left their seats or experienced any passionate rowdiness. Andrei was indeed an excellent musician, but the atmosphere was masked, and the vibe felt tight and controlled. The band would play, finish a song, and stop. Andrei would say a few words. People would clap.

They'd play another song. I felt like I was in a hamster wheel that was stuck on its hinge.

Halfway through the set, Andrei's guitarist broke a string. The song stopped and everyone – the band, the thousands of people, Andrei, Boris, and me – barely moved. It turned into a concert of statues. An eerie hush fell over the crowd as the guitarist calmly went about changing his string under the stares of ten thousand pairs of eyes.

"What's going on?" I whispered to Boris. "Why doesn't the rest of the band improvise or play a different song?"

"They can't. Every second of the show is pre-approved." Boris watched the guitarist's fingers slowly work along the neck of the instrument, taking their sweet time. "They're not allowed to drift at all from the show schedule."

"It's so awkward," I mumbled.

"Not for Russians," he said.

Despite the restrained, stifled control of the crowd, I could still tell Andrei and his band were big stars. To see the number of people there waiting patiently as the guitarist changed a string for the song to pick up, the blunder unable to quell their interest, emphasized the dedication people could have to these official groups. After the concert, when Boris and I went to hang at Andrei's apartment, I saw how big and beautiful his home was. It had open windows over a wide street and many rooms for just him and his family, a hugely noticeable difference between Boris' and the other unofficial rockers' tight, shared spaces.

Andrei couldn't have been nicer, and it was apparent from the start that he and Boris shared an important bond. Though their conversations in Russian escaped me, I can still remember the blissful evening so clearly: my head was leaning on Boris' shoulder as he was smoking his favorite cigarettes – Belomor – the distinct smell curling into my hair and the threads of my clothing fabric, his and Andrei's melodious dialog mimicking their songs. I noticed on many occasions that just being near Boris did something transformative for my soul, the way summer made the flowers bloom into a thousand different colors and forget about the drought or snow.

A couple of days later, I met back up with Boris in Leningrad. He invited Judy and me to a series of home concerts, where several musicians crowded into a cramped room to sweat and sing and smile. The homes, communal apartments designed to hold several families, were quite large, but at each concert they would shrink to the feeling of sardine cans packed with more than a hundred smelly, sweaty rock fans. Boris would play guitar, joined by a violinist, cellist, or bassist. It was beautiful. Again, I realized that I'd been missing something all those years back in America, as if my heart had been a lamp that wasn't plugged in. These musicians, though, they were electric.

Before Boris and the other musicians would arrive, the hosts would pass an old fur hat to collect money for the performers. When there was no money in the hat, a surprisingly regular occurrence, sometimes the band just played for alcohol. I could see that for underground bands like Aquarium, it was never about the money. Boris, Viktor, and the rest of the men I met performed because they loved it, because it was what put breath in their bodies and got them up in the morning. In those moments where I sat and watched them pour their hearts out through the pores in their bodies and the instruments in their hands, they seemed free and happy and unburdened by what the rest of us carried on our shoulders.

After the concerts, I would leave with Boris and the band, all of us linking arms and trudging about a mile in the freezing wind to catch a tram back into town. It always surprised me to watch Boris, a famous rocker who could wow his fans with just a strum of the guitar, take public transportation through the Russian winter months to get home. It made me think of their missed opportunities; I would lay awake at night with the wheels in my head turning, thinking how Aquarium and Kino should be recording, going on tour, and appearing on television.

In those sleepless, starless nights, I would also try to puzzle out the fascinating relationship Russians created between freedom, money, and the concept of time. I could see these rockers valued their freedom above all, chasing down that feeling for short periods in tiny apartment jam sessions while all others could do was tell me in their broken, accented English, "I want to be free like you." I remember telling them that Americans paid a price for freedom, waxing on about mortgages and college loans and investment for retirement. Freer access to capital and alleged opportunity forced Americans to plan ahead, to miss the moments in which they were living as they chased down the golden sunsets like the cowboys that they were. There was no borrowing money in the Soviet Union, so there was little reason to plan or save.

Everything happened as it happened: meals, drugs, laughs, fights, love. If I gave Boris one hundred dollars, he would spend it that same day. If I gave him ten bottles of vodka, he would throw a party then and there in the middle of a rainy afternoon.

◆

After one of the home concert performances on a trip I took in the first half of 1985, I got to have my second conversation with Kino's guitar player Yuri Kasparyan, with Viktor Tsoi standing between us, smiling and translating yet again.

"Can you escape from your group tour once more?" Yuri asked through Viktor.

"I've done pretty well so far," I teased. I couldn't stop staring at Yuri.

"We are going to Pushkin tomorrow. It's a town a few kilometers away with a big palace and beautiful gardens. You should come." Viktor added his own thoughts to Yuri's words, telling me "some people call it the Versailles of the Soviet Union."

■ Yuri Kasparyan, the guitarist from Kino, Leningrad, 1985. Behind Yuri is artwork by Oleg Kotelnikov (on the left) and other New Artists.

"Better," Yuri managed to tell me himself, as if I needed convincing.

"I would love to," I said, noticing the light birthmark on his chin and his high cheekbones. "What time should Judy and I meet you?"

We could barely speak to each other, but I was falling for Yuri. We had an instant bond, some strange mesh of energies that left me breathless and left him amused and smiling.

Pushkin's grounds are right on the water, so Yuri and I rented a small rowboat together. We pointed at the passing toy boats and brown ducks, making faces and laughing as baby waves rocked the boat and we pretended to fall out with our limbs touching and twisting. As we were racing Judy in the boat next to us, Yuri leaned into me and met my eyes. His kiss was like the water that splashed my skin and the white Russian air I was inhaling; cold, soft, and invigorating.

"And this one," I heard myself saying in my mind, as I had so many times over travel tours I was looking to take and instruments to bring back. Now I felt like saying it again, his heavy bangs in my eyes and his hands on my face. "I want this one."

There were no travel bans, customs restrictions, or jingoism that were going to keep me away now.

♦ The Wolf and the Phoenix

Working with Sergey, the "Capitán," was unlike anything I'd ever experienced. Growing up I'd been a professional gymnast and had had an uncompromising Austrian coach who would scream at us girls and slap us on the legs when we faltered, sending me home with red prints on my thighs and a bruised, sore ego. Sergey would coach me from the piano with his puppy dog eyes, an intoxicating soul with a mind that ran a mile a minute. My voice soared higher than I ever had on the uneven bars or balance beam, and unlike gymnastics I loved every minute of practicing with Sergey. He had a biting wit, glabrous ivory skin, and wrote songs whose melodies would have given Shakespeare goosebumps.

I'd seen him play in the first old house show and then as the keyboard player in Aquarium, but over the course of trips I took, I began to see that I was not even close to understanding the depths of his genius. While there was hardly a band in which he hadn't played or produced, Sergey was probably best known as the leader of Pop-Mekhanika (Pop Mechanics), a crazy group of misfit musical pirates specializing in everything from jazz, rock, and classical, to avant-garde. Sergey conducted using his whole body instead of a baton, cranking out rigid arm movements, grand twists, head jerks, and monumental jumps during every song. Somehow his musicians recognized every gesture. He was an inexhaustible source of energy, bold and bright and commanding like the north star. To him, the concept of time was irrelevant.

"We're spending something," he mused once about it, a rare moment of inactivity as he lounged casually on his side in the sun. "We don't know what it is yet." His life was a credit card without a limit.

Even in those early days, when Sergey, Boris, and I were together, Sergey would sit next to me with his legs entwined in mine and his arms around me. From my nest in his arms I'd watch Boris trying to change channels on the boxy brown television, shocked to see that there was only one channel available, featuring a choir made up of the Soviet mass youth organization, The Young Pioneers. I glanced up at Sergey, his eyes twinkling with thoughts and secrets and songs that were begging to be let out. He didn't need the television or even the smoke or the drugs to light his own fire; he was already burning up inside with the inspiration and motivation of a thousand men.

"Jo," he'd say to get my attention, and then shriek and howl like a wolf. I could feel the power of everything overflowing inside him.

"*Da pashol ty!*" he'd say to the authorities or anyone threatening to shut down a concert, harass his friends, or tried to wrap him in some type of regulation as he performed on the unwashed streets without official permission. "Go F- yourself."

Sergey would regularly send me out to embarrass myself. He loved to have me and Judy say dirty phrases to strangers. The first thing he taught me was "*Bolshoi kolbasa,*" which means "big sausage." We'd say it to one another all the time, and I loved to watch him throw his head back and laugh as I shouted it across one of the cramped apartments or whispered it in his ear. Sometimes when we were all invited to hang out at the Western consulates – French, Swedish, and American – Sergey would goad me and Judy into giving the diplomats what he swore up and down was a traditional Russian greeting. We could tell, from the curl of his lip and the electricity in his eyes, that he was teaching us something dirty, but we'd do it anyway because it was fun and because it was Sergey. We'd say things like "*tselui menia doorak*" and "*oo menia atsasi seichas.*" He would stand proudly off to the side as the diplomats coughed and drained their drinks and tried to smile politely in response to our demands of "Kiss me, you fool" or "Give me head now."

It was more than just dirty jokes and verbal communication though. We would write songs together, transcending any type of linguistic barrier. He'd play these ingenious pieces on the piano and record it on my Walkman, singing a gibberish melody in his soft and shaky falsetto like some cat stuck out in the rain. I could take the recordings back home with me to write and record lyrics in a L.A. studio. He was consistently amazed with the quality of what the American studios could produce, and I with what his mind could conjure. He took pride in making his own music that was not just another "pathetic imitation of the west." He was very specific about every song, its tones, crescendos, and

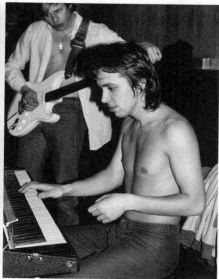

■ Sergey and me, Leningrad, 1985.

■ Boris on his Stratocaster from David Bowie and Sergey on his keyboard from Yamaha, 1985.

rhythms. He wanted to make things that had never been done before.

"Jo," he'd say again, pushing me to sing in different styles, challenging me to turn my back on my comfort level to sing in various speeds or in my head voice. For me it was better than any master class I could have taken in songwriting from a top conservatory.

As a highly respected classical pianist, Sergey could play at "official" venues that closed their heavy oversized doors to the other rockers. On one of my first trips I went to see him at a concert hall in Leningrad. He sat on two stacked chairs angled directly at the grand piano with a saxophone held tightly to his chest, first accompanying the famous gypsy singer Valentina Ponomareva and then the saxophonist Vladimir Chekasin. He would play and shake and become so lost in the music, hitting a snare drum while kicking it across the floor and making the most haunting songs fly into all corners of the building. The packed house was enthralled, and the government authorities left him alone. There was something about Leningrad, a looser version of Moscow, that allowed him to flourish, despite the fact that he had actually been expelled from the conservatory for nonconformity and nonattendance.

"I've got a very high opinion of my abilities," he said in an interview with me once. Sergey knew he was better than everyone else, but he still loved us regardless.

I always considered him a kindred spirit, wrapped around each other on the sofa as if

■ Performing with the Pop Mechanics, Leningrad, 1986. Photo by Natasha Vassilieva-Hull.

■ Sergey conducting a Pop Mechanics performance, Leningrad, 1988.

we were best buddies. To others he may have been The "Capitán," but I called him "Papa" for his confident, all knowing authority and the protection he offered me to explore what I wanted and how I sang. He was the leader of not just his own pack, Pop Mechanics, but of all of us – his strong personality and sharp eyes drove everyone around him wild and hungry for more music, more music, more music.

Grinning and growling, he asked me to be a part of Pop Mechanics the following year I was there. I performed a few times on stage with them, bashing drums, singing back-up, and dancing around in my combat boots and bright red lipstick. It was exhilarating to be on stage with him, a natural high that couldn't be cultivated with any type of stimulant. With the colored lights in my eyes and Sergey jumping around me sky-high, I felt a rush like no other. It was wild.

◆

Back home I had always been terrified of my mother, this gorgeous icy presence who had a hot temper exacerbated by three obstreperous and capricious daughters. As a result, I'd spent a majority of my life always trying to fly under the radar and be cooperative enough in the hopes that I could just enjoy my mother's glowing generosity and attachment while she screamed and swore at my older sister and Judy cried under the table. Being with Sergey was a taste of this unencumbered freedom I had never felt before, and I reveled in the riotous pandemonium he spread through the underground like an oil spill on fire. It was addictive, and as I stretched myself to explore this unrestricted space, Sergey would only encourage me and everyone else to see how big we could become.

■ Afrika and Gustav performing with artwork by Afrika as a backdrop, Leningrad, 1985.

One of my favorite Pop Mechanics concerts at the Rock Club that is still vivid in my mind is where I saw Sergey produce performance art at its fullest. Musicians of every style, visual artists, models, and pantomimes shared the stage with a shitting horse and a goat that danced with Afrika, whose pink hair, long earrings, and polka-dotted dress lit up the entire room. Sergey could somehow conduct chaos into craft, painting a picture with these wacky, prancing characters as he paced the stage and tried to hide his growing smile. The incident was typical – Sergey and Afrika always wanted to see what they could get away with doing.

After that concert, the KGB arrested Afrika. The way he looked on stage, some type of illuminated phoenix in drag, was the immoral alternative to their stiff, colorless suits and eyes. They told him his attire was a disgrace to the Soviet Union, but it was who Afrika was – this young, creative, expressive creature, driven, dedicated, and unapologetic for his wiles. A member of the New Artists, Afrika was an extremely talented mastermind in his button-down shirt and bow tie. I could see the similarity when people talked about him as a provocateur and contemporary to Andy Warhol, his pieces littered with Soviet symbols to raise attention and spark debate.

By now I was bringing musicians and artists alike numerous things from the States: clothes, accessories, acrylic paints, canvases. As a thank you, they were giving me pieces of their art that I managed to smuggle out of the country.

"They're just children's drawings and works," I told the grimacing, choleric customs agents as they eyed the contemporary graffiti.

The New Artists produced work that was childlike, colorful, multi-media, and

■ Timur, me, Gustav, and Afrika (posing as a Young Pioneer statue) with Timur's painting of the Russian Museum (left) and Afrika and Andrei's shower curtain painting on the right, Leningrad, 1985.

wildly imaginary. Since they weren't official artists, they didn't have any type of luxurious access to supplies, instead using plastic shower curtains, drapes, pieces of wood, and polychromatic t-shirts. Yuffa (Evgeny Yufit), a strange underground filmmaker with a stretched smile and brightly fierce eyes, would improvise blood and scars and use an archaic camera to make gruesome movies that turned his actors into fierce and unnatural creatures. Timur Novikov, Evgenij Kozlov, Ivan Sotnikov, Kirill Khazanovich, Gustav Guryanov, Afrika, Oleg Kotelnikov, Andrei Krisanov, and other artist friends would paint what they felt, the wacky materials an extension of their own instincts, and then analyze each other's works. They made weird contraptions of hanging weights and irons that sounded like a new wave synthesizer. They wrote and recorded avant-garde compositions and staged outrageous performances that almost brought me to my knees. Vladimir Mayakovsky, a futuristic poet/playwright/artist/actor of the early-twentieth century, was always in the back of their minds. Gustav looked like a reincarnation of him – a devilish and pensive man with a creative genius and scalding temper. Gustav was the drummer in Kino, who had a visionary force that shaped the band's striking fashion and was also the most difficult personality; a moody perfectionist, he was one of the few Russians I met that had such a short fuse. In the middle of Kino rehearsals, he would throw his sticks down as if they were poisonous snakes and stalk out if some unsaid, unseen thing pissed him off. He was complicated and tortured, an almost cliché artist with stormy eyes.

I was riding in the backseat of a car with Gustav once when he asked if I would be

■ Me, Viktor, and Gustav with Timur's collage of the Pulkovo Airport in the background, Leningrad, 1985.

his girlfriend. I told him I cared for him deeply but not in that way. It pissed him off so much he left the car and refused to talk to me for several days. Yet under that hard, inflammable skin, he could be genuine, funny, and kind. He, Viktor, and Yuri were so close as a group and as friends, and his extreme talent was crucial to Kino. In the video footage Judy and I took of him, he can be just as playful as he was sour, dancing next to me half naked with animated laughing eyes.

◆

Like Mayakovsky, all members of the New Artists were dedicated to creative innovation. On a huge floor of an old building Timur had claimed for them, with little more than their materials and a stray chair or two, they convened to make art for themselves and their friends. It was amazing to me to see people put so much heart and soul and sweat into the process as opposed to the end result. They were unconcerned with money or audience and did what they did simply for the love of it. Their work filled the walls and spread all over the floors, some stacked up and used as a substitute mattress for sleeping. Someone would create a piece and then move it out of the way so he could move on to the next idea, like some type of intellectual gardener growing a lemon tree and then getting a craving for oranges. They also made wonderfully huge backdrops for many of the concerts at the Rock Club or the Palace of Youth.

One day Timur and Afrika walked me over to a bulky painting of a mean, distorted man with sunglasses that was covering a tall window. They pulled the painting aside

■ Andrei Krisanov, Gustav Guryanov, and Viktor Tsoi, Leningrad, 1985. Andrei and Gustav played with Kino as well as being part of the New Artists. Viktor also made art. At this photoshoot, Gustav is wearing a long skirt; Andrei has garters on his bare calves.

and pointed across the street to a big apathetic building glaring grossly in the sunlight.

"That is Bolshoi Dom, our Big House," they said.

"What?" I asked.

"It is the building of the KGB." They quickly recovered the window, their eyes filled with comical irony as they put up that single barrier between their rebellious behavior and the condemnation of the state. Of all the places to set up a studio…

The New Artists also seemed to be obsessed with Yuri Gagarin, the famous Russian cosmonaut that completed an orbit of the Earth in 1961. In my eyes, these men were very similar to Gagarin, people never short of ideas who dreamed of soaring into the future. Timur, with his striking, pale, and magnetic features, was a quiet cosmic force with which to be reckoned. He didn't speak English, but just watching him I could understand that he was incredibly cultured, deep, and mischievous. He did wonderful self-portraits whose personalities still haunt me today.

There was a wintry day where I went with Timur, Afrika, and my sister Judy to go skating outside of Leningrad. Judy was driving us all in our rented Russian Lada down the icy roads. I remember sitting in the front passenger seat facing backwards without a seat belt, balancing a camera as I videotaped Timur and Afrika dancing in the back seat with Western music bubbling out of my Walkman. As the two guys twisted and shook in their seats, Judy spooked at a truck sliding forward in the lane next to us and

■ Members of Strange Games and Kino performing with Afrika at a Pop Mechanics concert, Leningrad, 1985. Left to right: Alexei Rakhov, Viktor Tsoi, Yuri Kasparyan, Grysha Sologub, Oleg Garkusha (front man from Auction) on knees with goat, Sasha Kondrashkin, Sasha Titov, Afrika in drag, and Vitia Sologub.

slammed on the brakes. We hit the truck and the cheap tin of the car crumpled around us. We climbed out onto the highway with headaches, Timur with a bad burgundy cut along his forehead and down the side of his face. Leaving the ruined car in the falling snow, we hitchhiked back to Leningrad to get help, stunned and silent. For the rest of my days in Russia, Timur and I were bonded over our close call, sharing the profound realization of how impermanent and delicate we all were.

Afrika, as always, had been unaffected by what the country threw at him. An arrest, a sliding truck – he had an extraordinary ability to dust himself off and throw himself right back into life. For his sweet youthful look and lanky awkward frame, he was as outrageous as his artistic pseudonym. He loved attention, up for bringing a goat on stage and humping its leg if Sergey told him to. He appointed himself as the cruise director for me and Judy, making sure we were having fun and inhaling as much life as we could in those short days. We'd meet in Moscow and Leningrad, and he'd take us to places foreigners would never see, flying around the cities like a bird and introducing us to artists, poets, musicians, nuclear physicists, and underground filmmakers. Afrika was not only connected and resourceful, but he was thoughtful and amiable and adored people. Looking back at all the photos Judy took, Afrika is always there somewhere in the middle with his arms wrapped around my waist and his smile contagious among all artists, a pop of color in an otherwise black and white image.

◆ Star Light, Star Bright

Yuri, Viktor, and I were becoming like The Three Musketeers.

We had so much fun spending time together, doing nothing, chilling out, listening to music and singing until our lungs felt as if they could collapse. They'd turn me on to new bands from England that they'd somehow discovered in Russia before those singers ever reached American ears. Viktor's favorite song was "Love Cats" by The Cure, playing it on repeat with our other favorites like The Smith's "How Soon Is Now," The Cult's "She Sells Sanctuary" and "Nirvana."

"Every day, Nirvana," I would sing, only to be drowned out by Viktor and Yuri's unison voices screaming out, "Every day, Joanna!" They were my very own solar eclipse, two radiant beings in line with each other, making me feel as if I was the whole world.

Out of the three of us, Viktor was the goofy one. When he'd smoke, he'd curl his lips back like a cat and suck in the smoke really hard until his cheeks became so concave that all that was left of his face were his big expressive eyes. Proper Russian pronunciation demands rolling your Rs, something I couldn't quite manage, and Viktor would get in my face and say "rrrrr!"

"Rrr,rrr,rrrr,rrrr!" like a motorcycle flying down the highway towards my hysterically laughing face as I tried to shout it back to him. He shrewdly avoided military service by checking himself into a psychiatric clinic for a few weeks that deemed him unfit to serve. He was a huge Bruce Lee fan, and he would constantly adopt kung fu positions as though he was about to kick or pounce on me while his deep, luminescent Asian eyes, a

■ Top left: Viktor and me at a drum concert, Peter and Paul Fortress, Leningrad, 1986.
Photo by Mikhail Makarenko.
Top right: Viktor, *Red Wave* publicity shot, 1985.
Below: Yuri and Viktor, 1986.

rarity in Leningrad from his Korean grandfather, would crinkle at the corners.

There was something about him too, though, that was solemn and dark, the enigmatic persona people saw when he was onstage performing. It wasn't a character he donned like a jacket but an inner ethos that was rooted in his very core as a Russian.

"Every person has a feeling that they are in a cage sometimes," he told me once when I asked him for whom he wrote Kino's songs. "A mental cage. You want to find an exit... a person lives and cannot find a way to be free of what stops them, what pressures them." He wanted to provide that escape people needed, his music a doorway to a brighter world.

"What's the balance between songwriting and performing?" I asked. "Are you first a songwriter and then a performer?"

He shook his head and leaned forward in his chair. "My understanding of just writing a song and performing it is inseparable. Sometimes you write a song right at the concert."

He was such a reflective, intuitive person, and he was fueled by the energy around him. Nothing was ever fully for himself, but also for the people he loved and observed. It was funny, though, that even with all of the Russian connections and friendships, Viktor got so much joy out of eating at the Peking Hotel restaurant when we went to Moscow. He loved the Asian food and being able to come face to face with people who looked a little more like himself. It was hard for Russians to get into the pale-yellow Stalinist Empire style building, but of course Afrika could somehow manage to get us in.

What was so unique about Viktor was that he was one of the few Russians who would actually look to the stars and plan for the future. He and I would sit around and dream about the things we wanted to do, filling our imaginations with places we wanted to go and see. He wanted to come to America and visit Los Angeles, planning his trip to Disneyland and listing which of the roller coasters he wanted to ride. I'd lived my entire life in California so it had lost its dewy, radiant charm, but Viktor made me realize how lucky I was to have grown up in the City of Angels.

What struck me the most about Viktor, though, was the way he almost seemed embarrassed by his surging fame. He was a regular guy who couldn't objectively see what a magical, enigmatic musician he was. As his records spread underground and he became more and more well-known, he seemed surprised that people were listening to his songs and amazed when people would follow him around in public. One time we were waiting in line at a bread store when a crowd of people gathered around the window, fogging it up and trying to peer through at him. When we walked out, they rushed around him, asking for autographs or handshakes, trying to reach out and touch his jet-black hair

■ Viktor Tsoi at his job, shoveling coal in the apartment building nicknamed "Kamchatka," 1985.

and bewildered face. Viktor didn't know what to do, so we took off running down the side streets, chased by the sound of footsteps and the screams of strangers. He giggled the whole way, unable to comprehend that all these people were fascinated by the sweet, shy man that he was. His humility always made it so easy to be friends with him.

"Viktor, what's your job?" I asked him once.

"I shovel coal."

"Like for a train?"

"No, into a giant furnace to make heat for buildings." He gave an exaggerated pantomime. "It's a good job. I don't have to work all that often, and it leaves me a lot of time to make music."

I stood there in a state of confusion, trying to reconcile such an ancient-sounding job with this present, modern man. Finally, I asked, "Can I come visit you at work?"

"Foreigners aren't allowed, but I'll try."

He worked in this dark basement room with no windows and thick stale air, shoveling coal into a big growling furnace like something off a postcard from the nineteenth century. The place was called "Kamchatka," the name of an Edenic volcanic peninsula in the Russian Far East, and standing there, watching his muscles tense and the hot black smoke rise, I felt like I was somewhere at the ends of the earth.

"One day, an old man came down to 'Kamchatka,'" Viktor said. "He started screaming 'It's too cold in my apartment! Why aren't you guys working harder down here?' Then I turned around and he recognized me. 'Wait,' he said, 'You're Viktor Tsoi. You're famous. What are you doing working here?' I just laughed."

"I agree with that guy!" I said, amazed at the transformation Viktor could make from this mysterious rebellious rockstar to this working-class plebeian.

"It's okay," he told me. "I like doing the work. It keeps my feet on the ground."

Not only was Viktor capable of such inner self-reflection, but he was an outwardly attentive and respectful person. At an early Kino rehearsal that I was watching, things began to escalate as Viktor started dancing around the stage with the microphone dangling close to the amp to create feedback. Gustav started banging the snare drum aggressively because Afrika had taken his other stick, creating this savagely wild beat that inspired Viktor to knock him over.

They were acting silly and manic, and as Afrika jumped up on stage to join them, he accidentally broke a piece of wood off the stage's facade. At the end of the long rehearsal everyone was laughing and panting, but if you watch the video footage Viktor walked over to the broken piece of stage and carefully put it back. As crazy as he could get, and he could get crazy, he never ruined or disrespected anything or anyone. For someone growing up with Miss Manners as her mother, I was always in awe of Viktor's courtesy to everything around him.

"So, tell me the dream," I said to him one evening, tossing my legs over his lap on the couch and watching him light a thin white cigarette. "What do you hope for the future, Viktor?"

As he sucked in his cheeks and inhaled, the butt and both his eyes glowing softly, I could see the smile in the corners of his mouth. "Other than Disneyland?"

"Other than Disneyland," I laughed.

"First, I wish that in the future no problems, no wars. And of course, I'm going to do music." If only people like Viktor were the ones governing our two countries, I could imagine a world where Disneyland wasn't the only "Happiest Place on Earth."

Viktor also had this innate ability to sense if I felt awkward. He'd glance at me and raise his eyebrows as if to say, "You okay?" When we performed at Pop Mechanics concerts, I would meet his eyes on stage and they would wink or sparkle with a little smirk as if to say, "How fun is this? How lucky are we? Isn't this cool?" While everyone else pounded on around us just breathing for the moment, Viktor and I realized what a life we were living. Whenever Viktor was in the same cramped apartment or concert hall, I could stand there surrounded by other strangers and never feel alone.

Viktor, Yuri, and I wrote a song together that would become known as "Tsoi Song (Ye man)." We were stuck on a freezing street trying to get a taxi or a ride home from a party, the air cold and dark and about forty below. I couldn't feel my hands or my face, almost crying as the wind cut through every layer of clothing and wrapped its ephemeral hands around my bones.

Viktor kept telling me to think of a warm place as he wrapped me in a hug. Yuri did the same. The three of us stood with our noses almost touching.

"Think of Jamaica, and tell me what you are doing there," Viktor said.

I imagined a soft white beach with beautiful crystal blue waters steaming in the hot sun. I started throwing out words and images.

"Ye man," Viktor and Yuri kept saying, drinking it in. "Ye man." They started to play along, speaking of warm tropical islands where the sun never set, and the hot tubs bubbled over into the ocean.

"Ye man," I said.

We added a reggae beat. Later in L.A. with my friend Paul Delph, with whom I recorded most of my early songs, I turned these words into the lyrics for "Tsoi Song."

Sitting on a bench in the summer
Eating a banana in the shade
A man asked me if I wanted some money
I said ye man

In the car which Yuri, Viktor, and I finally found to drive us home that night, I sat between the two of them with my frostbite thawing painfully in my fingers and toes. I didn't know what I'd do without them.

Through all the frustration and pain and exhaustion, these two especially always had ideas in their heads to inspire me.

"*My-ya krysha payekhala*," they would say, which means "my roof is moving." It's one of my favorite phrases in Russian, when there's so much about which to think that it can almost drive you insane. These boys were crazy, and they were the best.

Even when I would go back to Los Angeles, Viktor would send me little drawings and notes saying they all missed me and couldn't wait for me to come back. I would sit in my red wooden house on Beverly Glen with cars racing by and have these low moments where I could feel how far away Russia really was, but Viktor's words always made it feel a little closer. *Still I love you and care for you.* He was a soul reader, a deeply devoted friend who somehow heard me across two continents and an ocean when I missed everything

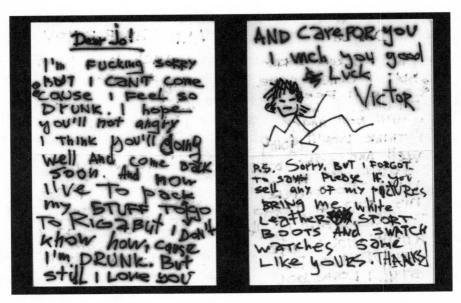

■ Viktor sent me a farewell note through a friend as I was leaving Russia on one of my early trips.

so much it was blinding. *Please if you sell any of my pictures bring me white leather sport boots and Swatch watches same like yours,* he added to one at the end. There was always a reminder they were waiting for me and expecting me to come back.

Despite the late nights we shared back in Leningrad, Viktor and I both loved a good night's sleep. At those *tusofkas* that could last until breakfast, he and I were both ready to head home around eleven p.m. I had forced myself one time back at Studio 54 in New York to stay up all night just so I could walk out of there in the morning to go get breakfast as if I was some trendy rockstar who kept sleep under the soles of her boots; I had felt so crappy I hadn't even been able to feel as cool as I thought I would, my eggs cold on the table in front of me. Viktor, like me, rarely stayed out past midnight. He believed there were laws in life, and one of them was that night was for sleeping. If you broke that law, there would be consequences.

◆

There was no one as pure, as transcendent, as irresistible as Boris Grebenshchikov. I had never met anybody less attached to material things. In Los Angeles people were worshiping at the wheels of their fancy cars and locking themselves away in their homes with expensive coffee tables and oversized candles and swimming pools. My sisters and

■ Boris' room was full of amazing trinkets and talismans.

I had spent years crying over toys that we wanted in store windows, enough that my mother would yell at us and tell us how selfish and greedy we were being. The next day those toys, new and colorful with the tags still tucked behind their ears, would always greet us in the kitchen, because even our mother couldn't resist the pull of buying her daughters material goods that filled up space and seemingly added value to our worth. Especially in Beverly Hills, it was all about possessions – what you owned and what others did not. Boris never hesitated to share what he had, smiling that worthy, wonderful smile of his as his blue eyes dared you to take what he offered.

Judy and I loved spending time in his room, running our fingers over his spiritual trinkets, drawings he made, and albums of pictures. He would light up as he told us about them, and I'd share in his enthusiasm and respond, "Wow, that's so cool!"

"I want you to have it."

I'd always say no, I just thought it was beautiful, I don't want to take it from you.

"Please," he'd respond, that smile and those eyes. "I want you to have it."

"Boris, it's yours, and it's important to you."

"That's why I want you to have it," he always said. "If I give you something I don't care about, then it means nothing. I want you to have it."

It's a philosophy I've since tried to follow my whole life.

Boris and I began to write songs together in those first couple of years. We would be sitting around chatting, most sunny days on his roof overlooking the colorful onions of the Church of the Savior on Spilled Blood, and at some point, Boris would invariably start strumming his guitar and we'd begin to jam. He would sing something over what he played in his cool, almost British accent, and then I'd jump in. He would make up lower harmonies as I'd scribble lyrics down and try a different melody, sharing ideas and grins until we had something resembling a song. There was something incredible about writing with Boris, like getting swept up in a wave of the freshest, warmest water. He was the only Russian musician with whom I worked who would write lyrics with me, a poet both in Russian and in English. He pushed me to grow in my own language and redefine my music.

Before I met Boris, I was trying to be a rockstar. I wrote silly songs and obsessed over the simple desirable things around me, like friends buying expensive cars or skiing in Aspen. After I started writing with Boris, I understood that rock 'n roll wasn't about being a star – it was about expressing myself and viewing the human soul as the most powerful muse. There's one song Boris wrote that ended up on the *Red Wave* album called "The Thirst," and at the end of an intense, driving instrumental section Boris sings a few lines many times like a chant:

I close my eyes

And I pray to water

Water cleanse us one more time

After the third repetition, the instruments drop out and he sings it almost in a whisper. I would sing this part over and over, one of the first lines I sang in Russian, when I was back in Los Angles and curled up with my heart aching for the life I was missing back across the Atlantic. It was so powerful and meaningful; those lines changed how I looked at the world. Instead of perceiving things in a concrete or material way, I became more aware of an internalized spiritual searching. Boris and his music taught me that to become a better songwriter, I had to first become a better, more enlightened person, and the rest would naturally follow.

Boris' song lyrics could be stream of consciousness, lines having nothing to do with one another feeding off each other in this intensely complex narrative. And here I had been thinking that songs had to be clear stories with a beginning, middle, and end. How boring! With Boris, I was using songwriting to express exactly how the music made me feel at the exact time I was writing lyrics, letting so many random thoughts and feelings and emotions impact the song.

■ Boris with his wife, Lyuda, and their son, Gleb,
Leningrad, 1985.

■ Boris, May 1986.

Everything I wrote with him helped shape me into a deeper, more honest version of myself. He was the sun melting away all the snow from my branches, revealing the changing, rich hues underneath the superficial white facade that had frozen my *Beverly Hills Brat* album in place.

The first songs we wrote together were called "Steel Wheels" and "Modern Age Rock 'n Roll." They were the kind of songs that made me proud to listen to them, flushed cheeks and a beaming face as I shared them with others. The lyrics for both aren't necessarily straightforward, but both evoke different themes with random, disjointed lines. I love listening to the chorus of "Steel Wheels" now, the call to "make love under the red sky" especially meaningful in retrospect.

There would be days, my favorite days, when I'd catch Boris in a playful mood. Once we were up on his roof with his guitar, the sun straining against the heavy clouds, and he spontaneously started jamming a bunch of oldies like "Johnny B. Goode," "Tutti Frutti," "Blue Suede Shoes," a Grateful Dead song, and a few others. He played them out of the blue like a magician pulling birds from thin air, his deep voice beautiful and the Celtic cross hanging from his neck giving off a spark that lit up the corrugated metal around us. To watch him was to witness a completely free and pure artist. It was so obvious how much he loved those songs and how much Western rock 'n roll awakened him and changed his life. I felt so incredibly lucky to be part of this time with him.

As we toyed with other ideas, Boris started strumming "I Got You Babe," by Sonny and Cher. Listening to his slower acoustics, I felt goosebumps up my arms.

"Let's record it," I said.

"Okay," Boris said slowly. "I don't know if my friends can steal the recorder from the studio while you're here."

"What if we try it the other way around?" I was getting excited. "I'll record it with my friends in the U.S., and I'll bring back the tape for you to sing your part over it."

That's how we worked. I would have ideas, and Boris would smile at me and say, "Why not?" I went home to Los Angeles and recorded the song in a silver studio bus on an abandoned property overlooking the Malibu beach. On my next trip to Leningrad, I brought in the cassette tape and we recorded Boris' vocals in the most roguish way, with Boris in his headphones listening to my recording on my Walkman while he sang into another Walkman. At the end where I repeated the phrase "I got you babe," he repeated it in Russian. I brought Boris' tape back to Los Angeles, and we fed his vocal back into the machine to line up with mine. Boris was up for anything and down for everything, always getting a kick out of my feverish suggestions. "Why not?" No matter what I proposed, Boris infused it with magic.

The two of us didn't do anything according to a grand plan. We jumped into everything on the spur of the moment like the devoted Castor and Pollux bouncing between Hades and Olympia, America and the Soviet Union. On another of my trips over, when winter had not yet turned to spring, we snuck into a completely empty Gorky Park to shoot scenes for our "I Got You Babe" music video and pulled each other onto the stationary rides and vacant stage. Judy played the part of the cinematographer, chasing us around Moscow with my camcorder as Boris and I danced on balconies and ran through big snowy squares. We were as inconspicuous as possible, but we were as free and unencumbered as the icy wind.

The next day, Boris came to our Moscow hotel called the Cosmos. Russians were not permitted to enter hotels, but Boris and I pretended he was a foreigner and made loud conversation about sightseeing that day.

"Wow, that square was so big!"

"I thought the murals were so powerful!"

"The domes on the cathedral were incredible!"

He sauntered past the guards. Upstairs in the boring Soviet hotel, we tried to think of the most ridiculous scene we could film. We ended up filling the stocky bathtub with bubbles and getting into it, writing on the tiled wall with my dark lipstick and singing to each other while Judy diligently kept recording. I messed up and wrote "I You Babe" so that Boris had to show me where to fit in the "Got" as the camera rolled, always a reminder that despite all my ideas, Boris was the master and I was the student.

When I came back to the States, I took that footage to an editor with the idea to turn it into a music video. The editor and I spliced it all together, and I ran it back to Boris

■ "I Got You Babe" video shoot with Boris, Cosmos Hotel, Moscow, 1985.

like a hotcake. I had never done anything like that before, but I quickly discovered I had an ability and talent to visualize scenes and put them together on film.

"Shit," Boris told me after watching it. For him, less words were always more, and I knew he loved it.

The video would become quite famous, and that tub scene one of the most iconic images of the two of us. People assumed we were totally naked beneath the bubbles, but to this day I'll swear we weren't. Boris was wonderfully good-natured about the whole thing. He had had no way of knowing my little video project would amount to anything or immortalize the two of us in a white tile bathtub on YouTube, but he was happy to have fun with it in the moment. He lived by the mantra that if you could do it now, then do it. For the wild spirit I was becoming, it was all the inspiration I needed.

"I hear that you and Joanna might be cooperating together," a Western interviewer said to Boris shortly after. "An American and a Soviet musician working together?"

"Well, we are cooperating for quite a long time already, like two years writing songs together. It was a big challenge for me to try and co-write the songs suitable for usual American people who don't know a thing about Russia and don't care. It was great fun trying to do this, and Joanna looks to me like a very promising songwriter right now."

"So, do you guys feel like citizens of the world or still your own countries?"

Boris laughed in that low way that I loved. "I think it's the same thing because Russia is part of the world and America is part of the world – not just countries, isolated. Here we have such a beautiful weapon of rock 'n roll, and everybody understands it. As long as rock 'n roll is common ground for everybody, it can serve as some kind of a bridge."

A bridge from one bathtub to the next. I think Boris and my music video surprised people because we both appeared so human and so similar. Face to face you almost couldn't tell who was on which side of the imaginary line.

As all this was going on, though, my mother was getting more and more concerned with my growing ties to a Communist country, her perfectly styled frosty blonde hair moving against her jawline as she shook her head and told me, "I really don't think you should keep going. You need to find a real job here and find a nice American husband. You're not getting any younger, Joanna."

"You're not getting any younger, Joanna," I mimicked to Boris as I complained to him about my mother's pressures and anxieties. That trip, before I left again, Boris handed me a soft manila envelope with an ash smudge on it.

"Can you give this to your mother for me?"

"What?" I stared at the envelope, totally caught off guard.

He said nothing more, giving Judy and I his customary bow as we left him standing at his door and headed down the familiar cement stairs. When I got home, I sat on the arm of the sofa as my mother got a silver letter opener and sliced through the envelope.

Inside was a handwritten note on grid paper. As my mother read it, I saw her entire person change in a way I always imagined would happen. Her cheeks softened, her eyes danced, and I could see Miss New York City in her face, a title she'd won in her youth.

Mrs. Nicholas! I'd like to thank you for all you've done and – the first thing – for your beautiful daughters. You have to put up with a lot, it's – as I can imagine, knowing my own mother's troubles – a hard thing to be a mother of a rock 'n roller, and I admire your patience and your faith. You're really wonderful. Greatest thoughts and lots of love from all of us, including my mother, my wife and my son, and all the people in the band. I hope I'll meet you some day. Love from Leningrad, B.G.

"She loved the letter!" I told him when I phoned him after, hoping the line wouldn't get disconnected. "I can't believe you did that!"

"That is good," he said in his thoughtful, articulate way. There was a pause where I was afraid that I may have lost the line, until I heard him clear his throat. "You come back now."

◆

The first time I saw Kostya Kinchev was in 1985 at the Rock Club in Leningrad. He performed with his punk rock band Alisa, having left Moscow and the heavy hands of the authorities trying to squash rock musicians in the capital to find air in Leningrad that could fill his lungs. His music was driving hard rock, but also dynamic and dreamy like Black Sabbath riding into town on dragons. Kostya was a shorter Billy-Idol-meets-Freddie-Mercury with an aura that could spill over the stage and wrap itself around your heart. He'd twist his arms and hands in knots while shifting his body from side to side and provoking you with his black-rimmed eyes. As strange and overpowering as his performance was, it was hard not to melt while watching him.

He was just as compelling offstage as he was onstage, a soulful and observant man with a cross on a chain hanging over his chest. He had a surprising Herculean strength when he hugged me that would always make me go weak in the knees. Kostya didn't speak English so we couldn't have long conversations, but I did interview him a couple times with Alex Kan as a translator. During the first interview, even though Alex was doing most of the talking, Kostya stared deep into my eyes the entire time without flinching. He was a literal star, this intense, burning energy that was both blinding and steadfast. After the interview, I asked Kostya and his bandmate Slava to do a short spot for MTV with me out on the balcony. As Alex began translating, Kostya started to touch my hair and my neck with the back of his hand. Normally I'd be shocked at such an aggressive and invasive move, but something about Kostya just made me go with it. I had never had anybody do anything as brash as that before, and even though I was a little embarrassed, it was impossible not to feel energized by his aura.

"Tell him I want his phone number, because the next time I come I want to call him the first day. I can't believe I've been here five times, and this is the first time we're meeting!" I said to Alex. As he translated, I looked back at Kostya, and he just stared down into my soul.

"*Tselui menia doorak,*" was the only thing I could say to him in Russian, followed quickly by, "Sorry, that's all I know." Being Kostya, he accepted what I'd said by kissing my neck. As I stood in the middle of Kostya and Slava, Judy dutifully kept filming. There, between the glare of the camera and the glow of Kostya, I faced the lens and said the only thing I could remember in that moment. "I want my MTV!"

I saw Kostya again when I went to see him recording at Lyosha Vishnaya's apartment. Vishnaya, or Cherry as everyone called him, had renovated his one large room into a

■ Slava Zaderi and Kostya Kinchev from Alisa, 1985.

recording studio draped with carpets with an oversized couch almost pressed up against the mixing table and a small vocal booth. I sat on the couch with Cherry's skinny blonde wife and filmed Kostya filling the space with his amplified eyes and cigarette smoke. He was always unpredictable, waiting for lightning and inspiration to strike. It was always interesting to me that he was the only one of the guys who didn't seem to have the patience for being filmed, his eyes darting around and his fists feistily on his hips. In one video I have of a casual dinner party, Kostya keeps his hands over his face the entire time the camera is on, only revealing his twinkling smirk once it panned away. He was so free a spirit he couldn't bear to be captured, even on film.

Nothing could tie him down.

"I sing about looking up to the sky, not to look at your feet. I sing about eternity," he told me once when I interviewed him with the help of Alex Kan. Kostya had his legs crossed, his elbow on his knee like the art model that he was. As he talked, he waved his hand along to the cadence of his words, a bird in flight.

"I'm not looking up enough," I told my mother when I returned home, sitting across from her at the dark oak table in her dining room.

She shook her head. "Tell me Joanna, are you looking for God or for a husband?"

It wasn't about either. For the first time in my life I was beginning to feel empowered, people like Kostya and Boris challenging me to start trying to find myself.

"How do you get an idea for a song?" I asked Kostya.

"It depends on the song. It's hard to explain. They just appear, depending on various moments in my life. It's just a state of my soul." I could see as Alex translated, even he was inspired by Kostya's sentiment.

Kostya was so effusive, so in touch with his feelings and ideas that he couldn't even consider keeping them down. His hand would write lyrics by itself, and he would only realize after that something had been written down.

"Would you want to become official?" I asked.

"No. Because I want to do what I want to do. For me, this is folklore." Kostya was writing himself into his own fairy tale, an amalgamation of the villain and the hero with his saturnine face and magnetic smile. I had to stop myself from swooning.

The beautiful thing about Kostya was that he never stopped shining and making you hyper-aware of yourself in his presence. Every time I saw him, he was smoldering with this passionate and profound power that I found addictive in a country of grey skies and dark winter days. A few times we snuck into a closet or a small room and fooled around. I knew he was married, but somehow, I rationalized that since I didn't know his wife it wasn't as bad. The way he could find his way around a woman's body was impossible to resist, and even though we didn't know each other's languages there was a strong physical chemistry that said it all. You don't need to understand the universe to be awed by its actions.

◆ The Beauty in the Beast

"Hey, I am a British tourist!"

It was the first time I ever saw Boris unnerved and panicked. As we were leaving through the lobby of my hotel off Nevsky Prospekt, discussing my ideas to bring his music to the States and try to bring Bowie to play in Russia, two men in black suits with angry eyes grabbed Boris for questioning. Around this time I'd begun noticing cars following me while I drove around town, and I often got stopped for numerous traffic violations that I hadn't committed; these were things I tried to convince myself I was making up in my own mind, but to see my master and my bulwark lose his cool was like frigid water splashed in my face. In that moment I suddenly became acutely aware of the fact that I was an interloper in this place I called Wonderland.

I was quickly growing attached to Russia. I had found this beautiful, spirited, patch-work family in the musicians and artists who filled my trips with their bright souls and dark humor. I loved sharing a sofa with them to write songs or chasing ideas through the subzero temperatures, sharing jackets and kisses like crazy kids on a playground. Every time I boarded a plane back to America, I'd feel lost and empty, tired of floating around Los Angeles like an alien who could never fully convince others of the wonder and excitement of my faraway planet. I hated the thought of all of my friends going on without me back in the Venice of the North, holding court in their communal apartments and making merry at basement concerts to which I wouldn't be invited. Sometimes I wondered if they ever hated that I could even get on a plane and escape Russia, trading those white nights for sunny days and poolside lemonades.

The Soviet Union was so different from anything I'd ever known growing up, but it grew on me like ivy-league vines. I adored that Russians were so comfortable with who they were; few had pretenses, and they never exaggerated to make themselves or anyone else feel better.

"Your daughter is beautiful," I told a couple once. My mother had trained me to always be complimentary to others, part of that Southern California charm that lined the tan, thin skin of competition and superiority.

"No, she's really not," they responded. "But she is a very clever, very smart, and funny girl."

I was in awe of Russian women. They all had jobs, took care of children and husbands, and made food for everyone in their home. I had never even learned how to bake a potato. Despite all these demands, Russian women weren't run down by their hard work but took pride in their strength and their bodies. Overweight women would wear sexy outfits and dance at parties as if gravity had no effect on them. Leaning against a wall and watching them in an oversized shirt and baggy jeans I would often think, *Do I as an American feel as free as these women?* They might not have much money, but they had fewer societal inhibitions and were less constrained by convoluted ideas about what other people thought of them.

"*Te tolsty.*" Some people would sometimes say to Judy and me when we'd return back to Russia. "You're thicker." It absolutely devastated me, but these women didn't see it as an insult. It was a fact of life, not a mark of self-worth.

The men in Russia seemed more affectionate between each other – fathers and their teenage sons comfortable holding hands and close male friends kissing goodbye on the lips. These men were so confident in their masculinity that they didn't feel inhibited in the way I would see American males interact.

Yet the most actively defiant, bold, and aggressive people on the streets were not these male figures but the *babushkas* marshaling their neighborhoods with their groceries and grandchildren.

"So, you think you have the right to be on the lawn?" one yelled in Russian at a group of us as we relaxed in the grass. We'd been taking photos in our black and white Guitar Center t-shirts and then started singing "We Are the World." She was not amused.

"Quickly now, get off the grass. All of you!"

Boris, ever the peacemaker, started to get up while the rest of us lingered.

"We do not speak your language," Afrika shouted at her in English with heavy accent.

"It's not nice," she continued to scold us. "I'm sure that in your country you wouldn't do it. Imagine what'll happen if you all lie on the grass!" As the rest of us began to push ourselves to our feet, she shooed us away and continued to call out, "There will be no grass if you lie on it like that!"

Here we were, a group of tough rockers, and we were slinking away guiltily from the words of an old woman.

The food was certainly not what I was used to. I'd spent my life snacking on Snickers bars or eating processed and over-salted TV dinners that my mom would leave for me and my sisters when she'd run out on dates with my stepfather, but as time went on I began to crave Russia's simple, pure dishes: carrots, potatoes, borscht, and the most incredible brown bread ever. *Bulochnayas* – bread shops – were all over Leningrad. You couldn't walk down the street without inhaling the thick hearty smell of the old-world bread and local ingredients, only overpowered by the scent of meat people hung on their balcony railings, using them in lieu of refrigerators. Each loaf felt like it weighed over a kilo, and just a couple of slices could be a full meal. It made me realize how fake American bread was. I guess Wonder Bread wasn't so wonderful after all.

The biggest downside to food in Russia was getting it. It seemed as if most mothers and wives spent their entire lives trying to buy food. Store lines would stretch for hundreds of meters down busy streets in the dead of winter, and once inside, the shoppers would be crammed into a steamy room as everyone pushed towards the splintered counter. There were times when the guy behind it would just walk away right as someone would reach the front, disappearing and leaving all the overheated, packed bodies pushing awkwardly against each other. Did he go to get something? Was he taking a break? Had he left for the day? It happened all the time. The whole process felt like someone chipping away with a hammer at a sculpture, all for just one loaf. At open markets or street stands, lines would be just as long, and the produce would be unpredictable. You'd stand in line for what felt like years, and then most had to walk, take a bus, and walk some more to get home with bags and bags of bread and fruit and vegetables weighing them down. None of these people ever had to go to the gym.

Russians were very homeopathic about their health. They seemed to rarely go to doctors but had ingenious ways to take care of themselves. In the middle of a conversation, Boris would pick up a whole garlic and start eating it.

"What are you doing?" I'd laugh.

"What? I feel like I'm getting sick, and this makes it go away."

"Oh my god, Boris, that is so gross…"

It was just one of the many home remedies that somehow seemed to work. Even garlic wasn't as ubiquitous as vodka, though. As someone who wanted to drink nothing other than cold water, I ran into a few problems. Everyone would boil their water, which gave it the worst tangy taste and a bit of a strange smell. I'd refuse to drink it, instead running the sink tap and cupping my hands to use as a glass.

"You can't drink that," everyone would say to me. "It is not clean!" Being young and thinking myself impermeable, I drank it anyway.

Every day, one of the biggest adventures I'd have was trying to use the toilet. A majority of people used newspaper instead of real toilet paper, which was usually pushed behind a pipe in the bathroom like a kite stuck in a tree. It was so stiff and didn't absorb much of anything, but I soon learned that even newspaper could be a luxury as it was absolutely better than nothing.

Especially on Aeroflot, there was rarely toilet paper or a hand towel in the bathroom on flights. I became happy if the toilet was just working. On some of those flights even the seats would be broken and completely bent forward. Most people smoked, and few bothered to wear their seat belts. It was such an informal environment, thirty thousand feet away from the nearest working toilet. It was a startling, stark contrast to the American 'safety-first' attitude.

Flying wasn't the only transportation feat. None of my friends had cars in the first few years I traveled to Leningrad, nor did most other Russians at that time. We'd either take the metro or tram, or we'd hitchhike the Russian way by waving a hand low at a car. If it stopped, you gave the driver a destination and prayed to whatever hunched, grumpy gods were crouching in the clouds that the driver would agree to take you. Upon arrival, you'd pay a nominal amount, and everyone seemed to know how much each ride was worth. This was the Uber of the '80s.

♦

There were the difficulties of life, but the friends I'd met made it so easy to forgive and embrace this grating, unmerciful motherland. Every time I was forced to leave, I filled my days as a missionary for the underground Russian movement until I could go back. In New York in 1985, I set up a meeting with Andy Warhol at his factory to show him photos of the New Artists and their art. He was a subdued, soft-spoken man, translucent as a ghost with electric yellow glasses and frosty white hair, who made conversations static and awkward. Yet as he was looking through those photos, he became animated and his face contorted into these boisterous, fascinated expressions. I explained who the artists

■ I brought Andy Warhol some examples of Russian art, including this collage by Oleg Kotelnikov, 1985.

were, and as he ravenously dug through my images, he told me he couldn't believe that halfway around the world people were creating graffiti styles parallel to Keith Haring and Basquiat. I gave him two pieces of actual art, one collage from Timur Novikov and one from Oleg Kotelnikov. Warhol, who had greeted me with a limp handshake, now grasped the works strongly in his hands as he tried to cling to his own piece of Wonderland.

I told him how all the Russians knew and idolized him and asked him if he would sign some Campbell soup cans to my friends if I ran out to buy some. Fifteen minutes later I was sitting with my legs crossed beside Warhol under the industrial lights while I spelled out name after name for him to write on the cans. He was such a trooper, laughing at himself as he tried to get the foreign names right. Before I left, he told me to keep in touch and let him know what was happening with "the guys." That day, Warhol put the "ordinary" in "extraordinary," a humble, gracious man with a nose for brilliance and a new vision of the Soviet Union under his white wig.

Flash forward to the customs at the Russian airport where I had to explain to the grizzly guards how I had terrible food allergies and had to travel with the only food I could eat: Campbell's soup. I had lugged them across two continents and an ocean in my backpack, refusing to let them out of my sight. I wasn't going to shoulder all that just so those pejorative authorities could eat it all up.

■ Colored pen drawing of Sologub, Grebenshchikov, Tsoi, and Kinchev by Oleg Kotelnikov, 2018.

All my friends were ecstatic about the signed Andy Warhol soup cans. They started to jokingly call me Santa Claus.

"Hey, Santa Claus," Gustav said one day as I walked into the apartment, my cheeks bright red from the effort of the stairs.

"Hey," I said. "Something smells good."

There was the signed soup can on the table, but as I got closer, I realized it was empty! Gustav saw my look of surprise.

"We wanted to know what American soup tasted like!"

Warhol died not long after this. We had all felt so connected to him, and the world seemed a little darker for a while. Sergey and Kolya sent me a telex that I passed on to the Warhol Factory. In Sergey's note, he wrote: *Since I got to know about him, I've dreamt of meeting him and working together. And though we never met, this death is a personal loss for me.*

Those were my Russians. Full of dreams, reactions, and haunting introspections that they were not afraid to share with themselves, me, and the rest of the world. If that's not free, I'll never understand what is.

◆

By now, I had been christened "The Tractor," or "American Tractor" for my ability to push forward and get things done. Music videos, collaborations, shiny guitars, and soup cans. Between Yuri, Boris, Viktor, Sergey, and the other guys in Kino, Strange Games, Alisa, and the Rock Club, I felt like the luckiest person in the world to be hanging out with these superlative humans night after night. I wanted to do more than just getting them instruments and supplies. I wanted to share their genius with my own country.

Before one of my trips through London, Sergey told me to get hold of a guy named Leo Feigin, a tall, bald, sweet-faced Russian immigrant there who was working for the BBC. A couple years prior, Leo had somehow gotten Sergey's music out of the U.S.S.R. and put out a few of his piano and Pop Mechanics recordings in the U.K. It was then that I got it in my head that I wanted to produce an album of Russian rock music to share with the northwestern hemisphere. My first thought was to put out an Aquarium record. I got back in touch with David Bowie's people to see if they could help, to whom I'd steadily been sending Boris' tapes. At the same time, though, I was increasingly aware that I might only have one shot to expose Americans to the unimaginable, meaty scene of Russian underground rock. It started to make more sense to feature more than one artist or band on a record so people could get a fuller plate.

"Hey, so I have another idea," I told Boris back in Leningrad in November 1985.

Needing privacy, we were tucked in the safe space of his roof on the metal shingles, talking and watching the dark pigeons fly over the city. When we spoke up there, I always felt so powerful and hopeful, removed for a moment from the urban waterfall of chaos and exhaustion.

"Go on."

"Let's release an album in the United States with a bunch of Russian bands. I'm pretty sure I can get us a record deal. I just feel that people need to be inspired by you guys."

"Why not?" He said as always, his incandescent smile starting the slow crawl up his face amid the cigarette smoke. "Let's do it."

"We need to decide on the bands," I said, already in tractor mode. "Obviously, Aquarium has to be on the record, and Kino, but who else do you think would be good?"

In the end, we decided to include Alisa and Strange Games because both had such energy and magnetism, and I considered those guys my friends too. Those four, about the biggest bands at the Rock Club at the time, would give the album a diverse, uninhibited sound: Aquarium's eclectic style, Kino's dark pop, Alisa's harder punk rock, and Strange Games' ska grit.

Unlike any sane, content person, I had this burning desire to also make music videos to go with the album and add a visual texture to the production. MTV had recently launched in the States, and videos had become the best way to market a band. But more than that, the bands I knew each had such a distinct ethos and backbones that they created an alarmingly colorful contrast I thought would be incredible on film. Boris was Boris, handsome and steady like Apollo; Viktor Tsoi, with his big hair, black makeup, and iridescent shirts was a commander of steady ebony seas; Alisa were a strong, exuberant group that was bold and showy or like some secret drug; Strange Games was a party of flashing lights and goofy, graphic musicians.

I never had to make a big 'pitch' to the guys, but the next time I'd meet each one I'd casually ask if I could have their music on cassette because I was going to try to get a record deal in the States.

"It's a long shot, but how amazing would it be," I told them. Their responses were nearly unanimously the same, just a shoulder shrug and an amused smile and a hand through the hair. No one was too excited because nobody thought we had a serious chance of getting a deal.

I wasn't one hundred percent sure of the risks, for me or the bands, but I knew they existed. Yet, through all my experiences up to and including this time, I lived with the cocky American confidence that my beautiful blue passport and citizenship could protect me from anything. "Just blame me," I told them all from the beginning. If shit was going to hit the Siberian fan, "blame it all on me."

Boris and I decided on code names to make ourselves more inconspicuous when talking directly through the telephone or using intermediaries.

"I would like to be Bowie," he said.

"I don't think that works," I said. "We're trying to get the real Bowie on board and that could get confusing, you know what I mean?"

"Okay, Jagger."

"That works!" I wracked my brain trying to come up with something for myself, but my head was already so preoccupied with thoughts of the videos, my industry contacts, and Yuri that I couldn't fill up space in my brain with anything else.

Back in the States I was driving with my friend Paul from Houston, Texas, to Bloomington, Indiana, in Paul's 1959 Corvette Stingray. As we shot across the empty, open roads, I told Paul about the album and my need for a code name to keep the plans hidden from the KGB. Racing past tumbleweeds and gnarled thirsty cacti, I glanced between my feet on the dash where the silver logo *Stingray* sat framed by my red sneakers.

"Stingray!" I screamed into the open desert cavity. "That's it!" The car swerved.

"What?!" Paul shouted.

"Stingray!" I was bouncing on the seat. "That's my codename for this Russian rock album!"

"Liability," Paul muttered, both hands gripping the wheel as he righted the car. "That's your codename for this American road trip."

It wasn't just any American road trip. We were headed to meet John Cougar's songwriter friend, Dan Ross, in his hometown, who John thought would help my career. I'd met John Cougar a few times through Billy Gaff, an English music manager who would always host me when I went through London to Leningrad. One night, I was dancing around in Billy's screening room to John Cougar's new music videos when the singer himself showed up in the doorway.

"Hey! What're you up to?" He asked with a smile on his devilishly handsome face.

I slammed off the television and threw myself down into a chair.

"Nothing! You?"

Back in Leningrad, as I was still somewhere in between the Longhorn State and the cornfields of Bloomington, the guys were collecting their recordings and band photos for the potential album project. Sergey and Boris both had friends in several international consulates in Leningrad – the U.S., French, and Swedish – who were fans of the underground rock music as well. Boris and Sergey would get invited to go see new films or listen to American records, but their diplomatic connections also gave them access to direct international phone services and international delivery service through diplomatic pouches that navigated around the clawing hands of any customs officers. A couple of people in the consulates agreed to send tapes out in their diplomatic mail, addressed to my mom in Los Angeles.

"Hey, Jagger, I got the Billy Idol music," I'd relay to Boris on the phone, referring to the band Alisa in code. "Still waiting for the Duran Duran pictures." Duran Duran had become the code name for Kino.

"Roger that, Stingray," Boris would say in a way that made me burst out laughing at the ridiculousness of it all, usually seconds before the line would get disconnected.

The first couple of industry titans I met in the States, like those at Warner Brothers and Capitol Records, were receptive to the tapes I had already brought back with me and played for them. It was so clear they saw potential in the project and could see the remnant pieces of Wonderland that the tapes represented, but as soon as the discussion turned to specifics, I could feel everything get sticky.

"Who owns the rights to this music?" I was asked nearly every time.

"The bands do. They're technically unofficial, underground musicians who record on two-tracks in their bedrooms. They're completely independent."

"I don't know," the titans would muse. "Are we sure the Soviet government doesn't have a stake in this? The last thing we need is for them to start suing us for copyright infringement."

"Absolutely not," I'd say, exasperated. Even when I was back home now, the Soviet government managed to plague me like some heavy morning fog that distorted everything and refused to burn off. "These artists have complete freedom to do whatever they want with their music."

I could see that my assurances weren't enough to convince a large record company that the U.S.S.R. wouldn't end up taking legal action. Much later, I'd be informed that the Kremlin's publishing arm VAAP had already cut deals to distribute Russian classical music with several of these firms, so that the American companies didn't want to jeopardize that tentative relationship with any type of clandestine rock 'n roll.

I realized I needed a smaller company willing to take a risk. Big Time Records was an Australian label that had hot stuffy offices on Sunset and Vine in the center of Hollywood. The thunderous cacophony of traffic swelled into the room as I spoke to Fred Bestall, an exec whose business attire included jeans and a t-shirt. I told Fred about my recent experience at Disneyland, where I asked some boys in line behind me what they thought of Russia.

"Russia is evil! We should blow them up!" These were young boys, whose extent of a social life ended at the plastic facade of Splash Mountain. I told Fred that if these boys could see my friends and hear their music, they would probably change their tune.

"Every one of the bigger labels recognized the potential of this project," I said, "but they all got hung up on the legal end of things. These bands aren't recognized by the government in the Soviet Union. Here, they have every right to publish their music freely."

"There's still got to be some risk," Fred pointed out.

"Well, yes. There's a huge risk for me, that I could never go back and see these bands, my best friends, again. I honestly think the record is so important that I want to keep going regardless. Their music is a gateway to bringing people together."

"I see…"

"And there's probably still some risk you could be sued," I acquiesced reluctantly.

"I'm sure we could." His face toyed with the possibility of a smile. "You know, they say any publicity is good publicity."

I knew I was finally getting somewhere, that underneath his business strategy he was starting to believe in the power of these musicians. "I could also have the bands sign something saying they were free to turn over their music, or anything that would make you more comfortable."

"Perhaps," Fred said. "But what's life without a little risk?"

I was so happy even the cars in traffic started to sound like songbirds. We started talking terms, and soon we had a deal. We agreed to a double album with an initial run of five thousand copies. The two records would be on colored vinyl, one red and the other bright yellow for the colors on the Soviet flag.

This was the beginning of 1986, about the same time I walked into my mother's house and saw her talking in the living room with a woman I had never met.

"Oh, Joanna, this is Agent Betsy Cordova from the FBI. She came over to ask me about your father's film, *The Truth About Communism.*"

I froze, glaring at the slender, bookish brunette and feeling the euphoria I'd been riding slowly start to deflate under me. A thousand thoughts raced through my mind. Why would this woman call my mother about my father's film when they'd been divorced for fourteen years? Was this all some elaborate setup to talk to *me*? What if any Russians knew this woman was in my mother's house? It would justify their belief that I was an agent, and I'd never get back in, that's what.

The FBI woman stood up and reached out her hand. "Your mother has been telling me all about your trips to Russia. I'd love to ask you some questions."

I had little choice but to sit down, crossing my arms over my chest to avoid nervously pulling on my face the way my mother hated.

"Can you tell me about these trips? Where do you go?" The woman had to be in her forties. She was way too old, I concluded, to have any appreciation for the boldness of the underground rock scene.

"I go to Leningrad and Moscow every three or four months on group tourist trips," I told her curtly.

"Whom do you meet? Did you meet with any government officials? Why do you go so often?" As she spoke, she was scribbling down notes on an oversized legal pad.

"My friends are underground Russian rock musicians. I'm just trying to bring their music out of the Soviet Union and publish an album here in the States."

She cocked her head at me. "Why on earth would you do that?"

I raised an eyebrow at her. "I want Americans to see how cool and talented these Russian rockers are. People here need to understand that rock music in this country is the same as rock music anywhere. Music has no borders. I'm trying to bring about a better understanding between people."

"I see." She was completely disinterested. *Listen to me!* I wanted to yell. *Listen to their music! It will change the way you look at the world through your nasty, narrow eyes!*

"Have you been to any Soviet consulates here in the U.S.?" She continued. "Or met with any Soviet immigrants?"

"No. Just musicians."

"And you say you've had no contacts with anyone in the government?"

Why didn't this chick just come out and ask me if I were a Soviet spy? The question was written all over her face.

"Just. Musicians." I repeated.

She leaned forward. "I don't think you quite understand the risks involved, regardless of your reason for going. It is possible for the Soviets to blackmail you by planting drugs on your person and then arresting you for possession of narcotics. Forced cooperation with the Soviets is still cooperation in our books."

I glared at her. "I see."

She handed me her card before she left. "If you don't mind, I'll probably have some additional questions later."

"Mom!" I screamed after the woman left. "Why in the world would you let this woman come over and interrogate me?"

"I don't know," my mom said innocently. "She called and sounded so nice and asked if I could talk about your father's film. It's been so long, so I thought why not?"

"Mom, you have to have my back for stuff like this," I sighed, throwing myself back down on the paisley couch.

"Obviously what you're doing there is raising eyebrows and putting you in danger. What if they plant drugs on you? I don't want you to get hurt. I don't think you should go back."

"I'm not having this conversation." I got up, pushing my way past her and heading for the large, oak front door. Outside I could see the afternoon sunlight, and hundreds of miles past the horizon the darkness of the Russia night. "I've got a record to finish."

◆ Making Waves

We arranged to have everyone meet in Mikhailovsky Park. It was safer there than the communal apartments, inside the wrought iron gates where the only things watching us were a few ducks and mature oak trees. I walked quickly along the waterside path covered in a thick brown coat, the garden empty, snowy, and dark in the short winter day. The bands were waiting for me, their devoted and nutty smiles radiating heat as I rushed into a dozen open arms.

"Welcome back, sweetheart," Yuri said, kissing me.

"Oh my gosh, that's amazing," I said, beaming at him. "You learned English for me!"

"Sweetheart," he said proudly. It was clear that was the extent of it.

Vitia and Grysha Sologub were the only two members from Strange Games there. I knew the rest of the band didn't want to be a part of my project for fear of getting in trouble, which I couldn't hold against them or their families. All of Kino and Aquarium were there, though, as well as Kostya and Slava from Alisa. Neither Boris nor I had updated anyone about the deal yet, so they really all showed up with no idea what the meeting was about. They stood there stamping their cold feet into the thin layer of ice on the grass and laughing at each other's goofy expressions, jostling one another with their lanky, long arms. At a *tusofka* years later someone mentioned to me that every time I came back it was like a party for everyone, and I was lucky that because of the excitement I always got to see the guys happy and teasing. I never witnessed any in-fighting between the bands or Soviet depression, just the glowing faces and cigarette butts.

I cleared my throat, looking up at their lively, bold faces. "It took a while," I said loudly, as calmly as I could. I could hear the excitement in my own voice, and the Russian lilt that had crept into my accent when I was talking to my friends. "But we have a record deal in the United States!"

I was met with silence. Stunned, incredulous silence. They blinked their big eyes and shook their heads like wolves shaking themselves awake. Then I felt someone sweep me up in his arms and what seemed like a hundred kisses across my face as everyone began to celebrate. We were a pop of color and light in the vacant winter wasteland, a surge of hope within a forlorn, miserable system.

"Each band will have five or six songs, so give me eight or ten to choose the best ones for the U.S. market," I said as we caught our breaths. "We're going to do a double album, so with four bands that means each group will get one side of the record."

"We are comfortable representing Strange Games for the album," Vitia spoke up, putting his arm around his brother.

"I also need you guys' lyrics so I can have them translated for the albums. We want people to be able to understand what you're singing about." I paused. "I have no idea how many albums we're going to sell, so I have no idea how much money we're going to make."

It was clear by the way they shrugged and leaned casually into the cold air that swept through the park that they weren't concerned with profiting from this.

"Whatever we make we can buy whatever equipment," Boris said easily. It was unanimous.

I took out a pen and paper, and in the freezing cold I wrote with red fingers a list of everything they wanted, from guitar picks to drumsticks, strings to synthesizers, and acrylic paint for the artists. Vitia looked over my shoulder, making sure I had everything they requested written down. Exactly.

"So, the last thing," I said, trying to see if I could still move my fingers as I shoved them back in my gloves and pockets, "I told Boris already, but if anything happens because of the album I want you to all say you don't know anything about it. I have an American passport, so I'll be fine."

Viktor was the first to shake his head. "Jo…"

"I'm serious. You guys need to protect yourselves. Just worry about changing the world."

Kostya, who had been standing with his arms crossed and his legs wide, wrapped his arms around me like a bony, sultry teddy bear. It turned into a group hug that could have melted the coldest heart at the Kremlin.

Later that day, as Boris and I slipped off our shoes at the entrance to his apartment, he turned to me with a more serious look on his face. "The KGB," he said in his slow drawl," they have been asking about you."

"What?" I asked. "Why? How do you know?"

"Sometimes they call us musicians and ask to talk. I like to play nice, and sometimes they want autographs. I have nothing to hide."

"You're kidding me," I said. It was so weird to imagine Boris chatting with a member of the KGB. "Does everyone do that?"

"No. Some ignore. Kinchev might disappear to Moscow when they start asking about him. Gustav refuses. Vitia always talks because he's scared."

"Well, what do they want with me?"

"I don't know. They ask me if we know one another."

"And what did you say?"

"I say, yeah, I know her. Everyone knows her because she loves Russian rock 'n roll. That's all."

This was the first time I had hard evidence that the KGB was interested in me. Before, it had always been little hints and assumptions – disconnected phone lines or trailing cars. I thought of the record deal, and of Yuri. The idea that someone wanted to prevent me from that... I could feel this new anxiety twisting itself between my ribs.

"I have nothing to hide," I said, getting defensive. "All I want to do is open American eyes to Russian music and show that our two countries are a lot alike. I'll tell them that to their faces. Can you ask them if I can come speak with them?"

I thought that maybe if I could show the KGB pictures of me speaking at several high schools in California and showing my videos there, they might understand I was trying to bridge a cultural gap and not trying to spy. I hated knowing these guys were out there tracking my activity and assuming I had an agenda that was not as honest and purposeful as the one I had. It made me feel ineffective and neurotic.

"You scared them a bit," Boris told me after approaching them with the request. "They got very nervous. They told me no, don't let her come here!"

I pictured these monumental gargoyle men who could paint an entire town red with paranoia running to close the windows of their Leningrad headquarters and hide inside as I walked by. The thought almost made me laugh, if I hadn't been so anxious about the fact that they wouldn't let me meet them or listen to me defend myself.

A few days later, the director of the Rock Club, Kolya Mikhailov, told Boris that the

■ Aquarium playing at the Rock Club in Leningrad, 1986. Left to right: Dusha Romanov, Seva Gakkel, Sasha Titov, Boris Grebenshchikov, and Peter Troschenko on drums.

KGB threatened to cancel an Aquarium show that Boris had invited me to join. Years later, I found out that during this period in Russia there had actually been an internal struggle between the old guard and the others in the government, a debate over whether or not rock 'n roll was a decadent Western disease that had to be outlawed or merely a generational trend that could be monitored. If an American got up and sang at the Rock Club, the old guard could have used that for their argument and shut down the entire thing, so that I would have single handedly suppressed a movement of which I was dying to be a part! I had been so excited to get to stand there and sing with Boris for the first time, to share our magical connection with a room full of shining faces and twinkling sparklers, but even without knowing the extent of the consequence I felt it would be too risky.

"If you can't play, then I won't play," Boris said very matter of fact.

"No! Boris you have to go on. I don't want to make any trouble before the album is released in the States."

As I sat backstage and listened to the show in the shadows, I tried to ignore the fact that the record could be obstructed by forces bigger than any of us and instead, think about the name for the album. Boris came up with the idea to use the word "wave," evoking the image of waves of music traveling across vast oceans and colossal continents to fill the American air. I liked the idea of using that word in the title, but I also wanted to make sure Americans understood that the album was about bands from the Soviet Union. Boris and I eventually came up with the name "Red Wave." There was still the question as to how we would describe the bands in the album's subtitle though. Were they "illegal" or "outlawed"? "Amateur"? As I continued to watch the show from the wings, I knew these were some of the greatest musicians I'd ever seen. They needed a name that did them justice. Saying "unofficial" didn't feel very rock 'n roll to me, and finally as I sat in that dark corner of the hall and felt the walls shake the very core of the earth, I landed on the term "underground."

I knew the Soviet government would be upset with that term, but the truth was that these guys weren't allowed to fully exist in public and the Kremlin treated them almost like monsters under the bed threatening the sweet dreams of Communism and a controlled state. I was terrified of really making the officials mad, but I knew in my heart that what happened to me wasn't as important as what happened to these bands. We had to be honest with the album name, to pull back a piece of the Iron Curtain to show to the Western world. After much discussion with the rest of the guys, we had our title. *Red Wave: Four Underground Bands from the U.S.S.R.* Put that in your papirosi and smoke it.

◆

Yuri and I had been spending more and more time together. I started getting rental cars on most trips and tried to teach him to drive, letting him hold the steering wheel and change the gears as I yelled out "two!" or "three!" as we sped down a wide street. We would blast my new songs that I had recorded back in Los Angeles. I loved playing one called "Give Me Some More of Your Love," and as the song ends with me singing, "Come on, baby," I would shout out, "Come on, Yuri!" The more time I spent with him, in his muscle shirts and sunglasses, the happier it made me.

When I was back from making the record deal, he took me to his apartment. It was the first time we'd been truly alone together and not surrounded by the other members of Kino or other drivers trying to get out of our way on the road. The place had a homey feel to it, similar to the other apartments I'd seen and a world away from my mother and stepfather's pristine house, which felt more like a museum than a home. In Yuri's apartment there were faded rugs hanging on the walls and bits of paper, shopping bags, books, and clothes draped over the floor and furniture like little sleeping dogs. Out of the windows I could see a big empty lot filled with grass and small trees surrounded by uniform beige apartment complexes, with tiny red garden sheds and an economical yellow play structure. It all looked cheap, like a row of lower income housing in New York that was characterless and quiet.

"This is such a nice place. Do you live here by yourself?" I never really expected much of an answer to my English from him. He smiled and pointed to the refrigerator.

"Oh, no thank you, you're so sweet. I'm not that hungry."

Yuri nodded, and then made me a plate of cheese, bread, and borscht soup. I sat down at the kitchen table and forced myself to eat as he strummed his guitar and sang. He didn't need a stage or lights; he was absolutely mesmerizing in a black sweater and high-top boots, meeting my eyes over my plate. He put down the guitar and stood, taking my hand and leading me into his bedroom. It was a small, square space with oyster-pink wallpaper and a single bed with striped sheets. There was a moment we stood on either side of the room and I could *feel* the distance between us – the crumbled rough stretches of Europe, the cold salty Atlantic, and the political topography of the United States – and I wondered if it would ever be possible to bridge that gap. Then he was there, kissing my eyelids and my lips, his hands pulling me close to him. There were his eyes, my yellow hair falling against his face, his smooth white skin and my flushed red cheeks, until you couldn't remember which colors belonged to which flag and suddenly both countries were irrelevant.

I started spending most nights there after that, some forty minutes outside the city center in a southern part of Leningrad called Coopchina where his family was able to have their own apartment. I never saw his parents, an entomologist and botanist researcher, but I could always hear them moving quickly around the apartment before I would fall asleep or get up in the morning. By now I was used to the fact that many Russians didn't want to be involved with foreigners. Often Yuri's mother would make some type of cake and leave it out for the two of us to share, as if the place was filled with invisible fairies or elves with a special talent for baking. When wallpaper would tear or a pipe would leak, Yuri's father would tape it up and disappear as well.

"Are you sure they're okay that I stay here?" I kept asking with a mouthful of cake, eyeing all the scratches and bruises of the kitchen that needed fixing.

"Joanna," Yuri would always say with a slow smile, drawing out each syllable of my name. "Jo-an-na." Then he'd lean forward and kiss my eyelids again.

A trip or two after I started staying with him, I finally ran into his parents. It was early in the morning, cold and dark, and I walked into the kitchen in Yuri's long shirt

■ I started spending more and more time with Kino guitarist, Yuri Kasparyan. In the bottom right-hand
video still, Yuri is pointing to a window from where the KGB monitors the crowds.

and a pair of socks to find both his mother and father eating at the table.

"Oh," I said loudly, shocked. I stood there, blinking like a tired owl, wondering
whether or not I should keep standing there half-naked.

"These are parents," Yuri said in his broken English, running up behind me. He
pointed at them, and then at me. "This is Jo-an-na."

"Hello," I tried to say brightly, crossing my legs where I stood.

The two smiled and nodded, letting Yuri and I sit down. His mother had just made
some hot food, and she served us some as the four of us tried to make a conversation
around the steaming plates. Her flowered sundress looked out of place in the monochromatic room. Yuri's father spoke just the basics of English, and his mother didn't speak
any at all, so Yuri tried to translate with what little English he knew. I felt like I was in
a strange, happy episode of the *Twilight Zone*.

"So, what work do you do?" I asked Yuri's father.

"I am entomologist," he told me.

I stared at him.

"He studies, you know, insects," Yuri explained.

"This food is delicious," I told his mother. "Thank you for always leaving us some."

She smiled warmly at me, with no idea what I'd just said. I could have told her that I was from Mars and her expression wouldn't have changed.

"My mother, she works at a plant research institute," Yuri said proudly, putting his arm around her.

At that time, many women in America didn't work, but my own mother did until she got remarried and then became primarily a homemaker. I was so impressed with Yuri's mother, with her strong, dusky features and cropped brown hair, that she managed to dedicate herself to a career as well as a family.

"My mother, she wants to know if your mother is worried that you are so far from home?" Yuri translated.

"Oh, of course," I said quickly. "But she knows I'm happy and that I have Yuri, and I still go home so much, too."

"And what you want to achieve in Russia?" Yuri translated from her before he could translate my answer. In that moment I realized that rock 'n roll was not the only thing that had no borders – neither did mothers! I found them no matter where I went, with the same questions and the same patient, concerned smiles.

I told Yuri's parents about my family, growing up as the middle child with two sisters and training as a professional gymnast who went to Nationals for eleven years and younger. I told them about my parents divorcing when I was twelve and how I was embarrassed by my mother's old yellow car in the drop-off line when we moved to Beverly Hills. As I spoke, I could see Yuri beaming at me, so happy we were all together.

"My mother, she says America is very far." As Yuri said this, his mother took his hand, holding it up and squeezing it like she was nervous I might try to take him away from them.

"Maybe you all can visit one day!" I said.

The three of them laughed like it was the silliest thing they'd ever heard.

Being with Yuri made me feel like I was floating. He could lay with me for endless stretches of time, caught between daydreams as he'd touch my hair or sing softly along with the music playing in the background. Sometimes he would hum the cello pieces he'd learned when he was younger. There was a sweet cloud of smoke that filled my head when I was with him, both mentally and physically. He'd puff through a few cigarettes an hour, like a slender dragon curled up beside me as I slept. I'd open my eyes and see him sitting against the pillows with the soft orange glow at his lips. There were and are still very few things I hate more than someone smoking, but for some reason when I was in Russia, I could be at a party surrounded by forty people with cigarettes and it didn't bother me at all. Other times, we'd be in the bath, and he would chain smoke as he ran the hot water with the stopper up for half an hour or so while we soaked.

"How can we do this?" I asked him. In the back of my head I could hear my father keep telling me not to waste water. *Los Angeles is a desert – water costs extra here. You can brush your teeth without the faucet running, Joanna.* I can't imagine what he would think of continuously running the bath water as it slowly drained itself.

Yuri shook his head. "Water costs almost nothing." He gave me one of his slow, goofy smiles and a sarcastic thumbs up. What the Soviet Union lacked in freedom, it made up for in H_2O.

It must have been the same for electricity. We always had the lights on throughout the whole apartment, and through the window I could see the cheap glow coming from the stacked windows that surrounded us. It was like a thousand cigarette butts piled on top of each other, warm and smoky.

Yuri used to stand in front of the mirror in his underwear and just admire himself, flexing his arms and legs and staring at his muscles. Other times, I'd walk in to find him posed in kung fu style positions just like Viktor, a testament to the Bruce Lee movies I'd brought back for them that they loved to watch. Though he always looked so strong and healthy, the plight of mere mortals would catch up with him at certain points, one time forcing me to jam a thick metal needle into his *zhopa* (butt) every day for a week that was never cleaned or replaced. Yet he and all other Russians I met disregarded most things with an apathetic shrug; they had suffered much worse as a people. Once when I was back in L.A., my whole body was on fire itching. After a doctor gave me medicine for scabies, a skin disease caused by an infestation of mites, I raced home and phoned Yuri.

"Are you itching really badly!" I screamed through the phone.

"Oh, yes," I heard his deep, unhurried voice. "Gustav too. I hope you are okay?" Nothing would phase them.

Even though Yuri and I didn't speak the same language, we bonded over our music. Yuri would strum a few chords on the guitar, his head falling forward and his foot tapping against the cheap tiled floors, and I would make up melodies on top of it. We wrote a handful of songs together including two that I released in the '90s, one called "Somehow," and one called "Walking Through Windows," which became the name of my second album on Melodiya in 1991.

It was so easy to write lyrics about Yuri. Our songs were heavenly and spacey, floating through the ears and allowing anyone who listened to relax into that sweet spot of love where it overshadows reality and brings the stars out to play.

■ Yuri and me, Leningrad, 1985.

Walking through windows
Flying on rainbows
Moving through mountains
Gliding on teardrops

Being with Yuri was like a cruise through shining crystal waters, even in the middle of a city. There was something about being with him that calmed down my frenzied, obsessive attitude towards life and made my worries go away.

"Jo-an-na, sit down," he would say as I'd rush around the house trying to leave for a plane or a meeting. "Breathe."

I would sit next to him on the bed and take a huge breath.

"Okay," he'd say after a minute. "Now, let's go."

I can still see his dark eyes as I'd watch him leave the airport, running a hand through his hair and glancing back over his shoulder. "Miss you, kiss you," he'd quote out of The Cure's "Love Cats" in his strained English.

"Miss you, kiss you."

I like to think there was something about me that excited or energized him a little bit too.

He was always so slow, considered, and appreciative of the moment, but there were times he would jump up and act silly with me and Viktor. We were yin and yang: me always bouncing off the walls and him always standing calmly, waiting with open arms to catch me. After that first meeting with his parents, they accepted us together, no longer hiding from me and even eating dinner with me and Yuri sometimes. The single bed in Yuri's room magically became a king overnight.

But don't forget that precious moments are precious
Keep them hidden in a song and they will linger on

◆

Even while focusing on taking stuff out for *Red Wave*, I was still having a whole ocean of experiences in Russia that were taking me deeper and deeper into this underground world. I started shooting interviews and concert footage not just of Aquarium, Kino, Alisa, and Strange Games, but also of a pack of new bands that popped up and were now playing at the Rock Club. Kolya, the director of the club, loved including them and had a great relationship with everyone, although for the longest time he would ignore me completely. To him I couldn't exist; I was just some apparition among the testosterone and guitar cases that he would have to report to the KGB if I became real. Luckily, the new bands were accepting of a platinum-haired American groupie and even seemed to enjoy my company. They all had sharp new sounds and hip, brazen names like Avia, Televisor, Auction, DDT, Chaif, Nautilus Pompilius, and Kalinov Most. The guys were from places like Sverdlovsk along the eastern Ural Mountains and Novosibirsk in southern Siberia; the lead singer of DDT, a scruffy guy with big bright glasses and a gravelly voice named Yuri Shevchuk, was from Ufa, one of the old cities of the Mongol Empire's Golden Horde. It seemed like rock was spreading across all of Russia.

A big hand in orchestrating the expansion was that of Artem Troitsky, a handsome and charismatic guy from Moscow who would travel the country to find new ambitious bands to bring to the Leningrad Rock Club and promote in the official media. Somehow, he managed to live between the official and unofficial worlds of Russia, and though there were a few who were suspicious of him being an informant, he was nevertheless respected and liked by all the underground musicians. He was the only professional Rock journalist and critic in the Soviet Union, an off-the-record provisional talent scout who did more to promote those radically alternative bands in the '80s than anyone else. I had met him early on in Russia at the party after Boris' first concert. He spoke fluent English with a small smile and attentive eyes, and he knew much about Western culture and its rock

■ Zhenya Fedorov and Rikoshet (Alexander Aksenov) from Obyekt Nasmeshek (Object of Ridicule), 1986.

music. Later he introduced me to contacts at the Russian publishing company VAAP and concert organization Gos Concert in Moscow, always telling me about new groups and heaping praise on the Soviet underdogs.

One day, I went to film a rehearsal of a punk band who sarcastically called themselves Obyekt Nasmeshek, or Object of Ridicule. They weren't actually allowed to play the Rock Club or any other halls, so I was intrigued to discover this darker, grungier world of Russian punk.

The leader of the band was a man called Rikoshet, skinny and charismatic with sleepy eyes and dark wet curls. He was one of those guys who would slip a cork or crust of bread beneath his earlobe and pierce it with a silver spike, barely blinking. He seemed apprehensive of me at first, crossing his arms over his concave chest and asking if I spoke Russian. I shook my head and told him only what Sergey had taught me, and then proceeded to ramble off all the dirty lines and words I could remember. He cracked up like it was the funniest thing, and from that moment they accepted me. Besides me that night, there were some chic, alluring female punk fans who looked as if they'd just fallen out of a *Vogue* or *Rolling Stone* magazine, cat eyes and perfectly styled hair, and a drunk in a knitted sleeveless sweater who was passed out on the couch the entire time. They told me he was the most legendary punk rocker in Russia, a round-faced musician called Pig.[2]

As I was filming Object of Ridicule, they were spazzing and tearing through the space so madly that they broke a glass mirror. Rikoshet sliced his arm down the side and used the blood to paint across his cheeks as the rest of the band kept playing. It was fiercely feral and incredibly reminiscent of the punk I'd experienced in the west. I found this overwhelming and authentic sense of human expression so illustrative of what I wanted to share with Americans. Pull down the Iron Curtain and you realize there aren't monsters – there are people, just like you, albeit a bit bloody and drunk.

I went from that trippy, macabre video shoot to filming Sasha Bashlachev, a bard singer unlike anyone I had ever met. Even though I couldn't understand a word of his lyrics, I could see the prolific poetry in his eyes as the words tumbled out of him like rain from a storm cloud.

"I never thought about what to say to Americans," he said to me when we met, and I sat down with Alex to interview him. "They will understand," Sasha said. He had the ability to see the same root of folk music that fed all our continental branches. "All we are is the sum of influences. It's the influence of love first of all."

His music and the power of his throaty, cavernous voice was spellbinding. Each song he sang as the camera rolled was a piece of his soul, some type of twisted, folkish story that spoke of the depths of human pain. He would start a song eerily soft and breathy and gradually gain volume like a steam engine barreling toward you. As I sat there, I felt like the roof was about to blow off the building with his power. Everyone in the room was motionless, mortals frozen beneath the mountainous voice of a god. I could tell he was far closer to heaven than the rest of us. As I listened to his emotional ballads, I wanted to wrap my arms around him and hold onto him tightly like some kind of lifeboat. It was incredible to me that when he stopped singing, he seemed to shrink back into this meek, shy, fragile man. After I filmed him in 1985, I played back some of the video for him to see in the camera. I believe it was the first time he'd ever seen himself on film, and even he seemed surprised at what he became while performing. He gave me an amused, abashed smile, and bowed his head.

"Have your poems been written down on paper?" I asked him. He shook his head, his long hair falling in his eyes.

---

2   Pig was the nickname of Andrei Panov (1960–1998), the founder and leader of the group Automatic Satisfiers (1979–1998), which is considered to be one of the first and most radical punk bands in the U.S.S.R. In their first composition, Viktor Tsoi played the bass guitar.

■ Filming Sasha Bashlachev, Leningrad, 1985.

"No, I'm not ready for that. I memorize them."

"What's more important, the singing or the poetry? Or both of them combined?"

"The spirit," Sasha whispered, his voice like a heavy oak burning on the Urals. "The soul."

Sasha Bashlachev died in 1988, and it felt like a loss not just for us as people who'd known him but a loss for humanity as well. I know that what I got to see of his emotional performances was just one part of him, the tip of the iceberg.

◆

Just before my return back to the States in the beginning of 1986, I called all the bands back to Mikhailovsky Park for photos and music video shoots. It was freezing, thick snow on the ground, naked trees, and a brooding grey sky. Judy and I took turns shivering and marveling that no one else seemed affected by the polar temperatures. Russians have this magic within them that makes them impermeable to the cold, though I think some of the time that magic can be called vodka.

Both Judy and I took photos, setting up shots of the four band leaders as well as group shots with everyone lined up. People passed by us and ignored us completely, as if we were these invisible creatures that didn't, or shouldn't, exist. As we posed and jumped around

■ *Red Wave* album cover shoot, Mikhailovsky Park, Leningrad, February 1985.

for the shots, these people rushed by on their way to somewhere, seemingly hellbent on the notion that if they saw no evil, they couldn't "officially" be asked about it.

The last photograph we took was a group photo with everyone lined up in front of a church. I stood in the center, hypothermic and laughing as the guys told jokes and put their arms around me. You couldn't have paid me to be anywhere else in the world – no tropical beach, coconut smoothie, or warm blue waters could have compared to freezing my ass off with these fiery guys who had become my family. As Judy devotedly tried to frame her shot before freezing to death, it dawned on me that I, standing in a long tweed coat between Boris and Kinchev, was the luckiest girl in the world. The picture we took became the back cover of the album.

We shot the videos next. I had already filmed part of Aquarium's "Ashes" video with Boris, playing my Walkman on his roof as he performed to it like a private concert, and Sergey playing piano to the song. He had Boris use a saw next to his long fingers in a bout of creative genius. We filmed the crowded, concrete streets of Leningrad and watched people rush by like rocks in a river, a sharp contrast to the footage of Boris and Sergey in a private rehearsal as they kicked around the intimate yellow space and made emotional love to the instruments.

I organized the Kino video to be shot in the courtyard of a building where Timur had set up his New Artists floor, with them playing around the parked trucks and metal slide. Unfortunately, Yuri had to miss the shoot. He worked at an electric utility plant, measuring the water pressure of five steaming hot, twelve-meter boilers and couldn't find a substitute to take his shift that day. This was a time way before you could photoshop someone into something, but as I stood there and watched Gustav and Viktor play with the industrial percussion section of Timur, Afrika, and Andrei Krisanov, in my mind I superimposed Yuri onto the scene with that meditative, amused glint in his eyes. I remember not being able to feel my toes as I shot the video, but Viktor and the others distracted me as they flirted and played around with the camera like it was some reincarnated lover. Viktor wore a cool long coat I think his wife might have made, always glancing up over the lens to share a quick, can-you-believe-this smile with me that was better than any handwarmer.

When we filmed the Sologub brothers for the Strange Games video, it was even colder than it had been for either Aquarium or Kino. By that point, the band had virtually split into two groups – the Sologub brothers had just become a band called Games while the others formed a group called AVIA, an acronym for "anti-vocal instrumental ensemble." Sergey and Gustav joined the Sologubs for the shoot, and Sergey ended up directing a lot of the silly scenes they pulled off while I laughed as my fingertips froze to the camera. There was something cool about shooting in that unforgiving cold, like the pain was part of this artistic struggle for all of us. We ran around the hard, frostbitten city acting crazy and bloodthirsty for that uninhibited creative high. They'd walk in a straight line swinging their arms in unison while shuffling on the ice, a band of elephants escaping the circus, and wrestle each other to the ground. As I chased after them, they'd climb benches and statues and jump around, making faces at the people who passed and refused to acknowledge our existence.

Every time we stopped the cassette player to take a break from the activity, the guys panting heavily in what was left of the snow, Vitia Sologub would start glancing around to see if anyone was watching us. It always reminded me that what we were doing could get us in trouble, but even Vitia didn't let that stop him from dancing or rolling down the stairs. I couldn't stop giggling as I watched these guys light up the somber overcast metropolis, acting goofy in a way people rarely allowed themselves to do in the Soviet Union.

Kostya Kinchev and Alisa filmed the last video. Timur managed to find an old abandoned building, probably condemned and thoroughly deteriorating. The wooden beams were broken and exposed, the brick crumbling and crying red tears of dust. If it had eaten us all alive as we stood there and filmed, I genuinely would not have been surprised. Nothing could have been a more perfect place for Kostya, though, his sharp, saturated eyes and sensual body slipping in and out of focus as he shot around like an arrow from Robin Hood and bounced off the shocking, warped setting, but then when he wanted to, taking to the camera like a fish to water, a mesmerizing apparition floating through the building's hollow shell. I didn't need to direct him at all; he was a force of nature, a true performer who could bring a house down by just opening his mouth.

Shooting the photos and videos brought out the best in each of the bands. I had brought a Sony portable 8mm video player into the country so we could play back film as we were recording it. Seeing everyone beaming at themselves as they sang or danced around made it so special for me, because I could tell how excited and proud they were about what they were doing. It confirmed that this whole project was real, and as the album and all of its pieces materialized in front of the bands, they began to radiate enthusiasm and a fearlessness that no one had seen on the black market.

For the first time ever, I was excited to go back to Los Angeles so I could edit the footage. My longtime friend Mark Rosenthal helped me get access to an editor and studio at Raleigh Studios in Hollywood, a world away from the homemade, hand-crafted studios in Leningrad. I felt really confident in my ability to edit, and when we finished the four *Red Wave* videos, it was all I could do to not run down Pacific Coast Highway waving them above my head. They were so compelling, and not much different, I thought, from what was playing on MTV at that time.

The last thing left was getting the bands' music tapes out of the country. I would meet with each band or their engineers to collect their tapes, lyrics, and photos, which I stashed in my suitcase in my hotel with a chunky metal lock guarding them from the prying eyes of the hotel workers. I had already brought out several of Boris' recordings and some other videos and photos, but this was so much more. I started to get super stressed about carrying out so many things, ramming into a brick wall of anxiety every time I lay down at night to try to go to sleep. I would lay there on my side staring out the window at a starless sky and try to talk myself out of the inner turmoil. *Think of all those tours you ditched* , I told myself. *Think of all the other music you've smuggled out. Think of the bands. Think of Yuri.* The repressive system may have refused to showcase these talented, divine humans to the rest of the world, but I had determined that come hell or high water or subarctic temperatures, I would get this music out there and all over the world.

It was actually possible to get some of the tapes out through the consulates, but that wasn't enough. As I sat in my hotel room one morning, I realized that my big Sorrel boots had removable insoles under which the printed lyric sheets could fit. The tapes I tried to hide in the big back pocket of my winter coat, planning to wear my backpack over it so that the irregular, lumpy shapes were totally hidden. The photos I slipped into the bottom of my suitcase, Boris' bright eyes the last thing I saw before I covered them all with a special flap.

It was a strange transition, going from carrying out Boris' cassette in my pocket over a year and a half ago to creating elaborate and secretive schemes to transport the music of four different bands. In the beginning, I had been so enchanted by the music that I had been completely blind to the real dangers of being caught, but now that I knew more about the perverted system, it was harder to ignore the possible consequences. There was something inside me though, this evocative desperation that grew with the swell of every song I heard, which helped me override rational thought and throw caution to the biting wind. This operation was going to work, I convinced myself, because it had to.

There was an initial adrenaline high as I walked to the bus to leave. I felt like I was doing something heroic, something with the power to change two enemies' perceptions of each other, something that would allow two hemispheres to become neighbors and friends in a cultural revolution. Yet as I got closer and closer to the airport, I felt a growing chasm in my stomach, a dark hole opening up and draining all of my optimism. I tried to fight it, taking deep breaths and singing songs in my head, but as the bus pulled up to the long concrete airport, I felt my whole body on fire with nerves. I don't remember standing up or walking into the building, and if anyone said anything to me, I didn't hear them over the ringing in my ears.

The next thing I remember is standing in line to go through customs. I was physically shaking under the weight of what I was about to do. It wasn't about me; if I failed, I'd be letting down so many people who had done everything in their power to make space in their hearts for me. The line moved quickly, and I was suddenly standing in front of a tall, pale guard pawing briefly through my bag and glancing at my paperwork. For a moment, we made eye contact, and I thought the world would slip out from under my feet.

"Go," he said, already on to the next passenger.

I was floating. Nothing could touch me. The ringing in my ears turned into the harmonized voices of Kino and Aquarium as I hurried to the plane that would carry them and the other bands into the radio waves and cookie-cutter homes of the United States of America. For a moment, as I felt the plane ascend into the air, I was Thor – thunder god of the sky, about to make it rain.

◆ Red Wave and Blacklist

From thunder god to studio gopher, I spent my days in Los Angeles holed up supervising the final assembly of *Red Wave*, getting my hands dirty in all aspects of the process. I had meetings with Big Time and their art department, adamant about how I wanted the album to look, feel, and sound. We remastered each tape at A&M Records on La Brea Avenue in Hollywood, sitting among empty coffee cups and listening to each track a thousand times inside the building's brick walls. I was so excited, bouncing on my seat and telling story after story about the bands back in Russia as the engineer tried to ignore my incessant yammer and balance out the levels. Vocal tuning wasn't a thing yet, but he was at least capable of tuning me out.

"KROQ has been playing a couple of the songs! They went from one of their songs right into a Russian one, and you couldn't notice a difference in quality or sound or anything. I feel like a lot of people just listened and took it in without even realizing the lyrics were Russian. It's that powerful."

The engineer nodded noncommittally.

"A funny thing is on Alisa's 'Experimenter' song in the middle he's screaming 'X! X! X!' and I think all the American kids think he's screaming 'Sex! Sex! Sex!' and that it's such a cool song."

The engineer slid his chair farther away from me.

"I did an interview with Voice of America and they were going to play some of the Russian songs, so I called up the bands in Russia and had to give them maybe eight different radio frequencies I got from VOA because apparently when Russia blocks one of them they can switch to another. A couple people heard it, which is great because they haven't ever heard their songs on the radio before!"

The engineer left and returned with two cups of coffee, placing both of them in front of himself.

Despite the engineer's disinterest, so many people were becoming intrigued by Russia and its people because of the pre-press I had been doing for *Red Wave*. Being on the radio especially gave me a direct line to people's homes so I could start convincing everyone that Russia was not the big bad wolf they all assumed was waiting to devour us.

"I want to ask her how she felt after she went to a socialist country and how she felt about all the rules and regulations they supposedly have compared to a free country like America?" a woman asked me on KROQ.

"You do have more freedom than you expect to have," I told her earnestly. "These musicians are really having a fun time and running around partying and doing what most kids do around the world."

"That's terrific! So, it's not as tight as we think."

First round: Joanna, one; government propaganda, zero.

"What do your friends do for fun?" Another caller asked.

"Russian people in general go to the movies. They sell ice cream at theaters instead of popcorn." I heard a slight chuckle and smiled. "Behind closed doors, they do pretty much what we are doing."

Second round: Joanna, two; government propaganda, zero.

"What do you think is the main difference between American and Russian rock?" A third person phoned in.

"I don't think there is much difference. What I've learned by going over there is rock 'n rollers really are rock 'n rollers everywhere. Their videos are going to be premiered on MTV next Thursday night at nine and when people see them, I think they'll see that they look like rock 'n rollers everywhere."

Final round: Joanna for the win!

It was like being in a boxing ring with two countries who were fighting each other, trying to dodge Russia's punches so I could knock some sense into America. *Red Wave* was the left hook that no one saw coming.

Despite any nerves I had over the legality and politics of the album, I knew it would be powerful. The fact that there was so much risk around it almost reinforced my belief that *Red Wave* was something worth noticing, something potent and moving regardless of the language barrier. When I was in eighth grade, I remembered being assigned a project to analyze the lyrics of Led Zeppelin's "Stairway to Heaven." Try as I might, my adolescent brain could not puzzle out the meaning, and still to this day I don't know all of what Robert Plant is trying to say. There was something about the song, though, that from the moment I heard the chords it captivated me and made me feel such strong emotions. It was the same experience I'd had when I listened to Aquarium or Kino for the first time, unable to comprehend the meaning but spiritually moved by the generosity and tolerance of the music. I knew the songs on *Red Wave* could move people even if Americans couldn't understand the Russian words. It would be all about feelings, about emotions, about love.

I hand-picked the front and back cover photos of the album as well as the plethora of photos on the inside pages and their individual placements. Despite the additional cost, I insisted on inserts with the Russian lyrics and their English translations, hopeful that if Americans could understand the humanity the Russians were expressing, they would feel more connected to these brothers across the world. One of the most important details for me, though, was the ad on the inside sleeve for shirts that said "Save the World" in Russian and English. They came with a free button that said "Peace" in both languages, something to signify the magnitude and urgency of the album.

On the back was a statement that the musicians "bore no responsibility for the publishing of the album." It was important to me that I would be the parachute that slowed the fall, should the KGB or Kremlin attempt to yank success out from under us.

The last thing I did was write a thank you column for the album. I wouldn't have gotten anywhere without all the help and love of these guys who had become the starlight and mountain movers of my life. I also specifically thanked the wives of Boris, Sergey, Viktor, and Alex because I knew it couldn't have been fun to have their husbands hanging out with me all night instead of being home. These were strong women, but I knew even strong women get lonely sometimes. I knew that when I was away from those men, I sure was. I also thanked those who had the courage to help me get the tapes out of the U.S.S.R., those figures in the shadows whose names I couldn't print since they worked at foreign consulates.

In the days before the release of *Red Wave*, I couldn't find sleep anywhere in my body. Ideas continued to pop in my head, making me jittery and anxious. Sometimes as I stood there with a fire tangled in my ribs and an overpowering itch to do something, I wondered if this was how Sergey always felt as the ideas and music created a tsunami inside him that was impossible to ignore. *Red Wave* had become what I felt I was put on this earth to do, and the pride and happiness I felt for the project didn't come without the anticipation of wondering if others would feel the same way. To call it *Red Wave* was initially a nod to the mother Russia, but it had come to represent so much more. The *Red Wave* was all of the blood and sweat we had poured out of our bodies and into creating some tangible representation of the solidarity of the human race.

◆

In spring 1986, I got a phone call from Agent Betsy Cordova of the FBI requesting another meeting.

"I appreciate your interest in me," I tried to say over the phone. "But nothing has changed, and I'm still going to Russia because of their rock music. I'm actually trying to put out an album of Russian rock in the States to improve our understanding of Russian people."

She was so persistent I finally agreed to meet her at the Hamburger Hamlet up on Doheny Road in West Hollywood. I was already trying to navigate dirty waters with the Kremlin – the last thing I needed was to fall out of favor with the U. S. government as well. I sat in the brown booth with my arms crossed over the sticky table, wishing I could be anywhere else but there as Agent Cordova asked leading questions.

"There's really no need for this," I interjected. "To be honest, I don't want meeting you to jeopardize my visa to get back into Leningrad if the Soviets find out I'm meeting with the FBI!"

I could see she was unconcerned with what Russia thought of me, a one-trek pony convinced I was some type of spy for the team that wasn't hers. She was like some brutish goalie who refused to leave the field even with no one playing the game. I was so irritated.

"I'm sorry, I don't know what else I can tell you. I have only been involved in music." I pulled the *Red Wave* cover out of my bag and slapped it down in front of her as proof. "I'm trying to make a difference here."

Her face was unreadable as she studied it for a while. "Can I have this?" she asked.

I declined and asked for it back. "It'll be out in Tower Records in a few weeks. You can buy one then." I was so angry and exhausted. The nerves from making the album combined with the frustration that neither the Russian or American government would ever appreciate what we were trying to do was demoralizing and infuriating. If the FBI was going to subtly accuse me of foreign espionage, then I refused to continue to participate in these pretend play-dates. I left the Hamburger Hamlet with a doggie bag and a bad taste in my mouth.

Almost twenty years later, I applied for and got a hold of my FBI record. They high-lighted my reluctance to meet with American agents and my numerous trips to Russia, citing both as possible evidence of my allegiance to the Soviet Union.

"'It is theoretically possible that Fields is currently already cooperating with Soviet officials… Fields does not have access to classified or secret documents, but her parents and stepfather are politically affluent and active'?!" I read out loud in disbelief. "'Fields' mother advised that Ted Kennedy had called their residence a week prior to ongoing interview'? They don't know anything!"

"You really should have just married an American," my mother sighed.

But leaving that Hamburger Hamlet, the only men on my mind were Russians. I decided to bring that same *Red Wave* album cover I showed the agent back to Russia with me so the bands could see the finished product. I sat up well into pumpkin time, the clock pushing past midnight, as I tried to figure out how I'd get it through customs. My answer was packaging. My first boyfriend, Paul, used to work at Tower Records on Sunset Boulevard, where I remember he would use a machine to shrink wrap returned records and stock them back on the shelves. I figured out that if I hid the *Red Wave* cover inside another album and then shrink-wrapped it in plastic, I might be able to disguise the whole thing. As soon as the sun rose and the stores opened, I raced over and made my way down every aisle to find an album that worked. I ended up purchasing a double album of some obscure country band, removing the plastic wrap and tossing the two country records to make room for the *Red Wave* cover inside. I then made my way back through the empty store and asked the teenager smacking his gum behind the counter if he could wrap my new package in plastic.

"Uh, yeah, we don't do that," the kid mumbled.

"Yes, you do," I told him. "My ex-boyfriend used to work here and said that's exactly what you do."

The kid blinked really slowly. "We don't have one of those machines."

I put both hands flat on the counter like a dog about to steal food off the breakfast table. I was tired, and I was desperate. "Look, I've got an album of underground Soviet rockstars that's about to be released. I need to sneak this album cover into the U.S.S.R. next week to show the bands."

I pulled out the *Red Wave* album cover. "See this guy? His name is Boris Grebenshchikov, and he's basically the Bob Dylan of Russia. And this guy? His name is Kostya Kinchev, and he's like Freddy Mercury and Billy Idol in one body. These are people who are revolutionizing what it means to be human. Can you just do me a favor

~~SECRET~~

The issue of Blackmail in regards to forced cooperation with the Soviets was addressed and the issue of possession of narcotics in the Soviet Union.

Fields appeared curious and willing to be interviewed but not in the presence of her mother.

It is theoretically possible that Fields is currently already cooperating with Soviet officials. She refused in the initial interview to identify her affiliate in New York with Soviet Union associations and was very curious about Soviet intelligence officers who she thought the FBI might have been surveilling or analyzing in the past.

In order to establish dates of travel, identifying data, and pertinent intelligence the following leads are being set forth. Subject is described as follows for this purpose.

Name:	Joanne Lee Fields
Alias Name:	Joanna Stingray Fields
Date of Birth:	July 3, 1960
Current Address:	880 Loma Vista Drive Beverly Hills, California
Former Addresses:	308 South Wetherly Drive, Beverly Hills, California
	1022 North Beverly Glen City Los Angeles, California
	330 South Spaulding Drive Beverly Hills, California
	9483 Date Street Spring Valley, California 92077
Mother:	[redacted]
Father:	
Sex:	Female
Hair:	Blonde full-strip center, dark brown sides, Medium length
Eyes:	Green
Height:	5'8"
Weight:	135 lbs.
Vehicle:	1982 Mazda license BFIESTY now changed to: license CBRATGO (personalized)
Convictions:	None Criminal One vehicle code violation on file
Memberships:	Musicians Credit Union, Local 47 817 Vine Street Hollywood, California

b6
b7C

~~SECRET~~

- 5 -

U.S. Department of Justice
Federal Bureau of Investigation

BETSY KOPP CORDOVA
Special Agent

11000 Wilshire Blvd.   (213) 477-6565
West Los Angeles, CA 90024   (213) 272-6161

■ The FBI investigator assigned to my case was Betsy Cordova.

and go wrap this record in plastic, so the border guards don't confiscate it and send us all to jail?" There was a moment of silence as the teenager considered me.

"This. Is. The. Most. Rad. Thing. *Ever!*" He screamed. He ran a hand through his greasy hair, and then held it out to take the record. "I'll wrap it. Wait here."

Then, on April 26, 1986, less than a week before I was going to the Soviet Union for the last time prior to the release of *Red Wave*, Chernobyl happened. When I saw the disaster on the news, I nearly passed out. I knew Kino was supposed to play a concert a few miles away from Chernobyl in Kiev on that exact day and was petrified for their safety. With no way to get in contact I sat in my pajamas all day and glued my eyes to the coverage, waiting until someone could contact me. It took all of my willpower and rationale not to hop in the car and drive to the airport to beg someone to let me on a plane then and there. I felt like someone was dunking me under freezing water and holding me there; every muscle in my body was burning and tense.

All of my American friends and family started calling me about it, which only helped keep the disaster in the forefront of my mind.

"I don't know anything yet," I repeated over and over from my living room, my voice robotic but my body shaking. "I'm heading there in a few days."

People thought I was crazy, warning me not to go. My parents were shocked I would risk my health to return, screaming at me over the phone until I gave up listening and put down the receiver. I was young and stupid, but I was also in love with Yuri and the bands and the city that had given me so many adventures and songs. That's what you do for love: despite radiation, you show up.

I had managed to get another keyboard for Sergey, a Fender P Bass for Vitia, and a four-track recorder to take back in with me, plus a load of rock t-shirts, punk bracelets, cuff earrings from different companies and magazines, and black lipstick straight from Melrose Avenue. I also had the cover-up country album and legal documents that all the musicians had to sign. I had never tried to bring so much into the Soviet Union at once. Judy was with me again, her pockets full of legal papers and her eyes as big as two strawberry moons.

"Are we sure about this, Joanna?" She asked as we drove a small red Ford from Helsinki to Leningrad. We had heard through Russian friends that we might draw less attention if we entered the U.S.S.R. through a more remote crossing at the Finnish border.

"No, I'm not sure," I told her as I flew down the empty road through the Land of a Thousand Lakes. "Let's keep our fingers crossed."

At the Helsinki rental car agency, I had signed a contract promising to keep the car within the country. Without so much as a sneeze, we were about to try to drive into one of the strictest countries in the world with a confiscated car filled to the windows with equipment that was technically illegal to bring in and hand out. At this point, though, I would have done anything for my friends. I would have army-crawled down through the Arctic Circle dragging three hundred pounds of equipment like some vicious foaming husky if it meant I could get everything to them safely.

The drive itself was actually beautiful, with snowy forests parting around the wet road and sparkling in the sun. I barely saw another car, only the low hawks and the smattering of resilient wildflowers to keep us company.

"Isn't it pretty?" I kept asking Judy, trying to distract myself from the turmoil that had begun to bubble in my mind.

"Mmmhmm," Judy would respond, craning her neck to try to see past the giant guitar case we had fit vertically between her legs.

As we neared the border, though, the landscape suddenly transformed into a desolate dystopia, Russian signs dotting the vast stretches of mud and snow. I became quiet, anticipating the inspection. Doubt flooded into my whole body, like a river rushing towards an impossibly high waterfall. At the border, there was only one car ahead of us, but the guards had practically disassembled it down to its final bolt searching for contraband. Judy and I looked at each other. I immediately questioned everything, down to the color of my hair and the tangy scent of the rental car. Every little thing seemed like something that could give us away.

The guards were taking their time, content to let us wait as they felt up every last centimeter of the first car. I had a horrible thought that they were so bored they might have nothing else to do but be super vigilant, the complete opposite of our initial theory that had convinced us to come this way. I felt my brain somersaulting inside my skull as I tried to come up with excuses explaining all the equipment, clothing, and album. Maybe I should feign sickness, make a run for it, try and fly. There were no alternatives.

"I can't do this!" Judy screamed, shoving the paperwork onto my lap and jarring me out of my thoughts.

"Shhhh," I hissed, shoving the papers into my pockets and yanking up all the zippers. "Shit, Judy, I can't believe you're doing this now!"

We both stared at each other, startled by our own outbursts. We stared at each other, and then... we sat. And sat. And sat. We sat for almost two hours, afraid to say another word and call any more attention to ourselves. We sat for what felt like five years, hyperaware of every article in the vehicle and terrified to touch any of it. We sat until I'd decided that I loved airplanes and airports and was never going to see my friends again.

"Advance car," said the border guard as he motioned towards us. He had a bitter face as if he'd just eaten an entire lemon tree, his eyes dark and volatile. "Open doors. Open trunk."

We pulled up and stepped out, standing in the empty windy wasteland beside the grey border patrol building. I watched them start to unpack the car before my stress kicked into overdrive and I began to prattle so quickly I could see even Judy struggling to catch what I was saying.

"I'm a musician, and after Russia I'm going to tour Europe. That's why I have to bring all this stuff with me. I don't trust anyone else with my things – they're like my babies." I then proceeded to list every country within the European continent that I remembered. There were definitely a couple I made up entirely.

After a few minutes, the guards found the country album. I transformed into a machine gun, my quick speech turning into rapid-fire. "I bought this country album of an American band in Finland. Isn't that so funny? I don't know who they are, but I thought it was funny that it was selling in Finland. We're so American! Isn't that funny? I never thought I'd find an American country band on sale in Finland of all places." If the guard had been able to understand English at all, he would have suspected me straightaway. Judy elbowed me in the arm, but I barely felt it.

The guard inspected the album. I could feel my heart crawling up my throat, unable to breathe. I watched him as he fingered the wrapping and wrapped his thick white knuckles against the insulated cardboard. I felt as if I was running a marathon, sweat darkening my hairline and shirt.

"Okay." He dropped the album into the pile of suitcases and instruments. It was that easy. I had to hide my huge sigh of relief as he continued scavenging through the rest of the things like some secondary carnivore. I turned to Judy, only to watch the back of her dark ponytail receding away from me towards the building.

"My sister?" I said loudly, looking back to the guard who was elbow deep in yellow t-shirts. "Where is she going?" He ignored me, tossing aside one of the shirts like a dirty banana peel.

"My sister?" I called to another guard sometime later, who was standing in front of the car as if it would drive away on its own. He gave a nod to the left, his eyes never leaving an imaginary horizon he'd found.

I turned to see a female guard escorting Judy back to me. Judy's face was pinched, her eyes glowing like those of a furious tiger.

"You okay, Jude?" I said in a hushed voice as she stopped beside me next to the Ford. She stared straight ahead, almost as if she were about to cry.

"Okay, go." We both jumped as the guard handed me back the paperwork and pointed down the highway. I couldn't believe it, staring dumbly at all our luggage, musical equipment, and car parts that they had left on the ground. Judy moved first, grabbing random parts and stuffing them all back into the car. I hurried to help her, jumping into the driver's seat once everything was picked up and hitting the gas like some cartoon character speeding away. As the whole scene fell away into the rearview mirror, I felt as if I was on some planet with zero gravity, my excitement filling me up like a balloon. I could feel Yuri and Boris and all the guys waiting for me, could picture their faces when I showed them *Red Wave*. For a moment, I rode a high, swimming in satisfaction.

Judy, on the other hand, burst into tears.

"What happened?" I asked.

"I was strip-searched!" She furiously wiped tears away from her brown eyes. "Do you know how humiliating that is?"

"I'm so sorry –"

"Never ask me to take anything into the Soviet Union again! I mean it."

I couldn't help it; I burst out laughing. All of the adrenaline and the anxiety that had stretched the skin of every one of my limbs now had nowhere to go but out my mouth in a fit of hysterical giggling. Everything – my relief at getting through the border, my anticipation to see the lights of my life again, the fear that had plagued me for the past couple of weeks, my pain for Judy, self-pity, and a sense of triumph, all came rushing out as Judy stared at me with her arms crossed over her chest. In a moment, she was laughing with me, the two of us giddy with a manic palliation. We were two hyenas speeding away in that moment, pushing one hundred and twenty kilometers an hour on an icy road. I was no longer scared of anything.

Yet as we pulled up in front of Yuri's house, I felt that familiar tug of paranoia creep back into my bones. What if the Chernobyl disaster had changed him in some way? What if he had become apathetic and lukewarm in my absence? I jumped out, sprinting towards the stairs and leaving Judy with the car and all the crap we'd packed into it. I rushed to the door, my combat boots pounding the crooked cement stairs as I suddenly faced the moment for which I'd gone through everything.

Viktor and Yuri were sprawled across the sofa, calmly listening to music as I burst in, almost in tears.

"Are you okay?" I gasped.

The two guys looked at each other, and then gave me two of the brightest smiles of which a human is capable.

"Yes, sweetheart," Yuri said, standing up and letting me throw myself into his arms. "Everyone in America was saying how bad Chernobyl was!" I said, hugging Viktor tightly too.

"We got checked when we arrived home from Kiev and had a high level of radiation, so they told us to throw away our clothes," Viktor told me.

"What? That's it?" I pulled back, surprised.

"Yes," they nodded in unison.

"Did you guys throw your clothes away?"

"No," they answered. The subject of Chernobyl never came up again.

As Judy appeared in the doorway with her arms full of stuff from the car, talk quickly turned to the album. I refused to show Yuri and Viktor the cover before everyone else, teasing them with it as Yuri brought out bread and cheese and we sunk into the couch. I could tell the anticipation was unbearable for them, Viktor getting on his knees and begging me to see it. I shook my head, covering his twinkling eyes with my hands.

We all ended up meeting in the park again, our own enchanted world removed from the reality of the city.

"I could only bring in one album, but at least you'll get to see how it looks," I said as the guys stood stamping their feet and exhaling into the evening air. "The release date is set for June twenty-seventh, and the first five thousand copies will have two albums: one in red vinyl and the second in yellow. I want to try and bring in a copy for everyone."

I unwrapped the country album and pulled out the *Red Wave* cover. They passed it around, examining the images and then inspecting the two inside spreads without saying a word. I stood in anticipation, my arms wrapped around myself as I tried to read their faces beneath their high coat collars. Sergey finally took the album in his hands and flipped it to the back, holding it up to me and pointing to the photo I'd chosen of us all lined up outside the church. The day we'd taken the shot had been cloudy, but in the photo, we'd managed to capture a rare ray of sunshine as it shown down to highlight the top of the church and the blonde in my hair.

"You see," Sergey said in his broken English as the others nodded in agreement, "God sent a message to the church, and sent a message to you."

♦

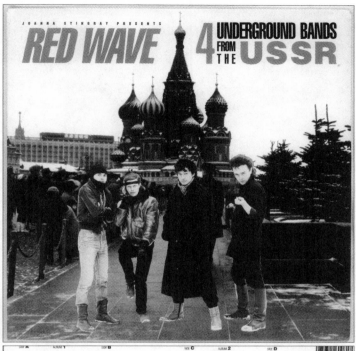

■ *Red Wave* interior covers.

I showed up at Hotel Evropeiskaya off Nevsky Prospekt five minutes early, my hands and feet freezing as I walked into the wooden and marble foyer. I could remember when Boris was grabbed in that same airy foyer as if it were yesterday, and for a moment I felt that same sense of hopelessness I'd had when I'd seen his golden halo of hair disappearing between two dark government figures. I shook my head to clear it, squaring my shoulders. This would be different. This time, the KGB wasn't coming for me. I was, in a sense, coming for them.

Just days before my flight back home, Boris had told me that two sociology professors

Left to right: ALEXEY, GRYSHA, VITIA

AFRIKA

STRANGE GAMES

Left to right: GRYSHA, ALEXEY, ALEXANDER, VITIA

GRYSHA

ALISA

KOSTYA

Left to right: SASHA, SERGEY, SLAVA, KOSTYA, PETER

KOSTYA

from the university asked if they could ask me some questions about America and American life. His tone, the even slower drawl and enunciated words, clued me in to the fact that this was not just a straightforward academic discussion. Apparently, after refusing my request to speak on the last trip, the KGB had had second thoughts. I'd said yes without even thinking about it, determined to try and win them over.

Now here I was, in my oversized vest and tight black pants, watching as two out-of-shape men in worn suits walked towards me through the gilded lobby. For a second, I considered that maybe these really were two professors genuinely interested in the day to day experience of the free world and that in my paranoia, I had convinced myself of an entirely false narrative. These men were hardly the image of the KGB in my mind… one of them sneezed, his entire body overtaken with the force of it.

"Ms. Joanna," the other professor said warmly. "We have a room on the second floor. It will be quieter to speak, yes?"

We walked up the wide, carpeted stairs, and he opened the door to a fancy room with a large table filled with food. Beautiful china and crystal decanters with water and vodka mingled with rosy meats and soft loaves of bread. I felt like I had walked onto a movie set from the czarist era; all that was missing were the troops preparing for invasion. *Or maybe*, I thought as the professors eyed me through their glasses, *that's me.*

Unbelievably, I didn't feel even a little bit nervous. I sat down and almost burst out laughing, wondering if regular people knew that the government had it so good. There was a bowl of cherries to my left that gleamed of their own light, brighter than anyone's apartment.

"What do Americans like to do in their free time? For vacation and such? What films are popular to watch right now?" the professor who'd invited me up began asking.

I responded easily. Like Boris, I knew my truth and that it was pure and good.

"Have you ever met with any Russian emigrants in the States?" The other professor cut in. "Have any contacted you? Does anybody else in the States ask you about your Russian travels?"

I shook my head, 'forgetting' to mention my brief hamburger date with the FBI. It was clear, as the man who had asked the questions leaned forward over his sandwich and dipped his tie in the sauce, that it was impossible for anyone to understand why I would be going in and out of the Soviet Union so often if I wasn't a spy.

"Music has no borders," I told them earnestly, repeating my mantra. "I'm just trying to bring about a better understanding between Americans and Soviets."

It was a circuitous discussion. They kept pushing, trying to find a pressure point while upholding their academic facade and ignoring the fact that I could clearly see who they really were and the agenda they had tucked into their breast pockets. It was like a game of cat and mouse where I was the mouse watching the two of them chase their tails in circles. I sat there and let them tire themselves out.

I knew my travel schedule looked suspicious, and I also realized with new gravity that I needed to be extra careful with the work I was doing. The album was everything to me, but I was having moments of selfishness where I was starting to question whether I was making the right choice. To put out the record was to jeopardize my relationship with Yuri, Boris, and everyone else if the iron fist came crashing down on us, as I'd told them I'd take the blame. The KGB hadn't scared me, but they had made me aware that someone was onto me and the ice on which I was skating wasn't as solid as I'd hoped. As I sat on the lumpy sofa later that day and watched Kino through the open door of the homemade recording booth, I knew I wasn't ready to give this all up.

"Every day, Joanna!" Viktor and Yuri sang to me in between a take. They had been riding a high with the album like a magic carpet underneath them, but as I laughed at their childish, puckered faces I felt tears swarm into my eyes. How can you love people so much that you would do anything for them, and then a second later hope nothing ever changed? I was on my own roller coaster of conflicting emotions. I thought back to Sasha Bashlachev's words, his contemplative and dark opinion that having a purpose confined people to a life of trying to achieve it and forced things like friends, family, and pleasure to take a backseat.

I knew I couldn't be in the Soviet Union when the record came out. I planned to travel home with Judy just before its release, instructing Big Time Records' publicist not to leak anything about the album until I was safely out of Russia. I knew they were over the moon excited for the publicity, but I was now being overly cautious about everything. I read their draft press release that said I had 'smuggled' the recordings out of the U.S.S.R. and forced them to change it out of fear it would piss off both countries' governments.

◆

Rumors about the record were starting to circulate before I left for this trip, so my Californian friend Mark Saleh and I came up with a couple of code sentences in case word of the album's release made the Western press while I was in Leningrad. We agreed that if he called and said the code, I'd make arrangements to leave immediately. A day or so before my scheduled departure, I got a call at Yuri's house.

"Hello?"

"The pigeon has shit." With no online news access, my awareness of my position in the world had been reduced to four words.

My heart sank. I wasn't sure exactly what had come out in the media, but I knew that any talk about the record could jeopardize my place in the Soviet Union. I began to torture myself with the thought that I might not be back, vacillating between realizing the power of this music and feeling sorry for myself as a casualty of this cultural war. At the border, I was convinced I might be arrested, practically hyperventilating even as I sailed through customs. Ironically, it was one of the smoothest exits I'd ever had. I later learned that there was such little communication between the authorities in Moscow and Leningrad that even if Moscow knew something and had blacklisted me, Leningrad would have no idea. I got out and was free, but I didn't feel good about it.

It turned out that *Der Spiegel*, a West German weekly news magazine, had published a small photo of the album cover on its first or second page. The caption read, "American girl smuggles out Russian underground rock'n roll." Not long after, the same thing came out in *Newsweek*. I was all over the West, but the only place I wanted to be was back in Russia. As I started doing interview after interview with music magazines, national and local newspapers, and television programs in the States, I couldn't help feeling disappointed that I didn't have any of the guys with me to share the experience. I needed Yuri there to put his arm around me, Boris to give me a long slow smile, and Viktor to look at me with that wink in his eye saying *can you believe this?* I was getting asked all about the music and the bands that were now over five thousand miles away. I knew I was so fortunate to get to share a piece of magic with the world, but I also felt exiled from my friends, a group of people for whom there were no words that could do them justice. I knew that my shock at the success of the album was only a fraction of what the bands must have been feeling, and I would have given anything to witness their long, celebratory nights. *I would have stayed up through the morning,* I told myself, *just to share it.*

"Aren't you happy?" Judy asked me at one point. "I have to be honest with you, I really didn't know if you could do it, Joanna."

I was wildly happy but still riding a wave of disbelief. We had all put so much into this project, and the fact that people were responding to it confirmed that I had indeed tapped into Wonderland and that I hadn't just imagined this truly extraordinary experience. But I missed the colors and the characters, sitting around the table as Sergey ate his canned sardines and Gustav played the drums in his underwear. Sitting through interviews and talking about it made me miss them even more.

"The main thing is to do what you have to do," Kostya told me once when I was interviewing him, his chin in his hand. "Do it honestly and bring people happiness with what you do."

What he didn't tell me was that happiness was the journey, not the end result. It was the songwriting and the filming and the dancing under a Soviet sky, hair loose, lips puckered, holding hands and singing songs.

It was that feeling of fullness that warmed the stomach before the pigeon shit.

◆

By June of 1986, American eyes were newly turned towards Russia and its underground rock'n roll, while my Russian friends gathered together in *tusofkas* and backstage with no way to let me know if they had any idea. I had sent fifty albums through the Swedish consulate in Leningrad and was rolling around at night wondering what the guys thought about the red and yellow discs and the sound of their songs on real vinyl. As soon as I had gotten home I'd signed up for a tour in August, packing a bag and leaving it by the door as a manifestation of the hope that my visa would be approved, but every day that brought me closer to that date took me farther from the last time I had seen any of the bands. I sent a telex to Artem Troitsky and VAAP's Anatoly Khlebnikov telling them I was doing lots of interviews in Los Angeles for the album and wanted to set up a press conference for the album in Moscow on my return. *Can you help arrange it?* I wrote as I played Kino loudly in my bedroom. I felt like I was racing the Kremlin, trying to explain and promote the album before the KGB could interfere. For some reason, I thought that if I could show the Russian government the positive reactions people were having in the West, they might be thrilled and embrace me.

While I waited, I had interviews to distract me, a never-ending onslaught of questions and coffee. I loved being able to talk about my adventures and the bands, but every memory also reminded me how much I missed them and how ready I was to go back.

"This is exhausting," I mumbled one afternoon in my mother's kitchen, my bleached head against the cool marble of the counter. I had had dreams all night of basement concerts and smoky communal kitchens, but every one of my friends' faces had been turned away and shadowed. I woke up completely stressed, the stars still out and my chest tight.

"It takes a lot of energy to change the world," my mother said over the sink.

I lifted my head and peeked at her over my arms. "What?"

"I'm very proud of you, Joanna." She said without turning around. "All the interviews, the album… I can see you're actually doing something important."

I felt my cheeks get warm. My mother finally seemed satisfied that I was doing something with my life. Moments like that, moments of praise, had been rare between us up until that point.

"Finally forgive me for not finding an American husband?" I joked.

My mom looked up, her eyes wide. "When did I say you had to find an American husband?"

◆

The press wanted to know the whole story: how I met the rockers, how they recorded and lived and what they ate, how they survived under a communist regime, and how I infiltrated the coldest country in the world to smuggle out these songs of passion and fire and love. No one would believe me when I told them Boris and Viktor and everyone else didn't want to leave Russia and live in the West.

"It's their homeland," I tried to explain. "They're very tied to it and are happy there. They realize their creative inspiration comes from the fact that they are Russians living in Russia. Of course, they'd like more freedom to travel and make money from their music, but their Russian blood runs very deep."

The interviewer would blink. "But if they could, they'd still want to leave Russia, right?"

While I had anticipated an interest in the chance to see behind the Iron Curtain, I hadn't imagined so many people would become so obsessed with the album and how the musicians and I did it. As lonely as I felt on the opposite end of the world from my friends, I also felt incredibly cool as I drove from one interview to the next in my dark sunglasses and leather jacket. I talked about the Russian black market and the under-ground *samizdat* (self-publications) that had stories about art and culture in Russia and in the West. I explained how unofficial rock and official rock music in Russia coexisted and differed.

"It is the same difference between love for love and love for sale," I quoted Boris.

I told stories about applying for visas, the fear and the anxiety that came along with trying to get back in, and left out the parts where I cried myself to sleep.

I remember an interview I did for Channel 7's *Good Morning America*, where they put me in a pillowy club chair with my knees almost touching Maria Shriver's. She squeezed in across from me as they were doing the ten second count down to the live airing, her green eyes on the teleprompter. At the commercial break she leaned forward towards me and whispered, "Wow, this is an amazing thing you did. I love it."

The best way I could convey the excitement and enthusiasm over the album to the guys back in Russia was with t-shirts. The perk of doing all the interviews was that I could get the publications or companies to give me memorabilia apparel to take back to all the bands in exchange for photos of all of us in the clothes. I also tried to get copies of everything that was published or aired so I could bring those back with me to show everyone how insane people were going over their music and lives. These things were all tangible reminders that I was doing something of real meaning, something that transcended our own hearts and touched others.

Leaving an interview with my arms full of t-shirts and promotional gifts, I was so fulfilled. It's amazing what an armful of commercial gifts could do to make the lonely nights and tears worth it.

◆

Around this time, I wrote a letter to send with the *Red Wave* album to both Gorbachev and Reagan explaining how I was working to establish a cultural bond between our two countries by introducing Americans to the exciting music that was created by Russian rockers. I said neither my intentions nor the music was political, but merely an attempt to redress misconceptions that Russians and Americans had about each other. I had no idea if either president would see the letter or the album, but I had to give it a try and distract myself with something else as I waited to hear back about the visa. Los Angeles became the land of eternal summer as I hoped and prayed to get back to the wind, snow, and rain. Finally, just as the season was reaching its peak, I received my visa. It was almost too easy.

◆ I Love Rock 'n Roll!

Everything had changed.

It was August of 1986, two months before Gorbachev and Reagan would meet in Reykjavík for a peace summit, and I felt the stirring of openness and *glasnost*. For the past two years, my visits in Russia had been plagued by an underlying ominous feeling that had magically gotten washed away. I realized how accustomed I'd become to never being able to fully relax, always aware of what I was saying and who was around. It's funny how humans can adapt to that kind of way of life so that the tension and apprehension are barely noticeable anymore. I had been living a life in Soviet Russia that was completely instinctual, always having to figure out whom I could trust and where I could go. Now suddenly people's doors and arms were opening.

On the last couple of trips, I still traveled with official tours but was able to stay longer than the usual week. Everyone, my closest friends and strangers walking past me, seemed happier and freer than I had ever seen them. People talked more on the street, cracking smiles and dirty jokes, some even daring to laugh. This was freedom at its best, where everyone could go home at night and still only pay pennies for using water, gas, electricity, for health care, and more. If only it could last.

My friends had all received their copy of the album and were beyond ecstatic. They had heard a little about the press they were getting, but when they crowded around to see all the reviews and articles I'd snuck in to show them, they pointed and talked over each other excitedly, amazed at how big it all was. I went to the *Beryozka* shops exclusively

■ Alisa in concert, lead singer Kostya Kinchev.

for foreigners and bought Marlboro cigarettes, Western alcohol, and food to celebrate with everyone. The days and nights rolled from party to party to party.

One night, I was with the band Alisa and Kostya, all their sweethearts, and Lyosha Cherry, the engineer in whose home-studio Alisa recorded. We were in the oversized apartment of a member of the official band Secret, the Russian knock-off of The Beatles. It was the first time I met Kostya's wife over plates of food and filled glasses we were holding, the air thick with cigarette smoke between us. I swear I was the only person there without a cigarette between my lips. In the background, David Bowie's album *Tonight* was playing as a few guys strummed along on their guitars. Kostya danced through the crowd, sticking his tongue out at the camera and using his hips to guide his body into a parallel universe where he could exist with the music that moved him.

After this celebration, I remember walking down Nevsky Prospekt with Afrika. It was a warm, humid evening with the early stars hanging low in the sky and people selling watermelons on the sidewalk. As we passed three young guys going in the opposite direction, one of them raised his fist and yelled, "Sting–ray!"

"Are you crying?" Afrika laughed as he looked at the expression of surprise and amazement on my face.

"I'm just sweating," I said, pushing him forward into the twilight heat.

There was nothing more fulfilling than knowing how much it meant to these rock fans to share their beloved stars with the world in the West. There was a sense of Russian pride surrounding *Red Wave*, and within weeks the album was being sold on the Russian black market for two hundred dollars!

"We have a lot of visitors – there are always people here. From morning to night, his fans," Boris' wife, Lyuda, told me at a party, laughing. "He's always a gentleman. He never pushes fans away. He even gets love letters from girls!"

"Are you surprised how responsive people are to you and *Red Wave*?" I asked Boris.

"This music is a one hundred percent spiritual thing," Boris paused and pressed a dark blue bottle to his lips. "And so, right now it remains more of a psychological curiosity. It depicts and reflects some kind of spiritual quest, which rock music depicted from the beginning, of course." Through it all, no one believed in the power of music more than Boris.

Even in the face of their music success, these Russians had deeper priorities. It was an emotional commitment to life that I saw not just reflected in the music but also in the fans.

"I love rock 'n roll!" someone yelled at me in Russian, clinging to the sleeve of my jacket. "It entered my life, my blood." Even today, I am still awed and impressed by how insightful these Russian fans were, and how acutely they felt.

Celebrating the album did not mean that any of us were slowing down. Judy and I still filmed and did so much on this trip, dragging the guys around like the hooligans we would always be. We went to one of my favorite Pop Mechanics concerts ever, right on the street in Leningrad, that was totally electric. There were lots of *tusofkas* at Timur's studios, and Aquarium played a beautiful acoustic concert at the Rock Club. Sergey and I also recorded a song we wrote called "Feeling" at Cherry's home studio, the only song of mine in the '80s where a majority of it was recorded in Russia. I wrote special parts for my friends to sing, and we all spent most of the day there with Sergey putting down the bubbly keyboard melodies and guiding Sologub and Yuri through their parts on bass and guitar. Sologub was also working the board and recording equipment as well as the drum machine I had brought them and to which he had developed almost an emotional attachment. Viktor was there with his impish eyes and loving laugh, helping with arrangements. The song was mostly in English with Sergey singing a couple of lines in Russian that he wrote: *I was sitting quietly at home, and then came the American.* For the video, I recorded each guy singing their part, and then we danced around like circus monkeys, crazy and full of color. *We were sitting quietly at home*, they screamed, *and then came the American!*

Sergey put together a drum concert with about twenty of his Pop Mechanics goons for a festival at Peter and Paul Fortress and asked me to be a part of it as well. It was more than a month since the album and wave of press came out, and I figured the Soviets had begrudgingly accepted it as ultimately a good thing. For the first time, I felt like all my problems and fears were behind me. The concert was outside with thousands of people crowding the stage and spilling into each other's arms and laps, hooting and whistling with sparklers and lighters singeing the air. Up to this point, I had never performed at any of the clubs, but Sergey was confident no one would care about one crazy American girl in the middle of such an overwhelming, excited crowd. It was one of those perfect days, the sun out and coloring the painted drums, wheelbarrows, and backdrops of the event. The audience started gathering as we were setting up the stage. I had brought hair gel from the States that the guys loved and was putting it into Sergey's and Afrika's hair when from the corner of my eye I could see two police standing on a roof overlooking the event, and I realized the sight of them didn't send my adrenaline pumping like it used to. With my hands full of hair gel, I waved. Much to my luck, just as Sergey had predicted, they didn't notice me.

Energy overflowing as always, Sergey finally pawed away my hands and jumped up. "We will perform a few pieces by a composer who has been working with this orchestra," he said in his resonant, considered voice to the hordes of round faces. "The composer Afrika presents us with the most radical music. Actually, all the members here are composers and work on the arrangement of songs that this orchestra performs."

All at once we started hitting our drums, some people banging pieces of metal with sledgehammers. I could see the eyes of people in the audience wondering what was happening.

"I want you all to get ready and listen to this brand new and modern music," Sergey would yell sarcastically, stopping the playing with a jerk and then egging us on again. We would hit and bang and kick and hit some more, and Sergey would stop and start it like a bad car motor trying to make it up a mountain. Halfway through, a quartet came on to sing old Russian songs.

"Our dear public, before you is a performance of the Palace of Culture and the Railroad Workers," Sergey screamed maniacally. I could see how much he was enjoying himself. "This is a commercial. You will see skits performed from the life of wagon workers."

Then back to the drumming. I sang "yeah, yeah, yeah, yeah" at the top of my lungs with everyone else, "yeah, yeah, cha, cha, cha!" My throat and arms were numb, but my heart felt like it was filling up my entire body. I had no idea if the audience understood what they were watching, but for the first time in my life I felt like I was a part of Russia. In that moment on the stage, I was no longer an American or a foreigner or a tourist – I was one of the guys, surrounded by my best friends, following the Capitán and making the kind of noise that could shatter any glass or iron. All around the world, I was sure people could hear us.

◆

The end of the summer of 1986 was one of the brightest, untroubled times I can remember in Russia. It was exciting and familiar in a way that gave me a false sense of security in a country of inconsistency.

In the middle of Leningrad, amid the city heat and beyond the traffic lights, there was a beautiful log house. It was a private home, one of the only ones left, that had been granted to the Falalayev family by Lenin himself. Andrei Falalayev, the friend who had introduced me to Boris back before my first trip, still had his mother Tamara and aunt Nina living in that house in Leningrad. They had even hosted Boris for a few years in the late-'70s. Boris brought me there for dinner one night, ditching our normal visits with our crazy Beatles Guy Kolya to make the one-hour walk through the late summer stickiness from Boris' apartment to the timber home.

Tamara and Nina, her bright orange hair almost magenta against the trees, met us at the doorway and ushered us into a room filled with food. They didn't speak English, but we all had a lively conversation through Boris over huge meals, a St. Bernard at our feet sneaking bites of warm meat from my hands beneath the table. They told me about their lives, funny stories about Russia and about each other, and anecdotes of all the rockers who knew these two hip ladies and visited them. As I sat there surrounded by low light and their genuine, eager faces I knew these were the people I was trying to show the rest of the world existed in Russia. They had enough warmth to melt a Siberian winter.

On the other side of town inside the plaster and stone buildings, I met a friend of Afrika's from Moscow whom everyone called Big Misha. He towered like a gentle, sweet pine tree around six-foot seven inches, claiming that a nuclear accident in his hometown Snezhinsk in the Ural Mountains was what contributed to his height. He was a physicist who was an electronics specialist, an intellectual lighthouse. He spoke perfect English, well enough that at times I wondered if he could be a spy, and he could give me so much background and insight on people or the bands that went deeper than just rock music.

"There is big competition between Moscow bands and Leningrad bands, you see?" He said once while helping me conduct an interview. "The Moscow bands think those in Leningrad are too influenced by the West and not real Russian rock."

"It's like the battle between New York and Los Angeles," I said.

Big Misha waved his hand in the air, his big rings like small silver birds. "Leningrad may not have the sunshine," he said with his usual air of confidence. "But it has the magic."

By now, I was going with Boris, Afrika, and some others to Moscow by overnight train and back again, huddled together behind the dirty windows pretending we were all completely Russian. I was still having trouble communicating totally in Russian, so each time the conductor came by to collect tickets or the service came by with the tea cart, Afrika would speak for me or I would pretend to be a mute. I hadn't even been able to buy my own ticket since these trains were not for foreigners, and sometimes I'd end up in a car with two or three strangers whose snores rivaled the rumble of the engine and made me feel like I was sleeping in the boiler chimney.

"Afrika, please, I need to sit with you," I would whisper to him on board as we made our way down the narrow, dirty passageway. Sometimes he was able to talk the guy in charge of our seating section into letting us switch rooms to be together. I had no idea how Afrika did it, but that was his thing, and I was eternally grateful as I curled up next to him and listened to his quiet, soft breathing.

Those overnight trains were always a crazy ride. The controls were all automatic, so the heat was either blasting so hard people had to open the windows and let the snow fly in or it was so cold I couldn't stop shivering for eight hours. I found something strangely fulfilling in those long, disorienting nights, though. Suspended between two cities, it was an austere, inconsequential existence, and I felt comfort in the simplicity and intimate solidarity of it. There was nothing like this back in Los Angeles, where everyone was safe and separate in their comfortable convertibles and station wagons, the days and nights bright and the streets lined with emporiums. It was exciting for me to exchange control for an uncanny and ironic sense of freedom, the freedom to accept suffering and be uncomfortable. I felt like I was really living, really sharing an experience with my friends. Sometimes in the artificial low light I could feel more alive than I ever had before, hitching a ride on the back of a dragon or a comet as it barreled through a landscape no one back home had ever seen.

In August of 1986 after *Red Wave*, a bunch of us went to stay at Sasha Lipnitsky's apartment and *dacha* as we had done before. Sasha was the bassist in an underground post-punk band called Zvuki Mu – "Sounds of Mu." While the leader of the band, Pyotr Mamonov, was one of the most revered and eccentric figures in the Russian arts, contorting his body and flipping through various styles of singing each song, Sasha was lanky and gracile and hid half his face behind a beard. He had an apartment right in the center of the capital where all the Leningrad rockers would crash. Sasha was a great organizer of social events and concerts, and there were rumors he came from an

■ Pyotr Mamonov of Zvuki Mu (Sounds of Mu).　■ Big Misha Kucherenko, a physicist and sometimes my translator, with Sasha Lipnitsky of Zvuki Mu.

important family.[3] He was so nice to Judy and to me and spoke to us with great English, but he had never seemed to want the two of us to sleep at his place or spend too much time there. Yet this time it seemed some of the rigidness of the city had softened, and the two of us joined Yuri, Viktor, Sergey, and Afrika for eggs, meat, and thick cut bread and a trip to the *dacha* to relax on the beach and swim in the Moskva River.

"Is it clean?" I asked Viktor as we headed out to the water hand in hand. "Of course," he said with his big, golden smile.

Years later, my friends at Moscow Greenpeace told me that they had tested the water quality and the levels of fecal bacteria were off the charts.

In the afternoon, Afrika and Sasha cooked us all a barbecue dinner that painted the breeze with its sweet, smoky color, and we jammed in the studio to rock music and the sound of laughter. It was one of the best days I remember having in Russia.

By the end of that trip, Yuri and I had also become a serious couple dazzled by the dream that things were opening up and maybe it would be possible to spend more time

3　In fact, his stepfather Viktor Sukhodrev (1932–2014), the son of a Soviet intelligence officer, was a Russian–English interpreter who spent his formative years in London and translated for high-ranking Soviet politicians including Nikita Khrushchev, Leonid Brezhnev, Mikhail Gorbachev, and Alexei Kosygin.

together in Russia. He gave me a quick kiss before Judy and I drove off towards the Finnish border in our rental car, confident he would see me and my crazy bleached and black hair soon. As I gunned the weak, coughing engine, I felt carefree and satisfied with my knees against the steering wheel and my arms out the window. Everything seemed to be working out for the best, and everyone seemed so happy.

"I got you, babe!" Judy and I belted into the clouds as we sped to the border.

I pulled up and pushed the button to let the guards know we were there so they could open the gate.

The minute we began to speak we heard them hang up. We called a few more times with no answer, and for the first time that trip I felt the hair on my arms stand up. I could see the guards in the distance, their dark silhouettes in their concrete structure, but they acted as if we were invisible. We sat for another hour, energy draining.

"I'm sure it's just their bureaucratic stuff," Judy tried to reason to me.

"We're going to miss our flight!" I screamed into the empty air.

We sat in the car all night, staring at each other and the impeded road in front of us, until the sound of jeep tires jogged us out of our helplessness. I saw a couple of the soldiers' cars pull into the facility. About an hour later a guard came to the gate and took his position for the day. I rolled down my window.

"Excuse me! Excuse me!"

He looked over at us, the purple bags under my eyes and the crazed look on my face. "What is up?"

I immediately started bawling. "You guys kept us captives here all night!" I wailed. "We missed our flight and everything!"

He shifted his weight, completely uninterested. "Border opens half hour."

"We were here last night before it closed, but they wouldn't let us through!"

"Border opens half hour," he repeated.

If only I had known that this trip would be seemingly one of my last, I don't think I would have been in such a rush to get out.

◆ Hold on to Your Pants

I was working for Ronald Reagan. At least, that's what the letter from the President's United States – Soviet Exchange Initiative implied. It thanked me for my thoughtful letter and *Red Wave* record I had sent to the President, reassuring me that "by introducing Soviet contemporary music in the United States, you are carrying out President Reagan's desire to expand cultural contacts between the peoples of the United States and the Soviet Union." I was then further instructed to keep them advised of my projects. Sure, it was a forced platitude, but it was the first time I had really heard it as an acknowledgment of my efforts. I was starting to feel that both countries finally understood that I was doing nothing more than music, and that music was a positive thing.

A few weeks later, I got my visa to return to Russia in October of 1986, as well as word from my friends that VAAP, the (only) Soviet publishing company, was trying to get the *Red Wave* musicians to sign a paper that said they had no idea about the album and that I had stolen their music. Suddenly I questioned if my visa would still get me through the border. For some reason, it was the easiest time I'd ever had getting in, the calm before the lightning struck and burned my world to the ground.

After *Red Wave* and all the publicity in the West, Russia was starting to open up more and welcome the curious guests of the outside world. What was so great for me is that bands coming in would contact me to hang with them and introduce them to some of the Leningrad rockers. The first to come through on October 6, 1986, was UB40. They showed up with ten musicians and Brummie accents from Birmingham to a double line of about a hundred stiff and stern soldiers guarding the stadium. I'd never seen anything like it. Russians were captivated by the number of black musicians and crew members, their eyes following the dark silhouettes from the bus to the stage door. The lead singer, Ali Campbell, gave me a wink and pulled himself up next to one of the soldiers.

"*Loosen up guy, we are going to have fuckin' fun!*" he shouted in the man's ear, shaking the man's cement shoulders. I was instantly a UB40 fan.

I had been given a backstage pass to go wherever I wanted and take photos of the concert. I watched as the band's roadies unloaded their equipment and as the musicians drowned out the sound of the audience with their shiny, loud, crisp music. It was so different from the intimate, provocative Leningrad band concerts to which I'd been that for a moment I felt disoriented. Where the hell was I?

After their concerts, the band would come to hang out at different apartments through the city, jamming and chilling with the boys I adored. Those Birmingham boys were the first people I'd met who could give the Russians a run for their money with drinking.

"That's fuckin' right," Ali sang after downing another shot. "You Russian boys better hold onto your pants!"

I was so amused by him, his vulgar language and sharp smirk. I went back with the band one night to their hotel on the other side of the river, watching as they stumbled across the streets and swung themselves in circles. At some point in the evening, I knew the bridges would open on the canals and I wouldn't be able to get back to the other side, but I was having too much fun to keep track of time.

"Uh oh!" Ali laughed, throwing an arm around my shoulders. "Looks like you're fuckin' stuck!"

"Lucky you," I laughed.

When none of us could keep our eyes open, Ali told me I could crash in his room. We squeezed into his small twin bed, and I fell asleep to the sound of wind passing the window. Early the next morning, before the sun had even colored the sky or the buildings, I snuck out and crossed town while Ali was still sleeping.

"You just fuckin' left!" He said to me when I saw them again in Moscow for their next concert, his brown eyes wide.

◆

Late one evening in Moscow, I was with the band in Red Square when one of the musicians told me that he had to piss. Before I could say anything, he unzipped his pants and peed in the middle of Red Square. I stood there dumbfounded as a guard ran up and tried to arrest him. Somehow one of the road managers with us managed to talk the guard out of it or pay him off, but the country had already been christened as a destination for Western bands. It was a piss poor welcome, but nevertheless marked a period of change.

More and more of my friends were informing me about the VAAP papers that all the *Red Wave* bands had been asked to sign against me in September. Gorbachev was in power now, though, and I truly felt that things had to be loosening up. How bad could it be? I found out that two of the original members of Strange Games signed the letter against me but Vitia didn't despite his fear for his family, and that Kinchev and Sergey basically told VAAP to go fuck themselves. Kino ignored the request. Sergey told me later he was at a friend's apartment in the center of Leningrad when he got a call from Viktor about it.

"I'm at a *dacha* with Boris, and he said that tomorrow when we get up, we should go together to VAAP and sign the letter," Viktor said softly into the phone. "What do I do? I don't want to sign against Joanna, but I don't want to upset or disappoint Boris."

"Are you fucking crazy!" Sergey screamed back at him. "You get on the next bus back to the city and leave immediately!"

No one said no to Sergey.

Boris ended up signing the letter against me, and many people were as furious as Sergey. It was strange, but I couldn't bring myself to feel that anger or betrayal that everyone else did. I had told Boris hundreds of times to protect his family and his band, and I knew that him signing the letter was what he had to do. Boris was the rain over my California desert – even if he did a little damage, I was still so grateful he was there. Nothing could ever make me love him less.

Boris and I never talked about him signing for VAAP. I never asked him about it because I knew he didn't like any confrontation, and for what would I be confronting him? He had never tried to anger or disappoint me or anyone else – he was a peacekeeper and a ray of sunshine who just wanted to bring the world together. He never wanted to be part of any problems. I knew that he did what he had to do in that moment, and it had nothing to do with me.

❖

Years later, I read a book on Sergey Kuryokhin that said when *Red Wave* was out, someone from VAAP brought it to Gorbachev.

"How can it be that these bands are released in the U.S. and not here?" Gorbachev reportedly said.

It's been documented that in the months after *Red Wave* came out in the West, the Soviet authorities started scrambling to try to make it look like the bands were "official" bands in an attempt not to embarrass themselves as the government suppressing such popular and accepted music. They chose Boris to be their darling of *glasnost* – of course, who wouldn't choose an angel for the top of their tree – and offered him and his band Aquarium the chance to play in Jubileyni. Jubileyni was the largest concert hall in town! Aquarium, Zoopark, Kino, and other Rock Club bands started to get played on the radio and eventually on TV, with Aquarium and their chamber orchestra getting the honor to be the first rock band ever to perform in the prestigious hall in Oktyabrsky.

"It was not at all by chance that Boris Grebenshchikov and his band Aquarium were somehow chosen as the sort of banner of *perestroika* and rock," Alex Kan later pointed out in an interview. "Boris changed. And he changed naturally. That was a natural evolution of an artist. He was not as aggressive, as sarcastic, or as satirical as he had been. He became much more mellow both in music and lyrics, and it coincided with the general evolution of the society, with *perestroika*. So, it brought together the cultural establishment and Aquarium. They fitted each other very well."

I remember that Boris could have become official many times before *Red Wave*, but he passed on the expensive apartments and shiny BMW cars that some of his friends had sheepishly accepted. He had stayed true to himself, and now he was finally being offered the opportunity to retain his music and his soul but take his place in the stars for which he'd been reaching. I couldn't dream of taking that away from him.

At this point, I hurried to Moscow to meet with VAAP. I wanted to explain the record and explain the positive impact of what I was doing. I knew I needed to go and try to protect myself. Anatoly Khlebnikov, my VAAP contact, had set up the meeting in a pale office room. I remember sitting across from three or four angry faces who were expressing their unhappiness with the album and how it was released without the artists' knowledge. I could see in their blinking, snapping eyes that everyone there knew consent had been given for everything. I kept trying to change the subject to focus on American and Russian relations and understandings, and even showed them some of the press the Russian musicians were garnering back in the States.

"The album was put out illegally," they kept telling me. "There are copyright laws."

"Fine, yes, the musicians didn't know!" I finally lied. I knew I had to protect my friends, but I was so angry about this whole charade. These people with whom I was arguing were the ones who had been working with me to bring Bowie to the Soviet Union as well as a bunch of Yamaha equipment for the Rock Club. I knew we both wanted to go forward with those projects, and I also knew we both were aware that the musicians had consciously contributed to *Red Wave*. It felt like a losing battle between toy soldiers. "I did it alone. It was all me. But it's serving such a good and important purpose. I didn't mean any harm."

I was asked to sign a statement admitting my guilt and pay a fee, promised that we could then put the incident behind us and work together. On October 16, 1986, I signed a paper admitting to copyright infringement and paid a fee of reimbursement for moral and material damage. For some reason, I chose to sign it Joanna Stingray, which was not yet my legal name. The second I signed the coarse white paper, their entire attitude towards me changed.

"We heard you have some music recorded. Maybe we could put your record out on Melodiya," one of them said to me.

Suddenly, I was their little American darling.

◆

I'm a big believer that holding onto a grudge is like holding onto an anchor and jumping into the sea. If you don't let go, you'll drown almost immediately.

The day after I singed at VAAP, I met with Gos Concert to discuss having Aquarium come to the States to play. I harbored no ill will towards Boris for signing against me and was still gung-ho about sharing his music and band with the rest of the West. Valery Kiselov from Gos was very open to my ideas and asked me to bring him a proposal upon my return in December. I had telexed my concert promoter friend to tell him the good news, letting him know the most important issue to the Soviets was the money. I was always amazed that something deemed "dangerous" suddenly was a safe bet if it could bring in the bacon.

It was a week after the infamous Gorbachev/Reagan Peace Summit in Reykjavík. I had made these black and white shirts for all the band guys that said "Save the World" in English on one side and in Russian on the other.

"Let's wear these to our concert at the Palace of Youth tomorrow and make it about peace," Viktor said excitedly when I gave them to him. "You should join us and sing one of our songs you recorded in English, Jo."

I felt a warm thrill at the thought but forced myself to shake my head. "Remember what happened when I tried to do that with Aquarium at the Rock Club?"

Viktor threw a lanky arm around my shoulders. "I don't care if they stop the concert," he whispered to me daringly.

■ My first EP, *Joanna Stingray*, which was released by Melodiya in 1990.

■ U.S. President Reagan greets Soviet General Secretary Gorbachev, Reykjavík, Iceland, October 12, 1986. Fed Govt / Public domain.

It was one of the proudest nights of my life. To see Kino decked in the shirts I designed as I got to join them on a stage flooded with light above a thousand silhouettes made me feel so important. It was affirmation of the gratitude the guys and the fans had for what I'd done, and after twenty-six years of wondering if I was ever making the right decision, it was confirmation of my life up until that point.

"I want to introduce to you our friend from America, Joanna Stingray," Viktor shouted in the middle of the concert. "We wanted to offset the non-agreement that took place in Reykjavík, Iceland, to demonstrate the fact that we do want peace and friendship with the United States!"

The crowd erupted, and I stood there shocked as all of my senses were overwhelmed. I looked over at Viktor and he gave me that sheepish grin. *How cool is this?* I could hear him saying in my head.

This was the first time I ever actually sang on stage with a band. Starting with Studio 54, I had only ever lip-synced my songs. I didn't realize how terrifying it would be, barely able to hear my own voice over the support and applause from the audience. I knew that for everyone there I couldn't mess up. The equipment was poor quality, and I'm not even sure if we had a monitor, but the crowd carried me as they sang along and waved their hands way over their heads.

Performing live on a stage like that is the most unnatural feeling in the world, something so unlike any other activity in the way it made me feel larger than life and almost untouchable, intangible. All my worries and paranoia about the concert getting stopped evaporated under the heat of the artificial lights. Everything at a concert becomes abstract – infused with symbolism and meaning and significance. When it was over, we walked outside to hail a car and I just kept noticing how hard the ground was beneath my feet. It was such a different sensation to before, when I was almost flying over the crowd.

"It can really make your roof move!" Viktor said with a laugh.

After this, I started joining some of my other friends on stage at Rock Club concerts. Each performance made me more and more confident that the next one would not be stopped either. One night, many of us jumped up to dance and sing at the end of an Aquarium concert, and another night I sang a song in the Pop Mechanics performance. Worlds were colliding, and groups were fading in and out of each other like stars behind the clouds. One night, Kolya Mikhailov finally acknowledged me, lowering the cold shoulder and saying hello after the performance as if I had been there all along.

Right around this time Melodiya finally agreed to release an Aquarium album exactly as it was given to them with no censorship. This was historic! It was what the guys always wanted, to have their music shared as it was created, with no propaganda or sticky strings attached. When we had made *Red Wave* to help Americans understand Russians, I'd had no clue the album could actually help change things in the Soviet Union. My friends and I were getting happier and bolder by the day. For the first time in all my trips, I was no longer afraid my visa would be declined. Everything now felt above board and legal, the winds of change arriving as the city trees changed from green to red and brown.

The first surprise came when I was back in Leningrad, driving my rental car through the narrow, shady streets. I could tell I was being followed and couldn't believe it. As I made my way through an intersection a policeman pulled me over for a violation I did not commit.

"I didn't do anything, and you have no right to pull me over," I said aggressively. "I'm working with VAAP on some important projects, and you have no right to pull me over!"

I could see it written across his hard, sullen face that he did not understand me and did not care. He took me to the police station, where I was questioned. I fought their inquiries, telling them I was doing business in Russia and had deals going with VAAP, Gos Concert, and the Ministry of Culture. Again, all I could see were colorless eyes that did not care. They fined me, satisfied with the hassle, and I stormed out. As I drove away, my eyes glued to the rearview mirror, I realized that just because I had smoothed things out in Moscow didn't mean Leningrad knew anything about that yet.

As I was leaving the Leningrad airport, I got another surprise when the guards confiscated one of my 8mm video cassettes that had an Aquarium concert I had filmed. Ever since our first Russian adventures, Judy and I had been extremely cautious with the footage we shot, immediately changing the cassettes after shooting and leaving a clean one in the camera just in case. This was one of the first times I hadn't changed the cassette.

"Please, you can't take that, it's for business!" I pleaded with them. I felt furious, unable to reconcile in my mind the fact that things had seemed to be opening up and yet here I was still getting abused by the Russian government in Leningrad. I had no choice but to get on the plane and leave the cassette and footage behind. As I watched the grey city recede through the dirty window, I realized with a jolt that my faith in the Soviet Union was maybe a little idealist. I may have never held a grudge, but there were officials back in Leningrad who seemed to feel very differently.

◆

The week of December sixth I heard about an article in *Ogonyok*, one of the most important magazines in Russia. Apparently, it threw a lot of negativity on the *Red Wave* album and distorted the truth about what we'd dubbed the underground rock bands. The kicker was that it quoted Boris from the VAAP letter he signed against the album, although VAAP claimed they had no idea how it had been leaked to the press.

"I thought things were changing!" I yelled at my roommate Tom. "I thought they saw the important work I was doing!"

"Oh, honey," Tom said, "they say love is blind."

Back in Los Angeles, I had been focused on getting Boris a record contract in the U.S. I had met with MTV's Steve Lawrence, who thought Boris was the coolest and introduced me to Kenny Schaffer, an eccentric fellow who owned a company called Belka International with his partner Marina Albee. While VAAP in Moscow had made him aware of a few of the official Russian rock bands, he didn't like any of them. On the other hand, after hearing all about Boris and listening to his music, Schaffer was hooked. The three of us – Schaffer, Albee, and myself – decided to join forces to get Boris a deal here. I put my back into the project full force, refusing to let any magazine or publishing company drive a wedge between me and my teacher. Boris had been the one who had made Russia home for me, who had taught me to open my thoughts and feelings and had introduced me to all the other bands. *Red Wave* had been my gift to Russia, but this record deal for Boris would be my thank you to him. *I want you to have it*, I would tell him, just as he had said to me so many times. *I want you to have it, and I don't care what the government says.*

In the middle of December 1986, I headed back to Leningrad with a visa to stay for over a month. I arrived to a frigid winter, bare trees and black sidewalks, the apartments steaming with body heat. As I ran from the metro to Boris' place, I was amazed how many Russians were still walking the streets to do errands as if the world wasn't an apocalypse of ice. I rushed past an ice cream cart with a line against the buildings, too cold to even look.

Boris' small room was lit by a little Christmas tree, casting cozy shadows against our faces as we sat, and I told him the news about Kenny and Marina.

"Well, shit," he said with a long, warm smile. Between that and Melodiya's plan to release an uncensored Aquarium album after the New Year, winter was warming up for us in that square, snug room.

After Aquarium's release, other Rock Club bands would also publish uncensored albums with Melodiya. The icing on the incredibly cold fruit cake was that Kino was blowing up in Russia, even more popular than before and playing tons of gigs. I went with Viktor to a concert they played in Moscow and then another one at the Rock Club back in Leningrad. Being in Russia was the easiest time to ignore the obstacles in my own life that the Kremlin seemed to be building. I was getting mixed messages around every turn, from Melodiya and VAAP to airport security, but when I was with Boris and Viktor and the others everything was certain – things were finally looking up.

This trip, I completely ditched the tour and spent the entire thirty-two days at Yuri's house. He made me feel like I was becoming a real Russian. Living with him became a habit that made me feel settled halfway across the world from my therapeutic mattress and mother's marble kitchen. True, I had thrown myself into the lives of my friends and let that carry me away from a lot of my problems, but there were moments when isolation and my foreignness hit me hard. Yuri helped rid me of that. I remember one day when I was alone in the apartment making tea, glancing out the window at the desolate, lonely tenement buildings surrounded by icy snow. A weird, dark feeling came into my gut, and for a moment I felt like I was on the moon, the most unnatural place in the world.

"What am I doing here?" I said out loud to the fuzzy reflection against the glass.

Suddenly Yuri was through the door, wrapping his arms around me and reaching for the tea. He made me forget I was an enemy in many people's eyes.

The opportunities for the bands kept coming. The rockers were playing concerts in bigger halls and different cities. They were happier, giggling like little boys with new bicycles to ride. I reveled in every *tusofka*, every hug, every concert, every laugh. My new engraved I.D. bracelet – Stingray on one side and the names of Yuri, Afrika, Viktor, Papa, Timur, Gustav, Andrei, Kostya, and B.G. on the other – became my armor, my guys the dazzling white knights singing "Silent Night" in Russian as we rang in the new year. We had started that night at the Swedish consulate where we drank, danced, sang and howled like wild animals. I'd painted my hair bright pink and Afrika and Timur wore these crazy rainbow wigs and pig nose glasses I'd brought. Sergey played jazz on the piano surrounded by champagne glasses and loud voices, until he switched over to our favorite UB40 song that he played over and over.

"I don't like the work but true I need the money! My life is like a joke but to me it isn't funny! People all around, telling me what to do – And all I want to do is stay at home with you!" We shouted into the old, moonless night.

Later that night, Afrika, Timur, Yuri, Gustav, Andrei Krisanov, our friend Alosha, Judy and I all went out onto the streets. Warmed by a medley of outstretched arms and chests dripping with vodka, whose taste I usually hated enough to refuse, we didn't feel cold at all. We were on fire, all of us, surrounded by the artificial lights of Nevsky Prospekt and screaming, singing children. It was the kind of festivity that I felt Old Hollywood back home was constantly trying to capture in its movies, but it was the kind of night a person had to see to believe. I watched a makeshift marching band, families with sparklers, and a huge giant plastic Dyd Moroz (Father Frost) fill every corner of space, like a lung filling with air as the city suddenly came to life.

"Assa ye ye!" Afrika shrieked as he slid across the ice and smashed into all of us dancing.

A month later, as I sat at home in Los Angeles under an unforgiving sun and sticky winter, this is a night that I thought of often. It was such a beautiful moment in time, the culmination of all of my work with these bands and these guys as we crested the ladder of success and slid into celebration. It was bright, it was promising, and it was unspoiled by the malignant suspicions and lies of Soviet magazines, publishing companies, and government. It was Russia at its finest, full of love, light, and warmth.

◆

"Was that supposed to be Bruce Lee?"

"Aww oooh!" Viktor and Yuri chimed again, leaning towards me with exaggerated faces and mouths full of brown bread and fish.

Laughing, I looked up from the big bowl of rice Viktor had made me since he knew I had become a vegetarian and taken an affinity to his favorite food. I remembered the noises from the newest film that I had brought them. "It's really convincing," I said teasingly. "Now stop that and pass me some *tsoi* sauce."

Viktor tossed me a packet of his favorite soy sauce I'd bought for him at the *Beryozka* shops with a wink.

It was my first time in Viktor and Marianna's apartment, where they lived with their fifteen-month-old son, Sasha, and Marianna's mother and grandmother. It was outside of the city center, its cramped kitchen filled with a stove top, cigarette packs, an ashtray, and Sasha's syrupy wandering hands that seemed to revel in the fact that there was no baby-proofing here. As the guys twisted open a bottle of Cuban rum they'd received at a concert in Riga and tasted it for the first time, I decided to interview Marianna. Marianna was an artist who spent a fair share of her time organizing and managing things for Kino. Out of all the musicians' wives, she seemed the most involved, and Viktor, Yuri, and Gustav seemed to love her input and help.

"In terms of money, do you ever wish that Viktor was an official singer so that he got paid for his music?"

She tossed her shoulders back. "No woman ever refused money, but if he had to sacrifice something with his artistic freedom, then I wouldn't need it." Her eyes were always blunt and blue. "Let everything stay the way it is. We'll make that money some other way. I don't think money is that important. Of course, when you have a kid you need more, but more or less we have it. Whether you have a lot or a little, it all trickles away like water!"

I loved her directness with words, unabashed and uncompromising in her experiences and opinions. "Tell me how you cope with all the young girls that jump around and try to attract Viktor after concerts?"

"Thankfully, our circle is small," she leaned forward with a mischievous face. "Whispers about my character have already reached the ears of all those young girls who go to his concerts. They know to stay away!"

If only the same could be said about me and the Russian government.

"Don't forget I'm taking you and Yuri to the American consulate tomorrow for cheeseburgers," I called to Viktor as Yuri and I left that evening.

"Thanks, Jo," Viktor called to me, winking again as always.

"It will be so much fun," I said to Yuri as we got home that night. "None of that pickled fish tomorrow!"

"I want you to be my wife," he replied casually.

"What?"

■ Yuri and me, 1986.   ■ Victor with his son Sasha, 1985.

"Jo-an-na, I want you to be my wife," he repeated with his sweet dark eyes and funny English accent.

"Yes! Yes!" I threw my arms around him. "*Ya prosta ne magu perezhit biz tibia*," I whispered in his ear. It was my favorite Russian saying. "I simply cannot survive without you."

That was it. On Tuesday, January 6, Yuri and I went to the wedding palace in Leningrad to register to get married. They gave us a date three months from that day: April 6, 1987.

"Why so far?" I asked Yuri. "In America you can get married the day you think of it." To this day I still see it as a genius idea with which Americans could benefit, being forced to really consider your choice and the consequences that may come with it.

That evening we had a party with all our friends. I had always felt like one of the guys, but now I would be legally connected to their group.

"Joanna Stingray – she was a real bombshell," Gustav said in an interview years later. "She did a great job for us. She was fantastic. We couldn't just let her go, so we sacrificed Kasparyan."

The whole thing felt like a fairy tale. I'd battled the great iron forces of Communism and prejudice and in doing so had found my prince charming. It seemed as easy as getting married and living happily ever after. If only I'd known that the world had other ideas that veered very far from Disney's vision.

"Congratulations!" Yuri's father said to us when we told them. His mother smiled, but I could tell she was nervous and already anticipating what the world had in store.

"Do you have a plan? Where will you live? What will you do? Where are you going to bring up the children?" She asked Yuri softly.

The problem with being in love is that it takes up so much headspace there's very little room left for logical thinking. I was like a cartoon character with big heart-shaped eyes and a head full of dreamy white clouds, assuming that all the details would just work themselves out. It never crossed my mind that in the end it wouldn't be a fairy tale but a fight for what I wanted, never even dawned on me that it might not be Yuri or Viktor who would have to channel Bruce Lee the most, but me.

◆

It was so hard for me to understand how anyone could think *Red Wave* did anything but good, positive things between Russia and the United States. As I sat with Boris in his flat the next day, he presented me with his Melodiya record. It was something that had never even been on the table before *Red Wave*, and I knew it meant so much to him.

Jo, with all the love of a fuckin' rock 'n roller – that's definitely all I ever was, he signed it.

That same day, Sergey and Alex stopped by to show me the *Ogonyok* article about which I had heard. "It is very strange," Sergey said in his quick, articulate way, barely pausing for Alex to translate. "The editor of the magazine, Vitaly Korotich, is supposedly very into Gorbachev's *glasnost*."

"How can a man of vision condemn this?" Alex asked.

That was all I needed to hear. "I want to meet with him," I said. "Let me try to explain *Red Wave*."

The guys nodded.

"I think it is a good idea," Alex finally said.

"I will come," Boris said ceremoniously, his eyes twinkling at me. It was settled.

On January 13, 1987, Boris and I were sitting in the Moscow offices of *Ogonyok*, across from Korotich. He was a charismatic man, worldly and smart and seemingly open-minded. I told him all about *Red Wave*, why I did it, the American response, and the settlement with VAAP over copyright infringement.

"We have Columbia Records in the States interested in Boris recording a U.S. album and we're collaborating on this with Mezhdunarodnaya Kniga,"[4] I told him. "It's

---

4 Mezhdunarodnaya Kniga was the Soviet government agency dealing with cultural exports/imports.

important stuff!"

Korotich turned to Boris. "And what are your thoughts on it all?"

Boris tossed back his blonde hair and folded his hands on his lap, his long muscles and limbs falling over the chair. "Evidently, rock music remains the universal language of communication of youth the world over."

"I suppose I cannot disagree with you there," Korotich replied. "Joanna, what you did was a wonderful project, and I would like to officially apologize for the negative article." He requested to have one of his journalists interview Boris and me right there for their next issue in February.

As if to balance out the universe, on January 28, another bad article came out against the record in the Soviet's largest newspaper, *Komsomolskaya Pravda*.

◆

"*Red Wave* on Troubled Waters?!" I read the headline aloud. "How can they say I didn't care about the moral and material damage to the Soviets that the album caused? They're saying I made up that Aquarium wasn't official just because they've released with Melodiya, but that literally just happened and *Red Wave* came out over half a year ago!" I was furious. I was also confused as to why this type of article was coming out three months after I had signed and paid compensations to VAAP. Just when I felt everything was coming together, the ground underneath me felt like it was splitting into fragments again. I chalked it up to the recently developing struggle between the old guard and the new, my friends telling me some people were just stuck in the old Soviet ways and saw rock music as a traitorous danger. In the end, I let it go, way too willing to let my excitement as an upcoming bride distract me from the subtle signs the Soviet Union continued its mistrust and chicanery.

My last memory of this trip was at the Leningrad airport. Yuri was there trying to keep his arms around me and kiss me, begging me to take some moments to stop and breathe and be with each other before I left. I laughed him off, consumed with wedding ideas and feeling so loved and happy that I couldn't take anything seriously. I felt like a real businesswoman now, respected and legitimate.

"Just let the authorities try and stop me now," I sang to Yuri as he tried to hold on for one more hug.

"Jo-an-na," he said slowly.

I remember so clearly gently brushing him aside and telling him, "I'll be right back in just over a month. Don't worry about anything!"

I didn't even take the time to look him in the eyes and say, "I love you."

"Love ya!" I called over my shoulder. He looked back, his hand running through his hair and his eyes bright and full, and then I was gone.

◆

I was blissfully dreaming about my upcoming wedding, my head full of soft music, early stars over the canals, and alabaster flowers.

"Do you have a plan?" Somewhere from the imaginary void full of sweet cakes and first dances I heard Yuri's mother's words again. "Where will you live? What will you both do for money? Are you planning on having children? Where would you bring them up? Do you know what his grandparents died of?"

What? I blinked.

"Do you know what his grandparents died of?"

Suddenly my mother's high cheekbones were in front of me, her pearly skin creased in consternation.

"No, why should I know that?" I asked.

"You want to know what you're getting into, Joanna."

"I love him and want to marry him!" I said.

"And I love you and want healthy grandchildren!" My mother shook her head, exasperated.

We stood staring at each other across the granite countertop, until finally my mother let it go.

"Have you been looking at white dresses for your wedding?" she asked.

"No," I sighed, leaning forward on my elbows. "I realized I don't really like dresses, and certainly not white ones! It's not my style."

"Oh no," my mother said, crossing her arms. "You only have a wedding once, and you want it to be a special day, don't you?"

"You get to pick, either a white wedding dress or grandchildren. You can't have both."

"Joanna, think about it. We could have you help design it."

Over the next week I thought a lot about my mother's offer. I could see how important my wedding was to her, and with everything she'd put up with as I flew back and forth to Russia over the past few years, I finally decided wearing a white wedding dress would be a nice thank you. There was a part of me, too, that fantasized about a traditional fairy-tale wedding.

Now everything was coming up roses and palm trees. I got word that Boris' album with Melodiya sold over a million copies in the first couple of months in Russia, and also that *RIO* magazine, a *samizdat* in Leningrad, released an in-depth article on my journey to Russia and my successes with *Red Wave*, dealing with VAAP, and confronting the negative press. It was called "California Girl," written by these cool young guys named Sergey Chernov and Sergey Agonin with the help of Alosha Ipatovstev. The article was full of details about which I hadn't even known at the time!

At this point, *Red Wave* had sold over fifteen-thousand copies and counting, and RCA Records agreed to release it in England in early spring 1987. I got offers for a lecture deal to speak around America about the record, as well as a book deal from Doubleday in New York; they ultimately wouldn't happen because of a storm of events, soon to be unleashed, that would change my life forever.

◆

Allan Affeldt, who was putting together a U.S.A./U.S.S.R. International Peace Walk, contacted me to help get a concert together around the event. I also planned a trip for legendary producer Phil Ramone to come to Russia in April to discuss the possibility of producing an English-language album for Boris. Isolar, Bowie's company, gave me the authority to put together a Bowie concert in Russia for the upcoming fall, with Boris and Aquarium as the opening act, and set off to make a film about the concert as well. Vladimir Litvinov from the Ministry of Culture, Valery Kiselov from Gos Concert, and Anatoly Khlebnikov from VAAP were all working with me as I stretched my reach across Moscow and Leningrad to try to make all of these events happen. Up until then, I had avoided going to the American Embassy in Moscow out of fear that the Soviets would become convinced I was a spy, but now I needed their help in arranging the large Yamaha donation to the Leningrad Rock Club.

On top of it all, a designer and I came up with a futuristic peau de soie white wedding dress that I lovingly dubbed my Jetsons dress. Between it and the special wedding invitations and "backstage passes" I made for all the invitees, the wedding suddenly felt real, as real as the sun on the horizon. My mother, stepfather, sisters, a few L.A. friends, Yamaha's Doug Buttleman, Guitar Center's David Weiderman, and the rockers, artists, and friends in Russia were all planning to be there at the Leningrad Palace #1, followed by a reception at the Austeria restaurant inside the Peter and Paul Fortress. For the day before the wedding, I planned for all the bands and myself to play a concert as part of the celebration. Timur Novikov agreed to paint the backdrop for the stage, an image of me sitting in a huge tractor with the word *Stingray* colored across it.

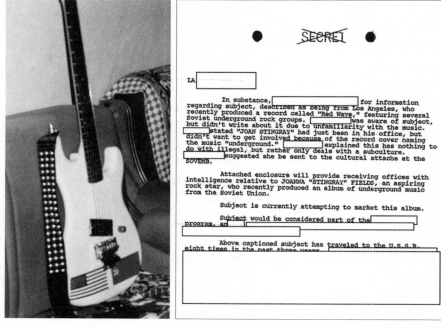

● ~~SECRET~~ ●

LA

In substance, ▮▮▮▮▮▮▮▮▮▮▮▮▮▮ for information regarding subject, described as being from Los Angeles, who recently produced a record called "Red Wave," featuring several Soviet underground rock groups. ▮▮▮▮▮▮was aware of subject, but didn't write about it due to unfamiliarity with the music. ▮▮▮▮stated "JOAN STINGRAY" had just been in his office, but didn't want to get involved because of the record cover naming the music "underground." ▮▮▮▮▮explained this has nothing to do with illegal, but rather only deals with a subculture. ▮▮▮▮suggested she be sent to the cultural attache at the SOVEMB.

Attached enclosure will provide receiving offices with intelligence relative to JOANNA "STINGRAY" FIELDS, an aspiring rock star, who recently produced an album of underground music from the Soviet Union.

Subject is currently attempting to market this album.

Subject would be considered part of the ▮▮▮▮▮program, an ▮▮▮▮▮▮▮▮▮▮▮▮

Above captioned subject has traveled to the U.S.S.R. eight times in the past three years.

■ The donated Kramer guitar and more of my FBI file. The redactions create more mysteries as they indicate there were sources, maybe Russian or maybe American, that the FBI was interviewing. It remains unclear what "program" is being referred to here and whether the US government ultimately wanted to try to recruit me.

"NBC called and wants to shoot the wedding!" I shouted into the phone, bouncing on the sofa cushion as I stretched the phone cord to its limit. "And *Life Magazine* wants to interview me about my emerging role as a musical diplomat!"

"Joanna, speak slower," Judy pleaded on the other side of the call. "I can't understand what you're saying."

"They called me a young Armand Hammer!" I screamed.

The icing on the wedding cake was that Kramer presented me with a U.S./Soviet flag painted guitar, the same time that Pan Am airlines agreed to fly all of the donated Yamaha musical equipment for the Leningrad Rock Club for no charge at the end of March. It was a Disney movie at its finest, all the pieces falling together in this perfect puzzle.

◆ Why Are They So Afraid of Love?

"Joanna, your visa has been declined."

It was just three days before I was scheduled to head back to Russia, and moments ago, I had been giddy with excitement, blasting Kino's punk song "Mother Anarchy" while packing. It was always hard to stay home among the red convertibles speeding on twisted roads and cold winter beaches, because I rarely got to hear from the guys or get any information on what was happening. The anticipation of being back with my second family and having my wedding made me feel like I was floating around my suitcase, dreaming of the fourteen-hour flight I normally hated.

I had just about finished, the leather and cotton commingling in the zipper of my bag as I danced around it, when I heard my phone ring. I quickly stopped the music and grabbed the phone, laughing and out of breath. It was the owner of the travel agency.

"Hey, how's it going?" I asked her.

"We were supposed to get the thirty visas today for the trip, but unfortunately we only received twenty-nine." I could hear buzz in the background – the sound of computers running, fingers typing, and printers coughing up papers. "Joanna, your visa has been declined."

I stood there in my socks, feeling caught with the strangest urge to laugh. *She's joking,* I thought to myself. *She can't be serious.*

"Joanna?"

The Russian idiom popped into my head which, to paraphrase, advises that there is always a little joke in every joke. In other words, most jokes contain more truth than jest. Then I realized what was happening. "What did you say?" I choked out.

"We received a note that said your visa could not be granted at this time. We put in a call to check if it was a mistake, but they gave us the same answer." She paused. "Maybe you should try to call the Soviet embassy in D.C.? I can give you the number.

I wrote it down numbly.

"I'm so sorry about this," the woman said. "We'll do whatever we can to help. Keep in touch the next couple of days."

I hung up the phone and stood there in such a state of shock I couldn't feel a thing. It didn't seem believable to me, and I thought for sure I could fix it. My whole life was waiting for me back in Russia.

I called the Soviet embassy in Washington D.C. and told the operator that I had to speak with somebody urgently about my declined visa. "I'm doing official work with Russia, and I'm getting married to a Russian. I need to speak with someone right now."

She transferred me to some guy to whom I told my story. As I heard the words fall mechanically from my mouth, I started to feel the reality set in, my voice getting tighter and tighter.

"Okay, calm down," I heard the man say kindly. "It's okay. Don't worry about it. It must be a mistake. Give me some time." He took down my number and promised to call me within half an hour. I took a breath for the first time in what seemed like forever, forcing myself to continue packing. I placed a hair dryer and a few other goodies on top of my packed clothes that I knew the airport baggage handlers would steal, sealed my suitcase, and curled up next to the phone. It had to be a mistake. I knew this kind and caring person from the embassy would work it out. Nowhere in my mind could I picture not getting back.

"Hello?" I grabbed the phone on the first ring. Something felt different – the energy was off.

"Sorry, no visa," the same man said coldly.

I couldn't breathe. It was like those moments in diving when I'd hit the water wrong, like a group of fists pounding straight into my stomach. "How could this happen?! I'm working with Mezhdunarodnaya Kniga and VAAP!"

"I can do nothing. Our telex from Moscow has informed me that Moscow is not expecting Joanna Stingray. No visa." He hung up on me.

I felt like I was in space. In the back of my mind I heard a little voice screaming *Joanna, snap out of it! Cry, scream, feel. Do something!*" But I did nothing other than stare blankly out the window at the saturated lawn and yellow hazy sky. I knew my life was being ripped away from me, everything into which I'd put my heart and soul for the past few years, yet I could not react.

At some point the phone rang again. I picked it up without saying a word and heard my mother start talking about something else on the other side. I started to sob.

"I'll miss my wedding! I'll miss my wedding!" I kept saying, trying to tell her about the visa. I was so hysterical that she couldn't understand what I was saying.

"Are you hurt?" She kept yelling into the phone, convinced I'd injured myself at home.

"My visa!" I wailed. "I'll miss my wedding!"

She finally understood. "Joanna, we will work this out," she said loudly over me. "Please calm down. We will help." My mother knew I rarely cried, and when I did, it was because of something truly traumatic. In those few moments I'd had in my life, she always came to my rescue.

"Please," I begged her. "Please."

I got in the car to head to my mother and stepfather's house, deciding not to call anyone else about the problem yet. Spreading the word set it in cement, validating that this was a real problem. I couldn't handle that. When I walked into the kitchen, my mother had a list of their contacts who might be able to help and was already on the phone with one of them. When I was at my worst, this was my mother at her best, coming to my rescue with her helmet of styled blonde hair and fiery blue eyes.

I told her about the telex the embassy relayed they'd received from Moscow. "They used Stingray," I said, which was not my official name and not the name on my passport for the visa. It was obvious that this was a very measured, purposeful act, a message sent to me that my work in Russia was no longer tolerated. I broke into tears again.

"We still have three weeks before your wedding," my mother tried to console me, her hand over the mouthpiece. She was calling Dolores Beilenson, whose husband Anthony was one of our congressmen and a close friend. Dolores told my mother that Anthony would help, and my stepfather Fred should call him right away. She also mentioned that we should contact Armand Hammer for help, who had arguably the most pull with the Soviets of any American.

As my mother continued her phone calls, I sent a telex off to Oleg Popov at Mezhdunarodnaya Kniga confirming our upcoming meeting and all the projects on which we were working, including producer Phil Ramone coming to Russia in April, the David Bowie concert, and the Yamaha donation to the Leningrad Rock Club. I included letters from Ramone, Bowie's management, and Yamaha, letters that verified they had given me consent to work on these projects on their behalf and be their representatives in Russia. I refused to give VAAP any opportunity for another accusation. In the telex, I mentioned nothing about my declined visa.

Popov usually responded very quickly to my messages. When I didn't hear back in twenty-four hours, I sent a similar message to my contacts at VAAP and Gos Concert. I also tried to call my friend Anatoly Khlebnikov at VAAP. All I got was silence, deafening and indelible. I felt sick. Everything suddenly seemed very ominous. After all I'd done, I had become a ghost, an outcast, reduced to being nothing. It was the worst feeling in the world.

My mother, on the other hand, had become a steamroller. From Dolores Beilenson she was also given the names of Mark Perris and Kathleen Lang in Government Foreign Affairs at the U.S. State Department. A close friend Marcia Weisman also gave her the contact information for Claude, Armand Hammer's secretary, as well as those of Joan Mondale and Guilford Glazer who had potentially traveled with Hammer to Russia. Someone else gave her information to someone who worked in Hammer's office. My stepfather reached out for help to his friend Leo McCarthy, the Lieutenant Governor of California, to see if he could get him to Mr. Hammer, as well as John Van de Kamp, the Attorney General of California, and his wife Andrea.

Word came back that my visa had been declined from the Ministry of Foreign Affairs in the Soviet Union. My mother wrote a letter to the singer/songwriter Kris Kristofferson asking for help too. He had played in Russia, and my sister Rebecca was currently the sound engineer for his wife, Rita Coolidge.

"I wrote that I'd seen his concert in Las Vegas, and it was so powerful and showed his humanity towards all people," she promised me as I sat numbly in her house. "I told him it made me more open-minded to listen to both sides of every political issue in the future. If he can help, he will."

Since I'd never heard back from any of my business contacts in Moscow, Doug Buttleman from Yamaha sent a telex off to Popov reiterating that they were authorizing me to handle the donation of the equipment to the Rock Club. He asked them to confirm the meeting with all of us in Moscow in April. We heard nothing.

There was one point I finally managed to get through to Yuri on the phone. I told him the news and promised my family was working on it, and I had hope I would be there in time for our wedding.

"I will try," he said slowly, "to do something in Russia. I lo-" and the line was cut.

With that, I became a machine in my desperation to fix everything. I sent telexes to Mark Taplin in the Cultural Affairs Department in the Moscow U.S. Embassy and to Vitaly Korotich from *Ogonyok* magazine explaining what happened and stating that I loved Yuri very much and just wanted to be with him. It was very unfair, I told them, for the Soviets to keep me away from the one person I couldn't live without. To Thom Shanker, the writer I had befriended at the *Chicago Tribune* in Moscow, I protested that after all my positive cultural work I was now being used as a political football.

"Why are they so afraid of love!" I screamed at the world as I wrote it.

I was dramatic and desperate, but I was also a twenty-six-year-old woman who felt like the life she had created was being ripped out of her chest along with her heart. I was terrified of losing my friends and my husband-to-be, and was deeply entrenched in the shock, hurt, and fear of the moment.

Somebody suggested I write to Vladimir Posner, a charismatic spokesman for the Soviet Union who had appeared numerous times on *Nightline* with Ted Koppel and on *The Phil Donahue Show*, but I heard nothing back. Not from anyone.

Congressman Beilenson sent a telex letter to the Ministry of Foreign Affairs, Consular Section Moscow, on March 26, 1987, and to Minister Zakharov at the Ministry of Culture in Moscow on March 27, 1987. He explained with regards to my recently denied tourist visa that I had plans to marry a Soviet citizen, in addition to my duties as a musical ambassador in Russia.

He urged those in Moscow to use their authority to grant me a visa and even he, an American Congressman, heard nothing back. I was eternally grateful to him to step up, but I was also inconsolably devastated.

Picture a sailboat. Picture it catching the right wind and turning into a group of other sailboats, their bright colors complimenting each other and their presence urging each other on. Farther and farther into the sea, strong as a pack, guiding each other as they left their ropes and docks and rushed into the great unknown to taste the freedom cresting each risky wave.

Then picture an Iron Fist, reaching up from the cold depths and swiping the rudder from that sailboat when no one was looking, when everyone was focused on the horizon.

Picture that sailboat, alone and drifting as it fell behind the group, stranded without direction, without the others, without any place to wear a white wedding dress.

♦

Before email, before cell phones and texting, before FaceTime or WhatsApp, there was me on my oversized burgundy couch in Los Angeles convinced that my Russian friends were going to move on with their lives without me. Russians knew you couldn't fight what you couldn't fight. What I didn't know but found out soon after was that the minute Yuri heard about my visa problem, he and some of our friends took the sleeper train to Moscow where he filled out a written request to the Consular Department of the Ministry of Foreign Affairs. In the long moonless nights that I spent awake thinking of him, finding out about what he'd done gave me a minute of happiness in an otherwise indelible nightmare.

Yuri finally received an answer to his request that said: *The arrival of U.S. citizen Joanna Fields/Stingray in the U.S.S.R. is not currently feasible.* They had written the end of the story.

Life went on in Russia, because none of us really had a choice. I usually had to wait days, weeks, or sometimes even months to get any information, and it was the same on their side. On April 6, 1987, there was no wedding. Yet the world didn't stop turning, and I was forced to wake up and sit motionless through the hours I should have been laughing, kissing, and celebrating. I have absolutely no recollection of that day though. I've tried to search the depths of my brain for a memory, clawing through the images I'd pressed into the cracks of my skull and hid away, but there's nothing except a blank white page stuck in the twenty-four-hour bindings of that fateful day.

The only thing that reoccurs is a different memory I have of my high school CIF Finals for diving where I was the star for the Beverly Hills High School and expected to contend for a medal that day. My last dive was a reverse 1½ flip, and as I took my three steps and made a leap, I suddenly heard a loud bang echo through the oversized indoor pool. I felt like I was floating, peaceful and disassociated from myself as I sank and a slew of people jumped into the pool to get me. *Wow, I wonder what that bang was,* I remember thinking. *I wonder why all these people are getting in the pool.* I felt two arms grab me and drag me into the air, everyone talking over each other and asking me if I was okay. The whole time I felt fine, so serene, like a bird being carried by the wind into the sky. It's a memory that reminds me how powerful the human psyche can be, and when the pain – physical or mental – is too hard to bear, it can shut itself off and deny any type of tangible existence. My psyche erased one of the worst days of my life for me. In my mind, no matter how hard I try to revive it, April 6, 1987, just doesn't exist.

Across the ocean that day, Yuri did the only thing he had the power to do to express his frustration and sadness – he had Gustav cut off all his beautiful, flowing hair. When I later saw photos of his crew cut and sharp frown, he looked like someone heading into the army. I guess this was our own silent war.

After I missed my wedding, my memories kick in of me, my parents, and their friends

■ Gustav cutting off Yuri's hair in protest of our missed wedding, April 6, 1987. The artwork in the background is by Oleg Kotelnikov.

pushing into overdrive to try to fix my problem. Unlike Russians, when we Americans are wronged, we feel redress or vengeance is our right as citizens of our country and of the world. My parents flew to Europe with my passport and tried to get me a Russian visa from some of the Soviet Consulates in cities in Poland and such. Before they left, my stepfather Fred was put into contact with Vladimir Posner, who promised to investigate the visa denial on his return to Russia after stopping through Los Angeles.

"Only Armand Hammer could get the Soviet foreign office to issue a visa to a U.S. citizen," Posner told Fred over the phone.

Not long ago I found a letter I received from Armand Hammer dated December 20, 1985. *Dear Miss Fields*, he'd written, *thank you for sharing with me your videos shot during your visit to Russia, which I am returning with this letter. It was kind of you to think of me. May I wish you a joyous holiday season and success with your career in the year ahead. Sincerely, Armand Hammer.* When I got this letter, I had thought it was fabulous! Now that I'm older and wiser and more aware of what was going on around me, I can read between the lines.

Who are you? I don't like rock 'n roll. These guys look like hoodlums, and I don't do anything illegal, even for a good reason. You and I are not alike. Take back your videos, I can hear him say.

And he never did anything to help with my visa issue.

My parents received some information off the record about how to contact Anatoly

Dobrynin, who was part of the Central Committee in Moscow and formally the Soviet Ambassador to Washington for more than two decades until 1986. Fred also reached out to Mayor Tom Bradley of Los Angeles, Senators Alan Cranston and Mel Levine of California, as well as Senator Ted Kennedy of Massachusetts, all close friends and men he had supported over the years. My mother had heard back through Dolores from the State Department: it was clear that I had entirely underestimated in the past few months the way the Soviets would have a problem with me and what I was doing. In their words, I had control of the Russian Rock situation, and they were not willing to give up their power to a young American with geometric hair.

I telexed another long, rambling letter to Anatoly Khlebnikov at VAAP, citing any new items that could help my cause. I included that Bowie was interested in licensing his albums to Melodiya and pleaded for him to telex me an invitation for a business visa so I could attend our meeting with them and Kenny Schaffer to discuss further plans for Boris and Aquarium to come to the States. I got nothing. I telexed Mr. Zakharov and Mr. Litvinov at the Ministry of Culture, explaining I had sent telexes to Mr. Kiselov at Gos Concert and others concerning the Bowie concert and Boris and received no response. With each desperate rejection and cruel silence, I was becoming more and more of a wreck.

"We cannot let my personal problems in Leningrad interfere with our business affairs. They are two different things, and I will handle each separately," I read aloud as I wrote them into the telex. "We have some very powerful projects happening to help open the cultural doors, and they are too important to let fall through! Please respond quickly!" I started to cry.

My visa denial and missed wedding became a bigger deal in Russia than I could have imagined. Many of my friends tried to do something or search for information. A rumor was circulating that one or more of the official Russian rock bands in Moscow was behind my visa getting declined, an immature and sadistic attempt to cure their own jealousy after not being included on the underground album of *Red Wave* – they were the stars in Russia and felt it was their right to be the first to have their music released in the West. Despite the speculation, I was less concerned about who had declined my visa and focused all my energy into getting back through the borders.

I found my champion on April 20, 1987, in Senator Alan Cranston and his incredible assistant Elmy Bermejo.

"Nothing here matters except that two people in love are being kept apart," Senator Cranston said to Fred when he received the information about my problems. "That is

■ I went to the White House to advocate for myself during this visa crisis.

■ Telex from Senator Alan Cranston to the Ministry of Foreign Affairs in Moscow on my behalf.

not okay. We need to fix this."

Thank goodness for Senator Cranston, especially when word came back from Kennedy's people that because the Soviets loved the Kennedys, the family didn't want to tarnish that image or precarious relationship by getting involved in my visa problems.

My days were spent either writing letters and telexes or lying on my bed sobbing while my friends' music blasted through the dark, square rooms of my house. The chorus of Boris' haunting song, "I Dream of Ashes," kept playing over and over. It felt so real to me. I knew I still had Bowie and his projects supporting me along with Yamaha and their donation and Boris' U.S. record deal, but as I fought to hold onto the light, I could feel myself slipping more and more into darkness. There were days I didn't bother to flip the light switch at all.

♦

"Hey Joanna, it's Kenny. How are you doing? I'm so sorry for your visa problem."

"Thanks," I said quietly. It was a no light switch kind of day. "It's been hard, but we just keep trying to fix it."

"You know, I had a great meeting in Moscow about our Boris project." He paused, and I could hear the static between the lines. "I'm afraid your visa problem could affect it. I hate to say this, but I think for Boris' sake you should step away from the project."

The only thing I could think of was that I was going to be sick. I curled myself into a ball, holding the receiver so tightly against my head that I could hear the plastic shifting uncomfortably. I was surprised by my feelings of possessiveness and overwhelmed with a surge of defiance. I was the one who had gone back again and again and again on my own expense. I'd worked three years to make Boris' dream of being an artist of the world come true. I had known from the first time I met him that he was a magical poet, a bard and a rocker whose soul was bright enough to cover the Western world. How could I let this go? It was my heart, a piece of me and a reflection of my own feelings and convictions, validation that I had found something special and that I, in turn, was special for recognizing it. It was supposed to be *my* gift to Boris, not anyone else's.

As I sat there, tears staining my cheeks and the room full of shadows, I had a sudden flashback to Vitia Sologub singing his badass, punk version of The Beatles' "Helter Skelter."

When I get to the bottom I go back to the top of the slide!

For some reason that line was in a continuous loop in my head, some type of meditative chant and holy comfort. In that moment I had an epiphany that shattered all the shadows.

If I give you something I don't care about, then it means nothing. I want you to have it, I heard Boris' voice like a whisper in my head. So many days in his apartment, so many trinkets and presents he'd surrendered to my hands or Judy's. Things that he'd loved, things that he'd cherished, things that were all he had, he'd willingly and even happily given them to us.

"Of course, I will," I said to Kenny. "I don't want to do anything to get in the way of Boris and this dream."

I was giving away one of the cornerstones of my life: Boris and his music. It was my gift to him and to the world, an expression of the gratitude I had for everything he'd selflessly given me. In the end he'd traded more than just baubles and objects – he'd given me the ability to feel without fear, to sing with conviction, and to love with the deepest and unflinching parts of my heart. For so long, I'd been so focused on him and the other guys that I hadn't had a moment to view these transformations of my soul, but suddenly I felt changed. I was lighter and more hopeful than I'd been in a long time. I picked myself up, brushing the bedsheet lint off my legs, and got ready to start climbing the slide. From where I was, I could only go up.

♦

If Green Day had found the Boulevard of Broken Dreams, I was paving my own way to Russia on the Avenue of Exhaustion. I would stop at nothing. I found a receptive ear at the Soviet Consulate in San Francisco, which motivated me to fly up north only to be rejected by another cold shoulder. I flew to London, waiting in a long, rigid line at the Soviet Embassy and trying not to fall asleep standing up. The person in front of me, Kate Karam, a young and articulate girl with bright, attentive eyes and long brown hair worked for Greenpeace and was there to get her visa in advance of discussions to open a Greenpeace office in Russia. I'd always had a great affinity for the organization and a resounding respect for warriors fighting for our earth. I told her about my troubles, and we exchanged numbers to keep in touch. It was the only good thing to come out of that day, and I flew home empty handed and sleep deprived.

"What will you do if you can't get back in and Yuri can't get out?" Jane Pauley from the *TODAY Show* asked during a satellite interview I did about my "enemy of the Russian state" status.

The question caught me off guard. In my despair and my anger had I never actually entertained this idea. But once this possibility was put out into the universe, vocalized and echoing out into the void that separated me from my second home, I physically shuddered.

"No," I told her loudly. "Not seeing Yuri and not getting married – it's not an option for us."

Somewhere over six thousand miles away, at least some people seemed to agree with me.

I received news about a three-page letter to E. V. Yakovlev, Chief Editor of *Moscow News*, Russia's most liberal newspaper, written by the Rock Club of Leningrad and signed by all its rockers, the administration, and the director Kolya Mikhailov. The letter gave some background on what I did in Russia and addressed my visa problem, ending with the statement: "This letter is neither a complaint nor a request. This is most likely an ascertainment of a number of facts and our bewilderment about them. Or maybe a question, the answer to which sooner or later we will have to give by ourselves, the Soviet people."

It was such an unexpected surprise, and one that only drove me further in my conviction that there was no alternative to my return. Russians didn't often stand up to fight the system, and the fact that these guys did that for me gave me new strength to continue my push for justice. I was so proud to be a part of this gang of pirates and would fight tooth and nail to get back to them.

The American-Soviet Peace Walk organizer, Allan Affeldt, heard about my visa troubles and extended an official invitation to me as a special guest to participate. He said his organization was getting everybody's visa as a group for the walk from Leningrad to Moscow, June 8 – June 12. It was worth a try, but unfortunately not even this scheme could work.

On May 25, I finally got correspondence back from Russia. It was a telex to Doug Buttleman at Yamaha from Mrs. L. D. Nechaeva, Chief of the Department of Culture at the Leningrad Regional Trades Union Council. Even in my exasperation I was continuously amazed how many titles people had in Russia for their jobs, how under Communism the authorities just kept making up more and more titles and jobs for all men and women to work. Mrs. Nechaeva's letter noted that they would be happy to receive the Yamaha gift of equipment for the Rock Club and graciously agreed it would "serve a wider development of musical and cultural contacts between our nations." I remember thinking it took a woman to finally be the bigger person and decide to emphasize what was important. At least one thing I'd planned was still on track.

It was at this point that I started to write English lyrics to many of my friends' songs and record them in my free time. While in this exile, I could feel more connected with them this way despite the fact we weren't together jamming, laughing, and singing. They had such glorious, luminous songs that moved me every time I listened. Words just started coming into my head. From Boris' "Ashes" and "Babylon" to Tsoi's "Beatnik," Kinchev's "My Generation," to Games' "Cry in Life." I managed to rope Judy into bringing my recorded versions back to the guys for me, something that made me still feel like part of their world. One of my favorites was the English version I wrote to Tsoi's new song "Peremen" – "Change" – that would go on to be one of his most important and famous songs, even quoted by Gorbachev.

I called this song "Petty Men" to rhyme with his original title, and it became the outlet into which I channeled all of my confused, conflagrant anger at the Russians who shunned me.

Petty Men

I tell you this tale of a vision I've seen
Such a dangerous sight
Frustrated boys, deadly toys playing all night
Cigarettes in their mouth, hats on their heads
Power and greed, blind fear
Left spineless and weak with cement in their tears

Petty Men
Troubled water will fall from your eyes
Ambitious features, bureaucratic teachers, have
made petty men Petty Men
You will fall with your lies

I hang by a thread, vultures over my head
Patiently waiting my fall
While they keep building up their ice-cold walls
They should turn back around, stick their heads
in the ground
And fade to dust
On borrowed time heartless souls get what's just

Petty Men
Troubled water will fall from your eyes
Ambitious features, bureaucratic teachers, have
made petty men Petty Men
You will fall with your lies

I sing you these words of a battle I've lost
Maybe you'll rise where I've failed
Trapped by a game, rules insane, so beware
Of Petty Men
Troubled water will fall from your eyes
Ambitious features, bureaucratic teachers, have
made petty men Petty Men
You will make Petty Men

■ *Help Stingray* cassette cover, 1987.

◆ Help Stingray

In 2014, a member of the Russian parliament made claims that allegedly stemmed from studies done by the former Soviet KGB. In his words, "A whole CIA department in Hollywood, California, were professionally writing songs for Viktor Tsoi after studying the situation in the U.S.S.R. and then picking the correct words that would play on the listener's sentiment." Were they talking about me?? They say that Russia is a country with an unpredictable past, but it's also a country with a sometimes-fictional past as well.

◆

To circulate the news about my situation, I decided to follow in the footsteps of my friends and take the fight 'underground' and back to their own fans. I put the song "Petty Men" and others I lyrically rewrote on a cassette and created a home-made cover with the title *Pomogee Stingray* – translated as *Help Stingray*. Judy got it into Russia, and the network of rockers distributed it the old-fashioned Russian way. The irony wasn't lost on me that now, after I'd smuggled out their music on a contraband album, my guys were doing the same for me. These moments, these pockets of secretive pursuit we shared, was the lifeline that carried me through a dark ocean of bureaucratic neglect.

On June 16, 1987, Congressman Beilenson received an answer to the cable he had sent in March. The negative letter, from the Consulate General of the U.S.S.R. in San Francisco, was the one and only direct response from the Soviet government any of us got, and it was a crippling, emotional punch.

From the initial denial to the curt or nonexistent replies that filled months and months of tear-soaked nights, stretched a chaotic time saturated with disappointment and uncertainty. I was riding a roller coaster of confusion, despairing then hopeful then despairing again within minutes.

"Joanna," my mother said one day on the phone. She sounded cautious, guarded. "A letter arrived from Russia..."

I was out the door and into the car, racing over to her house. "Oh my god," I gasped when I opened it and saw a full-page letter from Yuri. He had never written before and rarely said more than a few words during any conversation, yet suddenly here he was in the black ink that coated the thick paper. It took me a moment to focus on the sentences and realize with a panicking heart that, of course, the whole thing was in Russian.

"I have to translate this letter!" Again, I was out the door with my tires complaining against the fast, sharp turns I was taking. My brain was frantically trying to figure out an easy solution in the days before Google Translate. Every second that ticked by was killing me – every second I could have been a little closer to Yuri and heard his low, thick voice in my head. I had turned off Sunset Boulevard just past the famous Beverly Hills Hotel onto Benedict Canyon when a flash of light in front of me turned into a white VW Rabbit convertible, driven by what looked like a god with flowing, blond hair. It took me less than a moment to figure out who it was. I sped up next to the Russian ballet dancer and actor and dangerously crowded his car towards the curb.

"Godunov!" I screamed as I rolled down my window. "Godunov! I am an enemy of the Russian State, and I can't get married!"

Godunov had been the star of the Bolshoi Ballet until he defected to the States in 1979. The look on his face told me he couldn't understand what I was saying, his eyes wide and his face scrunched as if to ask *What the fuck?* Miraculously, he slowed down and parked against the curb. Breathing heavily, I pulled behind him and hopped out of my car, opening his passenger door and throwing myself in next to him.

"I am an enemy of the Russian State and they won't allow me to get into Russia to marry my fiancé, but he just sent me a letter and I can't read the Russian can you please translate this for me?" I pushed the letter into his hands as I gasped for air.

Alexander Godunov looked down at the sweaty page and then back at me. His stormy blue eyes met mine, cradled on his magnificent face. "Sure," he said casually.

Nothing could have been more powerful that day than the premier danseur reading Yuri's thoughts to me in his rich Russian accent. "Yuri says, 'Baby I am sorry we could not get married, and I know how hard this is for both of us. I tried to do what we could in Russia and will keep trying. I want you to be my wife, and I will wait as long as it takes. Do not worry. You must take deep breaths. I want you to have my baby.'" Godunov didn't even flinch.

Yuri's letter filled my heart like warm water or a ray of sunshine in an empty flowerpot. As the seconds ticked by on the small round dashboard clock, life was suddenly bearable, doable. I looked up at Godunov and smiled.

"Thank you so much. This means so much to me." I jumped back out of the car, not wanting to take any more precious time from this icon. In my frenzied rush, I left him sitting on the curb of the canyon with Yuri's letter still in his hands as he watched a complete stranger he'd met not five minutes before race away.

◆

We feel that it is most important that Joanna Stingray be on the charter flight at 7 a.m. on Tuesday, June 30 to Moscow, Lieutenant Governor Leo McCarthy of California wrote to concert promoter Bill Graham.

Bill, with his far-reaching reputation around the world, had somehow thrown together a concert with the Soviets to culminate the Peace Walk on which I'd been invited. He was convinced that I should just hop on the plane with him, James Taylor, Bonnie Raitt, and the Doobie Brothers and head with them to Moscow without a visa. Leo McCarthy promised to make every effort at his end to get things in order, but if worst came to worst, Bill assured us that he would make it work upon landing. To this day, I'm still amazed at his willingness to help someone he didn't know. This felt like the best chance to get back into Russia. It was a big venture, with computer entrepreneur Steve Wozniak donating five hundred and eighty thousand dollars to cover organizational expenses. If there was anything that could sway a Russian bureaucrat to turn a blind eye, it was money. But even five hundred and eighty thousand dollars wasn't enough to soften the hard hearts of the Soviet government, because word came from Moscow that if I was on the plane, they would not allow it to land, nor would they permit anyone in the group into the country. Twenty-four hours after Bill's offer, I stood with my suitcase in my hand and a bubbling sense of rejection and panic as the plane left without me.

It had been almost six months since my visa was initially declined, and as the days wore on and hope became elusive, Russia felt farther and farther away. I got word that I'd missed a crazy Pop Mechanics concert where the boys had shaved the heads of two girls on stage, and also that Afrika was starring in a new film with the renowned director Sergey Solovyov in which Aquarium and Kino were going to perform. Things were changing and speeding up for the better in Russia, and it broke my heart that I couldn't be there to see it and be a part of it. I felt exiled on another planet, watching the world turn.

When I needed him the most, Viktor somehow magically must have understood what I was feeling. In July, he succeeded in sending me a silly drawing of himself with *Happy birthday Jo. July 3* and *Rrr,rrr,rrrr,rrrr* written beneath it. To know he hadn't forgotten me was the extra air in my life vest that I needed to keep me afloat.

Senator Cranston had informed my stepfather that he would not give up helping me despite the brick wall we were all hitting. My mother had different ideas.

"Maybe this is a sign, Joanna," she broached carefully to me. "We're almost out of options.... I don't know, have you considered that it may be time to leave Russia behind and focus on moving forward here?"

I absolutely lost it. "I can't live without Russia!" I cried hysterically. "It's in my blood! I would rather be sitting in a Russian prison than here in your big fancy house! Don't you *ever* tell me to leave my home behind!" I stormed out on her, overflowing with fear and loneliness and the adrenaline of too many sleepless nights.

The sun kept rising day after day. I wasn't really sure why.

I was continuously haunted by the last time I saw Yuri. I kicked myself over and over about not taking the time to wrap my arms around him and tell him that I loved him again and again right to his angular, alabaster face. It would have been so easy, yet I had been so careless. This event changed who I was forever. After that, every time things get really good in my life, I become nervous and afraid that something bad will happen if I don't pay closer attention. I never go to bed without resolving any fight I've had with family or close friends, and even when my elderly parents are feeling strong, I say prayers at night to keep them healthy. I love my life now, but when things get even better, I might check our earthquake kit or the water bacteria in the faucets. It's impossible to ever be completely in control of life and to prevent bad things from happening but being mindful and attentive at least prevents some things from slipping through the cracks and widening them.

"Stingray luck," I whispered to myself on those lonely afternoons or early mornings when I felt farther from my friends and resigned to the desert smog, reminding myself of how lucky I'd been to have all my Russian experiences just fall in my lap. It had never been planned – I had been lucky in my life, and I forced myself to believe that such luck could and would continue.

As luck would have it, two good things happened at the end of July. Senator Cranston wrote my stepfather another letter saying that in a recent meeting with the Russian ambassador, he asked that priority be given to my case. He had gleaned that Yuri and I were only one of two blocked marriages on the Soviets' list and questioned how anyone could be on that list in what he dubbed "Gorbachev's new Russia." Along with that, my managers at the time – Harriet Sternberg and Ken Kragen of "We Are The World" fame who were helping work on my case – got a tip that I should look into an overnight boat from Finland into Leningrad for seven hours and back. I found that to do this twenty-four-hour trip I wouldn't have to give my full passport with my name and photo but only a passport number for approval.

"If I legally change my name," I explained to my mother. "I'll get a new passport number!"

My mother, resigned to the fact that my love affair with Russia was too deep to be cut away like a dark curl of hair, dug up contacts to help me do a quick name change and receive a new passport within a few days. I was now officially Joanna Stingray.

I applied for the Finland trip and got approved. It was like breaking through the ice after being dragged beneath it for months. My hands were numb, and my spirit was bruised, but I had survived!

"I'm going with you," my mother said curtly when I told her.

"Are you kidding? No, mom, I'll be fine. You can't go."

"What if they recognize you going in and arrest you?" She was sitting up incredibly straight, her body long and motionless, her sloping Slovakian jaw set and her eyes cold as stones. She was the kind of person I wanted on my side. "There's not a chance you're going," she warned, "without me."

We decided not to tell anyone about the Finland trip, just to be safe. We arranged with Judy that she'd be in Russia and could tell Yuri and the others in person the day I'd be arriving for seven hours. If all went well, we would meet at Boris' apartment in that square, sunny room I knew so well.

A week later, I landed in Helsinki with my mom, NBC producer Linda Ellman, and an NBC camera man named Tim. NBC had decided they wanted to record my reunion in Russia and were planning to use my hand-held video recorder. Trying not to make eye contact with the pale faces and icy blonde heads that surrounded us, we headed to the travel agent to get our tickets and visa for the boat. My whole body felt like my nerves were on fire, hyperaware of every movement and every flicker of light against the cool linoleum tiles of the floor. I welcomed the feeling, the rush of excitement and anxiety so different from the months of stagnant isolation and hopeless depression I had felt.

"We should have dyed your hair or gotten you a wig," my mother said under her breath for the hundredth time.

I shook my head. I knew the Russians would either figure out that I was coming and arrest me or not. This wasn't about being sneaky or undercover. This was about barreling into the weakest part of the defense and hoping I managed to break through. This was about a wolf running straight for the bear and hoping I was fast enough to make it to my pack.

◆

While my mother went to get our visas, I waited around the corner. I hopped up and down, my feet unable to stick to the shiny floor, until I saw her walking towards me with a smile.

"Two visas," she said proudly. "They said to be at the boat by six p.m."

Up until that moment I really wasn't sure she would get it. I reached out and took the piece of paper in my hands, more precious in that moment than any silver or gold. I could feel my heart beating faster and faster at the realization that I would be seeing Yuri and my friends so soon, after months of believing it would never again be possible!

"I just want to call Russia!" I whispered excitedly. "I want to say it's okay and that I'm coming. You don't know how many times they were sitting and ready for me to come and then I couldn't."

My mother shook her head with authority. With her head held high, as if she were still a Rockette on stage, she could command an entire room, including me.

"Don't you think we can just call Marc in Los Angeles and tell him?" I pushed.

She shook her head again. She's beauty and she's grace, as the Miss America song goes, but it fails to mention she's also the one who gets the last word.

The light was getting dimmer as we headed to our cabin, walking past a lone man playing the accordion as we boarded. I could feel my mother start touching and tugging at my hair.

"Mom, what are you doing?"

"I think we have to cover your hair or something, so it doesn't look so obvious," she said. If the visa had boosted my confidence, it had only made my mother more nervous.

◆

A few years back I had dyed the front of my brown hair a shocking, angelic blonde, and then a little while after that had dyed a big strip of hair underneath the back of my head blonde as well. I loved the blonde look but was afraid to go all blonde because I didn't want to be known as another Hollywood blonde bimbo. I ended up with a three-layer skunk pattern with the top and bottom blonde and brown in the middle.

Against the uneven rocking of the boat my mom tried to cover my head with a scarf, both of us laughing at how ridiculous I looked. She tried so many styles, bracing her long legs against the boat's jerky movement, but one was worse than the other.

"At this point I'm either going to have to shave it off or dye it blue," I said, exasperated. "Just let me put it back and tie it with a pink ribbon." I knew I looked silly, but it was the best option I had.

We met with Linda and Tim to make a plan for when we arrived in Leningrad.

"Two hundred passengers are in the bar with their belts around their ankles and their shot glasses getting refilled," Tim told us. "Alcohol is too expensive in Finland, but out here off-shore the price goes way down." We could hear the rowdy crowd on the floor above.

"When we arrive, we're supposed to disembark, go through customs, and get on buses for a seven-hour tour of Leningrad," Linda said, trying to ignore the stomping and laughter that sunk down through the ship. "We will all go together and try to walk past the buses to go into the city on our own. Just follow us, and we can all head to Boris' to film Joanna and Yuri reuniting."

Hearing her say that gave me chills up my entire back. For a moment I saw myself from afar, hunched below deck on the Baltic Sea with a couple hundred drunk Finns heading for Leningrad. Linda and my mother sat memorizing Boris' address in their heads in case something happened or we got split up. Then I was back in my body, jittery and chewing my lips with nerves. I was so revved up and impatient that my mom gave me half of a sleeping pill. The next thing I knew, there was sunlight pushing out from behind the window blinds and the boat was slowing down. I sat up and peeked outside. The first thing I saw was an old rusty boat with Russian letters on it. The sight of it made me catch my breath.

"Mom, wake up!" I called to her. "We're not far!"

We went to the top deck, my hair stupidly pulled back again. No one was there, just the two of us watching the boat slowly creep between all different kinds of Soviet ships. The boats looked tired and bulky sitting low in the water, but the sight made me impossibly happy. I remember thinking how weird it was that these old broken transportation machines made me feel nostalgic, like I was coming home. There was something eerily beautiful about it, like that first night I'd walked through Leningrad with its dark corners and lingering smoke.

By the time Linda and Tim joined us, I had tears in my eyes. The four of us stood and waited for the rush of passengers, but nobody else seemed in any rush to get to Leningrad or even off the boat. We floated silently forward and docked with no sign of any other tourists. Down on the shore a group of musicians were playing some mediocre Russian music to welcome us. It made me hungry for the rockers, for my family, for my home. I had to get off the boat.

Below was the oversized, angry, concrete building that housed the custom control area. There was a huge empty square past them with a tiny figure standing on the far side.

"Judy?" I whispered under my breath. I was so nervous I was hallucinating, trying to find a sliver of comfort in the world around me.

Ten buses were lined up at the side of the square closest to the port. Everything felt strangely quiet and vacant, the soft pitchy music fading into the early morning. I felt the adrenaline kick in like a shot of espresso, rushing down two floors to stand by the exit as my mother and the two from NBC followed at my heels. Suddenly, so close to the freedom I was craving, I got a pit in my stomach so huge that it almost broke my heart. Within minutes my feet would be on the soil of my mother Russia, but how long would it last? Passport control rose like an old lighthouse warning of the sharp rocks that surrounded me.

"Maybe we should wait for a few more passengers so we don't stand out?" Linda whispered as the workers clamped on the walkway and open the gate.

I couldn't wait any longer. I was like a horse out of the barn, head lowered and blood pumping, walking briskly with only one thing on my mind. I had to just get to the square. I had nothing with me but my passport, so I walked right by the customs guys and headed towards passport control.

This is it, I thought to myself. *Don't puke, don't faint, don't die.*

◆

I stood face to face with the soldier at the kiosk and handed him my passport. I forced myself to smile, trying to ignore the earthquakes in my hands that were making both my arms tremble. Behind me, up high was a mirror that the soldier kept glancing at to check the back of me as he studied my passport. I tried to stand absolutely still, hardly letting myself breathe.

The soldier started slowly thumbing through the pages of my passport, his face changing as he realized all the pages were blank except for the Finnish stamp. How could I not have thought of that! It was a red flag. It was the end.

"Aaaaaaah!" There was a loud thud and then a rush of commotion. The passport officer and I turned back towards the entrance to see my mother on the ground right in front of the customs people.

"Oh, ouch, help me!" She called out demurely, her manicured hands spread out against the dark ground. Around her the contents of her Louis Vuitton bag were rolling across the paved ground – curlers and lingerie, jellybeans, numerous mini alcohol bottles, and soy sauce for Viktor. The band stopped playing as the customs guys ran over to help her, stopping in front of the lacy brassieres and makeup as if they were unsure how to proceed. I saw it happening in slow motion, everything black and white like an old, almost comical silent film.

A loud clicking sound jolted me back to where I stood. The soldier stamped my passport and handed it to me as he took off towards my mom. I couldn't believe it. For a moment I watched in shock as he rushed past me, but then I was gone, leaving my mother and her dramatic act – my true saving grace – behind as I beelined for the square. The buses were all lined up, but I saw no drivers on the sidewalk.

"Keep walking, keep walking, keep walking," I muttered to myself under my breath. My whole body was burning with a sensation of immunity, a sensation of victory after half a year of doubt. My head was almost paralyzed looking straight ahead the whole time as I forced myself to keep a steady, slow pace. I was afraid to look around, afraid that one little glance behind me would set off an alarm above my shoulders. My body was so tense it would be sore for days afterward. I kept waiting for something to happen like it always did in those movie escape scenes. Everything was so still, and in my mind, I imagined voices calling out to shatter the silence and bullets racing past my cheeks as if I was some kind of female James Bond. The square was huge, and it felt like I just kept walking and walking, forever damned between the shore and the city.

When I was younger, my mother and father drove with me and my two sisters out into the desert. For some reason they'd taken separate cars, and my mother had gotten mad at my dad when we stopped for lunch on the side of the California highway heading east. I remember my mother piling the three of us girls into her car and speeding off without our dad, making our way down Pear Blossom Highway in a long line of cars.

"Oh shit!" My mother screamed, adjusting the rearview mirror and staring into it. "You've got to be fucking kidding me!"

I looked behind us out the back window and saw my father speeding along happily in his car. We had left a solid twenty or so minutes before him on a road where gunning the gas to catch up was almost impossible between the severe bumps in the asphalt. Yet there was Dad, smiling and waving to us as he caught up right behind. I could see for my mother that in her rush to blow off steam, in her need to shake off what was behind her and just get to our destination, she felt like the tires were rolling and the car was going nowhere. Now years later, I was watching the sidewalks of the square slowly inch past me, and yet I felt trapped on a treadmill just waiting for the antagonists of my story to rush up behind me. It wasn't anywhere as romantic as a marital fight, and I knew that any car behind me would have sirens and dogs.

Somehow, as I was imagining all of that, I reached the end of the square. I blinked as a few cars passed by on the road, and then swung my hand out. A car stopped almost immediately, as if that person was scheduled to pick me up all along.

"*Ulitsa Sofia Perovsky, Dom Piyat,*" I said, giving the address through the open door. The driver motioned me to get in and sit.

The car was a cheap old Lada with the thick smell of cigarettes and greasy food clinging to the headrests and peeling ceiling. As we sped towards the Venice of the North, I felt a smile blooming across my face. I was back – I had somehow made it through everything and was heading home. I wasn't concerned for my mother or the NBC people at all, having just seen how clever and capable my mother was as she provided a covert distraction for my escape. I knew I'd see them again soon enough, and all I wanted in that moment was to be folded into the arms of Yuri and the rest of Kino and Boris. I glanced behind me, out the back window to the empty stretch of road behind us.

"You've got to be fucking kidding me," I whispered. There was nothing there except the sweet taste of freedom.

♦ Unions and Reunions

Russia is a country with an unpredictable past.

Just like the uncredited quote above, it will never be clear exactly what the Soviets did to manipulate *Red Wave*'s release history and the identity of the underground bands, as well as marking me as an Enemy of the State. As the car turned down Boris' street, I felt like I was back in this crazy, wonderfully terrifying land of unpredictable and inconceivable things. One minute I was shaking in the backseat of a car, watching dark streets go by as I tried to remember the facial features of all my friends, and the next thing I remember I was in Yuri's arms as if we'd never been apart. The strength of his arms around me made the past seven months melt away.

"Your hair," I said when I finally pulled away. His beautiful long hair was gone, replaced by a buzz cut that framed the squareness of his face. I smiled. None of it felt real, this moment I'd been dreaming about for so long. All I could do was run my hands through his short spikes and kiss the shallow wrinkles around his eyes and mouth. We were completely in the moment, as if we would be standing there forever while the roofs moved above us.

"Joanna!" I looked up to see Judy and Viktor running towards me. Before I knew it, I was staring into the dark fabric of Viktor's shirt as he bear-hugged me with my sister.

"R, r, r, r, r, r," he rolled his tongue in my face with a huge smile.

"Ts, ts, ts, ts, tsoi," I laughed, sticking my nose against his.

The four of us finally scrambled up to Boris' flat. Back in the communal kitchen I

■ My mother, Joan Nicholas, with me, Yuri, and Viktor in Boris' flat, July 1987.

lost all my words, like a pond of water that evaporated in the sunlight. I just sat between Yuri's legs enjoying the feeling of his body around me, beaming under the weight of Timur, Gustav, and Alex as they joined us and overwhelmed me with hugs.

"You got in!" Alex exclaimed. "We didn't think you'd actually make it!"

After a while, Judy left to go buy some food and drink. We were all lounging around, happy and comfortable as if the world had stopped spinning, when I heard Judy's voice echo up the cement stairway.

"Mom! What are you doing here?"

I looked up and my mother was suddenly standing in the doorway, bright and blonde against the dim light and tight walls. She narrowed her eyes at me.

"They took everything!" She said, exasperated. "All the alcohol, makeup for the bands, jellybeans, even the napkins from the boat, and who knows how many packets of soy sauce." I could see the guys eyeing each other, surprised at all the stuff she was trying to carry in. I was surprised at the strange accent she'd magically developed between the time I'd seen her last and now, as if she thought speaking English with a different lilt would make it more understandable to my friends. "Somehow, I found this place, but I got nervous coming up, so I went back down to check if I was in the right place and I ran right into Judy! No hello or how are you doing at all. After all I do for you girls!"

I got up and wrapped my arms around her, pulling her inside. We settled in, drinking tea and sharing stories just like we'd always done. I had missed the *tusofka* way of life more than I'd realized. Judy filmed us lip syncing to my "Feeling" song so I could make a video on my return home – Viktor, Yuri, and I sitting on chairs pulled closely together with our arms draped over each other, with Timur and Gustav bouncing up and down in the background like wonderful, wicked birds as my mother tried to conceal her laughter. I had brought all the guys Swatch clip-on watches and we climbed out on the roof to take some promo shots. As I stood there and looked out over the sharp slant of the roof and the magnificent Church of the Savoir on Spilled Blood sparkling in the wet summer sun, I felt the blood return to my own body. I felt alive again, giddy as the rest of my friends as we sang and jumped around in our own little world.

When I crawled back into the apartment window, I saw Linda sitting with my mother. I could tell she was disappointed about having missed the reunion, but she was very eager to interview Yuri. She sat down across from him with a confident look in her eyes, a seasoned interviewer ready to pull on the heartstrings of her subject. Little did she know that Russians, especially Yuri, were men of simple expression and few words.

"How do you feel now that Joanna is here?" She started, leaning forward and placing an empathetic hand on the table.

Yuri blinked. *Wasn't it obvious?* I could see him thinking. "I feel fine."

"Well how do you feel about the whole situation of Joanna's visa being declined?"

"Not great."

Linda shifted in her seat, raising an eyebrow. "Why do you think it should be okay that she marries you?"

"Why not?" He asked, playing with the curls in my hair as I sat on his lap. This was pure Yuri and part of why I loved him. He wasn't concerned with games or explanations. He always said it like it was.

"When Joanna wasn't here, what did you think about?"

Yuri wrinkled his forehead, already bored of the frivolous, dramatic questions. "I can't understand everything now... my roof is moving very quickly."

"When she was not here, Yuri was very gloomy, always in black," Timur spoke up.

"Yuri, what did you do on the day of your missed wedding?" Linda asked, encouraged by Timur's answer.

"Sit at home," he said bluntly. "And do nothing."

"Did you drink?"

"No."

"If you could tell people in America why you think it's okay for her to come to Russia and marry you, what would you say?"

"Marriage is generally good." He smiled as the rest of us laughed.

"Oh, tell them Yuri," Judy prodded from off camera.

"I love Joanna very much!" Yuri shouted, putting his arms around me. The room cheered.

I could see NBC got what they wanted, but more than that I got more than I had ever dreamed.

♦

"What if I didn't get back on the boat?"

Yuri, Viktor, and Alex eyed each other, shifting uncomfortably. I could tell none of them wanted to tell me I had to go. Finally, Alex rubbed his hand across his short beard and shook his head.

"That wouldn't be wise," he said slowly. "It would be breaking the law, and then the government would have an actual reason to kick you out. They would never let you in again."

Still, the thought lingered in my mind. That day Yuri and I had decided to go to the Wedding Palace #3 and try to register again for a wedding. I'd had no idea what to expect but being back with my boys had made me bolder and more determined than ever. We went, holding hands up the wide, carpeted stairs, and received a date three months later.

"November 2, 1987," I repeated miraculously. It was amazing how easy it was. Not only did it reinforce what I believed was my fairy-tale destiny, but it also confirmed what I'd already learned about this oversized bureaucratic country – Russia was not a scary, well-oiled machine. It took months for information to move from one organization or city to another, and sometimes details were never substantiated.

"I don't even understand the motivation behind Joanna's visa problems," my mother admitted in a conversation with Linda and Alex back in Boris' apartment. "Isn't it the age of *glasnost*?"

"My guess is that she somehow very unfortunately got stuck in the middle of the whole struggle about rock that's being waged right now in this country." Alex sat on the edge of the chair, his arms on the faded table. "After the very strong and severe restrictions rock has had for years, it has quite suddenly been given a nearly complete go ahead during the last several months. In no minor respect that was caused by the *Red Wave* album, which was one of the very strong arguments for letting rock out of the underground. But there are people who are very nationalist and say they are trying to preserve Russian culture, the Russian spirit, and for them everything which is coming here from the West is in itself decadent. Rock is the purest manifestation of that."

"So, they see Joanna as a vehicle of potential danger?" My mom asked, her eyebrows crinkling as she knit them together. She glanced at me skeptically, my crazy hair and mouth full of gum.

"Yeah, she's a sort of person who was pushing Russian rock. Making it heard. Making it known. Making it internationally recognized and making it sort of a vital force. It became much stronger than it had been before." Alex paused, his bright eyes deep and dark in thought. "We very often tend to think of this society as solid, and of the government here as a solid state. We think of it as something that always votes unanimously, and we think the voice in the government is always one strong voice. It has been like that for decades, but it is not like that anymore. There are some very, very strong arguments and some very, very strong struggles in the highest echelons of power in this country on every major issue. Economics, politics, and rock 'n roll."

Guess I'd rather be a controversy than a cipher.

Time slipped by like a weighted hourglass in the sun, sparkling and magical and slowly draining. I didn't want to leave Boris' familiar kitchen and the warmth of the past three years that stuck around the cozy space. We had little time left, though, and Boris was rushing back from another city to meet us at a park near the boat.

"Good to see you, Jo," he said as he gave me a long, soulful embrace beneath the thin amber trees. It felt like the first time I'd met him, that mesmerizing smile framing his beautiful hippie body. It felt like nothing had changed, and his energy made me feel peaceful and hopeful in a way I'd almost forgotten. The sun slunk behind a cloud, bitter and unable to compete.

"Boris," Linda piped up, "why do you think the government won't give Joanna a visa?"

Boris stood there with his long legs and a mild breeze in his hair. "I can give no explanation. I don't know the answer myself. I think what Joanna did was one of the most positive things in cultural exchange, and the fact that it happened before *perestroika* stepped in says a lot on her behalf. For me, it's completely illogical. I think there are some people who have some kind of old conservative values and they just don't want to know about any fresh ideas. The same people who were banning rock music for a long time, they are banning Joanna's visa right now. I think it's exactly for the same reasons."

"Well let's not give them another reason," my mother said gently, indicating it was time to go.

"I don't want to leave, but I feel like I don't have a choice!" I said sadly. "You guys know I'll be back…"

One by one, my friends squeezed me in their lanky arms.

"Jo, we're waiting for you," Viktor said, his eyes locking with mine like a bridge across the sea.

"Everything will work out." Boris gave me his curling, radiant smile.

I stood there trying to memorize everyone's beautiful features, the sun angling off the backs of all their heads and creating a mirage of angels. Finally, Yuri draped his arm over my shoulders and walked me to the boat. We stood in each other's arms for as long as we could and listened to the water lapping at the feet of this unflinching country.

"Baby, all will be okay," Yuri whispered, holding me close as if he could tell I was about to run back towards the city. "We will be together. Kiss you, miss you."

Yuri's calmness came over me quickly, and staring up at him, I was no longer scared to leave. I believed him, and I also now knew that I wasn't forgotten when I was gone. My friends had given me back three years in less than a day, and I knew I'd get it back again when I returned.

"Are you worried at all that you won't ever be able to come back?" Linda asked me back on the boat.

I stared out the window at the receding gray shore. Somewhere against the horizon was my pack, the guys joking and jostling as they made their way back to their homes, whistling and singing the songs that we'd shared. I could almost feel their eyes glancing over their shoulders, down the thick streets towards the place where I stood on shaky ground looking back towards them.

Despair was no longer my companion. My wolves were waiting.

♦

It was right around the time that I snuck into Russia for seven hours from Finland that, unbeknownst to any of us, U.S. Secretary of State George Shultz was discussing with Soviet Foreign Minister Eduard Shevardnadze an upcoming meeting between President Reagan and General Secretary Mikhail Gorbachev. Thanks to the relentless persistence from Senator Alan Cranston, Secretary Shultz brought up my blocked visa. I'll never know exactly what he said, but whatever it was coupled perfectly with the fact that the Soviets more than likely had learned of my break-in and re-registration at the wedding palace.

"What is it?" My mother asked with concern.

"I... I don't believe it!" I said. "I just received a visa to go back to Russia in September!"

I guess the Russian government figured I was never going to give up, and it was easier to step out of the way of a charging bull than to be in its way. I felt like I was flying, on such a high from my short trip and now this. *Thank you, thank you,* I wrote to Senator Cranston. *I cannot thank you enough.* I sent him a super cool old Soviet watch, and his wife a beautiful Russian lacquer box, but I'm still not sure if the late senator or his assistant Elmy Bermejo ever understood the immense gratitude I had for them both. I still hold what they did for me close to my heart today.

Things could not get any better, until they did.

"Is this Joanna Stingray?"

"Yeah," I said, twisting the chord of the phone around the rings I wore, evoking my own Boris style. "Who's this?"

"I'm calling from David Bowie's office. He's heading out to Los Angeles and would like to meet with you."

What?? Bowie?? I swallowed my gum. This was the legend, my first big crush and teenage obsession whose music got me into my twenties and inspired me to walk the path I'd been traveling. *Bowie!* The guy about whom I'd fantasized my entire life. *I was going to meet Bowie – and he wanted to meet me!*

"Of course, that would be great," I said calmly into the phone. I hung up and screamed so loudly the birds flew out of the trees.

A few days later, I was sitting in a hotel room at the Westwood Marquis in Los Angeles, holding my breath as I watched the cars speed down the slanted street outside. I kept telling myself to play it cool, to not act like a crazed fan. *Just don't jump on him, Joanna,* I repeated to myself in my head. *Don't you dare jump on him.*

"Hey, Joanna," came the silkiest, silvery voice. It was both like fresh rain and a warm fire. "I'm David." He opened his angular arms and hugged me close.

This is it, I thought. *This is how I want to die.*

"It is so nice to finally meet you," he continued. "What you've done in Russia with the underground rock music is really something." He was so relaxed and easy going, like a regular guy with a lion's mane and electric smile. I'd seen so many stars in TV interviews who seemed so full of themselves and so messed up, but Bowie was pure and sweet – an Apollo in leather and sneakers. It was mind blowing for me to be able to see the real person behind all his enigmatic characters. He was the kind of person it was so easy to be around, who made me feel like his friend from the moment he sat down. He taught me that just because you're a star doesn't mean you have to act like one. I carried this lesson with me through the rest of my time in Russia.

We sat on the sofa, as comfortable as two cats, and he began to tell me all about what he had done creatively in his life. He talked about his music, his writing and producing, acting and filming, and how he'd been involved with all sides of the camera. I sat there and listened, hanging onto every word.

"I think what you've done is incredible," he said after a pause. His dual-colored eyes met mine. "And I would like to buy the rights to your life story."

I can't even write how that felt. No words in the English or Russian language are sufficient to describe my reaction to hearing Bowie say that to me. Here was a person whom the whole world loved and by whom I had been inspired my whole life, asking to be a part of it.

"I would like to play Boris in your story," he continued to pitch, his whole body sparkling.

"That would be so cool," I managed to stammer. I knew my experiences in Russia were amazing to me personally, but it never crossed my mind that somebody would want to make it into a movie – let alone David Bowie!

He went on to ask me lots of questions about *Red Wave* and my Russian adventures. He genuinely seemed so interested in it all. He gave me time, let me talk, and invested himself in the story I was telling. To this day when I think about it, I feel like I'm covered in gold.

"Why don't you take a few days to think about it and let me know if you have any questions," he finally said. "Either way, let's keep in touch, Joanna." His smile was magnetic.

Then I sat there, watching The Thin White Duke float through the dark, plush room like an angel with wings on his heels. *What was that*, my mind kept asking me. *What was that!!*

His representative came back in the room and sidled up next to me. "Bowie really enjoyed meeting you and loved hearing more about your Russian experiences. He'd like to offer you $35,000 for your life story even though he thinks you probably won't take it." The representative gave me a glance, almost daring me to agree. "Why don't you think about it and let us know."

I have no idea how long I stayed in the hotel room, letting time briefly go on without me. For the first time I felt like the absurdly wonderful and inescapable world I was building for myself was expanding. If I was dreaming, I didn't want to wake up, and if I was crazy, I didn't want to be sane. If I was selling my life story, I didn't want to give it to anyone but Ziggy.

◆

It became one of the biggest regrets of my life.

"This will be such a big, big mistake," I muttered to myself, curled up on the floor of my house as I tried to block out everyone's strong opinion after telling my friends and family about the Bowie offer.

"You could make a lot more money than that." – "You could get a big studio interested." – "You have to get an agent, and they will get you a bigger deal."

Everybody I knew was suddenly offering up a connection or friend in the entertainment industry. It was Hollywood at its finest, clichés and all. My parents checked with their friend who said I first needed a good entertainment lawyer to make sure I was protected. Sitting there on the floor, though, my gut told me to go with Bowie. I knew he was passionate about Boris and my story, and I really wanted the chance to work with him on the project – what could be better than that?

For the last three years I had had no plan, and things always managed to fall into place as I followed my instincts. A tiger doesn't get fed by looking at a map but by diving head-first into the dark forest. It had been an incredibly fulfilling three years, yet in 1987 I was starting to realize I was finding more ways to spend money than to make money. Even with my sporadic travel agent stints, I was helped by my parents and their hesitant generosity. Now the two of them had everyone telling them my life story could be big money, and I felt the pressure to follow their friends' advice. After getting the big deal lawyer, that meant I had to get a big deal agent too, but since I was finally heading back to Russia to get married the last thing I wanted was to be shuffled from one studio to another to meet production teams and pick one. Everyone was very taken by my story and had great ideas, and in the windswept weeks before leaving I'm not sure why I picked the team that I did. It ended up leading to a feature film deal with Kathryn Galan at Atlantic Releasing and made me an advance of $10,000. The film itself was supposed to make me another $75,000 to $100,000 when the film was made, an exciting idea but one that didn't make up for the pit in my stomach from passing on Bowie.

I flew back to Russia in the fall of 1987 with David Weiderman from Guitar Center and Doug Buttleman from Yamaha. With them came a whole sound system of equipment for the Rock Club. These two guys were rowdy, fun, and lady-loving cowboys, a shadow of the Wild West still chasing the sunset and throwing back their heads in laughter that became contagious. They helped lighten the work I had to do to get the approval and logistics for getting the gift into the country, a sorely complicated and time-consuming process, and it was beyond worth it in the end.

"Today is historic," Kolya Mikhailov, the beloved director of the Rock Club, said softly into the microphone. "It's the opening of the Rock Club for the season, and I know you have been hearing in the press about the company Yamaha. I'd like to invite on stage Doug Buttleman from Yamaha to say a few words."

The building shook as the crowd swayed and cheered. Everyone knew about the incredible donation.

"Rock 'n roll everybody!" Doug shouted over them, a huge goofy smile on his face and his hands holding a plaque high in the air. "This plaque is for everyone – the fans, the musicians, everyone that's making Russian rock 'n roll happen. With this donation of equipment to the Leningrad Rock Club, we salute musicians everywhere who are bringing joy and peace to this world through their music. Long live rock 'n roll from Yamaha and Joanna Stingray!"

I jumped up and down with everyone else, enveloped in this world of craziness and love. It was the kind of place where time became irrelevant; the months I'd spent away no longer existed.

"We hope, and we are sure that this step from Yamaha will lead to the tightening of friendly ties between our countries," Kolya said, stepping back up.

If Doug or David thought that they'd get a full demonstration of the equipment, they were wrong. The bestowed equipment was calibrated for 120 volts, which Russians didn't have yet.

So, that night they were treated to an authentic rock concert on the age-old Rock Club equipment, the deep and studded sounds reverberating through the building as Auction and Kalinov Most performed.

Rock 'n roll seemed completely above ground now, and everywhere. There were more concerts than ever before, spilling their light and sound onto the sidewalks. Games were playing two concerts at the Palace of Youth, and I joined them to sing two of my songs – "Keep on Traveling," a Games song to which I wrote English lyrics, and my version of The Beatles' "Back in the U.S.S.R." with the chorus in Russian.

"*Abratna v S.S.S.R.*!" I shouted into the microphone. I was really back, with my long flowing black shirt, wide-rim black hat, and tambourine. We were leaning over a sea of hot bodies and smiling faces, and it felt like nothing could touch us. Games was one of my favorite bands to play with because they had this punk-flavored rock that was right up my alley and saturated my soul. We barely ever rehearsed, and just let the songs pull us in every direction possible. It was the best classroom for me to learn the world of performing.

After that concert, I was interviewed by Russian TV about *Red Wave*. Later that

■ Grysha Sologub and me in concert, Leningrad, 1987.

■ Slava Zaderi, me, and Kostya Kinchev at my first performance at the Leningrad Rock Club, 1987.

evening, I tuned in to watch myself speak, and for the first time I felt like a real person. No more skulking in the shadows, dodging shady cars, and silencing my English.

"Today at twelve o'clock in the afternoon, Leningrad took part in a Wave of Peace. Here in the Leningrad Palace of Youth, there is a concert in which Joanna Stingray is participating. Hello, Joanna. Here we have your record, which was released a few years ago, called *Red Wave*. It is a wave of peace!"

The next night Kolya Mikhailov introduced me for my first performance at the Rock Club. Yuri was on a Fender white guitar, Igor Tikhomirov on bass, Sergey on keyboards, and Afrika and Gustav on drums behind me. They started playing my song "Lonely Boy" as I walked out to cheers in all black with a leather jacket accentuated with a Soviet and an American flag side by side on the back. I felt so proud, my oversized red star earring with an American flag in the middle bouncing against my jaw as I sang my heart out sandwiched between the people I loved.

My second song was "Modern Age Rock 'n Roll" that I wrote with Boris. There is a moment at the end of that performance I'll always remember, as Yuri did feedback on his guitar and I jumped as I kicked one of my legs up to my face. I felt like myself, like I'd finally discovered who I was and who I wanted to be.

Before singing "Turn Away," which I wrote with Sergey, the amp for the guitar of course needed to be fixed. While we were waiting, I heard a guy scream out.

"*Perestroika*!!" he shouted with his fist in the air.

"Rock 'n Roll!" more people responded.

"Assa!!"

"Stingray!!"

I sang "Turn Away" for all of them. The song really rocked, and my musicians were so good that even with only the few makeshift rehearsals we'd had, they blew the roof off the place. We sang "Steel Wheels" that I also wrote with Boris, and then my version of "Back in the U.S.S.R." again. Kostya and Slava Zaderi joined me on stage to sing the choruses with me. Things got wild, punks jumping on stage and dancing, which somehow morphed into pushing and fighting. Everyone loved it, that punk energy loud and driving and overwhelming.

The last song we played was my version of Viktor's song *"Devigaisia Devigaisia Tantsui Sa Mnoi"*: "Move, Move, Dance with Me." Sergey and I both played the guitar, me jamming out to the three chords I'd learned with the guitar around my neck and Sergey with a face full of joy. We jumped up and down while we played, the crowd singing along at the top of all of our lungs.

The last thing I remember was at the very end, just as the music was fading out, some guy from the audience screaming out in a thick Russian accent, "I love you, Joanna!"

It was so beautiful, his voice still in my head like it was yesterday. *I love you too!* I wanted to shout back. *I love you all!*

◆

"For America and the Soviet Union to get closer, what's more important? Politics, economy, or culture?"

"First of all, I think that music is above politics," I responded. "I always thought that if we could get Gorbachev and Reagan dancing together to rock music, they'd get a lot further than they do talking."

In 1987, there were still only two television stations in the Soviet Union that two-hundred and fifty million people were watching. I was performing on the new hit TV program "Music Ring," lip syncing to my songs and answering audience questions. There were all kinds of people there – government members, rock fans, average Russians with dark clothes and round faces. It was probably the biggest platform to be seen and heard in those days of *perestroika*.

"What is rock music?" Another audience member asked. "Is it food for the brain? For what is it needed? The soul, the brain, for entertainment, or for a little bit of everything?"

"I think rock music first of all is an energy," I responded. "It's for the brain, it's for the feet, the soul. But it's a very powerful tool. It's the easiest way to show people around the world that we have a common bond."

When someone said that all the music that I co-wrote with Russians had little national character, Kuryokhin jumped in. "How exactly do you imagine national character or folklore of Soviet rock? You can't define it. When I write music, I don't think about what is national or not. I like the music that I write, and if it gets performed, then I'm very happy. I try to write more good music. I've been making music for twenty-eight years. I belong to a huge musical universe. I consider myself a Russian person, and therefore my music is national."

While I never minded a chance to try and explain myself, Sergey had no tolerance for questions he found to be naïve or silly. His eyes would flash like electrical storms before he would shrug it off entirely, bored with the faulty accusations or inexperienced assertions.

That evening I watched the recorded show with Yuri and his parents on their small, square, black and white TV. It felt like I was watching somebody else, someone bold and dynamic and strong. I loved who I got to become in Russia. Even shrunken and monochrome on the screen, Yuri and I looked so in love, singing together and exchanging glances throughout the show. I put my head on his shoulder in the apartment, amazed by it all.

The Russian winter had arrived by the time my parents came for the wedding. My mother, in her oversized fur coat, exited the plane carrying a bouquet and boutonniere of lily of the valley flowers. They were wrapped in little plastic bags with water sealed by some silver foil.

"Are you crazy?" I asked her when I met her. "You brought those all the way across the world?!"

"Aren't they beautiful?" When my mother was inspired, nothing could stop her from being over-the-top amazing.

I'll never forget driving out to Coopchina with my parents and wondering what they could be thinking of the bland landscape. Fred was wearing a beautiful suit and tie, and my mother was like a porcelain statue wrapped in her black fur coat. They were sophisticated and worldly standing next to me slouching in my black choker with the silver antique locket in which I kept a photo of me and Yuri, and as the three of us tried to squeeze into the dank, tiny elevator in Yuri's building I saw a little trepidation in my mother's eyes. *Where the hell are we?* she seemed to be thinking. As the lift started to move, it wasn't actually clear if we would make it.

The little elevator coughed and twitched like a toddler with the flu. As we made it to the top Fred let out a full-body laugh, a lover of adventure and these unpredictable experiences.

Yuri and Viktor opened the door to greet us. The two of them, like me, were in all black.

They enveloped us all like a night sky – their eyes stars and their arms warm. Yuri's parents were all dressed up to meet my parents, Irina in a sweater and soft skirt hidden under an apron, and Dimitri in dark pants and a white shirt and tie. As I watched our two sets of parents meet, I could see how similar we all were. We could have been anywhere in the world, parents shaking hands and lovers smiling.

"It smells delicious," my mother commented as Irina moved over the big meal that she'd made to celebrate the upcoming wedding. As the food steamed, I took my parents on a tour of the three rooms the four of us shared. I couldn't imagine what they could possibly think. My parents' large house was a museum, with its impeccable décor and art, shiny floors and freshly painted walls.

"This is great," Fred said, fascinated with the unattached wooden toilet seat and old flush chain.

My mother laughed nervously. "Didn't we teach you to always put the lid down on the toilet?" There was no lid here at all! I could see the shock on her face when she realized the newspaper stuffed in the side of a pipe was supposedly a substitute for toilet paper.

Irina and Dimitri were incredible hosts. They had set up a long wooden table with a flowered tablecloth and filled it with colorful pieces of china and different dishes. There was a big bowl of fruit nestled between a tea set, crystal glasses, and other antique objects. My stepfather inspected all the bottles on the table, reading the curled labels of the wine, vodka, and Russian Pepsi. In no time the popping sound of bottles filled the small space.

"Party started without us?!" I heard a deep voice say. I turned to see my sister Judy coming in with my old friend Marc Saleh. "I've got Pat's brownies!" He held up a box of my favorite brownies, the ones that I used to steal from my best friend's freezer when her mom Pat would make them. He'd lugged them all the way from Los Angeles. "Gum for you and two cans of coffee for the Kasparyans!"

I dragged him to the table, and we all dug in. The food just kept coming, with homemade desserts like cherry pie. Marc, who had gotten right to business and was incredibly tipsy, swiped the video camera and jumped up on patrol.

"If you've seen a lot of David Letterman, you'll know what I'm doing," he announced. I followed him as he walked into the bedroom where Viktor was on the phone.

"Is this where Joanna Stingray lives?" He called out, narrating everything he saw like the photos and art on the walls, opening the closet and pointing out every piece of my black ensemble.

"I want to show you what Yuri got me for a wedding gift," I laughed, playing along. I opened a box and pulled out a beautiful long necklace made from jade and coral.

"What, no diamonds? He thought the one on your finger was enough? Oh no! There's no diamond on your finger either!" Marc teased.

"Be nice!" I shrieked, shoving him back into the kitchen.

As the night got darker and our voices got louder, I stood up to fill myself a cup of cold water from the sink.

"Don't do it, no, you must boil it!" Yuri's father called to me.

I couldn't help it. Cold water was the only thing I liked to drink, and I couldn't get enough. I was smart enough to realize there were probably chemicals and contamination in it, but I was always too thirsty to care. I had survived stalkers and car chases and six months of isolation, fought back blows from the Soviet government and resuscitated a wedding that had seemed impossibly lost. That night, as I sipped my cold water and watched the people whom I loved move through the room, I knew that I'd finally won.

The next day Yuri's parents hosted a lunch at their house for their relatives. The film people came, as well as Tamara Falalayeva, Sergey, Alex, and Viktor's wife Marianna in a beautiful flowered dress and green scarf tied around her neck. Judy had taken my parents and Marc sightseeing, so I stood with Clay, the writer for my film, as he peered through the glass on the wooden cabinet in the corner of the room.

"Wow, these are first edition hardcover books," he said.

"I know. Isn't it amazing? Most Russians seem to have things like this, if you can believe it." I knew they had no idea how valuable these old books would be in the West.

Yuri's relatives were warm, and the meal was delicious. Champagne bottles were opened and toasts made. Sergey stood up in the jean jacket I'd had made for him, *Captain* jeweled across the back of it, and made a heartfelt speech about his happiness for Yuri and me. Russian hospitality was unparalleled, but this was more than that. This was my new family and my best friends, and the happiness that felt like it was becoming ingrained inside my heart. Boiled water be damned.

◆ Rock 'n Roll Wedding

The hall was packed with fans and friends, my parents and Yuri's parents and relatives, Marc, Kathryn Galan from the film company with producers Jim Rodgers and George Paige, and writer Clay Frohman for my film deal. I stood in front of the backdrop Timur painted of me, an oversized version of myself waving from a tractor christened *Stingray*. It was Sunday night before the wedding on Monday, a huge concert at the First of May Palace of Culture that we'd organized in honor of the upcoming celebration.

The blaring punk rock of Games filled everyone's ears, the Sologub brothers taking turns singing lead and harmony for each other. I could feel their intensity and high energy performance charging through my veins. When Grysha sang the song "Cry in Life," his tormented voice distorted all the faces looking up at him with pain and heartbreak. I've never heard someone sing and convey such sadness or hurt the way that he did. After a few songs they started to play my song "Keep on Traveling." I remember I was wearing a wide-brimmed hat with a tambourine in my hand, a tight black top and flowing monochromatic checkered pants. When I raised my hand the silver tassels and beads hanging off my glove shone like celestial disks, reflecting the light that radiated off everyone else.

"This next song is for my friend Kolya Vasin," I shouted into the crowd, introducing "Back in the U.S.S.R." Vitia followed it with his version of "Helter Skelter," his whole body effervescent and red like he was going to explode as Boris, Dusha, and Garkusha and I crouched down to watch behind the curtains. To this day Games is one of the greatest performing bands I've seen.

"The power of music," Boris whispered to me, kneeling with his acoustic guitar tucked awkwardly under his arm.

He and his band Aquarium came out next to heavy cheers and a swelling crowd. Boris, with puffy white shirt and long ponytail, glowed. Sasha Titov joined him on bass and Dusha on recorder, with Misha Feinstein playing the bongos. Each song Boris started to play brought cheers as every person in the hall sang the lyrics they all knew at the top of their lungs and added to the harmonies that Dusha and Sasha were singing. Then suddenly it was silent as Boris started to play one of his most popular acoustic ballads "The Golden City," a medieval baroque melody with lyrics by the Russian poet Anri Volokhonsky. I could feel it all the way to my bones. I peeked out at the audience to find my parents, so overwhelmed with gratitude that they finally got to see this legend I had spent hours telling them about.

"*Zachem!*" I heard Natasha Vasilyeva, one of the main underground rock photographers in Leningrad, say loudly as Aquarium finished their set. "Why? I have permission!" I hopped up and hurried into the hall to where she was being confronted by one of the women who worked there.

"What's wrong?" I asked. "Natasha is shooting the concert for me on my video camera."

"Yes, Joanna asked me to film!" Natasha translated. She turned to me. "This *babushka* tells me she knows nothing about that but needs proof of permission." It was *glasnost*, but like most things in Russia it could still be slow going.

"Who allowed you to film?" The woman continued to demand, her eyes darting between Natasha and now me. "What is this?"

"I'm here with the groups," Natasha repeated. "Joanna Stingray asked me to film."

"So what? You are coming into a stranger's house. You abide by the rules, right? I'm asking you to stop filming. I don't know Joanna. We have a director of the Rock Club administration here."

"Yes, I am aware. I am a photographer for the Rock Club."

"Stop filming."

"I cannot stop, I am doing this for completely official reasons."

Even though I couldn't understand their exchange, I could tell this *babushka* was going to hold her ground. Somehow, as some other men got involved in the argument, we snuck Natasha away backstage.

"Do something silly, this is a video camera not a photo camera," she called out as she pointed it at Dusha. It was still very unusual to have a video camera at that time, and many people hadn't yet seen one in person.

The Kino band and Sergey joined me onstage for my set. This was the first time my parents saw me perform, in my tight black pants, silver studded belt, and black leather jacket with fringe hanging to my waist. I danced like a wild animal, twisting and kicking and banging the tambourine against my legs. I had so much energy, so much love in my body. As I ran off the stage Viktor grabbed my hands and gave me that look of his. We were so lucky.

I could hear the crowd go insane as Viktor started performing his new hit "Groupa Kroovy," which translates to "Blood Type," about the Soviet War in Afghanistan. He stood in the center of the stage in all black, his face stoic, his legs hip-width apart, exuding a power over every face in the room. With a tap of his foot, a slight nudge of his shoulder, or the protruding lift of his chin, he could make love to humanity and the universe surrounding us. It was during this concert, as Yuri hypnotized everyone with his solos and dark Ray-Ban sunglasses he'd borrowed from me, that I realized that I was about to marry a real badass guitar player. I watched from the wings as the group transitioned to their song "Tranquilizer," its addictive, slow rhythm and Viktor's deep voice vibrating through my body. Sergey did some incredible improvisations on the keyboard that weren't on the recordings but sounded as if they were meant to be there.

"*Lubov eta ne chutka*!" Viktor sang out, grabbing the microphone off the stand and swaying his body like a snake slithering through a sparkling desert. The song translated to "Love Is No Joke," something I felt in my entire being. Love, that moment right then, is something for which it's worth fighting.

After their next song "Watch Yourself," the crowd screamed for more. Viktor and the guys huddled to figure out what else to play when Afrika and Gustav both started pounding on their drums to one of Viktor's new songs titled "War." Their drums sounded like the heartbeat of a giant. Yuri started jogging in place as he moved his hands over the guitar like a car speeding across a country, and Viktor became emotional as he sang the chorus.

"Between the earth and the sky, there's war!" His voice rang against every ear in the hall. I felt so affected. As I stood in the dark and watched my friends shine, I realized that god had made all of us such wonderful creators, but it was man who made war – we could destroy each other and everything beautiful we conceived.

Viktor ended the song with a cold stare at the audience, a messenger who took to this stage to show us what we could become. What I could become.

◆

"You guys American?"

Clay and the other film people looked up from where they were chatting in English during a break. A group of Russian kids with excited eyes and shy smiles crowded around them.

"Trade, trade!" The kids started chanting before Clay could answer. He watched as they started to pull out all these intricate Russian pins from their pockets.

Immediately Clay and the others tried to find any and all things they were carrying that they could trade. Jim had a cigar that he exchanged for quite a number of pins, while Kathryn handed over her lipstick and Clay found some gum and U.S. coins. As the lights dimmed for the second half of the concert, both groups parted ways, two separate species sharing a watering hole and moving on. It was the dream I'd had from the beginning, of a cultural camaraderie. In the last seconds of the break, I could see it in Clay's smile as I ran past him to the stage.

I stood with a black Fender guitar between Sergey and Yuri. The three of us were in a row, and as Viktor leaned back on some amps and watched us jam, we started strumming along to Kino's "Devigaisia Tantsui Sa Mnoi." As the wedding concert continued, I became one of the guys, all of us one big family under the high ceilings and artificial lights.

"Give it to me, give it to me, give me some more of your love," Viktor and I sang to each other in English.

Oleg Garkusha, the master showman from Auction, ran on the stage as the audience cheered, dancing around us as his black suit with diamond pendants lit up his entire body. Viktor ran over to my mic and threw his arm around my shoulders as we sang the "whoa, whoas" together. As he continued the song in Russian I went back to the guitar with my boys, as if I'd been there my entire life. Garkusha joined Viktor for the choruses, and Sergey and I sang them together on another mic.

"Whoa! Whoa!" Viktor sang at the top of his lungs, holding out the mic to each of us to sing with him. Yuri screamed so loud, something I had no idea he had in him. That night we were pushing the edge of our very existence.

Yuri and Sergey were the last people left on the stage. Sergey never got tired, never hung limp like the microphone Viktor had left dangling from the stand. He could have kept playing for hours. Yuri ended the concert with all his new guitar pedals I'd brought him from Roland, putting them on echo, distortion, and loops so he could just stand there, and every thirty seconds play one chord that would ring out and slowly fade away. The crowd roared, all the lions of a new Soviet generation.

Backstage we could still hear everyone cheering, whistling, and chanting out in the hall. "*Kino! Kino!*" They screamed.

"Tsoi, you guys have to go back out," someone finally yelled in the dressing room.

As Kino jumped up with sparkling eyes and set jaws, I grabbed my tambourine and followed them out. Between a chiseled, shirtless Gustav and Afrika, I sang along to their driving, hypnotic song "Electrishka." As it ended, the audience became euphoric. They couldn't beg for any more, couldn't even move their bodies to keep us on the stage. Everyone was suspended in their own minds, riding the highs of the night with Viktor's song filling their heads.

"Good, no?" Gustav asked as he grabbed part of the stage curtains to wipe his wet face and underarms.

As always, the guys changed their clothes between mobs of people backstage. I pushed through everyone to find Natasha.

"Thank you so much," I said, taking my camera and giving her a hug. I gave her a pack of photo paper from the States in gratitude that I could tell she appreciated.

It was only decades later when I looked at the video of this night that I could see what I refer to as the changing of the guard. Boris will always be the godfather of Russian rock 'n roll, and his place in history is hammered in granite, but on this night, Viktor became the most adored and famous Russian rocker of that time. I also knew that I would never escape my image as the American in Russia, but that night, between the sweaty, effervescent bodies of my friends, I felt as if Russian blood ran through my veins.

"Happy?" Yuri asked me with a kiss backstage, his bare torso pale against his long, dark pants.

It may have been a wedding concert, but it wasn't just about Yuri and me. I was so happy for all of us, for Viktor and for Boris who was so proud of his mentee, for the bands and the boys and the howling crowd. We put the pride in a pack of lions, golden and sweaty and ready for the next move.

After the concert there was a reception with fish or cheese open-faced sandwiches with red or black caviar and Russian Pepsi in one of the spacious, decorated rooms of the Palace of Culture. The original art nouveau building, the elegance and lavishness suddenly felt fully legitimate and reminded me how above ground everything had become. I watched my friends and family sip wine and eat open-faced sandwiches as Sergey improvised on the piano. It was life at its best, the maestro at his instrument and the party in full swing.

◆

We woke up on Monday, November 2, 1987, smiling at each other.

It's still almost impossible for me to explain how I felt on the morning of my wedding. It was like waking up in the rain and being totally dry, a feeling of impossibility and wonderment, like I was the most special person in the world. We motivated slowly to get ready to head to Wedding Palace #3, Yuri in black-tie tails with a white shirt, red bowtie, and red cummerbund. He looked like a prince, his hair swept across his forehead and his eyes like diamonds.

I decided to get into my dress later at the Wedding Palace. I could only stand being dolled up for so long, even if it was part of the fairy-tale wedding. We had two silver bands that had sat by my bedside for eight extra months, engraved with the words *Yuri and Joanna April 6, 1987*, a reminder of our missed wedding and the dragons we'd fought to get there. I watched Yuri put them into his pocket as I stood behind him in my pants, and off we went.

The Wedding Palace #3, at 2 Petrovskaya Embankment, was built in 1913 for the grandson of Emperor Nicholas I, the last palace built in St. Petersburg for a member of the Romanov dynasty. Its neoclassic face was built facing the Neva River, marble exteriors and gilded interiors reflecting all the light off the water and into the windows. After the revolution, it was used for various government purposes and then became the Wedding Palace in 1985. The day of our wedding was cold and grey, but there were no clouds or rain in sight, and the building glowed like the bright embers of a fire.

The people at the palace escorted us into a small room, where I had a woman do my makeup. I tried to sit still under the thick brush, but I was so excited I just wanted to jump up and run through the carpeted rooms. My mother walked slowly around the room, one eye on me like when she used to take me to a department store and make me sit quietly in a chair while she shopped. This time, though, there was no punishment for my high energy and jittery legs. She gave a small smile and continued scoping out the wood panels and carved crown moldings.

"Jo!" Viktor and Marianna flew into the room, breaking the silence. Viktor was carrying an enormous ceramic plate that he'd made, over two feet long, whose round surface was painted with a dancing Yuri and me. As a trained artist, Viktor mostly did woodworks, but this piece was magnificent and pulsed with his heart.

"I love it!" I told him.

He laughed, pointing at my half-decorated face. "What's this?" He teased. None of them had ever seen this tomboy with lashes before.

Yuri came up behind me, my own personal hairdresser, and shook both his hands through my feathery layers. "Duran Duran style," he said with a proud smile.

I slipped into my wedding dress, barely able to put in my American flag and red star earring as I felt the cool fabric move against my arms, which made my hands shake slightly. When I came back to the room, I could see Viktor and Yuri were as stunned as I was. They fumbled to help me slide a blue garter on my left thigh for my "something blue."

The three of us walked together as we were led to a grand, palace-sized living room with huge antique tapestries and beautiful old cases filled with period garments along the walls. In the middle, there was a low table surrounded by four heirloom chairs, where I refused to sit in my tight, textured dress. As Viktor, Marianna, and Yuri kicked back, I stood beside them in my heels with my shoulders squared and my ankles turned inwards, making pigeon feet.

Viktor and Marianna were our best man and bridesmaid, which in Russia meant they were our witnesses. They sat side by side, Marianna in a boldly printed dress, double amber necklace, and a cigarette hanging out of her mouth, while Viktor wore all black save for the leopard print on the top half of his jacket and beige sports shoes. I had originally asked Yuri if Boris could be my witness because of all that he'd done for me and meant to me, but Yuri had told me it wouldn't be polite to not have Marianna as a witness if Yuri was asking Viktor. I loved Marianna so of course I agreed, and as I watched her and Viktor whisper and laugh, I felt so blessed to have these two radiant patrons with us.

"See that small house there?" Yuri stood and led me to the window. "That is Peter the Great's."

Viktor said, "That is the original wooden log cabin, and it was the first house in what became St. Petersburg!"

I stared into the glass pavilion with its encapsulated cabin, and the reality of the fairy tale set in. I was no longer in the middle of a busy city with my name on a registration list, but existing in a time period removed from buses and Communism and television. The magic of the day intensified, fogging the windows.

"Joanna?" My mother appeared with her perfect blonde bob and navy pin-striped skirt suit, moving delicately over the wide floor with her low pumps. She gave kisses to everyone and then handed me the beautiful lily of the valley bouquet before turning to Yuri with a boutonniere. Viktor, Yuri, and I took turns seeing if there was any smell left to the flowers. I inhaled a sweetness so lovely, innocent, and happy, exhaling it all around us.

"Aren't they wonderful?" My mother purred.

"They really are," I told her softly.

"They symbolize a return to happiness," Marianna said, approaching us and touching the small buds. "They are also one of the most poisonous plants to eat! You see, happiness must be protected fiercely, with every fiber of your being. If you hold it in your body, you must never give it up."

◆

As we waited in the living room, all of our guests were arriving and being ushered into one of the other spectacular rooms. I could smell the heavy smoke as people burned cigarettes freely in this romantic haven, a surprise that with all the rules in Russia, it was acceptable to smoke in these historic buildings. Boris wandered in, covered by a dark suit with a red shirt and monochrome scarf tied around his neck and under his low ponytail. He looked like a painting, the edges perfect and the face bright. Kolya Vasin was there in a Beatles t-shirt over a collared white shirt, tie, and green velvet jacket. Afrika would appear on one side of the room one minute and the complete opposite side the next, a visitor from Warhol's "Factory" in his self-made military jacket with its sparkling brooches, colored gems, hanging golden tassels, and braided cords.

"The mayor of Leningrad," he joked proudly, referring to how he was known to many.

◆

Russians always took celebrations and traditions to heart, and it was obvious everyone went out of their way to dress up for the occasion. Most men were in suits, and all women were in their best dresses and skirt suits, with white pins depicting a red heart and Каспарян и Стингрей (Kasparyan & Stingray) written across it. In everyone's hand was a bouquet of flowers with an odd number of buds. Sergey held bright orange ones I think of as the color of his soul, and Seva cradled a deep rich red bouquet like a kitten.

"Why odd numbers?" Judy asked.

"Always uneven number of flowers as a gift," a woman said. "Only for funerals is even number."

Yuri walked in and out of the guest hall a few times to say hello, walking proudly with his head held high and a big smile on his face. He stopped and watched Fred lift the Nikon camera off his chest and take a photo of my mother against the wood paneling, nodding at them both.

Gustav joined Viktor, Yuri, and Marianna on the chairs in my room as we waited for things to begin. He was dressed in a black suit, teal tie with white designs, and wire-rimmed spectacles that may not have even had glass in them. Viktor started joking and making funny poses for Judy's camera, and Gustav quickly joined in. I laughed as the two of them draped themselves back over the chairs and bicycled their legs in the air. Teasingly I tottered on one foot while I stretched the other one towards them. I could tell Viktor couldn't believe I had three-inch heels on under my dress!

"Never before," he said in wonder, shaking his head.

"And never again," I assured.

Finally, all the guests made their way into the main wedding palace chamber. It was a vast room with only six chairs on one side for Yuri's parents and mine and his elderly family members, and two chairs on the other side for our witnesses. Everyone else packed behind the wooden seats, standing shoulder to shoulder with their bouquets against their chests.

As the stately music of the city's anthem played over the speakers, Marianna and Viktor opened the large door on one side of the room and invited Yuri and I into the hall. I smiled when I saw all our family and friends, nodding at them bashfully as I shuffled in my dress and shoes. Yuri's face had become serious, a man on a mission as he led me to our spot in the middle of the room and turned us to face the front, with him on the dark half of the carpet and me on the lighter half. He was so into the formality of it, holding my hand in a traditional ninety-degree angle and counting the steps at the proper speed. He nodded confidently at our marriage officiant, a bold looking woman in a deep burgundy dress with matching-colored hair and a chunky pendant necklace.

"Today on the second of November 1987, is the wedding of an American citizen, Joanna Stingray, and a Soviet citizen, Yuri Dmitriyevich Kasparyan," she announced in Russian. As she continued speaking, I remember thinking *what on earth is she saying? I wonder if it's anything important I should know...*

At one point, Yuri turned to me, so I turned to him. He smiled broadly and raised his eyebrows, as if to say *isn't that profound?* I smiled back. *I have no clue what she's saying, but you are an absolutely gorgeous husband.*

"*Da,*" Yuri replied moments later to something the woman said. There was a long pause. Yuri finally turned his head to me and watched as I was clueless for a couple seconds.

"*Da!*" I repeated as we all laughed. Looking back, I find it so funny that I agreed to a question I couldn't understand. In Russia, you just had to go with it.

The woman in red kept talking, and Yuri kept looking at me and nodding as if to tell me these were important words. I still don't know if the officiant knew I couldn't understand a word.

Yuri finally tugged me forward towards the wooden table and two chairs at the front of the room. He pulled out one of the chairs for me. In front of us there was a large booklet open to its thick pages. The officiant pointed to a pen laying across the open face, which Yuri picked up and handed to me. With the flash of numerous cameras, I signed my name in two places, watching as Yuri did the same after. What exactly I was signing was a mystery, but I was swept up in the formality and ceremony of it all.

"Dear witnesses," the officiant called as Yuri and I stood again. "I ask you to come forward and sign."

Wearing the black Swatch watch I gave him and carrying five white flowers in his left hand, Viktor led Marianna up to sign. As I watched Viktor raise and then lower the pen, I saw something in his movements, in the reverence of it all, that was similar to the way he put the mic back after an important concert. Indeed, for all of us this was a grand and deeply personal performance.

The officiant approached Yuri and I with a small wooden bowl. Our rings were sitting in it, and with a flourish Yuri wiggled the ring onto the third finger of my right hand, the Russian way. I did the same, and as he spun the ring into place he leaned down and kissed me.

"In full accordance with the law of the Soviet Union, the marriage is registered," the woman said solemnly.

Yuri became so euphoric at her statement that he almost lost his balance. I stood there stone-faced, not understanding. As Yuri tried to whisper a translation to me in English, she proclaimed over him, "I announce you both as husband and wife. Congratulate each other!"

Yuri grabbed me and kissed me as the music swelled and everyone cheered. "*Oorah!*" screamed Afrika at the top of his lungs.

As the woman continued with a short congratulations speech, I was giddy and ebullient beside my stoic husband. Even though I still couldn't understand her, I could tell her words were sweet and kind. The ceremony was only about seven minutes long, seven minutes to be given a lifetime.

♦

My hands were filled with so many flowers I could barely get my arms around anyone. Boris leaned over the sweet, colorful bouquet to whisper some words of wisdom, words that got lost beneath the photographers all shouting. "*Boria, Boria, suda! Joanna, suda!*" After a hundred kisses I had over a hundred flowers in my hands, pinks and reds and whites with the exclusion of yellow. In their world of omens and superstition, Russians

■ Yuri and me on our wedding day with Viktor and Viktor's wife, Marianna in the Wedding Palace #3, Leningrad, November 2, 1987.

saw yellow flowers as signs of a break-up.

"Can someone take these?" I asked finally.

"It is tradition to keep them in your arms for the walk down the staircase," Marianna told me apologetically.

After all the photos at the top of the stairs, everyone had to wait and watch Yuri and I descend first before they could all follow. Viktor went behind us, posing in his stoic onstage stance before breaking into laughter. Yuri and I couldn't stop smiling as he held my arm and tried to keep me from drowning in all of the blossoms.

"*Opa*!" Everyone screamed when we reached the bottom, tossing more flowers towards us as we hurried outside to a black Chaika, a Russian version of a limousine. Before we slid inside, someone handed us two beautiful crystal glasses and filled them with a bright, shiny champagne. Yuri and I crossed our arms and drank, tossing the crystal glasses onto the ground where they shattered into a thousand sunlit fragments on the cobbles. As Yuri grabbed my face in his calloused guitar hands and kissed me, Viktor followed with another crystal glass and smashed it against the ground. Each broken piece signified a year of happy marriage to come, and from the looks of the sparkling pattern around our feet we really would live happily ever after.

Viktor, Yuri, and I piled into the back seat of the limo as Marianna sat in a jump

■ At the Neva River with the wedding party after the ceremony, November 2, 1987.

seat. We sped around all the historic sites throughout the city, our guests following in a bus as we stopped at the Neva River to take pictures. Yuri hopped out of the car and knelt on one knee to help me out.

"We're not alone," Marc said, filming as another couple came to wash their hands in the Neva River as well.

"I've got all I need right here," I told him, clinging to Yuri's warm body as the icy water froze my fingers. With a smile he grabbed another champagne bottle and held it to my mouth. He and Viktor played around along the bank, grabbing me and backing up as if they were going to drag us all into the indigo waters. We took pictures as Viktor acted out kung fu and I teased my dress higher to show off my garter, with Yuri pretending to unzip his pants to pee on the wall.

"*Krysha payekhala!*" We called out to the guests that were arriving and climbing out of the bus. "Our roofs are moving!"

There's such an iconic shot of me, Gustav, Boris, Yuri, Tikhomirov, Titov, Krisanov, Afrika, and Viktor standing in front of the river. We all look so young, so convinced of our purpose and lost in the moment. Decades later, Russian media wrote that this "rock-wedding" was the most beautiful, pivotal wedding of the '80s, the day when the Cold War finally seemed to end.

■ Traveling around Leningrad in the Chaika with Viktor and Marianna and stopping at the Neva River. Photos at the river by Valentin Baranovsky.

Our next stop was Senatskaya Ploshchad, Senate Square, which had been erected in 1704 as one of the first squares in St. Petersburg and marked the spot of the Decembrist Revolt of 1825. It was getting so cold as the day wore on, and after a shot of vodka in the car we all raced out to take some photos in front of the bronze horseman statue of Peter the Great with the wistfully magnificent St. Isaac's Cathedral behind us.

"Welcome back, here we are, who knows where!" Marc shouted behind the camera, well enough past tipsy to be smiling despite the sinking cold. "Shot of vodka and Joanna is about to do the old roll. She had a little too much to drink. Let's see if we can get the lovely lady's face here up close and personal. Let's see, excuse me, excuse me!"

"No, no, that's not fair!" My eyes were so glassy and my words slurring together like ice into the ocean as I laughed. "You're hitting below the belt, below the belt, Marc. Stop!"

"Are you Joanna Stingray Kasparyan?" Marc sung out.

"Marc, Viktor wants to kiss you. Viktor, kiss him!"

Viktor leaned in and kissed the video camera lens. His warm breath fogged the screen. "Oh my god," Marc bellowed. "I've been wounded!"

There must have been some bottles on the bus too, because everyone seemed to be becoming immune to the cold. Boris emerged with his arms stretched out like a falcon ready to drop into a valley. We all placed white flowers at the bottom of the horseman, sharing bottles and lining up for a photo the photographers called "Red Wave 2!"

◆

■ Yuri and me in front of the statue of
Peter the Great, Senate Square.

■ Afrika, Yuri, me, and Tikhomirov on stage at the First of May
Palace of Culture the night before our wedding.

"Don't laugh! You're laughing, I can hear you!" Marc taunted Yuri and me as the car drove in circles to see how long we could continue to kiss.

"Fuck off," I mumbled through the kiss. I could hear Viktor and Marianna howling with laughter.

"Fuck off, Marc!" Yuri managed to get out.

Russian weddings notoriously go on for days. It looked like ours was going to be no exception. As we piled back into the limo yet again, I felt high on excitement and alcohol. The car turned down the wide street, and I leaned against Yuri.

"*Krysha payekhala!*" He said happily, raising his hand to the ceiling of the car as we sped towards a restaurant. "Our roof is moving!"

"Come on, my darling wife." Yuri smiled so wide it was contagious. "Let's go to our party."

Yuri and I, with more champagne in our hands, walked into the airy Austeria Restaurant in the Peter and Paul Fortress. The guests clapped and whistled, as someone made a loud toast and we all downed our entire slender glasses.

"*Gorko! Gorko!*" Everyone screamed. "*Bitter!*"

In order to make it sweeter, the couple is supposed to kiss for as long as possible while the guests count. I was more than happy to oblige. Little did I know, this would be a ritual repeated dozens and dozens of times throughout the intimate evening.

The room was warm and comfortable with its white walls and exposed wooden beams overhead. There were two very long tables down each side of the room, connected by another long table at the top with a banner strung above it. *Happy Wedding Stingray and Yuri!* it read. There was also a beautiful portrait of me and Yuri by our friend, the artist Zina Sotina.

The whole room was full of delicious smells, over one hundred dishes of food filling the tables between the vases filled with our wedding flowers. White and silver balloons reflected the hot steam, with one large red heart balloon bearing our names like our pins.

"Where do we sit?" I shouted at Yuri over the popping of champagne bottles and drunken laughter. He took my hand and led me to our places at the middle of the main table. The minute we got there a toast was made to our parents.

"*Gorko! Gorko!*" Everyone screamed again. Yuri and I kissed until our friends started roaring like banshees.

The dinner was the most beautiful, joyous mess. Plates rang against silverware, corks flew across the tables, and people shouted over each other's heads. Every time a plate was empty, it was replaced with a new one, the glasses never not sparkling. Russians really do know how to be in a moment and honor the love they feel. I was swept up in a tidal wave of bright eyes and open hearts.

The details of the evening became increasingly fuzzy. It was a party of the who's who in the Leningrad art and music scene, with a few Western diplomats and the eclectic British artist Andrew Logan. Yuri and I received incredible paintings from some of our friends.

At some point, I miraculously found a way to change out of my dress and heels and put on some tight black pants, suede boots, and a leather jacket with fringe. I slid the blue garter over my pants just below the knee.

"She's back!" Viktor laughed when I appeared beside him. This was the girl with whom they were all familiar – pants, leather, and a wild look of freedom in my eyes.

"Oh, Joanna, let me get a picture of you and Viktor!" My mother had become one of the hits of the party with her polaroid camera. Everyone was awed by the fact that the photo would instantaneously print and appear.

"Careful with that camera, Mom," I joked. "If the party runs out of food, we could probably trade it on the black market for a ton of beluga caviar."

Through the cigarette smoke, a few of us made our way to the small stage set up with an old drum kit, amps, and mic. All of us sang mixed together – the Sologub brothers, Andrei Krisanov with a pipe hanging out of his mouth, Oleg Kotelnikov, me and Viktor. Later that night, a guy put on a record player through some speakers and everyone got up to dance. It was the Russian way, with no partners, where everyone faced each other

■ Playing guitar at the wedding party with Viktor singing, and in the background, the portrait by Timur Novikov of me in an American tractor.

and danced in a big, effervescent group. Yuri and I were dancing with our arms around each other, and the next thing I knew there was a whole circle of friends linked around us and pulling us into pace with them. There were no walls up, no barriers or customs booths. We belonged to no countries that night, only to each other.

As the night went on, some continued dancing while others fell asleep against the chairs or tables. Slava Butuzov, leader of Nautilus Pompilius, passed out in the arms of the engineer Fearsoff, who had recorded many of the underground bands and their concerts. I can't even remember how Yuri and I got home or into bed. All I remember is the feeling of falling asleep against his chest and knowing I was right where I was supposed to be.

◆

After sleeping into the afternoon, Yuri and I headed out for a midnight train to Moscow. Sasha Lipnitsky had arranged another party at his *dacha* for those who couldn't make the trip to Leningrad. My parents headed back to the States, and as most others were fast asleep, Yuri, Viktor, Sergey, and I cozied up in our cabin for the witching hour.

The heat on the train was turned up full blast, fogging the windows completely as the cold clamped down outside. Sergey and I painted our pinky nails black while we all sat around talking.

"Smoke?" Yuri finally asked. He and Viktor stood by the door, stamping impatiently in their coats.

"We'll come," I said, glancing at Sergey. We followed the other two out to the shaking platform between two cars, trying to keep our balance as icy wind and a biting cold clawed at our exposed skin. As far as I knew, Sergey didn't smoke, so I was surprised when he took a couple of hits.

"Cold," he said, smiling sheepishly and pointing to the air.

Shivering, I decided to join in and take my first hit too. We passed the cigarette from one mouth to the next, out in the dark and the noise as the train roared south. I felt like I was tripping, watching blurry shapes go by in the night as we stood silently with their arms rubbing against mine. Our conversation had no words, just energy and expression. *We're all mad here*, Sergey seemed to say with his eyes.

Before heading back inside we took a polaroid photo of each of us to mark that time and space forever, somewhere in limbo between St. Petersburg and Moscow.

"Yeah, we go together, running in the shadows. We must never break the chain, never break the chain," I sang softly as we laughed and tried to hold the camera steady. In that moment, those lyrics from Stevie Nicks meant everything to me. I could feel the power of our bond, of our connection. The train tracks flew under our feet as the train cars clung to each other's cold metal fingers. Never slowing, never stopping, never breaking the chain.

"Because of their tour schedules, the Moscow friends weren't able to congratulate Joanna and Yuri in Leningrad," Sasha explained in a video years later. "So, Stingray did as Mohammad in that famous saying. She brought the entire wedding to Nikolina Hill!"

I hired a bus in Moscow to take us all to Sasha's, forty-five minutes outside the city. His *dacha* was in Nikolina Gora, sitting pretty in the Russian equivalent of the East Hamptons. The four of us from the train along with Judy, Afrika, Kostya, Vasily Shumov of the Moscow band Center, and the Zvuki Mu band arrived to a beautiful setup of hot food and drinks that Sasha and his pretty wife Ina had laid out. We spent hours sitting, eating, drinking, talking, and drinking some more. Peter Mamonov, the eccentric singer of Zvuki Mu, seemed unusually relaxed and happy. At one point, he grabbed an acoustic guitar and sang a song at the table.

"Tonight, we'll be drinking, as long as it's raining. Tonight, we'll live, but don't wait for me. Let's eat yesterday's cake, and even sleep together – forget about this strange argument," he crooned.

Later, as Viktor, Kostya, and I reclined in one of the bedrooms filled with rock posters and photos, Kostya began to play one of his own songs. Even singing to an audience of two, Kostya transformed completely to meld his spirit with the spirit of the music.

"Where prophets are careless and gullible, where the crap-house is revered like a temple, that's where I'm going. I raise my eyes, and I look upwards. My song is a wounded crane. I raise my eyes."

After a swig from the bottle, Viktor returned an eye for an eye. His song was so powerful and pure – these two guys were truly the best of the best. It was so cool because they didn't hang together too often, but inside that room the music was palpable.

By this point, I wasn't surprised by the amount of alcohol Russians could consume, but no one compared to the drunkenness of the Zvuki Mu guys. They started a jam session in Sasha's studio on the top floor of his *dacha*, pounding and slamming and shouting way into the night.

Music, even more than alcohol, drove these men to their limits, pumping blood through their veins even when daylight began creeping towards us. The few of us that could still walk stepped over the passed-out bodies of our friends to have some tea and breakfast as the sun rose. Sasha smiled at us all, a collection of mavericks and freaks with the world to give to each other. He really knew how to throw the best kind of party.

◆

Back in Leningrad, leaning against Yuri in a cooling bath, I realized my tourist visa was almost up. I had to leave the next day, but Yuri and I had totally forgotten to make a plan as to what we were going to do after being married. We had fought so hard for the wedding, but now that it was over, I had no idea what to do next.

"I know I love you and that I want to be with you," I told him. "But where and how?"

I blinked and there we were again, sitting on the curb at the Pulkovo Airport with his arms wrapped over my shoulders.

"Breathe," he told me as he always did. "We will figure it out."

As is certain in life, everything is temporary, and change will happen regardless if you're ready for it or not. I left Russia in November of 1987 with an overflowing heart and the happiest of memories imprinted against my eyelids. My best friends, this magical group of characters, had taught me to believe in impossible things. I boarded the plane knowing, in the immortal words of Lewis Carroll, that "I can't go back to yesterday because I was a different person then." All I could do was go forward and hope it took me back to my Wonderland.

◆ 1988–1996 ◆

◆ Out of One, Many

As the plane lifted off from Pulkovo airport, I felt a serene sense of calm. Tracing my finger over the stamp in my passport from the wedding palace, I thought of my husband, Yuri Dmitriyevich Kasparyan, and smiled. As the plane bounced through turbulence, I could feel the winds of change bringing us all together. I was no longer split between America and Russia but had both of them woven together in a tapestry over my heart.

"*Chai?*" The stewardess offered me tea.

As I sipped on the bitter hot water I thought about Russians and their love of drinking tea. It was part of their daily routine, like brushing their teeth or cooking breakfast, a ritual that no weather or feeling could interrupt. It was something that marked every occasion – writing songs, doing interviews, planning concerts, the concerts themselves. This act of taking a moment of silence, whether alone, with friends, or with business partners, is something I still try to incorporate into my life to this day.

I choked down another sip of the tea, allowing all the associated memories to come back to me, and then placed the plastic cup as far from me on my tray table as I could. I was really more of a hot chocolate kind of girl.

◆

The appreciation and peacefulness Russians cultivated with drinking tea they balanced nicely with the surging crowds in the Leningrad airport. As I stepped back into Wonderland a month later, I was suddenly swept off my feet, pushed and shoved in a crowd that forced itself against the walls of the building and became a swollen mass against the doors. Turning my head, all I could see were blank faces and cigarettes hanging from their frowns. I almost laughed. That was Russia for you! I was back.

Back to a slightly different place. I hadn't realized how much over the year I'd been mostly away had been changing with Gorbachev's newly instigated freedom and openness for creative expression. I had gotten used to the isolated, secret commune-type oasis the rockers and I had carved out for ourselves. Whenever I had come to Leningrad previously, everyone was there waiting for me with their feet up on the sofas and canned sardines on the table. We would never break the chain, against which Fleetwood Mac so poignantly warned, because they would always be there – it was a closed Communist country, so where could these boys go? All we'd had was each other, until now.

What had once been our underground Russian rock was now all the rave, and Kino, Aquarium, and Alisa were being played all over the radio. They were asked to be on TV programs and offered concert tours across the Soviet Union. After the historic release of Aquarium's non-censored album on Melodiya, Kino and Alisa were offered the same deal.

This was the kind of thing about which we'd dreamed as we sat in a basement or in Cherry's dark, makeshift recording studio. None of us could be happier, and I felt so proud of my friends that it overwhelmed me. I could feel something else though too, a growing suspicion of sadness inside me, as I witnessed the new crack in the chain that had bound us together at the hips.

The biggest game changer for our group was Sergey Soloviev's film *Assa* that immediately became a cult classic. Sergey was a renowned film director, and he cast Afrika as the movie's star to the soundtrack of Aquarium and other underground bands. Yet what became the most famous and remembered scene in the movie was the last part that symbolized the liberation of Russian music from the state-imposed restrictions. It involved Viktor Tsoi, playing one of Afrika's band mates. In the scene Viktor shows up to play at a restaurant, condemned by the ridiculous rules by which a performer in the establishment had to abide. As the dictates are read aloud, Viktor leaves the room with the official manager and walks through the empty, inanimate space to the opening chords of his song "Peremen." Against the cheap backdrop in the restaurant he begins to perform, only to have the camera swing around as the credits roll to reveal a huge audience in an amphitheater, their hands raised in the air with lighters and fists that provide a sharp contrast to the lifelessness of the restaurant. That final cut so captured Tsoi's power that the energy was palpable, and Viktor suddenly became the biggest star and hero to the Russian people. Kino now had real managers that booked them tours and sent them flying out of Leningrad just as I was landing. Our tribe was becoming many, the reverse of the Latin phrase that sat on the United States' seal that claimed out of many, one.

It was December 1987, and for me it started not with my oldest friends but with a mesmerizing concert at the Palace of Youth by one of the newest stars of the expanding Leningrad rock scene. The folk band Kalinov Most, or Kalinov Bridge, drew inspiration for their name from a bridge in Russian epics and legends that connected the worlds of the living and the dead. The band was from Novosibirsk in Siberia, led by a charismatic vocalist and songwriter Dmitry Revyakin. His face reminded me of Jim Morrison, and he had a sensual aura that almost felt psychedelic as he performed. It was very spiritual and powerful as he stood there in a flowing blue shirt with his hippy eyes. The crowd was glued against the stage, screaming and howling after every song as the stage would go temporarily dark.

Suddenly, as the lights reappeared after another break between songs, I saw Kostya onstage with his brown eyes winking mischievously. I'd heard he was a huge fan of this new band, and as I jumped up and down with the rest of the crowd, he began passionately singing, almost pulsating with music. As Kostya and Dmitry sang together, the crowd surged forward as everyone sang along and reached out their hands to touch the two guys. I heard hysterical screaming throughout the hall as a bunch of guys lifted Kostya up. I caught sight of him above the crowd, surfing the bodies like a dark angel, and felt electrified. This was the place I remembered.

When they stopped singing, I watched Kostya pull Dmitry into a big hug and stand there swaying with him, and for a moment I wished that was still me wrapped up in Kostya's warmth. Then I felt arms surround my own shoulders and as I looked around, I watched the entire audience lean into each other and throw their hands in the air with the rock symbol. It was like floating in a sea of love, and I realized that as long as I had their rock music, I was never alone. I threw my head back and howled.

◆

"I've left Marianna."

"What?!" I stared at Viktor. I almost didn't recognize him.

"I've left Marianna," Viktor repeated calmly.

In my mind I swore I could hear the sound of a chain breaking. I looked frantically around the room, half-expecting to see the walls crumbling down around us. Viktor and

■ Viktor Tsoi, Afrika (seated), Andrei Krisanov, Marianna Tsoi, Timur Gasonov, and Sergey Kuryokhin, Leningrad, 1985.

Marianna were such a staple – two smiling, mischievous faces that I'd followed through the streets and apartments of Leningrad.

I felt the question of *why* on my tongue, but as my eyes found their way back to Viktor's serious, bright face I realized how much faith I still had in him. He was a steady guy, no rash decisions or impetuous behaviors. If Viktor left Marianna, I knew it had to be for a valid reason. They had always seemed like such a solid couple, but I had always thought of them more as best friends to each other than romantic lovers. They had spent more time together than many of the other guys had ever spent with their own wives; she basically managed Kino, and Viktor trusted her judgment and strength. For all of his music and performances, Viktor wasn't the type of person who had very many friends. He would grace parties for a couple of hours before disappearing into the darkness, preferring the hangouts Gustav, Yuri, and I had on the couch or the private nights with Marianna and their son Sasha at home. For him, a handful of true, blushing souls was all he wanted.

In Alma-Ata, Kazakhstan, where he had been filming his first lead in the movie *The Needle* with director Rashid Nugmanov, Viktor found a soul that matched his own. As he told me about Natasha Razlogova, I saw how much he had changed in those many months that I couldn't be there prior to getting married. He was emotionally stronger, more powerful in his convictions and fulfilled in a way that allowed him to relax into his seat and toss a lazy smile at his own words. There was still a sadness in his eyes, the burden of hurting Marianna and Sasha still weighing him down, but it was balanced out by the levity of happiness I could see he also felt. Viktor was indelibly loyal to his inner circle and very careful to never hurt any of us. I could see his intention had never been betrayal.

"I was introduced to her when I visited MosFilm Studios, and we became friendly when I saw her again in Yalta for the filming of *Assa*." Natasha had worked as a lecturer and translator, but she decided to move into the film industry. She was married with a son, although separated from her husband and with a new boyfriend. "I told her I had a son and a formal marriage that is part of my business," Viktor continued. "I was very serious, but I was smitten."

Years later, Natasha laughed as she told me she had never thought about a romance with Viktor on that first visit to Yalta. "He was so nice! That's all I thought. We were from two different worlds with no real reason to communicate further."

When Viktor came back to Leningrad in 1987, all he could think about was Natasha. He managed to glean her number from her coworkers and called, asking to see her again.

"You can always come back to Yalta," she said, joking.

"If Soloviev will organize a second visit for Kino, I will be there," Viktor replied.

Natasha brushed it off. The man said he would visit if he could come down for business!

Tickets were so cheap that she thought that if he truly wanted to see her, he could just come himself without another reason. What Natasha didn't know was that at the time Viktor and Marianna were very poor, unlike the Moscow elite of which Natasha was a part. They lived with Marianna's mother and grandmother in a cramped, stale apartment.

Still, Viktor continued to call Natasha quite often.

"To hear her voice made me happier," he told me sheepishly.

On Viktor's second visit in Yalta, the two of them spent hours together just talking, staying up through the night. Viktor told me he'd never felt this way about anybody else.

"She completes me, Jo."

"I'm so happy for you!" I threw my arms around his neck and held him in a big hug.

Later Natasha told me she had been very impressed with Viktor's intelligence, kindness, and internal independence on that second meeting. A few days before they both left Yalta to go back to their respective homes, Natasha moved into Viktor's hotel room. As she sat on the bed beneath the window and listened to him play one of his new songs, "Groupa Kroovy," before anyone else heard it, she realized how serious their relationship was for him. Viktor wasn't the type to share initial versions of his songs with just anyone. He had already told her it was instant love, that he had never loved anyone before, but she had taken it as words spoken in the moment. Now, though, as she watched his dark eyes blink nervously as he sang, she realized the truth.

The next day, Natasha was back in Moscow and Viktor back in Leningrad. They met up briefly in Leningrad again, but by June, Natasha had left for her *dacha* where she had no telephone. Viktor realized only once she'd left that he didn't know the address.

One night, amid the soft breeze and creaking of trees, Natasha was awakened in the earliest hours of the black morning to a voice calling her name. To this day she still doesn't know how Viktor found her in that small, remote village, but she was smitten ever since.

The two decided to live together, but it was something easier imagined than done. Viktor moved out of Marianna's apartment, crashing with friends and trying to find a cheap place of his own. He would travel to Moscow and stay with Natasha, meeting her mother and son and smiling at the way Natasha introduced him as her boyfriend. There was so much back and forth – Natasha working in Moscow full time while Viktor had his band and his same job shoveling coal (along with other rockers) at "Kamchatka" in Leningrad, which would later become an iconic place because of him, a museum and a club.[5]

"She came a few times to Alma-Ata while I was shooting," Viktor said. "We stayed at Rashid's brother's home. It is complicated, a lot of traveling, but I will do anything and go anywhere to be with her. I will do whatever it takes."

I had always felt that Viktor was searching for some small missing part inside of him. I don't know if he had even known it was there, but this longing and emptiness had been small and insidious. Natasha was the cork in the bottle that kept the wine sweet.

"Why didn't you tell me sooner?!" I asked.

"I was anxious to tell you, but because you were exiled for most of 1987, I had to wait. It was not something to bring up during your wedding days either. Jo, I know how much you love the group being together and how hard change is for you. I did not want you to be unhappy."

"Are you kidding?" I took his hands in mine and squeezed them. "You found what we all want! I am thrilled beyond belief for you."

---

5   The Kamchatka peninsula in Russia's Far East has a mythical association for Russians as being the place where the country begins. Viktor also wrote a song in 1984 called "Kamchatka." Sasha Bashlachev, the punk Rikoshet, the sound engineer Fearsoff, Alisa bassist Slava Zaderi, and the artist Oleg Kotelnikov also worked there.

I truly was. All I ever wanted was for my friends to find happiness, especially Viktor. Yet as I walked away from him that evening, heading down the paved road by myself, I felt a bubble of fear in my chest. Viktor had been right about the fact that I didn't like change. I had felt part of something great, but now it was splintering into many different, extraordinary things for all the guys I loved, and I was left in the winds of change trying desperately to adjust my sails.

That night I held onto Yuri, the only thing that felt safe and consistent. I watched the sky repaint itself as the hours melted into the morning. The new colors, even though they were different, were beautiful.

♦

As soon as I walked into my rental house tucked away in a corner of Beverly Glen canyon, I called New York.

"Hey," I said, trying to untangle myself from my luggage strap. "I'm waiting for Boris Grebenshchikov."

I had waited for four years to have Boris in my hometown, four years imagining how I would drive him up to Mulholland and down Rodeo Drive. He was now enormously popular in Russia and about to have his dream of recording in the West fulfilled. With a one-month visa in his pocket, he was planning on traveling to New York with a visit to the City of Angels as well.

Boris would be the first of my friends to actually see the United States and walk across its pavement. Even though I was no longer part of his American record project, I wanted nothing more than to be able to see his reaction to the country about which he'd been dreaming. He knew so much about America and its culture, more so than any of the others, and I had to see if it would match the way it looked inside his head. I knew he imagined a vast land of blue skies over loud cities that were flanked by deep forests and yellow deserts, the homes of his favorite poets, writers, and philosophers like Alan Ginsberg, Jack Kerouac, Richard Bach, and Robert Heinlein. He had soaked up so much information from Western music magazines and press that he'd gotten off the black market or foreign contacts, and he even listened to obscure Western bands that Americans didn't even know. Finally, he would get to see a continent from which everything he'd read had come. Or so we thought.

I should not have been surprised when the Soviets made up some bizarre story that they lost Boris' visa documents. He hadn't even left for New York! How could Boris not get to America when Gorbachev was already in Washington, D.C., for his third summit meeting with President Reagan? I guess *when the cat's away, the mice will play* their conniving, damning games. The mice were the old guard of the Politburo and the Central Committee of the Communist Party, the steadfast officials gone rogue to save as many as they could from Gorbachev's *glasnost*. One of them, the Minister of Culture Zakharov, still vigorously and openly condemned rock 'n roll. The same snarling wolf of a man I had telexed on April 19, 1987, about having Bowie play two concerts in Moscow and donating twenty-five-thousand-dollars-worth of musical equipment from Yamaha for the Rock Club. The same Zakharov who had ignored me completely, in addition to never responding to the telex from U.S. congressman Anthony Beilenson about my visa complications. It seemed the Soviets always had convenient issues when they needed them, and any attempt to thwart their backstabbing met with silence. Was it a coincidence that Boris' U.S. album was named "Radio Silence"?

"Jo!" He cried when I finally saw his radiant face with the palm trees behind him. "I never thought I would ever be able to leave Russia."

"What happened?!" I asked him, jumping into his hug.

"I didn't have high expectations of going to America from the start. When I was in Moscow, ready to go, they said they lost my papers. I shrugged and thought *okay, back to Leningrad and back to music.*" I almost laughed at Boris' zen philosophy. He was like a boulder in the waves, calm and meditative as the water swirled around him.

"I wish I could be more like you," I told him. "I would have lost my shit."

"You already did," he said with a teasing smile.

Boris had met with the head of CBS Records, Walter Yetnikoff, and was now going to meet with Dave Stewart of The Eurythmics about producing his album. It was so surreal to see him there, folding into my side of the globe. He took everything so calmly, but to this day I wish I could know what it feels like for someone who had only ever been in Russia for thirty-four years of his life to find himself surrounded by his dreams.

I took Boris to Guitar Center Hollywood and watched his eyes light up as he studied hundreds of guitars hanging on the walls. Equipment was the constant complaint of all the Russian rockers, and yet here were more supplies than could fuel a year's-worth of concerts. We went to Gelson's grocery market near Beverly Hills where my mom had a store charge card, and I told Boris to buy everything he wanted. At first, he was amused by the long rows of fresh vegetables, not just seasonal ones but a selection from all over the world, but I soon saw his bafflement as he tried to decide between twelve different choices of apples. When we got to the coffee section and he saw all the different choices, he became very overwhelmed. I'd never seen him like that, so out of his element and his comfort zone. Here was a man who had never broken a sweat as he pushed back against his own government and produced illegal music to inspire rebel youth, and yet it was a large selection of coffee options that managed to rattle him.

When I went to Russia and had thought it was crazy that the stores there had only one choice of coffee, he genuinely could not understand how any store could have dozens.

"People do not need this many choices," he mumbled, mixing three different coffees in his plastic cup at the counter. "How can they make music if they stand here all day choosing between all this?"

As I stood there, I realized how ridiculous either extreme was. Yes, I was grateful to have options, but did people really need that many choices? To have every vegetable, year-round now seemed almost gluttonous and unnatural.

I drove Boris around in my sporty Toyota Supra. I still laugh when I think back and picture him in the passenger seat clinging onto the door handle with white knuckles as I gunned it down Sunset Boulevard's curves with the music blasting through my amazing stereo system. Almost none of the people I knew in Russia drove or had their own cars, and driving was still a very alien skill to most of them.

"You drive," my mother had told me at the age of fourteen when she was supposed to take me somewhere. Without even questioning my mother, I got behind the wheel. Driving for me was instinctual. When I finally got my own used car at sixteen, I chose a stick shift, two-seater sports car with a personal license plate that boasted *speedy jo*. While I felt free and on fire, Boris looked terrified. I had never seen him so tense before.

Boris left for New York the next day, and I met up with him there a couple of days after that. I was lucky enough to be there when he met Bowie. I stood there in awe of these two icons, so similar in a way that blew my mind.

"Let me take a polaroid," I said. Here were Bowie and Boris, two men who inspired me to do what I did. My hands shook as I held the camera.

"Whatever Joanna says," Bowie joked. He was always so kind when he saw me and made me feel like an old friend.

I could only stay in New York briefly because I had an art show to open in Los Angeles with the Russian artists. A couple of days later Boris called me to tell me what I'd missed. It made me smile.

"The ophthalmologist tells me I have very poor vision. He tells me I needed glasses. When I put them on, Jo, just wow! This is what the world looks like!"

◆

Over the last four years, while I had been smuggling in equipment and art supplies for all the rockers and artists, they thanked me by giving me pieces of their work. At that point none of them had been "official" artists, and they had almost no access to staple supplies like acrylic paints or canvases. Like the rockers, the artists improvised to express their creativity and occupy their hands. They painted and made collages on plastic shower curtains, pieces of discarded wood, dishes, shirts, straw place mats, and fabric. I would stand with these unusual, raw, and dramatic pieces of work over my suitcase with no clue how to carry any of it out to the West. There was nothing I could fold and just stuff in the bottom of my suitcase; one piece of wood was five feet by one and a half feet! Somehow, with persistence and a delusional imagination, I got through customs with a total of two hundred pieces over the years.

Fields advised that on one occasion she was stopped from leaving the Soviet Union and questioned regarding some canvases she was taking out, my FBI file from a meeting on August 4, 1986, reported. *Fields stated that she told customs officials that the canvases were her works of art. Although they were signed with Russian names, the customs officials allowed her to remove them.*

Lucky enough for me, the bureaucratic officials didn't understand the paintings and creations. There were even times when I lied and blatantly said it was just children's art that had been gifted to me. Unaware of the style of graffiti and pop art, the guards would roll their eyes and let me pass.

"Oh, I just stuck that image on the material because I thought it looked pretty," I lied one time as they unfolded a large piece of fabric with a small image in the middle that Timur Novikov had made. The two officials in front of me eyed each other.

"Very strange, yes?" one said to the other as they waved me through.

◆

Back in Los Angeles, I had borrowed money from my parents to frame each and every piece of art I acquired. They were displayed throughout my house in beautiful wood frames, under Lucite covers, and on metal stands, like a special exhibit in some small corner of the MoMA. One day I came back to the house and wandered the small, tight rooms, looking over all the paintings that had brought me so much joy over the years, and helped me when I missed the guys and was hungry for their inspiration. It wasn't enough to keep the art – I wanted to share it.

I had kept in touch with Kate Karam from Greenpeace ever since I met her in line at the Soviet Embassy in London, and she was the first person I called. Just as strongly as I felt about my friends' expressions of individuality and soul, I knew that our existence was dependent on the environment and animals we preserved on this planet. We were all in it together, and I saw these Russian artists' fight for the human spirit relevant to Greenpeace's fight against negligence of our ecosystem. My discussion with Kate about an exhibit with the Russian work to benefit Greenpeace turned into the National Premiere of *Red Wave 'Unofficial' Contemporary Art and Music from the U.S.S.R.*

"Peace through art and music!" I sang to everyone who would listen to my new mantra. The event on January 28, 1988, exhibited eighty works at the Jerry Solomon Gallery on La Brea Avenue in Los Angeles, and the one-hundred-and-fifty-dollar ticket benefited Greenpeace's East/West Fund. Hard Rock Café provided all the refreshments, and Yamaha loaned the event a plethora of musical equipment for entertainment. The advisory committee consisted of David Bowie, David Byrne, Keith Haring, music industry executive Clive Davis, Christie Brinkley Joel, Lt. Governor of California Leo McCarthy, Carl Sagan, art collectors Frederick Weisman and Count Giuseppe Panza, and my stepfather Frederick Nicholas. Vitaly Korotich from *Ogonyok* magazine also took part, the only Russian authority who had never shunned me during my visa crisis.

Greenpeace printed beautiful invitations with one of Viktor Tsoi's drawings on it and produced an accordion-like pamphlet explaining about the artists. None of the artists were permitted to actually leave the U.S.S.R. to attend the opening, so we had monitors around the gallery that showed videos and interviews with them, and a sound system playing the avant-garde music of the New Composers who included many of the Russian artists.

To feature on t-shirts, we picked five strong images by Timur Novikov, Gustav Guryanov, Oleg Kotelnikov, Andrei Medvedev, and Maya Khlobuistin. Each had a tag that read *This shirt features new art from the U.S.S.R. The original paintings were done by a group of young Leningrad artists who call themselves New Artists. Peace through art and music* – Мир через искусство и музыку.

On Monday and Wednesday before the opening, Greenpeace received calls from an unidentified man. "I always hated Greenpeace and always thought you were in league with the Soviets. … If you don't cancel the show, I will bomb the gallery."

Kate Karam told me about the calls but said she'd like to go on with the show. "A Greenpeace ship was blown up in New Zealand in 1985, and we take threats very seriously. The day of the opening we will have police comb the gallery and a security firm there to monitor the event."

Later that day, she spoke to the *Los Angeles Times*. "This is precisely why Greenpeace is trying to promote understanding between the East and West. We have to be able to understand each other better than this."

All we wanted was for the exhibit to show American people a different side of Russia than the heavy bias depicted in movies like *Rambo*. There was still solidarity in young people making contemporary art around the world. *How was it*, I wondered as I made my way through the gallery before the opening, *that some people still didn't get the picture?*

A few weeks earlier, Atlantic Releasing Movie Company had filed for bankruptcy, and I didn't even blink. I was too focused on *Red Wave* the art exhibition to care much about the end of my film deal.

◆

The house was packed. Faces blurred together, eyes sparkling and fancy shoes scuffing the gallery floor as people jumped from painting to painting talking loudly. I saw the architect Frank Gehry, musician Graham Nash, MoCA director Richard Koshalek, Hard Rock Café owner Peter Morton, and a collection of art collectors with deep pockets and shoulder pads. I could see on their faces that they were impressed by the exhibit, their eyes searching the vibrant canvases to see what people on the other side of the world envisioned.

Essentially primitive in style, distinctive in their humor, and childlike in whimsy, the works use bright colors to depict mythical beasts, dancing figures, real animals, and carica- tured human beings, Daniel B. Wood of the *Christian Science Monitor* reported. Local critics and curators at the opening waxed on about the rebellious attitude manifested in non-political artistic realities, dropping phrases like "renegade" and "unconstrained."

I quietly stepped up beside Richard Koshalek as he and a reporter stood and stared at one of the works. "This collection is proof that innovation and experimentation in art is not something that is restricted to the Western industrialized nations," he said, waving the dark drink in his hand around excitedly. "The young Russian artists have shown us that creativity has flourished there, despite government restrictions."

It fascinated me, as I wandered through the conversations that night, how different the judgment of Russian art was compared to Russian music. The rock music, with its lyrics that many Westerners couldn't understand, was always categorized and seen as Russian rock 'n roll. This art, on the other hand, seemed to be accepted as universal, not just an exclusive expression of the Russian experience.

Art speaks where words are unable to explain, I'd heard once, but I hadn't realized how true it was. Somehow, in a gallery graced by the California sunset, the New Artists' work

■ Afrika with one of his paintings on fabric, 1986. Gustav Guryanov can be seen through the cutout.

■ Andrei Krisanov with his work and others in the New Artists' studio space, Leningrad, 1986.

managed to explain all that people needed to know.

"It has a sense of humor that I didn't think existed in Russia in the few times I have been there," I heard Frederick Weisman say. "It's kind of an uplift to me." Weisman had one of the largest and most eclectic art collections in the United States and loved the bold, whimsical themes of many of the exhibit pieces. Though the artworks weren't for sale, he couldn't stop looking at them.

"The humanity," he said, with his arms crossed.

"What are we if not art?" I asked with a smile. This started a dialogue between us that led to a great friendship and future trip together to Russia. In the end, I decided to sell him five or six pieces. He had a foundation that lent much of his art to museums around the country, but he was also one of the most delightful men I'd met who really *got* it – what Russia was all about. He also agreed to buy a piece that would be donated to the Museum of Contemporary Art, one of the main museums of Los Angeles and a pioneer of contemporary expression. MoCA chose one of the most avant-garde pieces of the show, a clear shower curtain with a large face of Lenin drawn in black marker. It was Afrika's piece, one he crowned *First Portrait of Lenin on Plastic.*

"The most provocative of the exhibit," Weisman agreed.

"These are my destructible paintings," Afrika had said of his ephemeral, uncompromising drawings on plastic. "I intend for them to last only two years." I have never checked to see if the MoCA piece survived.

At some point during the event, a shiny Rolls Royce showed up in front of the gallery.

Barbie Benton, the Playboy model, stepped onto the curb and waltzed into the room wearing a mink coat. What was she thinking? At a benefit for Greenpeace? She didn't stay very long, just long enough for someone to comment on the coat and send her slinking back to her car.

The success of the art exhibit overwhelmed me. I was so happy for my friends, and I felt closer to them than I had for a long time.

"What do you think?" I asked Judy when I found her in the crowd.

"I think you should stand to the left a little," she said with a camera up to her eye. "Next to Yuri's frame. Oh wait, can you move a little to the right? Maybe step back a little so the light is better. Right there!"

"They're space people," I said with a smile, pointing to the little figures. Yuri didn't make much art, but it was great to have him in the show.

"They're out of this world!" Someone shouted to me as he walked past.

It was true, although all I could think about was *this* world in which I was standing, and how soon I could cross its blue ocean and vast continents again. I couldn't wait to get back to Russia to show everyone the press and the photos from the event. I had never felt more grateful or more grounded, standing there in Oleg Kotelnikov's decorated shirt and my oversized denim jacket, while my head was in the clouds.

◆

I've heard that the goal isn't to live forever, but to create something that will. On February 17, 1988, I stood in my socks on a dim Los Angeles morning and hummed the immortal tune of one of Sasha Bashlachev's songs. At the age of twenty-seven, one of the greatest Russian bard singers was dead after falling from the window of a ninth-floor apartment. He was gone, but in my mind, I could still see the indelibly impassioned poet and storyteller, his bare fingers making love to a rare twelve string guitar until they bled and dripped down the stained wood like aged wine.

Unfortunately, Sasha hadn't lived long enough to leave a big body of work behind, and his songs had never been professionally recorded for the public's ears. He would play for the intimate groups of people he called his friends, and not many other people knew who he was or what the country had lost when he died. I am now so grateful that my sister Judy and I filmed Sasha singing many of his songs, which has helped keep his memory alive and introduce new generations of Russians to his epic poems and trembling sagas. He may not have been Russia's most revered and beloved bard singer like Vladimir Vysotsky, but for me and my friends he was always a demigod with his hair around his shoulders and his sad, twinkling eyes.

Sasha became part of the 27 Club, a list whose exclusivity dissuades rather than tempts people to join. It is a group of well-known musicians, artists, and actors who died at the age of twenty-seven, a cross-cultural phenomenon including Jim Morrison, Janis Joplin, Jimi Hendrix, Brian Jones, Kurt Cobain, and Amy Winehouse. Maybe Sasha was up there behind the stars, jamming with the greats and dazzling them with his poetry. He was always shy, and I wondered if death would change him on the other side as he stayed forever the same in our hearts.

Sasha was buried in Kovalevskoye Cemetery, a small, imperceptibly blue church surrounded by a rugged composition of graves and dirt. No landscaping, gardening, or paved walkways. Leningrad was a city with many historic, impressive cemeteries full of notable Russians and aristocrats like Dostoevsky, Tchaikovsky, the twentieth-century poet Anna Akhmatova, and the literary historian and author Dmitry Likhachev. The Volkovo Cemetery even has a section called *Literatorskiye Mostki*, or Literary Bridges, with tombstones crowning the poet Alexander Blok, composer Andrei Petrov, conductors Ilya Musin and Karl Eliasberg, and the famous director of the Kirov Ballet School, Agrippina Vaganova. Yet, Sasha received no perennial throne. What he had created was not a tangible ripple in the history books but a subtle, albeit powerful sense of love and imagination among our group. My lyrics were shaped by him, by the way he encouraged me to look at the world and understand struggle and endurance.

I was not in Russia at the time of his death, but I received the message through the complicated, twisted channels we all used to communicate in emergencies. It broke my heart that such a beautiful, sweet, unique soul was gone. Even with all the distance and all the changes that had been happening, I had never considered for even a moment that I could ever lose any of the magical beasts I knew in Russia. I was not prepared for it. My mind couldn't understand going on without Sasha while I was still humming his songs.

The occasion made me miss my friends back in Russia even more. Their separate projects and plans now seemed to be tumbling away from each other with an even more alarming speed now that Sasha's life had frozen in time. All I wanted in that moment after the tragedy was to be with Yuri, but he was far away while I had been home trying to organize all the documents to get him a visa to the States.

■ At Sasha Bashlachev's gravesite in Kovalevskoye Cemetery, Leningrad, 1988.

I returned to Russia a few weeks later. I had missed the funeral, but Kostya Kinchev, his bandmate Peter Samoylov, Object Nasmeshek's Evgeny Fedorov, the Rock Club administrator Nina Baranovsky, and Marianna Tsoi took me to the burial site.

"It looks so ordinary," I said, staring at the lumpy dirt framed by large puddles of water and a grey, low sky.

"It is a sad place," Marianna agreed. "Not much of a celebration for great lives."

There was something about Sasha's grave, though, that hit me with a feeling of warmth and happiness as I walked towards it. His young, pondering face watched me from a large black and white photograph, an expression that brought back so many memories of summer afternoons and long songs. The ground was covered with red tulips and yellow daffodils, arranged in a layered circle that was bright and heroic. I could hear his voice, the passion he spent with each word, like spring in the middle of a wintry day.

Kostya groaned, and I could see the pain on his face as he glanced down to the ground where his friend's body was held by the earth.

"We don't have a soul – we *are* souls. We have a body," I said, repeating a Quaker quote I knew. Sasha had been luminescent, transcendent, and even though his body was below us he was still just as strong and vivid as he had always been. In his words and voice our memories could find him easily.

"To Sasha," Marianna said as they all filled up shot glasses.

As the alcohol slid past our broken hearts, I swear I could hear someone singing.

Time of Little Bells
By Sasha Bashlachev

We roamed on and on, roamed to no end through
heat and frost
Endured it all but remained free
We gobbled snow mixed with birch tree bark
And soared up level with belfries

If we wept – we spared no salt
If we feasted – we spared no cakes
Bell-ringers with their black rough hands
Tore apart the loudspeakers' nerves

But days go on and the times, they change
Onion domes have been stripped of their gold
Bell-ringers roam around the world
The bells flung down and smashed apart

And why on earth are we still drifting
In our own field as if we're outlaws?
The Bell has not been cast for us
So the time here must be that of little bells

Chime on, my heart, hidden under my gown
Ravens hastily scattered away
Hey! Bring out the troika
And we'll dash away to the four winds

But the horses, they haven't been shod for years
But the wheels – none's ever been greased
There's no whip in sight, the saddles all ransacked
And the knots – they're all long undone

In the rain, all the roads are soaked in rainbow
Woe is looming, it's no time to laugh
But sleigh-bells ring in the harness
So rope it in and off we go

We'll roar, we'll whistle, we'll rattle
It'll strike us to the marrow
Hey, brothers! D'you feel it in your gut?
The thunderous laughter of the Russian little
bells?

For ages we chewed prayers and swears.
For ages we lived black as hell.
We slept at no end, and we got beastly drunk
And we no longer sing. We just don't know how.

We're waiting and waiting and waiting.
All dirty as heck and alike
But the cleansing rain revealed – we're each as
one's own.
But mostly honest, good and kind.

The Tsar Bell is broken – so what?
We're here with our black guitars.
Big Beat, Blues, and Rock 'n Roll
Bewitched us with very first strokes

Our chests sparkle with electricity.
Hats off on the snow – and bam!
Rock 'n roll is our holy paganism.
I love this time of little bells.

(translation Alexander Kan)

◆ We Will Not Be Silent

The passport book was small, blue leather with gold lettering carved into the soft cover. *Leningrad Rock Club.* My hands trembled as I held it, and I beamed up at manager Kolya Mikhailov and Rock Club secretary Olga Slobodskaya as they smiled back.

I flipped open the book to see my photo staring back at me, flanked by my name in Russian and the membership number of my book, 005.

"It is one of the first ten books for honorary members," Kolya told me proudly. "Like Boris and Kolya Vasin."

"I could not be happier," I replied, imagining this was what movie stars in America felt upon being handed an Oscar.

My friends were touring the country, their faces and music all over the TV and press, yet as I stood there with the Rock Club's book that cemented my legacy inside such an iconic place, I felt like I was getting somewhere too.

As much as I had done in Russia, there was still so much more that needed doing. The reality of Russia at this time was a bird's eye view of roses. Things looked better, and they *were* better, newer, and more colorful, but there were still thorns in our sides hiding under the beauty of change. The biggest problem was that top-quality equipment was scarce. Some months before, Billy Joel had come to the Soviet Union to play concerts in Moscow and Leningrad. He put on one of the most professional shows I and the Russians had ever seen, and my friends were blown away by the quality of the sound.

Joel, like UB40 before him, had brought all of his own equipment, which made the stadium feel like a spacecraft in a sonic boom. Watching from backstage, the Russian rockers saw what the West had available, and what they were still missing.

"It is horrible," Boris said at a concert in one of Leningrad's large halls, a place that a short time before he would never even dream of playing. "The equipment we are given to perform on, it does not do justice to the music."

The halls were packed, and Boris' fans loved him, but fame in Russia still didn't hold a candle to fame in the West.

"We are in a very enviable position right now, but nothing gets better," Boris explained to me later when I caught him before he vanished to another venue, another concert, another city. "I was really angry the other night because I'm thrown out of my room right now. Lyuda, Gleb and I don't have a place to live. At friends', I'm sitting and watching the TV with Boris Grebenshchikov and Aquarium all the time on it, and I put on the radio and it is the same thing, and I am sitting here catching cockroaches in my teacup."

"But why is it still like this?" I asked. "We've fought so hard. What else should we be doing?"

"It has nothing to do with us. It all depends on LenConcert, on concert organizations. They had better equipment, but they decided not to put it on. They think, *why should we bother? These guys will play on any shit.* They are not really interested in doing us a favor because they have their money. Tickets are sold out. As long as they have what they want to have, they are not interested in doing anything more. They do not love the music."

"But we do," I pushed back. "We'll fight for it."

"The public thinks we are now rich," Boris said unhappily, preoccupied with the disparity between imagination and reality. "But nothing has changed."

At a Kino concert in Moscow that Viktor and Yuri asked me to attend, I could see the same disappointment and embarrassment from Boris on Viktor's face as he sang into the cheap mic for his sound check. "*Ras, dva, ras, dva, tree, ras, ras.*" High pitched feedback screamed through the space as we covered our ears with our hands and waited for it to pass.

"It is not me," Viktor joked, but he picked nervously at the bottom of his leather jacket. "I swear."

Bad equipment had been the norm for Viktor since his days in the Rock Club and Palace of Youth, but now that he was the biggest star in the country and could play in many different cities and halls, I think he felt a responsibility to his fans to put on the best show that he could. And that show did not include an awful sound system that mangled his voice and puked buckets of feedback.

"The equipment we have tonight is lousy, but our spirit is good, so…" Viktor trailed off as he and I stood behind the curtain waiting for him to take the stage.

"So, make the music so good that not even the equipment can ruin the song," I whispered. I watched Viktor and the band, that now included Igor Borisov as a second guitarist, drown out the poor sound and blast the audience with music that overwhelmed the spirit. Kino's album *Groupa Kroovy* had become a huge hit, triggering what became "Kinomania" around the country. The crowd was crazy about the guys dressed all in black and Gustav in his green tank top, singing along to hit after hit while tears poured down faces and hands waved in the air. As I watched, I saw no difference between Kino and any top band in the West.

"Now, I'd like to introduce to you our good friend from the United States, the singer Joanna Stingray. She has done so much for all the musicians, or at least many of the musicians here. She released the *Red Wave* album in America. She has been bringing along lots of instruments and equipment for us. And now, she is gonna sing with us."

Just before the show had started, Viktor had asked me if I wanted to come up and play a song with them. No matter where Kino traveled and how far they went, Viktor never forgot to include me. Yuri kissed me as I finished my song, the crowd roaring like a hurricane of absolute joy. Their shouts only got louder as the night wound on, and when Kino finished their set everyone refused to leave without an encore. They clapped, whistled, and chanted until Viktor reemerged.

"Everything is broken here. We can hardly hear ourselves. We just can't hear anything… Give me a minute – I'll go backstage and try to talk to them."

"Viktor, they don't care what the quality was," I tried to convince him backstage. "They won't let you leave!"

Kino and I finally walked out and sang Kino's song "Boshetunmai," the Russian slang for pot. Everyone below us ate it up, laughing and screaming along to the reggae rhythm and lyrics. As Viktor sang, I stood with the other musicians, dancing and playing the tambourine. At one point, Viktor looked back, beaming at his tribe. I watched him shine, living proof that music isn't about the sound but the soul. It was such an intense revelation, and as I heard the bells rattle against the palm of my hand, I knew that no crappy equipment would silence us. I had my name in a blue passport, and a fire in my soul.

◆

Pop Mechanics' wildest, most extravagant concert was scheduled at one of the largest venues in Leningrad, the Sport & Concert Complex. The SKK, as it was known, held

■ Viktor, me, Vitia Sologub, and Sasha Titov, Leningrad, 1986. Vitia is wearing one of the shirts I made that
says "Save the World" in Russian on one side and in English on the other.

twenty-thousand people. It was more space than Sergey had ever commanded or created,
and besides the oversized stage there was a large area below it that he could use as well.

"The ideas," he said, "are limitless." His brain was working overtime, bouncing
outrageous ideas off of Afrika and Timur whom he knew would do anything he asked
of them. The three of them hunted through the city for ostentatious, gaudy people and
items for the performance. Sergey was a conductor on a wild train off the tracks.

Viktor, Yuri, and I all ended up in Leningrad to participate in the show. Yuri and I
hadn't been together in our bed since I'd arrived. Viktor had been gone so often filming in
Alma-Ata, touring with Kino, and spending time with Natasha in Moscow. I felt like one
of The Three Musketeers reuniting with the others. I was out of my mind to see them, but
it felt strange, as if we'd gotten too used to being apart. I held their hands in my own and
was afraid to let them go. As we waited for the day of the Pop Mechanics extravaganza,
the three of us tried to help Viktor find an apartment in the city. He desperately wanted
his own place, but he had very little money and no desire to manipulate the system to
make things happen faster. Those were cards up Afrika's sleeve, but not the way Viktor
could operate. He was daring not in the streets, but on the stage.

The hall for the concert sold out completely, although I don't think anyone in the
Russian public understood what kind of crazy ride was waiting for them. They filled into
the cavernous room with little idea that they were embarking on a journey into the folds
of Sergey's frantic, passionate mind. Here, existence was not enough, and experience had
to be tangible, visceral, and bright.

As I sat down to write this chapter, I put on an old video of the concert to help me remember the nuances of the explosive performance. After watching it, I felt drained and exhausted. It had been a relentless concert, impossible to duplicate.

The show started with Sergey on his keyboards, hunched over the black and white bars in his favorite *Captain* studded jacket. Angelic chords swept us slowly into a new world as a flutist appeared, then a man with a big, non-traditional drum, and a guy playing an unconventional brass piece that sounded like a crying baby being carried away by singing birds. Suddenly an entire wind section emerged, both modern and ancient instruments, while a group of Hare Krishnas with their odd music devices and guttural chants took the stage. Sergey let the introduction unfold; he hadn't even started conducting yet.

After a gypsy began dancing with three large snakes wrapped around her, she untangled herself from the creatures and handed them off to Afrika and Timur. The two guys jumped down into the crowd, letting the audience run their hands along the scales and curves. The Krishnas joined them in the crowd. The gypsy somehow reappeared with an even bigger snake, a boa constrictor of some kind that wrapped around her body. Behind her, Yuri appeared on some sort of pyramid of bleachers, playing his electric guitar with a distortion pedal. Yuri had become the lead guitarist for Sergey and working with the creative genius had turned him into a bigger beast, his sound reverberating through the entire hall. A trumpet player with a mutilated, twisted instrument joined, alternating his playing with bluesy singing. A lady with a monkey in a dress wandered the stage with a small flower basket, then suddenly mounted a little scooter and buzzed off. As more and more characters filled the stage, Sergey observed his creation while plunging his thick fingers into the keys on his two Yamahas.

A group of guys singing a hymn saluted their arms in different positions, tumbling to the ground as Yuri grinded a dysmorphic chord. Sergey switched his melody to something almost like a harp, and together with Yuri's music it became something seductive.

Suddenly, two old fashioned cars drove out below the stage, followed by Afrika leading a pony. Behind him were three ladies in dark, scant clothing reminiscent of both orthodox priests and S&M practitioners at the same time, followed by three antiquated soldiers with rifles and another pony.

Afrika swung himself onto the pony, watching over a strange guy with a pig nose and fake pistol as he pretended to rob one of the ladies in the crowd. A violinist, a fiddler on the roof of sorts, started a traditional Russian jig and danced while he played. Nobody knew where to look, including myself. I felt my eyes rolling around as Sergey hopped from the piano to join the two other guys dancing like spinning teapots that leaned over

■ Video stills from the Pop Mechanics extravaganza at the SKK, Leningrad, 1988. Yuri is on guitar (right); his mouth has just been covered by one of the dark ladies.

to serve themselves.

"Rock musicians, come on!" Sergey shouted, spinning back to the piano. "*Payekalee!*" He repeated this over and over as a whole rock section began to play. Seva Gakkel was on cello, Igor Tikhomirov on bass, Viktor Tsoi and the new Kino guitarist, along with Lyosha Cherry, jammed along. As the horn section joined in, Sergey stepped back and began conducting.

His whole body twisted with directions – his head jerked, legs jumped, almost as if they would jump away from him. It was so incredibly powerful. Every flinch, every movement, his disciples understood. Strange characters walked across the stage in homemade, royally apocalyptic costumes. Circus met rock met performance art.

Then, for a second, the sound came crashing down, and all the music stopped. Everyone in the crowd froze, not knowing what to expect. I could feel all the blood rush to my head as I strode onto the stage to the first notes of my song "Turn Away," black jacket, black sunglasses, even a black wig. Black everything, except for electric blue lipstick. As the horns and strings joined the guitars, Sergey tapped the mic and smiled at me. I could see in his eyes an explosion of imagination and camaraderie.

This live performance was so different than the recording; Sergey slowed down the song and turned it into this forceful, driving piece backed by a ringing euphony of jazz, classical, and rock musicians. Before the last verse, I tore off the wig and felt my blonde and black hair shine under the lights. *This is what I want*, I thought as the screams and chants almost made my ears bleed. *This is what I need.* Too soon, I disappeared back the way I came in.

When I looked back to the stage, I could see Sergey crawling across the floor like a wounded animal. Laying on his back, he started conducting with his limbs flying up and down into space. It was absolute mayhem, a human body turned inside-out like a shirt, exposing all the chaos and circuits inside. I stood there, shocked, wondering how in the world he came up with this stuff. It was out of this world, authentic and raw, his brain like a planet spinning through space.

"Assa ye ye!" Afrika shrieked in my ear as he ran past me and back to the stage. I jumped out of the way as Timur and other artists crashed after him with large pieces of scrap metal they ended up banging with sledgehammers and sticks. As I watched, they all disappeared into a cloud of fog from a machine pumping it out of the curtains. The noise transcended their existence.

As the concert blazed on, my favorite piece ended up being one of the best I'd ever seen from Pop Mechanics. I stood on the bleachers at the back of the stage with the guitarists, smacking my tambourine against my palm and my thigh. One of the dark ladies came out and wrapped black scarves around Viktor's eyes, Yuri's mouth, and Tikhomirov's eyes. The smoke built so that soon I felt as if I were wearing blindfolds as well, unable to see anything except the black figures crowding the stage for the finale. I could sense everyone, all the different musicians and creatures, as they screamed and fell and lost their minds in the mayhem. The last thing I saw was Sergey's lanky body up in the air, his teeth flashing in a huge smile before he vanished from the stage and the concert crashed to a finish.

I didn't know at the time it would be my last Pop Mechanics concert in Russia, but after we finished, I did know that I would keep performing no matter what. I stood there, panting like a ghost in a graveyard of broken statues, scrap metal, smashed instruments, and exhausted bodies. Yet somehow, we were alive, we were beating hearts, we were everything. We were the music makers, and the dreamers of dream. I collapsed at my own feet, but in my heart, I was soaring.

"Sergey!" I screamed at him, jumping into his arms after we cleared the stage. "What did you think?!"

"You know," he said, giving me his Cheshire smile and a wink. "It was okay."

✦

For the first time ever, I was the last to leave Leningrad. Boris had headed back to New York to record his U.S. album, Afrika was setting up art shows across Europe, and Viktor was still finishing up filming in Alma-Ata and spending time with Natasha in Moscow despite finally renting his own apartment in Leningrad. The gang had spread their wings and caught different tailwinds into opposite directions. It made me sad, sitting in the apartment with Yuri and looking out over the bare, cloud-covered streets devoid of any other familiar faces. Yet my heart still pumped away happily – no matter where everyone else had gone, Yuri was coming with me.

It would be his first visit to the States. My parents had planned a second wedding celebration at their home in Beverly Hills, and I was so excited to show my husband around and introduce him to all my friends. British Airways gave us business class tickets for the flight.

"Wow," Yuri said slowly, a smile on his face as he looked at the food and coffee they served for free. He slept, he smoked the duty-free box of Marlboro's we'd bought at the airport, and he didn't stop smiling.

A day after we landed in Los Angeles, my second Russian art exhibit opened at the Stock Exchange in Downtown. It was curated with a focus more towards the general public, with a cover cost of seven dollars to benefit Greenpeace. It included an exhibit at eight in the evening, followed by dancing to Russian rock 'n roll at nine.

It was a large, curious crowd that filled the space. Yuri and I walked in, both wearing semi-tuxedos, me with a red bow tie and him with eyes that lit up like rockets.

"I am very proud of what you put together," he told me in his heavy accent, tugging on the bow tie.

"It's like we're all together again," I answered wistfully.

Igor Butman, our old friend from Pop Mechanics who had emigrated to the States in 1987, hung out with us. He was thrilled to be with faces he could recognize from years before. He was considered a virtuoso saxophonist and was championed by American saxophonists Grover Washington Jr. and Wynton Marsalis.

"My favorite living saxophone player," President Bill Clinton had called him. It was an honor for him to show up at the exhibit.

From that night forward, the trip was a whirlwind of activity and color. I took Yuri to Guitar Center on Sunset Boulevard, where he sat in the guitar section playing one instrument after another. He would have played through the night with the stars as his lights. We went to dinners around town with my friends and parents, walked on Rodeo Drive, and flew up to Pismo Beach to ride four-wheelers on the sand dunes. My friend Mark Rosenthal had invited us to ride with him in his single-engine, red and white plane.

"Are you sure this is a good idea?" I asked as I squeezed into the back and let Yuri sit up front.

"Yes!" Yuri declared excitedly.

■ Yuri loved the beach.

We went flying up the coast, the cerulean ocean to the left and bone-dry mountains to the right.

"How about some tricks?" Mark asked Yuri, halfway through the flight.

"Oh no!" I called out from behind.

"Oh yeah!" Yuri said at the same time.

I felt the plane circle onto its side, to the left and then to the right, and then stall out so it felt as if we were falling through the cold, thin air.

"Wow! Wow!" Yuri repeated.

"Oh my god!" I screamed, before throwing up.

The tricks came to an abrupt halt. Everyone was silent. Mark cleared his throat. "Did you…"

"Just fly," I said through clenched teeth.

Once on the ground, I went wild on the dunes, a helmet strapped to my head, trying to lose all of my nervous, nauseous energy. Yuri and I switched places as we climbed back into what I saw as the death-trap, and Mark calmly flew us home.

"Better?" Mark shouted over to me.

"Much!" I hollered back. It was a moment that reminded me we were young and wild. Young and wild and free, except from the plans of my mother.

"I've booked Yuri an appointment at the dentist tomorrow," she informed me when we got home.

"What? He's here for fun, Mom, he doesn't want to do that."

"His teeth look black from all the smoking. Who knows if he's ever had them checked in Russia. It's not healthy." My mother's perfect button nose crinkled unhappily. She had to fix him – I could see it in her pale, pleading eyes.

"Why not," Yuri said, coming up behind me.

One month and over fifteen hours of drilling later, Yuri had fillings, some crowns, and a root canal in his shiny, white mouth.

Two decades later when my mom saw a photo of a reunion between me and Yuri, I watched her face fall. "What happened to the teeth I spent thousands of dollars fixing?!" All I could do was laugh.

A highlight of the trip was meeting with Senator Alan Cranston, the man who had pushed and pushed the Soviets to not keep two people in love apart. He was thrilled to see us married, giving each of us a hearty hug.

"You were such a big part of this," I told him as Yuri and I faced him, arm in arm. CNN reached out and asked to interview Yuri. I had done so much press for the *Red Wave* album and art shows as the spokesperson for my friends, and when CNN got news one of those guys was actually going to be in Los Angeles, they flipped. Interviews were not something Yuri enjoyed doing, but as usual he went along with the flow and followed the salty, Southern California breeze down to the studio. He was fascinated by their control room, the big sound mixing board and other equipment.

"Want to see how it works?" the skinny engineer offered. Yuri nodded vigorously.

After Los Angeles, Yuri and I flew to New York for an exhibition I'd arranged of Tsoi's work at an art gallery. Yuri's father flew from Russia to meet us there – he too had never been to the States before, nor had his wife.

"Why didn't Irina come with you?" I asked Dimitri recently. I had always assumed she didn't feel comfortable leaving her scheduled life at home.

"Why," he repeated. "Why is because we only had money for one ticket."

I wished more than anything they had told me back then. My parents would have gotten a ticket for her in a second. It was so Russian to not say anything, to put pride before supplication, regardless of the loss.

Yuri, Dimitri, and I walked around Broadway, through Central Park, and had dinner at a friend's café who collected old watches.

"I would be happy to buy your Russian issue nineteen fifty-five watch for a good sum of money," he mentioned to Dimitri over a thick New York sandwich. Dimitri quickly shook his head. My friend looked at me curiously, shocked that money didn't always talk.

"Oh my gosh," I whispered to Dimitri when Yuri had gotten up to go to the bathroom. "That's Laurie Anderson over there." I knew her because of Sergey, who raved about her genius talents and his adoration for the avant-garde music she composed and performed. I had to get her photo for him. When I asked, she was so nice, posing sweetly with Dimitri as well.

"She's an incredibly famous artist," I told him. Laurie Anderson beamed, looking expectantly at Dimitri.

"Very nice," he said to his sandwich.

Yuri, Dimitri, and I all headed back to Los Angeles together.

"Can you take me to the mountains?" Dimitri asked me shyly on the west coast. "I would like to collect bugs."

I drove him to Franklin Canyon, a nature reserve near my house. He jumped out with his backpack, ready to explore a climate and ecology that doesn't exist anywhere in the high latitudes of Russia.

"Can you come and get me in four hours? Maybe five?" He called over his shoulder. Later that afternoon, Dimitri laid out a bunch of dead insects on my oak coffee table, pointing and telling Yuri and I about each bug. If only Laurie Anderson could witness his adoration for the silverfish.

The three of us spent the next day at Disneyland, and then drove to visit my dad south of the city. Dimitri decided to stay with him and his girlfriend for a few days so he could explore the Mojave Desert and collect more specimens to take back home for his colleagues. When I saw him days later, in a shirt and jacket at my parents' house for the wedding celebration, he was tanned and grinning from ear to ear.

It was a beautiful spring night, the kind where the moon gets close to the grass and the pool, and the air is cool. The John Lautner-designed house had accordion doors that could open onto the backyard and extend the huge living room into the green twilight. My mother had bought a three-tier white cake with pastel flowers for us.

"Feed it to each other! Give her some sugar!" A few people started yelling as Yuri and I cut our first piece together in the American tradition.

I coyly smeared some frosting across Yuri's nose and cheeks. He blinked, then shoved an entire piece of sticky, sweet dessert into my face.

There we were, almost six-thousand miles from where we'd started, covered in wedding cake. All around us in various parts of the world, our friends were strumming guitars and up to their elbows in art, but for the moment all that mattered was that open space of back yard backlit by my parents' home. I didn't realize it, but my Russian guys weren't the only ones moving farther from our group and the underground scene we'd shared for so long. The boundaries that had defined my life were expanding too.

♦ Please Welcome Joanna Stingray

Between Los Angeles and Russia is half the world. Half the world is a lot of ground to cover, and suddenly I was covering it about once a month! I was now working on getting Kino an American record deal for their *Groupa Kroovy* album – Andrei Krisanov designed the post-war, Russian avant-garde cover that reminded me of Kazimir Malevich or El Lissitzky – as well as working with Melodiya to have my first record released in Russia. I managed to get Kino's song "Boshetunmai" and my song "Tsoi Song" on an upcoming Western album release called *MIR – Reggae From Around The World*. What time I didn't spend on planes I spent on hold with some music executive or in the studio sipping tea with lemon and honey.

In June of 1988, I went with Games to play a big hall in Tallinn, Estonia. It was set up through the Rock Club. While I was stoked to be part of the Games trip, I was disappointed I wouldn't be with Yuri on his birthday. Every so often I would think back to the days that all the boys and I would sit in Boris' kitchen with the smell of cigarettes and music filling the room. Now, Kino was on tour in the complete opposite direction of Games, and Yuri, Viktor, and I were apart.

Tallinn was a beautiful city – cobbled streets, dark alleys, red roofs, and streets as colorful as if licked by pastel paintbrushes. At the concert I sang three of my songs that I'd written with the guys in Games, jumping up and down with them and getting high off the energy. It was ironic that in this haven tucked just outside what would become the boundaries of the Russian Federation, I found my voice as an American-Russian performer.

When I returned to Leningrad, only Yuri was there to meet me. He told me that Viktor had lost the small studio he'd been renting and that he'd gone with Natasha to her *dacha* in Riga for the summer.

"It was too complicated, and expensive, to rent in Leningrad," Yuri tried to explain as I fell onto the couch, disheartened. "He will be based in Moscow after the summer and go with Kino for tours."

I could tell it disappointed Yuri as well, his angular face contorted into a thick frown. Our silver lining was that we both knew Viktor was incredibly happy with Natasha, but even that happiness couldn't alleviate the stress of having to figure out how to find money.

"It's the only thing that makes me nervous with your new manager," I said to Yuri cautiously. "I don't really know him, but he controls the whole business side of Kino. Are you sure he's not taking advantage of the band? He's the one who books the tours, and without Marianna how do we know he's not keeping some of the money for himself?"

"Jo-an-na," Yuri drew out in his thick accent, as he always did. It was his catchphrase, a mantra I knew so well. He shook his head. "Do not worry."

I promised I would try not to.

◆

I decided to have a few of the artists – Oleg Kotelnikov, Andrei Medvedev, and Inal Savchenko – help me shoot my music video for "Tsoi Song." We barely had any money to make it, but these prodigal masterminds came up with the most brilliant, artistic ideas.

The three of them made collage drawings of themes in my song and did stop-motion animation to make it ebb and flow. With an old super 8 film camera, they filmed Yuri and I walking around Leningrad and then drew right onto the negative of the film. We went to a classroom next, and Yuri and I danced through rows of desks filled with wide-eyed children, their faces painted and us in dark sunglasses and black clothes. I extended my hands to them and we danced in a circle, a group of mismatched banshees holding hands. The camera work was raw and shaky, but the angles were bright and mesmerizing. To this day it is one of my favorite videos I have ever done.

I talked my way through customs at the Leningrad airport to smuggle the film footage back to edit in Los Angeles, along with more pieces of art from my friends. I had no clue that this would be the last time I or anyone else could leave Russia with this kind of art. A day or two after I left, the Soviets were preparing for the first ever Sotheby's auction of Soviet contemporary art, when Sotheby's appraisers going through the official art saw some unofficial works and informed the government these crazy pieces would

■ Stills from the music video for my song "Tsoi Song (Ye Man)" with collage stop-motion animations by Oleg Kotelnikov, Andrei Medvedev, and Inal Savchenko.

bring in the most money. The Soviets suddenly realized that the colorful, silly, amateur art with which people were just walking out of the country was in demand and valuable. They immediately had customs stop any art being taken abroad.

"Finally," I muttered some time later when a pair of agents at the airport confiscated a small drawing I had. "Now you understand how innovative and worthy my friends' art is!"

At the end of August that same year, I flew with Sergey, Afrika, and a big group to Stockholm for a performance of Pop Mechanics and an art show of the New Artists. The Swedes went nuts for the concert and art show, incredibly receptive to Russian contemporary culture.

Sergey was over the moon to finally be playing to an expanding audience. The event was advertised as a "spectacle" instead of a music concert, which he also loved.

"What can you tell us about this performance people are going to see?" they asked him on live radio. "In English, please."

He rolled his eyes. Sergey did not like to speak in his limited English. "Hello, my name is Sergey," he replied. That was that.

From Sweden I flew back to Moscow to join Games at a big Moscow festival called "Youth, Culture, *Perestroika.*" It was a concert set to initiate a regular series of events to be called The Rock Clubs Parade. That day, rock clubs of Moscow, Leningrad, Sverdlovsk, and Kharkov came together to organize it.

At one point, Sasha Lipnitsky stepped onto the stage. "Good evening. It's my second time on the stage tonight, but I'm more nervous now. It's difficult to find words to describe the person who will come out on stage with Games now. It's an American singer. We have seen and heard quite a few American singers in Moscow. But there's no one in the U.S. or anywhere else in the world who has done so much for the Soviet rock as Joanna Stingray." He paused, beaming. I felt goosebumps down my arms. I had done so much for everyone else, I hadn't even thought to ask anyone to do anything for me. And yet they were, all of them, unprompted. Vitia nudged me and winked, and I jumped onto the stage with him. "Please welcome Joanna Stingray and Games!"

◆

While I was in Moscow, I met with Melodiya to finalize my upcoming album. I also met Natasha for the first time, at Lipnitsky's *dacha*. Viktor, Natasha, Afrika and his stunning actress wife, Irena, and I spread out around a dark table as Lipnitsky's wife Ina made us a delicious meal.

It was so obvious how in love Viktor was. Natasha was very different from Marianna, thin as porcelain with sharp eyes and a warm air around her smoky laugh. To me, I always saw her as a Russian Audrey Hepburn – stoic and wise, natural without heavy makeup or loud words.

"Thank you," she said to me teasingly, throwing an arm around Viktor, "for sharing this great man with me."

It was the first time I'd seen Viktor in a while, so later in the city I asked if I could interview him about the changes that were happening.

"I will try in English," he told me nervously. It was not particularly easy for him. As he crossed one leg over the other on the chair, leaning to one side imperceptibly uncomfortable, he lit a cigarette and let it smoke.

"Why did you decide to act in a film?" I started the interview.

"Well, I don't know why," he said with a shrug. "All the things I do in my life, is because it's interesting for me. That's the only reason."

"So why do you think you found acting interesting?"

"There is no films for young people. I would like to try to make a film for young people." He paused, sucking in his cigarette and exhaling slowly. "Here, in cinema, there is no real hero. No hero like Superman, a hero like a god who can do everything – fly the streets, fight everybody. Young people here do need a hero, and maybe I'm not good enough to do a hero, but if there's nothing then I want to begin it. I want young people to have their own heroes. They look to the west [for] heroes, to Arnold Schwarzenegger or Bruce Lee, but it's not their own heroes."

"You're already a hero, Viktor," I told him softly. "Your music, it's fearless." He shook his head, his dark hair falling towards his bright eyes.

"Speaking of music, tell me why you haven't recorded an album with Melodiya?"

■ Left to right: Igor Tikhomirov, Afrika, Sergey Kuryokhin, me, Yuri Kasparyan, Gustav Guryanov, and Viktor Tsoi, Red Square, Moscow, 1986.

"They published one of our records without us, without asking us. That's a problem. I don't want anybody to do things like that. Also, they don't want to give us enough time in the studio to do this record."

"But wouldn't you be able to sell more records with them? They've got such a big business."

"It's better if I do this record on the tape and lots of cooperatives can sell it everywhere," Viktor declared. He had the type of spirit unshaken by empty promises of fame and fortune.

When I asked about the theme of his lyrics on his hugely popular album *Groupa Kroovy*, he paused, thinking through the English words in his head carefully.

"This album is very heroic," he started slowly. "And very romantic. The main idea in all the songs is the person. If you are human, you have to do something. I don't know what, but just do. Not only live your life, but do something in the world. Just break anything, just break *any jail inside you*." He leaned back. "Difficult to explain. It's not because my English is not well – I cannot answer this question in Russia too. Everything I mean is inside this album."

The way he talked was pure poetry, enlightened and humble. He was considerate, expressive, heroic.

◆ Holidays 1988

The "Capitán" was coming to the City of Angels.

On November 13, 1988, *The Washington Post* published an article titled "The Anarchist at the Keyboard," a profile on Sergey Kuryokhin who was on his way to America for an exhaustive tour. He would be participating in the Thelonious Monk Jazz Competition, jamming at a session in the Arizona desert with New Age musicians, playing concerts in New York, Philadelphia, Chicago, Washington D.C., and Boston, visiting MIT's state-of-the-art Wang Media Center, and spending a week's residence with a student band at Oberlin College. The visit would end at the New Music America festival in Miami, in early December.

But Sergey's first stop would be Los Angeles. I quickly put together a party at my house to celebrate his arrival, packing my red house tucked into Beverly Glen with my friends, parents, Senator Alan Cranston's son and environmentalist Kim Cranston, Frederick and Billie Weisman, and a large group of Russian emigres who were old acquaintances of Sergey. In the entirety of the four years I'd been going to Russia, I had spent very little time with Russians living in the States. I found them to be very different than my friends in Russia. Many of them expressed hatred for Russia with deep scowls and gruff words – gone were their strong ties to the Motherland that the guys I knew well kept in their songs and their hearts.

Sergey and his Russian friends were all incredibly surprised with the small house. Every inch of space was filled with Russian art, posters, photos, and memorabilia. It was

■ Sergey and me at my house in Los Angeles, November 1988. The collage with Stalin that we are standing in front of is an artwork by Viktor Tsoi.

a shrine and a manifestation of obsessive years spent with evocative music.

"A mini-museum," someone said with a toothy grin.

Sergey, in a pair of jeans, multi-colored sweater, and page boy haircut, performed on my old brown piano. He made it sound like a Steinway, filling the tight room and improvising new songs that swept everyone away. I remember watching him under the Russian paintings, his sparkling eyes traveling through the room and connecting with his audience.

At the end of the night when most had gone, I fell asleep on the sofa next to Sergey and one of his oldest friends as they spoke for hours. I could tell they had never expected to see each other ever again, a feeling that I knew well – fear that pieces of your heart would end up scattered across the globe, rotting and sore.

The next day I drove Sergey up Laurel Canyon to drop him off at Frank Zappa's house for the day.

"Jo, come?" Sergey asked as we sat in the driveway.

I was already halfway out of my car. Who could pass up seeing these two eccentric icons face to face?! Zappa was in a plain white shirt with a mustache and stubble like freckles against his chin.

"Sergey!" he said easily. "I've heard a lot about you!"

I sat with them as these two wild and crazy geniuses talked about sound and music, airplanes and their thoughts about the world. Finally, as they retreated to the studio for

■ Sergey with Frank Zappa and composer Nicolas Slonimsky at Zappa's Laurel Canyon home and studio, Los Angeles, 1988.

■ Website for Sergey Kuryokhin Center for Art, founded in 2004, St. Petersburg. Accessed July 15, 2020.

the day with the famous Russian emigre composer, Nicolas Slonimsky, I decided to say goodbye and snapped a shot of them with my Polaroid camera, freezing the three characters in ink. *Legends*, I thought to myself as I turned towards my car. *Sergey can only go up from here.*

When I recently asked Alex, who had been with Sergey on the East Coast, how he did in the Thelonious Monk competition, he almost spit out the water he was drinking.

"He failed completely! They hated him. He didn't obey the rules and went completely against everything." Alex stopped to laugh. "He is a rebel. He idolized Monk as a revolutionary, but this contest was part of the establishment. Sergey followed his deviant nature and ruined it."

"What!" I screamed. "I didn't know that!"

"What did you expect?" Alex asked with a soft smile.

"Sergey must have loved that. All the commotion."

"He was furious," Alex informed me.

Sergey was always furious, though. Furiously passionate, furiously wild, furiously throwing himself into the deep end until the ripples of sound turned into waves of tsunami proportions. It was his dream to overwhelm the self, to be absolutely unavoidable and unmistaken. At the Knitting Factory, dubbed by *The Washington Post* as "a Manhattan nightclub that books the rudest of the new," Sergey dragged himself under the grand piano he was playing and lifted it above his torso with his legs before letting it crash back down over him. These stunts were somehow acceptable as a compliment to his visionary music, and the crowd there loved him. He was caviar, he was king, an acquired taste but indisputably of the highest, top quality.

Speaking of rock kings and gods, Boris was meanwhile having some drama of his own. While he was touring the States for his Radio Silence tour, his bassist Sasha Titov's wife, Irina, joined the group and suddenly she and Boris were together. I think this had been brewing for years. I always saw Irina's affection for Boris. Supposedly after the tour, Sasha and Irina went home together and Boris went back to his wife Lyuda, but neither relationship lasted that much longer. Boris and Irina left their respective spouses and moved in together. Very few of us were surprised.

There we were though – Sergey, Boris, and I – in the same country and worlds apart again. It would continually baffle me how divergent everyone's paths were becoming, and as proud as I was of all the success, I missed the more intimate days of the underground movement. In the center of my living room surrounded by all the Russian graffiti art, loud and bold colors and faces that, though beautiful, were inanimate and silent, I stood in sock feet with hands on my hips.

"Just because their dreams may be in America," I told the painted, frozen figures. "Doesn't mean mine ever were."

The next week in November 1988, I boarded a plane to Russia. Viktor had sent me word that there would be a big concert in Moscow in memory of Sasha Bashlachev.

"Do you think you could get back for it?" he had asked, his voice far away.

I smiled into the phone, remembering Sasha's sweet face and his inspirational words. *But days go on, and the times, they change… chime on, my heart… we'll roar, we'll whistle, we'll rattle.*

"I'm already on my way."

♦

On November 20, I stood in a packed Dvorets Sporta to honor the greatest bard poet with rock 'n roll.

It was one of the rare times I saw Mike Naumenko and his group, Zoopark – a solid sound through the bigger and better system the hall finally provided for the former underground bands. Kino and Alisa had gotten so big that they had some clout to negotiate for the things they wanted. Kinchev came on stage with his group, descending through a cloud of smoke and stalking the length of the stage until his heart poured out of his words.

"*Muie Vmeste!*" he screamed over and over with the crowd, backed by just the drums and the energy of thousands of pulsing bodies. "We're together!"

He gave me a kiss as he passed me in the wings, his body small and soft after such an intense performance. I watched as Kino took the stage and Viktor stepped up to the damp mic.

"Guys, now Joanna Stingray will sing one song for you. She flew in from the U.S. especially for this concert. She knew Sasha very well."

I walked onto the stage as Viktor caught my eye and nodded. With my sunglasses on I purposefully couldn't see the massive crowd through the dark shadows, but I could feel their heartbeats and lungs.

"*Privet!*" I heard my voice echo around me like a planetary ring. "Good evening. I knew Sasha well, and in his music, I always felt the power of his soul. He will always be with me in my heart." I glanced upwards, where I knew that through the ceiling the city met the sky. "Sasha, this is the first time in my life that I'm going to sing in Russian, and it's a tribute to you."

I had wanted to do something special to honor Sasha, so I'd learned the words to a poignant Games' song called "Memorial." The lyrics were written specifically for Games by Leningrad poet Andrei Soloviev. I hoped Sasha appreciated it as much as the audience did. When I finished, they roared and I blew a kiss upwards, thinking maybe somewhere up there, the bard would catch it. As I left the stage, I kissed Yuri as well for good measure. I heard people scream and stomp.

Viktor returned to the stage to join his band. I crouched behind the curtain, exhausted and invigorated, to watch him just as he'd watched me.

"I'd also like to say a few words to defend myself from the *Moskovsky Komsomolets* newspaper," he said softly, bowing his head over the mic. "Moscow seems to be the only city, and I have been to many recently, where dancing turns out to be criminal, where a wish to give a bunch of flowers to artists is a cause to be beaten. I do not want to raise any scandal here. But if there are any members of the press here, maybe we can somehow change the situation. At least at this concert it dawned on officials to remove chairs from the stalls. We had an agreement – they invited me to their office and asked me, Viktor, what should we do? Your audience have broken all the chairs. I told them, the only way to save your chairs is to remove them so that people could dance. They said fine, if I talk to the fans and appeal to their reason and order. But when we arrived at our second concert, I saw that the chairs were not only there, but there were more of them than before. And, of course, they were broken during the concert. I now feel free from any obligations." To the cheers and raised fists of the crowd, Viktor opened his set. Every single person there,

■ Sasha Bashlachev in one of his rare concert hall performances, Leningrad, 1987.

over ten thousand people who knew the words to each song, stood and started to dance.

It shook me to my core, the way the building rocked with the inspiration and aggression of rock'n roll. *Holy shit*, I thought as I sang along from behind. *Rock'n roll will never be a subtle art. To not get swept up in it is like fighting the ocean tide during a storm.* It made me want to keep singing, to keep performing.

All of a sudden, a Bashlachev song started to play over the sound system. Viktor smiled, initially playing along on his guitar and singing, but his mic and amp were turned off. He turned and walked to the back of the stage, sitting on an amp and listening to the power of Sasha's recorded voice and wise words. I'm sure many people in the audience hadn't heard Sasha before, having only come for the bands they knew were performing, but their reverent silence confirmed the importance of the young bard. To hear his voice reverberate so loudly in such a huge space brought tears of joy to my face. He deserved this, to be heard and remembered as something big and great. In that moment, I saw his immortality in front of me, and I continued to sing along.

When the recording finished, a woman's voice came over the sound system. "Dear members of the audience, this concludes our concert. We thank you for your attention. Please keep order while exiting the auditorium. We wish you all the best and hope to see you again."

The crowd refused to leave. They started stomping, hollering, screaming for more of Kino. Viktor came out to say something, but his mic was still dead. I could feel the fury of the crowd.

"Dear members of the audience! You are leaving the Palace of Sports! The first to leave are people in the stalls, followed by those in the upper rows. The program of our evening is finished. We ask to keep the order and be careful when descending the stairs."

No one moved. They stood together, legs braced and arms raised, shouting over the woman's voice and instruction. This was the new Soviet Union, and I realized it no longer bred citizens but tigers. Finally, Viktor heard feedback as his mic was turned back on. He jumped up and grabbed it.

"Guys, it's really unclear what happened here. It had been agreed in advance that once we have finished our set, Sasha's song was supposed to be put on – this very song 'The Time of Little Bells' that we have just heard. But for some reason, I don't know, it was put on much sooner than planned. It's really a shame that again things worked not in the way we wanted them to!" Huge applause. Viktor waited for a moment, his angular face deep in thought, before continuing. "This song was supposed to be the concert's finale. So, you understand that it would not really be appropriate for me to keep playing after it…"

Viktor knew it was Bashlachev's night, whose words should be the last to end the concert. As he walked offstage towards me, I could see it in his eyes that he knew we'd have many more chances to have the last word. Not just him, but me as well.

"Next time," he said, throwing his arm over my shoulders. "We will sing more. And you will too."

◆

"I just want you to see what my life is like in Russia."

I had said these words to Geoffrey and Dee consistently for the past couple of years, so the day after Christmas, 1988, they landed in Helsinki with me and our friend Deb.

At the Hertz rental car counter, a huge sign demanded that UNDER NO CIRCUMSTANCES ARE ANY OF THESE VEHICLES TO BE TAKEN INTO THE SOVIET UNION. We climbed into our car, Geoffrey, Dee, and Deb squeezing in with the massive amount of gear I'd brought for the life I was building with Yuri.

"We ready?" I called from the driver's seat.

"Let's do it!" Dee and Deb hollered.

"Um, Jo, is this part of a treadmill?" Geoffrey asked, his head touching the top of the car as he looked down at the black object he was straddling.

I drove us down the winding, blue roads of Finland until the entire forest turned into stretches of damp tree stumps and then nothing except the Russian tundra. The snow stretched for miles in every direction. As we passed a military pillbox on a rise with Kalashnikov rifles sticking out of it, right before the border, my friends became silent.

At the checkpoint we all exited the car and went in. I could feel the familiar anxiety like a cage of butterflies in my chest as I approached the official and met his dark, dull eyes.

"You don't have an auto visa. You cannot come in here with this car," he said numbly.

"What do you mean?!" I could feel Geoffrey and Dee's eyes nervously shifting between me and the car outside. "Do you know who I am? You have to let me in!" I started pulling out my *People* articles and all the Russian articles about me, letting them spill onto the ground and cover his shiny shoes as I shoved the rest up to his face. I had pictures of Yuri, of Kino, of Boris and me.

The border guards blinked at each other, perplexed and uncomfortable. I could tell they knew I was legit, but they had no idea how to take this into consideration.

As the guards grouped closely together to confer, the three of us were approached by three Finns, who had the only other car at the border. They had gotten there before us but had been detained for the past ten hours.

"All because of a fucking hunting rifle in the trunk!" One spat out. We all turned and looked at the guards. They jumped, shifting farther away as we stared at them. They had no idea what to do with any of us!

"Hey," I said, an idea brewing. I could tell Geoffrey and Dee were nervous. Deb sat on a hard chair by the windows, knitting. There was absolutely no way we could stay for another ten hours plus in this dingy, concrete cave, watching Deb try to make a pair of socks. I had to get us out of here.

Inching closer to the puddle of guards, I asked to use the phone on the wall to call my mother-in-law. In an excited voice I began rapidly talking into the phone.

"What do you mean I have to be at the Rock Club by eight o'clock? They're holding us at the border, I'm afraid we're not going to make it. They won't let us through." I could see the guards getting as nervous as my friends. I hung up the phone, made my way to the car, grabbed a duffel, and disappeared into the narrow bathroom. Five minutes later, I reappeared in full concert regalia, a la John Gautier, all in black with lace, and a pound of makeup under my styled hair.

Every jaw dropped to the floor.

"You have got to let me go," I pleaded, marching right up to the group of officials.

■ Kolya Vasin.

■ Everywhere you looked at Kolya's house, there was another mini-shrine to The Beatles or to John Lennon.

"Please, you have to help me. I'm going to miss the concert."

Next thing we knew, Deb, Dee, Geoffrey, and I were back in the car, being waved through before they even checked the contents of the vehicle.

"Oooooh mmmmmmy gooooooooood," Dee drew out, bouncing in her seat.

"This is actually a treadmill, isn't it?" Geoffrey asked from the back.

From the border we followed a two-way highway through a forest dripping with wet snow. As I came through a line of shadows on the road, all of these Russians appeared out of nowhere. They drove up right next to our car in the opposing lane and hung out of the windows, shaking big square bottles of vodka at us.

"You want to buy? Buy! Buy!" They shouted, honking and motioning for us to pull over.

"Keep driving, Jo," Dee instructed. "You are not allowed to stop this vehicle again until we get there."

In the rearview mirror of our rogue car, I could see some of them rolling their fists over each other, indicating change money – hard currency. I gunned it. My friends hadn't even been in Russia a full hour and already they were kind of traumatized.

We checked them into the Pulkovskaya, a Finnish hotel in a spacious, illuminated square.

The first night I took them to a party at one of my friends at the Swedish Consulate, and the next day they came with me to Yuri's to see my new home and meet his parents. We had dinner at Kolya Vasin's place, surrounded by The Beatles.

"It's quite a remarkable place you've got here," Geoffrey told him. Kolya beamed. "I am the walrus!"

Geoffrey put his arm around Dee, unsure how to reply.

Kolya approached them and put his arms around them both. "All you need is love," he added merrily, as the three stood together in the middle of the room.

"Should we go visit Tamara Falalayeva?" I asked, jumping to the rescue. She had a private home in Leningrad, and her son was married to Dee's sister.

"I! Love! Him!" Dee said as we left Kolya and his big smile.

"Did you hear that, Kolya?" Geoffrey shouted back up towards the apartment building.

His eyes sparkled. "She loves you, yeah, yeah, yeah!"

♦

Another day we tried to have lunch at a big hotel, but despite the lavish exterior, inside they had no food! We tried ordering everything on the menu, and they couldn't give us any of it. We ended up staring at a table of beets, brown bread, and hard-boiled eggs.

"This is a very Russian meal," I finally said.

"Oh, we're in Russia?" Geoffrey said dryly, giving me a wink. "I hadn't noticed."

We were sitting on two twin beds – Dee, Geoffrey, and I – facing a black marketer. I had arranged for him to meet with my friends, and now here we were smelling cigarette smoke and staring at black lacquer boxes and caviar.

"I can trade you this," Dee said, holding up Levi Jeans.

"Eh, whatever," the man replied, clearly not interested.

"I didn't know I was supposed to bring great, expensive stuff to Russia," Dee whispered to me. "All I have are these shitty, second-rate clothes."

"Okay, you can have this. Or this." The man directed our attention away from the shiny lacquer boxes and bulging caviar.

Dee looked at his stuff skeptically. "I don't know..."

"Alright girls," Geoffrey said, standing up. "Watch this." He pulled out his Brooks Brothers pants, his L.L. Bean sweater, Woolridge shirt, and a pile of preppy, classy clothes.

"Ooh!" The black marketer's eyes lit up. "Very, very good!" He knew all the brands, throwing anything Geoffrey wanted at us in exchange for his coveted clothes.

We got back to the hotel room and threw bags and bags of stuff onto the bed.

"Deb, you've got to come see this sweetie!" Dee sang. "We got *so much stuff!*"

"Oh really?" Deb said, looking up from her knitting needles. "I called some black marketers from the hotel phone and told them I'd meet them in the lobby."

"What?!" Geoffrey yelled, making us all jump. "What on earth have you done?! In what world do you think it's a good idea to invite them here? I want nothing more to do with it! If I meet any more black marketers I'll be walking around in the snow in my underwear!"

We decided to leave the hotel when they were scheduled to come. As we were piling back into our blue Volvo with Finnish plates, we saw the guys pulling into the parking lot. I could recognize their denim jackets, penny loafers, jeans – the way they tried to look Western in the middle of the Siberian winter, ten degrees below zero.

The two guys caught sight of us and came up to the car. Geoffrey scowled as he rolled down his driver's window and they began speaking in Russian, with shady deals and crooked offers. Deb leaned forward from the back seat, nodding with a toothy smile with no clue what they were saying.

The next thing I remember were two men in suits running out of the hotel, yelling at us. As I watched from the passenger seat, the two black marketers jumped into the back seat beside Dee and Deb.

"KGB! KGB!" They screamed. "Drive! Drive!"

Geoffrey peeled away from the curb, suddenly a wheel man driving us around with eyes as big as coffee mugs.

"I'm going to lose my law license!" he shouted.

"We can't go back there." Dee was leaning forward, shaking my shoulders. I could feel both of their fear.

"I'm Deb," Deb said with a smile to the black marketeer sitting awkwardly next to her, smashed between two seats. She extended her hand.

We dropped them off on a nondescript street corner.

"It's gonna be okay," I said quickly, my mind racing. I was furious at these black marketers using us as a way to escape. "We'll go back to the hotel and just go to our rooms. If they come to question us, I can come up with something."

We spent hours in the hotel room waiting, the four of us sitting and staring at the walls and coming up with excuses and answers to questions we, ultimately, were never asked. Lucky for us, nothing happened. That was the thing about Russia. You either couldn't do anything or could get away with everything.

◆

On New Year's Eve, Yuri and I joined my American friends on Nevsky Prospekt. We walked down the street between booths of steaming food and bubbling drinks, people talking, singing, and eating pink and brown cones of ice cream. As we got close to Boris' apartment, we could see a huge crowd in front of the door. Pushing past the warm bodies, I remember inside the eight flights of stairs were packed with kids crouched and sprawled on every step. Everyone was singing Boris' songs, drinking vodka, burning candles, and writing on the walls. It was one of the only places I ever saw graffiti in Russia.

"We love you, Boris," people howled up the stairs as they wrote the same words. "Boris, you are god!"

When I got to the top floor, I saw Boris appear at his door, motioning me, Yuri, Dee, Deb, and Geoffrey inside while his fans started screaming his name. He held his hand high and waved, a vogue Jesus blessing the disciples.

Inside, everyone was spread through the apartment not dissimilar to all the people lounging in the stairs. How funny that all that separated us was a door. A color TV was playing Gorbachev's New Year's address, the same speech that marked all the different, passing years. Boris moved in front of the set and popped in a home video of him and Annie Lenox in the back of a giant convertible, cruising down Ventura Boulevard and singing. In the video, the sky was a bright and sunny blue, and we all crowded around its imagined warmth while our asses froze to the apartment chairs.

The next night, January 1, I took my friends along with the Kino band to Moscow. We went by train to Sasha Lipnitsky's house, the bassist for Zvuki Mu who, as Geoffrey recalled, was in the icon-smuggling business. Dee, Geoffrey, and Deb headed out for a bus tour of the sites while I went around with the band. At that time, there was a big scandal that the new American Embassy had been bugged by the Russian workers who had built it, a rumor that the bus guide apparently denied.

"Okay, guys," I told them the next day. "I need to stay with Kino in Moscow, but my friend Big Misha is going to take you to the train tonight. It will be easy!"

That night, under a slice of moon curved like a gash in the sky, Misha dropped my friends off at the Russian train with the articulated instructions not to speak any English. Foreigners were not allowed on these cheaper trains. Deb was in one train car, and Dee and Geoffrey were in another.

"My friends are tired, and they are going to sleep," Misha told the conductor. "So, don't bother them."

At some point in total darkness, Dee and Geoffrey heard a knock at the door. The conductor opened it. As Dee and Geoffrey stared, the man said something in Russian. They blinked.

"*Nyet*," Geoffrey finally said.

The conductor narrowed his eyes, squinting through the dim cabin to make out my friends' figures. Without another word, he disappeared.

"What do we do?" Dee whispered.

The conductor reappeared, knocking as he entered through the sliding car door.

"Okay, the gig is up, honey," Geoffrey whispered back to Dee. He stood. "*Ya ne gavaryu pa rooski*," he said with his hands up. He heart was visible through his shirt thumping wildly against his chest.

Dee started pulling out cigarettes, ball point pens, and pantyhose, shoving them into the conductor's arms while pleading. "Please don't stick us out in the Russian tundra. Please."

The conductor started laughing his eyes lighting up at the gifts. His arms full, he nodded at Geoffrey. "I just wanted to know if you wanted your receipt?"

In the morning, the three of them had to drag their tired, frozen bodies from the train to the subway in Leningrad, back to the hotel and the rental car.

"Okay," Dee said, rubbing her hands together as snow fell around the blue vehicle. "What are the chances this baby is going to start?"

They followed Cyrillic signs they could not understand out of the city, somehow making it to the border.

"Boy, I hope they let me out of here," Deb said from where she'd been silent in the back. "I don't have any stamps or anything showing I've been in the country."

"What?" Geoffrey slammed on the breaks, too close to the customs to turn around. "Deb, tell me how that's possible!"

"I don't know," she said, curls falling into her eyes. "No one gave them to me!"

"Great," Geoffrey said, as the guards began making their way towards the car. "You have no proof of admittance, and I'm driving a car in someone else's name that was never supposed to leave Finland!"

"Well, at least if we go down, we go down together," Dee sang.

Miraculously, my friends managed to get out of the country. Years later we still laugh about the unpredictable, risky business we had together behind the Iron Curtain.

"I truly don't know how you managed to last there for longer than a month," Geoffrey told me as we sat at a dinner table in Beverly Hills and reminisced.

"I never got used to the cold," I told him.

"Oh, it was cold? I didn't even notice." Geoffrey leaned back, indulging in the warmth of the fireplace behind him. "I was too busy handing my pants out to black marketers and smuggling a Volvo and Deb in and out of Finland!"

♦ The Happiest Place on Earth

The day 'the three musketeers' united there was an ebullient sun in the sky over the hot roads stretching through Los Angeles. I surprised Yuri and Viktor at the airport with a stretch limo and champagne, wrapping my arms around their broad shoulders and ushering them into the car.

"First stop – Guitar Center!" I told them excitedly, watching them pick through the small bottles of alcohol and roll around the long seats. I wanted to show them everything, do whatever made them happy. There was no better feeling than seeing the goofy smiles on their faces as they stuck their heads out the windows and sang.

Like Boris and Yuri had, Viktor wanted to spend the whole day in the guitar room trying the hundreds of shiny, colorful instruments hanging on the walls.

"This place was made for people like you," manager Dave Weiderman said proudly.

"People like me," Viktor said from under his feathery hair, "were made for places like this."

On the way to my house, we stopped, and I took a classic shot of the two of them on a Beverly Hills street, their dark eyes and chiseled faces shaded by palm trees.

The first night we went to a Japanese restaurant where Viktor could have all the '*tsoi* sauce' he wanted. I took them to Venice Beach to watch the surfers, skaters, and street kids eating corn dogs and smoking weed. We went into all the hippie stores, rode horses, devoured whole lobsters in bibs at the famous Palm Restaurant with my grandma, and relaxed at my parents' Malibu beach house.

"Look, a dolphin!" I stood on the balcony that stretched over the icy blue water, face to face with the horizon. Met with silence, I turned around. Viktor and Yuri were spread-eagle on lounge chairs, wrapped in terrycloth robes and passed out under the salty sun.

I think Viktor was so happy to have a little time to be somewhere nobody knew him, where nobody asked for autographs or took photos. It was just him and his best friend, the way it had been before fame, the two of them taking walks on the beach with me and watching the sun set over the ocean.

On their third day there, I decided it was time to blow their socks off completely. They both knew I never, ever cooked, mainly because I couldn't. I sat them down at the dinner table with napkins over their eyes as they joked that I would burn the house down.

"Quick, what's our escape plan?" Viktor said loudly to Yuri.

"I can hear you!" I yelled from the kitchen.

"Just get the fuck out," Yuri replied to Viktor. "Run, don't stop."

I brought out a huge salad with cheese, chicken, tomatoes, croutons, lettuce, and hard- boiled eggs. As the guys stared at it in disbelief, I loaded the table with grapes, home-made chocolate chip cookies, and wine.

"Who are you?" Yuri asked, his mouth full of food. "And what have you done with my wife?"

That was the first and the last time I ever cooked for anybody.

The next day we went to Disneyland. I stood at the entrance gates between Viktor and Yuri with tears in my eyes. Viktor and I had dreamed of being here together so many times throughout the years, sitting in the corner at *tusofkas* while he talked about all the rides and foods he imagined were there.

"Jo," he whispered from my left. "This is a dream come true."

It was like being a little kid again. Here was the biggest rockstar in the Soviet Union, a hero to the youth and practically a deity to his fans, going around and around on a carousel with a smile so huge it could burst.

We went on almost every ride in the park. My favorite photo I took is of the two of them standing under a sign that said *Disneyland! The Happiest Place on Earth!* Viktor's boyish smile consumes his entire face.

Back in Los Angeles, I took them to Frederick Weisman's house to see his world-renowned art collection. He had over one thousand pieces crowding his home, the work of Henry Moore, Warhol, Alberto Giacometti, Picasso, Rodchenko, Rodin, Hockney, De Kooning, and Lichtenstein.

"I buy from the heart," he told Yuri and Viktor. "That's why I've got such an unusual collection. The only thing any of my pieces have in common is me."

Viktor and Yuri giggled their way through the house, staring at the naked sculptures.

We drove an hour south to visit my dad, me speeding along the desert with both guys singing at the top of their lungs to the cassette music I brought. My dad was ecstatic to see them, asking them about their lives and laughing hysterically at their straight faces and sarcastic words.

"Let me take a photo," I begged.

My dad sat proudly between Viktor and Yuri on his salmon-colored sofa, a hand on each of their legs. Afterwards, he drove us to a restaurant in his big, brown Cadillac.

"Do either of you drive?" My dad asked Viktor and Yuri as we climbed back into the car, full and warm. They both shook their heads. My dad nodded, turned on the car, and drove us to an empty parking lot.

"Well," he said, sitting back in the driver's seat. "Who's first?"

Yuri and Viktor took turns putting their cement feet on the gas pedal, speeding in inconsistent circles and refusing to stop.

"Freedom!" Viktor sang, making donuts with the car. "Freedom!"

Right when it seemed as if we had done everything we could possibly do, my friend Mark Rosenthal called me.

"How about a shooting range?" he asked me excitedly.

"Shooting?" Yuri said, overhearing. "I like that." Viktor nodded enthusiastically.

Next thing I knew I was standing in noise cancelling headphones between the two guys, holding a Magnum .357 revolver. Yuri had picked the same weapon, but Viktor had chosen a machine gun just like the ones he saw in action movies.

"Ready?" Mark yelled. "One, two…"

Viktor opened fire, his whole body pounding against the pavement.

We all stood, staring.

"Woo!" He screamed when he'd finished his round. He turned to us, beaming.

"Well, I guess I'll call it a day," Mark said, putting his own gun down.

I looked at Yuri and Viktor. I wasn't quite ready to call it a day yet. I didn't know if I ever would be. The three of us could be on a deserted island, nothing but sand and salt and Viktor's machine gun, and it would still be the happiest place on earth.

◆

Henry David Thoreau said that "success usually comes to those who are too busy to be looking for it." After Viktor and Yuri headed back to Russia for more touring with

Kino and for Viktor's film *Igla* to be screened at the Berlin Film Festival and released across the Soviet Union, I threw myself into preparing my second art show as a way to combat the loneliness.

New Art from Leningrad at the Sawtelle Gallery featured a hundred works by thirteen contemporary artists from the U.S.S.R.[6] One of my favorite pieces was done by Afrika with an artist named Zverev. It was a beautiful black acrylic on canvas, a portrait of a woman's face with random letters and words, yellow hair and green spray paint. It was a painting infused with beauty and wonder. Another piece I loved was by Khlobuistin, a dancing Stalin on the back of a jacket. Of one hundred works, though, my absolute favorite was an acrylic on canvas by Oleg Kotelnikov, a world of color and scary faces that demanded attention and bled a series of emotions. I traded Sasha Lipnitsky my Soviet/American flag painted guitar for it. Today it sits above the fireplace in my home, watching the world go by and daring me to be bold.

The special thing about this second art show was that, finally, one of the creators could attend the opening! Afrika was by far the craziest, most personable of the artists.

"And how would you describe him?" the *Los Angeles Times* asked me.

"He pushes the border furthest and does things before his time. He's been described as the ever-present Afrika." Case in point, when Afrika landed in Los Angeles a day before the exhibit, he somehow managed to design and install a number of last-minute pieces.

"Poetry," he said as he dangled different objects from a long rope we strung across the walls.

"Are you sure about this?" I asked as he slathered twelve dark-brown straw placemats with acrylic paint and nailed each one on the wall so together they formed the shape of a cross. I genuinely couldn't comprehend how Afrika managed so many ideas in his head. It wasn't just that he was a profuse dreamer – he was a prolific doer who could seemingly execute things he imagined even before he imagined them.

Afrika was the hit of the evening. Director and actress Penny Marshall and comedian Sandra Bernhardt would have eaten out of his hands if he'd let them. The press were obsessed with him and the exotic opinions he spun for them.

"I do all kinds of artistical activities," he related in an *Los Angeles Times* interview. "For example, I put two jugs of water into one big one, symbolizing unity between the United States and the Soviet Union."

---

6   Artists: Afrika, Gustav Guryanov, Andrei Khlobuistin, Maya Khlobuistin, Oleg Kotelnikov, Evgenij Kozlov, Andrei Krisanov, Andrei Medvedev, Timur Novikov, Vadim Ovchinnikov, Inal Savchenko, Ivan Sotnikov, and Viktor Tsoi.

■ Afrika sleeping on top of random materials and
art in the New Artists' space, Leningrad, 1986.

■ Afrika and Penny Marshall at the L.A. opening
for *New Art from Leningrad*, March 18, 1989.

I spent the evening eavesdropping on Afrika's stories and doing sales for the paintings. Since I had spent a fortune on all the framing and preparation for the event, I decided to sell the artwork as a way to pay my parents back for their help. A guy from New York named Paul Judelson became very interested in Afrika and Timur and bought a number of pieces. Not long after, he became their manager and opened a gallery in The Big Apple.

Sergey Soloviev, the Russian director who had made the Soviet film *Assa* with Afrika and Tsoi, also managed to come to the opening. I had never had a chance to work with him because of my visa problems when he was filming *Assa*, but we both loved the rockers and artists and spent the evening gushing over their names.

"We should not only speak of their successes. Look what you've managed to do. You are beautiful, creative," he said to me. I beamed. It was on nights like these that I wanted to freeze time.

Success was happening more and more for all of us. When I returned to Russia, the film *Igla* had transformed the Russian movie-going public. Young people finally had a new wavefilm with a romantic hero they rushed to idolize, whose on-screen personality and beliefs were relatable, identifiable. Viktor had become mythical. The fact that the film was shot in Kazakhstan, by the young Kazakh director Rashid Nugmanov, only enhanced Viktor's mysteriousness and magnetism.

The movie was a thriller that dealt with drug addiction, manipulation, and a counterculture of rock music with slackers and mafia-types. Viktor's music fed the story as

■ "Modern Age Rock 'n Roll" video shoot in Kazakhstan with my bodyguard Misha, 1990.

it unraveled. There is one scene in the film that is seared into my brain, and to this day I can't stop thinking about it – Viktor standing on the shores of the Aral Sea, finding it completely dry and barren as the eye can see. Somehow, he managed to infuse beauty into this scorching, lifeless place.

It became one of the most watched movies in the Soviet Union. Like me, the public couldn't stop thinking about it or about Viktor.

"*Mamouchka*," I said to Rashid, a nickname Viktor and I had given him because of his sweet, gentle, maternal nature, "I want to film the music video for my song 'Modern Age Rock 'n Roll' in Kazakhstan." I was so inspired by the movie and by Viktor, and I wanted an excuse to travel to such a striking, powerful land.

Rashid set up a shoot with the help of his brother Murat, who was a cameraman. We landed in Alma-Ata after a shaky Aeroflot flight. I stepped off the plane at the foot of the Trans-Ili Alatau mountains, surrounded by Soviet buildings and Asian faces. Since we were only there for one night, I didn't make it to the far-off place that Viktor shot my favorite scene in *Igla*, but we made it into the desert where I rode a classic Yugoslavian motorcycle across the sparkling, irreverent sand.

"Yes!" the cameraman shouted as I flew past him, unsteady and disheveled. I reveled in it, chasing my own success. I knew I was no Afrika or Viktor; as I sped into the piercing sun, I was nobody's hero but my own.

◆

"Hacky sack?"

Kolya Mikhailov, Games, and I were waiting for a train to Minsk, Belarus where the Rock Club had set up three concerts for us. Vitia Sologub held out the knitted, misshapen ball, dropping it and kicking it towards us – his brother Grysha Sologub, Igor Cherednik, and Andrei Nuzhdin wearing shirts with my upcoming album photos and myself in a new black vest coated with colorful stones that felt like it weighed ten pounds. As the boys hopped around to pass the time, I stood back and watched, almost unable to move.

The venue was a stadium, filled to its concrete edges with thousands of people. They drove us out to the stage by van, but when we got there, they hadn't gotten the equipment up and running and we had to lip sync for the first show.

"Please welcome the girl from Los Angeles who put out *Red Wave* and helped many Leningrad musicians," Vitia would introduce me after the Games' set. I remember walking out to a cheering, irrepressible crowd. I brought out my 35 mm camera with me to take photos of them – it was such a powerful sight. They loved it, raising their hands and making faces for the photos, riling themselves up as a man in a military suit went around and tapped people on their shoulders to sit down.

"Vitia," I whispered as I passed by the side of the stage. "It is actually so nice lip syncing!" I could just let go and dance, twirling and kicking without worrying about getting winded. It was the first time I could get swept up in my own music. It was such a striking moment, to realize for the first time that what had evolved to become my songs were so well received.

In that concert, I still hadn't yet found my stride as a performer. I was backed by some of the most accomplished and powerful musicians, and my live singing (once the technical difficulties got fixed) was getting better and stronger. Yet I was still unsure, and that fearlessness my friends had in their performances was something I'd yet to learn.

Speaking of my friends, Boris' U.S. album had been released, and he began spending a ton of time doing press for it. Go figure that when I was finally back in the Soviet Union, he was halfway around the world. I would listen to his songs every day, pretending he was still there in that snow globe of a country while I danced on my bed and cried with happiness and missing the best friend I'd once had by my side almost all of the time. One song in particular, "Radio Silence," was on repeat in my head. It was the kind of song that took me to the ends of the earth in my mind, where there was no more travel time or distance but just the two of us walking home on dark streets like we used to. It also reminded me of my punk days in my early twenties, when me and my friends would knock into each other dancing in mosh pits. Boris' song was reckless and wild, but it was meditated and thoughtful in a way that embodied him. I sat, the song tapering off, and felt nostalgia besieging my heart. I guess the U.S. was Boris' own 'Wonderland,' worlds away from my own. At least he was still here in his music, just as palpable and charismatic as before. And now I was making my own music too.

Bob Ezrin, a famed record producer from Canada with intelligent eyes, became a new acquaintance of mine. "Pink Floyd is playing in Moscow, Joanna. Do you want backstage passes to see it?" he asked me one day.

"Sure," I said with a shrug. I wasn't a big Pink Floyd fan because I hadn't heard many of their songs, but I knew my rocker friends loved them and wove elements of Pink Floyd's music into their own. I got a press pass for the Olympic Stadium concert, allowing me to walk wherever I wanted and take as many pictures as I could. Unfortunately, many of my friends were out of Russia at the time, as they were so often now, but I did manage to get Alex Kan into the concert. I have the most vivid memory of me standing just under the stage taking photos of David Gilmour, the light making everything look shiny and polished. The sound was incredible, the light show defiant of gravity and rationality, an entirely new level I had never witnessed. Behind the band was a large oval screen that played video graphics throughout the show. A huge papier-mâché pig flew out over the audience, thousands of Russians screaming with tears running down their faces. I never realized how many Pink Floyd fans there were here.

I didn't recognize many of the songs, but as David Gilmour ripped his guitar solos above me, I was completely hooked. My favorite song they played was "Another Brick in the Wall" – it felt iconic, rebellious, and as I jumped up and down with my camera above my head, I knew I wanted to make music like that.

"The energy, and the music – *WOW*," Alex yelled into my ear as we tried to elbow our way out at the end. "What did you think?"

"I think I'm gonna do that," I yelled back, dodging a group of fans in leather and eyeliner.

"That?" Alex asked, incredulous. "You mean you are going perform like them? That is a lot to ask of yourself. You got to learn how to act like that on the stage."

"Weren't you listening?" I asked, locking my arm around his as we began to run with the dispersing crowd towards the doors. "I don't need no education!"

◆ The Space in Between

Frederick Weisman and I started working together in Los Angeles. We met with the mayor Tom Bradley to try to make Leningrad the sister city of L.A., as well as pushed to expand an ongoing art exchange with the Soviet Union. It was amazing how fun it was to collaborate with a man many years my senior, a man who had memories in his mind from decades before I was ever born. Despite his seniority and wisdom, Fred was one of the silliest people I had ever known. His whole being was made of a young heart and juvenile jokes, a combination that fueled a vibrancy and spontaneity. I never knew what to expect.

"Let's go to Russia," he said one day as we sat across a table from each other flipping through photographs of artwork.

"Sure," I said, surprised. "The artists know all about you, and I'm sure they would love to show you their art and the city!"

"Great," he said, standing. "I'll book my private jet."

"What did you say?" I called after him, not believing my ears.

Sitting on a thick leather sofa eating a Snickers bar, I didn't think I could ever fly Aeroflot again. I didn't even notice when we took off. Fred was sitting with his future wife, art restorationist Billie Milam, and her nephew Sean, and the curator of the Frederick R. Weisman Art Foundation, Henry Hopkins, was across from me. As the plane leveled out, Fred came around with a basket of more candy. He put on a movie, and as we all watched, M&M's started flying over the seat at Sean and me. We both climbed onto our seats and peered behind us, shocked to see Fred's red face as he laughed deeply and continued tossing pieces of chocolate at our dumbfounded faces. You always had to be on guard for Fred's antics.

On the way to Leningrad, we made a pit stop in Minneapolis, Minnesota, to visit the Frederick R. Weisman Museum of Art at the University of Minnesota. Both Fred and Billie had been born in Minneapolis. We wandered through and had a late lunch, and then the museum staff arranged for us to have a late-night private tour of Prince's Paisley Park. They drove us over in a huge mobile home that had a crystal chandelier in it that swung with every bump in the road. The Warehouse, as it was called, was massive, with different studios and concert halls fit together like palatial puzzle pieces. I remember motorcycles, artwork, musical instruments, and Prince's costumes lining the high walls, and a few mannequins that were allegedly built with Prince's exact measurements.

"But they're tiny!" I whispered to Fred. I couldn't believe how small the superstar was.

"Small but mighty," Fred giggled. "What a man!"

We got back on the plane and all passed out. I woke up when we landed, looking out the window to a strip of runway in Reykjavík, Iceland surrounded by absolute darkness.

"Anyone want to stretch their legs while we refuel?" one of the pilots said, appearing at the cockpit door.

We all walked off the plane into a deserted airport. It was closed, soulless, and soundless. With a whoop, Fred dashed down one of the terminals. We chased him, hooting and laughing like adolescent hyenas on the open savanna.

On August 1, 1989, the plane landed in Copenhagen and we checked into a hotel. In the afternoon we visited the famed Tivoli Gardens and followed Fred around to all the rides and games. At one small roller coaster, he and I stood waiting for the gates to open. I watched as all the kids rushed toward the cars, waiting my turn and laughing as I saw them fighting with each other for their favored cars.

"Oh my gosh, they're ridiculous," I said to Fred. "Fred?" I looked around, but he was no longer beside me.

"Joanna!" I heard from the crowd of children. I looked down, and there was Fred, elbowing his way through the kids and fighting for the front car. He was one of them – youthful, joyous, and present. I hurried to catch up, apologizing profusely to the short, ruffled heads that bobbed around me. Fred's eagerness was contagious, and I felt myself get swept up in it.

The next day, thirty-five kilometers north of Copenhagen, we had a private tour at the Louisiana Museum of Modern Art. It was a vision of modern Danish architecture and a synthesis of art and landscape. To this day it's one of my favorite museums. I remember standing in the sculpture garden, baffled that in all the years I'd spent going back and forth from one side of the world to the other, I'd somehow missed all the space in between.

We finally landed in Moscow, and as we taxied I told everyone about the whirlwind of events I had planned. We'd be going to artist studios, museums, and meeting all of my friends that weren't away on tour or business.

"Wonderful," Fred said, standing and stretching his legs. "And we are having dinner at the U.S. Ambassador's house – we're staying with him."

◆

"If you buy from the heart," Fred said to me, "then it's respectable art no matter what any hot-shot art critic tells you."

We were standing in an artist's space in Moscow, in front of a pair of blue jeans hung on a canvas.

"I love it," I said.

"I'll take it!" Fred beamed, ecstatic.

From Moscow we headed to Leningrad, where they stayed at a hotel right on the harbor with dark green velvet drapes and gold fringing.

"Joanna," Billie pulled me aside in their large room. "The water coming out in the bathtub was brown. I decided not to bathe."

"Welcome to my world!" I tried so hard not to laugh.

Afrika showed up, buzzing and smiling, to guide us from one artist's space to another and over to Timur's expansive New Artists space. Fred had also bought pieces from me of Andrei Krisanov, Timur Novikov, Oleg Kotelnikov, Inal Savchenko, and Gustav Guryanov, and was so happy to finally meet the creators in person. Two pieces he got from Gustav were a few of his favorites; both were acrylic on canvas – one of a Soviet girl on a tractor and the other of a pilot, both in vivid pinks, purples, reds, and greens.

The next day the Hermitage was closed to the public. Our group went to meet the director, Boris Piotrovsky, in his office.

"Go look around the museum. Go wherever you want," he said to us, leaning back in his chair with a cup of tea in his hands.

Cautiously, almost guiltily, we began roaming the halls of the giant museum. We were silent, reverent, intimidated by the incredible collection and cavernous, vacant rooms.

"Oh my gosh!" Billie's shout broke the silence.

■ Painting of Boris by Sergey Debizhev, a graphic artist and film director, early 1980s.

■ Portrait of me in marker on black and white photo by Gustav Guryanov, 1987.

We ran to find her in one of the rooms. She was standing in a patch of dim sunlight, her hands covering her mouth.

"The window is open, and air and light are coming in right on the artworks. This is outrageous!"

It was strange that the works in such a magnificent, special place were not protected very much – not from light, outside air, or people themselves. The barriers, lasers, and ropes I expected in American museums were nowhere to be seen here. I loved it, the way it felt like I was truly experiencing a place, not as a ghost on the fringes just floating by.

We went down to a dark and cold room in the basement. As we looked through the large selection of paintings not on display, we started to realize that these were some of the most important paintings in the collection.

"I like to think we're seasoned art collectors," Henry said slowly.

"We've spent hours and hours in museums all over the world…" Fred chimed in.

"But we've never seen anything like this," Henry finished, bending down and trying to comfort the pieces slumped against the wall.

To roam free among the hidden pieces of the world's greatest and most iconic art was a feeling I will never forget.

"The residue of imagination in this room," Fred muttered in the basement. "Does anyone hear angels singing?"

■ Fred Weisman with two paintings he purchased by Gustav Guryanov, Los Angeles, 1989.

♦

It feels surreal to watch your own record being sold in a music store. My first album in Russia, a small record with a black and white cover of me in a fringe jacket, hat and sunglasses, and my name embossed in blue Cyrillic letters, was released on Melodiya. It had just four songs – "Feeling," "Turn Away," "Lonely Boy," and "Highstrung" – two that I had written with Kuryokhin, one with Boris, and one by myself. There was a contorted photo of me and the Games guys on the back. Vasily Shumov, from the band Center, wrote an introduction. He and my sister Judy had become an item and were moving to Los Angeles together. I was so appreciative of everyone's help, although no one ever thought to ask me if I even received a *kopek* from Melodiya. I am pretty sure that I never did. At the time, I wasn't even thinking about that; all that mattered was that my songs were out there, on vinyl, in Russia.

The only bummer was that Yuri wasn't there to share it with me. Kino was touring most of the time now, and I was spending more and more time in Moscow working on my own stuff. It was the real business hub in Russia, so I had decided to get an apartment there to try and make things happen with my music. Yuri and I hadn't been seeing very much of each other, and our marriage felt more like legend than reality. All of us who had once been huddled together in cramped, heated apartments in Leningrad were now sprinting towards trains and planes to catch to different cities and countries.

Still, as my friends and I found interest in separate endeavors, Russians were becoming more interested in me. Vasya, who became Judy's husband, introduced me to a jovial manager named Timur Gasonov. He hailed from Azerbaijan and was the kind of guy who could work the system and turn stones into water. Timur was the person who ended up finding me a large room to rent in Moscow, on the second floor over a *pierogi* shop where the smell of stuffed dumplings filled the room with a sweet and tangy scent. Only later did I realize that where there is food, there are cockroaches! I couldn't complain, though, as foreigners could not rent places in the city. I paid Timur an amount of money, and while I'm sure most of it went directly to him, I had a roof over my head and some critters to keep me company.

Timur helped me put in a wall towards the end of the large room. In the new, small space I taped posters and photos all over the walls of my rocker friends. I had the *Red Wave* poster from the back cover of the album, *Red Wave* art show pamphlets, Aquarium posters and posters of Boris, as well as ones of Televisor, Mike Naumenko, Kino, Alisa, and even a couple of mine.

"Wow, Joanna, it's a lot," Judy said the first time she saw it before moving to L.A.

I loved it. It was my rock room, a safe space where I could still imagine being surrounded by my friends.

In the end, having places to live in both Moscow and Leningrad actually gave me more opportunity to run into my old group of rockstars. Viktor's base was now in Moscow with Natasha, and when Yuri had to be with Viktor, he could spend his nights with me. I also spent some time at Sasha Lipnitsky's *dacha* when the cold metropolis filled with strangers made me feel lonely.

One day I got a phone call from Judy and Vasya in Los Angeles. "Vasya's musicians, they're just sitting around Moscow with nothing to do," Judy explained. "Vasya wants to know if you want to use them to do a tour in Russia?"

"Timur could arrange," I heard Vasya's deep, smoky voice say through the landline.

"Why not?" I replied. The whole idea almost seemed impossible, like it would never actually happen. It was something about which I had been dreaming – there was no way it could come true that easily, right?

Suddenly, Timur Gasonov was my manager, setting up rehearsals with the Center musicians and writing me optional set-lists for a concert tour he was working out. I showed up to the rehearsal and was met with three beaming, friendly faces.

"Joanna," the musicians all greeted me. "We are so excited to be playing with you!" I couldn't believe it. I took a deep breath. When had Russia transformed into a place where I felt in charge?

"Hey!" The drummer called from behind his drum set, a cigarette hanging from his mouth and a devilish look in his eye. "Are we going to play or not?"

The guys were younger than I thought they'd be, but as we rehearsed, they kept up and sometimes outpaced me. My music was so different from what they played in their own band, and I was still too unseasoned to direct them in each song. My tracks came out sounding like pretty candid pop, but it worked, and I loved every second of what I was doing.

Timur ended up scheduling us an eight-city tour around the U.S.S.R. It was really nice to be able to bond with the Center guys over it. Before we left, the four of us met up at the bowling alley at the Kosmos Hotel. We had the whole place to ourselves, sliding around the lanes and climbing on the plastic seats. The guys drank and smoked, and I laughed along with them. I still didn't speak Russian, and they all spoke very little English. Sasha Vasilyev, the drummer, never said a word to me, and that drew me to his enigmatic, standoffish personality. I became determined to get not just Russian music fans, but Sasha as well, to love me.

♦

On tour with us were Timur Gasonov and two security guards, Kostya and Misha. We had backstage passes for our guests, as well as a poster for the tour. It felt official, and we reached our first city Zaporizhia, in the southeast of Ukraine, with a sense of excitement. We showed up at a stadium filled with maybe one thousand people for the day performance, and a little more at the evening one. I came out in blue denim shorts that had an American flag painted across them and a short leather jacket. I had started wearing a big hanging earring in my left ear and just studs in the right. With my Kramer Soviet/American flag guitar hanging off my neck, I strummed the three chords I knew to my song "Give Me Some More of Your Love" and felt like I could fly. During our set, there were some young guys standing and dancing. One of them was waving a big Soviet flag that looked like a large bird with yellow and red feathers. At the end of the night, I jumped onto my bodyguard's shoulders and had him run in front of the crowd so I could touch all their hands.

"Joanna!" Timur tried to call over the sea of fans surrounding me, who were holding up their hands, money, even official passbooks for me to sign. "That's all! Autobus!"

Holding his breath, he plunged into the human ocean to pull me out. He really handled everything, and I felt so safe with him in charge.

The next stops on the tour were two more cities in the Ukraine. We went to Krivoy Rog, the longest city in Europe, followed by the industrial city Donetsk. There wasn't much for us to do in these cities besides sound checks and the concerts themselves. We'd spend the day laying on our backs staring at the ceiling, waiting for the performance. After the concert we would all go out for dinner, and it was one of the few times I ever really participated in drinking. The whole band loved drinking, and they were very good at it, and I didn't want to feel like the odd man out. Being a new touring performer was already all the attention I could handle. I didn't want to make another scene by being the stiff, sober one in this dancing, laughing group.

The only problem was that after one shot of vodka, I was completely drunk. So drunk that I would pick up the bottle and drink some more like it was water.

"Look at Stingray!" I would hear the guys hooting vaguely in the back of my mind while I tried to climb onto a table in a restaurant. Somehow it seemed like the only plausible action. "She's out of control!" The boys loved it, and I honestly don't remember much. What I do remember was how funny Sasha was. He had a wry sense of humor and a sweet, almost puppy-like face with a charismatic smile.

"My doctor," he would say as we all sat in a circle and drank, "says I need glasses." He'd hold up two shot glasses and down them both.

We were in what felt like the middle of nowhere, and because nobody in our entourage spoke much English, I was starting to learn some Russian. It was survival mode, a primal instinct to try to communicate with others. Just as we were all beginning to have real conversations and bonding as a tight, crazy group, Timur told us the rest of the tour was canceled.

"There are not enough ticket sales," he said sadly, stoically. "We are going home."

Nobody knew me in those cities yet – not one person had my record or knew all the songs. The concerts had just been promoted as an American singer, which was certainly not enough to bring out big crowds. I was bummed, knowing that my friends were out on stages swarmed with faces and lighters and I was heading back to Leningrad and Moscow early.

Maybe I wouldn't have appreciated my later tours as much, when people sang along and screamed my name, if I wasn't so humbled on that first one.

"We're going to get them next time," I told the guys in my band as we headed east. "Sell out everything."

"To selling out," Sasha toasted dryly, lifting his glass in the air. I raised my bottle of water to meet it. "To selling out."

■ My locket from the mid-1980s.

♦

"Have you been sleeping with girls on tour?"

Yuri and I were relaxing together in bed, a chill just starting to creep into the warm room.

I had heard rumors about Yuri and other women, but I had never brought it up before. I had never thought he would admit to it.

"Yes," he replied. "They jump on me, and I cannot stop them. It is not a big deal – they are like your sisters."

"I have two sisters," I told him, sitting up. "I don't need any more!"

Part of me was grateful that he had at least been honest with me, but the other part of me wished he would have lied, like the Sheryl Crow song that came out a couple years later: "*Lie to me, I promise I'll believe.*"

"Oh my god." I doubled over, sick to my stomach. It was a horrible feeling. "I shouldn't have asked."

Yuri wrapped his arms around me, kissing me along the ears and down my jaw. "I love you, Joanna."

It was such a strange feeling. I could feel he loved me, but then how could he treat me like a disposable person? I was so confused. Standing, I went into the narrow, boxy kitchen and leaned against the window.

A conversation I had with Viktor a while back popped into my head.

"You're such an amazing man," I'd told him. "So many people here cheat, but you don't!"

"Don't praise me for that, Jo, because it is not hard for me. It is who I am to be faithful."

"What does that mean?" I asked him.

"There are three kinds of men, you see. Ones like me don't have a bone in their body to cheat. It is natural for us to be faithful. Then there are those who feel like cheating, and so they do it." He paused, leaning forward with a serious look in his playful eyes. "The last kind of man is the only one who deserves praise. That is the man that has urges to cheat but controls himself. He tells himself not to. Now that is a strong man – that is a good man."

Standing in that kitchen, the cold tiles and groaning sink keeping me company, I began to cry. Was my husband not a strong man?

♦

To distract myself from my marriage, I became obsessed with making videos. That had always been my thing; whenever I was at home in the States, I would always watch all the hip videos on MTV, which would inspire so many ideas in my own head. After filming footage in Alma-Ata for "Modern Age Rock 'n Roll," I decided to film myself singing the song at Rossiya Hall to edit together with the motorcycle footage for a music video.

I learned from hours of watching music videos that a person needed two or three different elements to make a music video interesting. For the "Modern Age Rock 'n Roll" video, I decided to film one more scene, and found a studio and cameraman. I invited Sasha to be a part of it, after all the time we'd spent together, and my friend Big Misha as well. We filmed in front of a white screen so we could superimpose other footage onto ourselves and use simple computer graphics that were available those days in the editing bays. There's a fourth guy in the video as well, but I honestly don't remember who he was. I had brought some different items we could play around in. Big Misha wore a dark coat that hung over his knees with grey socks, no shoes, and big turquoise glasses. He drew beard scruff onto his face to make it look as if he'd just gotten up.

"Joanna, why do you laugh at me?" he said, standing without pants against the white backdrop. He looked so goofy, but there was something about it that was cool and alluring. Misha was a rockstar without even trying.

We had brought some alcohol for the occasion, and by the time we were ready to start shooting Sasha was already past tipsy. In capri leggings, a bright blue velvet vest, my black and white hat with a bow, and narrow reading glasses with fake diamonds, he danced around and agreed to anything.

I loved my look for this video – black clothes with a studded belt, thin retro sunglasses, and black and white paint on my cheeks like an anthropomorphic zebra. My lips were bright blue. This was the beginning of my own 'Stingray style' – the dark clothes, crazy sunglasses or hats, and colorful lips. I felt powerful, uninhibited, safe inside my bold costumes. It was Oscar Wilde who knew that if you give a man a mask, he will feel comfortable enough to reveal his true self.

As I was singing along to the song, the three guys just did whatever they felt was right.

There was no choreography, just vodka, music, and the urge to outdo each other. Big Misha would either just stand behind me and stare down the camera or start smoking a cigarette and occasionally take a big swig of whiskey from a bottle. Sasha was holding a flower in his hand and would bob back and forth with it or lay on his stomach with his feet in the air like a little girl in a park who was plastered out of her mind. I was totally sober, but being around these stewed, nutty guys felt intoxicating. I was giddy with laughter and excitement – I just wanted to spend the rest of my life making videos like that. I had no idea that soon the image the video would promote of me – a rebellious, vibrant, powerful female – would change me and my career forever.

I don't need a man to love me, I thought as I watched the playback of myself tumbling behind a projected outstretched hand in the music video, waving my hands and escaping its grasp. *Screw modern age romance – I want rock 'n roll!*

♦ The Needle

In January, Viktor's film *Igla* was accepted into the Sundance Film Festival in Park City. Rashid wanted us all to go. Since the festival was only covering Rashid's expenses, I applied for and received a George Soros Grant to cover Viktor and Yuri's trip.

Next thing we knew, Rashid, Viktor, Natasha, Yuri, and I were all lounging in front of a radiating, thermal fire inside a three-story mansion the festival provided for us in the quaint mountain town. I was shocked at how different Natasha was away from all the Leningrad people she didn't really like – she was relaxed, silly, her sharp laugh floating up to the high ceilings. I reveled in the fact that I could leave the reality of Yuri's unfaithfulness back in Russia and, for this short moment, curl up in his arms again.

The tickets to *The Needle* screening were sold out in a matter of hours. I couldn't believe I was sitting in a packed house of Hollywood's most critically acclaimed members. After the film, everyone stood and applauded Rashid and Viktor.

Unlike at a normal screening, after the movie the lights didn't come up yet. Everyone sank back into their seats, unable to find their way in the dark. There was rustling, whispers and movement, as everyone wondered what was going on. In the dark I saw Yuri and Viktor sneak up to the stage and heard them test their guitars. Suddenly, the lights came up and they started playing "Peremen," a driving and full sound that was so resonant it sounded as if the whole band were there playing. Viktor was on his new white guitar, strumming acoustically as Yuri waxed wild melodies on his own electric guitar. A reddish light shone down on the two of them, illuminating just their faces and

Viktor's white guitar against their black clothes.

The instrumental part ended abruptly, and the crowd erupted into cheers.

"Thank you," Viktor said shyly, in English. He turned back to Yuri. "Pachka Sigaret," he said softly.

As they started their next song, "Pack of Cigarettes," I watched the faces of the audience. I knew they couldn't fully comprehend how impactful the lyrics were to the Russian people and their soul, but the music still floored them. The guitars sang, cried, soared, and wallowed, and I could tell every person in there was swept up in the sound.

As the crowd cheered again, I shared a glance with Natasha and Rashid. The three of us, the only ones in the room who knew the true reverence held for Viktor's music back home, felt unseen between the crowd, sharing this secret knowledge about the mysterious musicians up on the stage. If only everyone else knew with whom they were sharing the room.

The last song Viktor and Yuri performed was one called "In Our Eyes."

"Thank you very much," Viktor said when they were done, his eyes hiding behind his long lashes. "That's all."

People in the room started clapping and stamping, shouting for more. With a bashful smile, Viktor draped his guitar back over his shoulder, and the two played "Groupa Kroovy." At one point, Yuri played a solo on his guitar, and I swear the entire room held its breath in awe.

"I am so proud of you guys!" I yelled after the event, throwing my arms around both their warm necks where the guitar straps had rubbed. "It was such new territory – people who didn't know you or your songs, and such a simple setup with just the two amps and microphone, but you rocked it like you were in a stadium back home!"

"Excuse me," a group of producers from America and Japan cut into the compliments. "May we speak to you about investing and working with Kino in the West?"

"Okay," Viktor said as Yuri raised his thick eyebrows at me.

"You should perform at a local nightclub this evening, a great follow up to what you just did," someone offered. True to who Viktor was, he politely declined. He just wanted to hang back at the house with his buddies, and no amount of fame could change that.

◆

The next day Rashid had to do some press about the film, so the rest of us decided to go snowmobiling.

"Why do you get the white goggles?" Yuri asked Viktor, pointing at the round white goggles on his face. Yuri's, like mine and Natasha's, were a vivid pink.

We sped through the Uinta Mountains outside the town, snow spraying up around us and licking our exposed noses. Yuri and Viktor were fearless, full throttle through the winter like frost demons chasing the sun. Natasha and I were a little more cautious.

"Screw it," Natasha finally said to me. "Let's catch up with them, shall we?"

It was absolute freedom zipping across the landscape, the wind at our backs.

"Keep going!" I shouted as the four of us plowed forward. It felt like we could speed all the way back to Russia, back to the early days and the long afternoons where we could snuggle onto a sofa and make music just for ourselves. We were needles in a haystack, immune to the duties of the real world, shiny and sharp in the snow.

◆

After the Sundance Festival, Yuri, Viktor, and Natasha all came back to Los Angeles with me for a few days. It was so fun to have them tucked away with me in the canyon, sitting around sipping coffee and humming tunes. Viktor couldn't stop talking about taking Natasha to "The Happiest Place on Earth."

As the three of them planned out which rides they would do, I stood and tossed my Jeep Cherokee car keys at Yuri.

"Hey guys, I have to edit today. Yuri, you're in charge of driving."

Yuri looked at me in shock – he had only just gotten his license and had very little experience driving, especially anything the size of an SUV.

"Jo-an-na," he said slowly, holding up the car keys. "Are you sure?"

"Of course, she is," Viktor cut in, giddy with excitement. Yuri couldn't refuse his best friend.

"Have fun," I called as I watched Yuri swing the car into the street and reverse about a quarter of a mile before the car jumped forward. Somehow, he navigated his way onto the 10 freeway towards Downtown Los Angeles and managed to make it through the multi-freeway switch up, where about ten lanes merged into two levels of twists and turns, to reach the 5-South to Anaheim.

When I asked Yuri about it now, he remembered this drive as one of the scariest and most tense moments of his life.

"My hands, they gripped the steering wheel for an hour straight," he told me.

Finally, as Yuri flexed his fingers, the three of them were standing in line for Pirates of the Caribbean.

My dad couldn't wait to see the boys again and invited us all to lunch at the famous

Friars Club to which he belonged in Beverly Hills. It was a private club for show business that was opened in 1947 by my father's friend, actor and comedian Milton Berle, and a couple of other famous actors. I could tell my dad was so proud to bring us all to the sleek white building.

Natasha remembers that the club was full of old ladies, a few of which commented on her perfect teeth.

"They seemed so happy to have some young people at the club!" Natasha laughed. After lunch, the four of us headed home.

"What next?" I asked, back in the driver's seat.

The three of them just wanted to relax in my backyard on lounge chairs, under the timeless Californian sun.

"True happiness," Natasha murmured, eyes closed and arm slung over her forehead. Never had they been able to sit under a warm sun in February, listening to birds and the faint hum of hot and heavy traffic.

"I never want to leave," Viktor told me.

I had forgotten how lucky I was to have a life in Los Angeles. For however many years it had been that I'd spent all my time trying to get out of this city, seeing my home through my Russian friends' eyes made me realize how easy my life had been here. It was always warm, always full of places to go. We had housekeepers and gardeners and food deliveries, everyone running around between a green ocean and actively tectonic mountains. There was very little hardship, very few layers to a place like this – everything simple, shallow, and bright.

On the last day before Natasha left, we went to Fred Weisman's art collection so she could see his vast treasure trove. Afterwards, we spent the afternoon in Venice. Yuri and I wandered slowly down the sandy pavement, looking at the skateboarders and stalls set up along the pedestrian walkway. Viktor took off ahead of us, pulling Natasha into all the hippie stores he'd visited before and weaving her through the street performers, bicyclists, and rollerbladers. It was so colorful, and there were the two of them in black moving through the crowd like a thundercloud.

"It was unforgettable," Natasha said when I asked her about it recently.

Natasha left a couple of days before Yuri and Viktor and missed their photoshoot with the extraordinary rock 'n roll photographer Henry Diltz. The *Groupa Kroovy* album I had just released on Gold Castle Records, which was a branch off the Capitol Records money tree, had come out with great reviews. When the record company heard the guys were in town, they set up the photoshoot. Viktor, over the moon to have his music on

■ Kino publicity shot by Henry Diltz for their U.S. record release with Gold Castle Records, 1989.

■ Kino's *Groupa Kroovy* album with cover art by Andrei Krisanov.

CD, cassette, and vinyl, quickly agreed. Diltz had started out in the 1960s as an American folk musician but became one of the most iconic rock photographers. He had been the official photographer at Woodstock as well as the Monterey Music Festival and had shot many musicians living in the laid-back neighborhood of Laurel Canyon above the grind of Hollywood.

I opened my door to a man with a long, white ponytail and wise eyes. He brought no makeup or hair artists, no lighting guy, no photographer's assistant. He did it old-school, just him and his beat-up camera. Yuri and Viktor loved him immediately.

"Let's head up the canyon and see what we find," he said casually, leaning against the doorway. We got into his car and he pulled into a little market halfway up the canyon. It was squeezed between the Bohemian houses, the front wall covered with bulletins and messages people had taped up offering things to sell, lessons to teach, and group events and seminars.

"Stand in front of this, will you guys?" Diltz asked the two guys, nudging a shopping cart near Yuri. "I think I'm going to shoot in black and white."

"Cool," Viktor replied with a smile. He and Yuri stood in their black clothing, staring into the camera. Diltz took a few shots and raised his eyes.

"We got it," he said simply.

Without all the bells and whistles of a typical photoshoot, the guys had felt so comfortable. Diltz's camera captured who Yuri and Viktor really were, straightforward and edgy, thoughtful and sarcastic. If a picture is worth a thousand words, this one was worth a thousand songs.

◆ What You Wish

Molly Ringwald wanted to have lunch with me.

"*That* Molly Ringwald?" My mom asked when I told her.

"Yes!" I shouted into the phone.

"Molly Ringwald from *The Breakfast Club*?" My mother asked.

"Yes!" I replied again.

"From *Pretty in Pink*?"

"Mom! There's no other Molly Ringwald."

As part of the Brat Pack, Ringwald was one of the hip, young Hollywood actors. I couldn't believe she wanted to meet, but even more than that I couldn't believe she supposedly wanted to play me in the new film deal with Fox TV.

"Joanna Stingray is such a rich character," she said, sitting across from me at the Kate Mantilini restaurant on Wilshire Boulevard in Beverly Hills.

I could only nod and try not to smile with all my teeth. It was so strange hearing my name mentioned like that, as if it were some third person who wasn't at the table with us. Joanna Stingray had somehow taken on a life of her own, and the events in Leningrad felt so long ago I truly didn't feel like I was talking about my own story. It was surreal, like coming out of the rabbit hole for the first time and blinking in the sun. Everything had changed.

We left the restaurant, and a few days later I heard she was interested in the part but wanted to sing and record my songs herself.

"What?" I almost choked on my cold water. "Who does she think she is?" I felt so protective of my songs – they were a part of who I was, so how could I just give them away? I could hear Sergey's voice in my head: *Don't sell out. Stand your ground. They are your songs. It isn't worth it.*

I declined Molly's conditions, and she passed on the part. I hardly noticed. I was in the middle of starting a music career and didn't have time for future regrets.

Back in Russia I was making more music videos. I hired Dima Dibrov and Andrei Stolyarov, two young guys working at the TV in Moscow, to make two videos to my songs "Keep on Traveling" and "Give Me Some More of Your Love." We signed a contract, and I paid them 18,684 rubles, around $622 at the time. Their idea for "Give Me Some More of Your Love" was to film in a factory with a conveyor belt and machines clanging and twisting inside each other. It was provocative and obviously about sex, but I just went with it. It was hysterical to make; they had all these average Russians working in the pretend factory and trying to walk across the screen in time to the music. Most of them had no rhythm, but they had beautiful eyes and round faces. Dima and Andrei had me laying down with a blue screen behind me with my arms and legs up like I was flying one minute and just sitting and eating a banana the next. The finished video was wacky and ridiculously sexual – boys' minds in Russia and America were basically identical. I had to laugh. Somehow, I got it aired on Soviet TV, but to this day that shocks me! How was it not censored??

The second video the two guys directed, "Keep on Traveling," was one I really loved. They used so many vibrant computer graphics, novel for the time. In the beginning of the video there's a shot of me wearing a shirt that says *SHUT UP*, and while I'm standing there moving my arms up and down and opening and closing my mouth, the colors change constantly. I wore so many different outfits in that video, with unique hats, oversized sunglasses, and costume jewelry. At one point, we shot in a dilapidated building. I was pedaling on a bike with someone lifting up the back tire so I wouldn't ride away.

The guys edited it so that it looked like sparks were coming out of the bike. They again brought in extras, Russians with such interesting faces, maybe because of all the hardship they had to endure. They shot me dancing in slow motion with the people in fast motion around me and painted flowers blooming up on the screen. It was so innovative and creative. Of course, Big Misha was in the video too. He stood there looking enigmatic and tough and fabulous. At this point I was rarely anywhere without him. He had become my sidekick, and he had me constantly cracking up and smiling.

Early days in Leningrad felt so far away, almost like a dream, but somehow when I was shooting and editing music videos, I felt like that same free spirit I'd been during those years. I may not have had my band of crazy pirates with me, but the creativity and the joy of the videos made me feel like they were still there, lurking in the corners pulling silly faces and wrestling each other in the snow. It was my way of throwing myself back into the land of imagination. I became addicted to making videos, just chasing the feeling of yesteryear.

I especially wanted to make a video to the song I wrote with Boris called "Highstrung." I decided to shoot myself singing the song while walking down Tverskaya Street in Moscow, right near the newly opened McDonald's. For me, McDonald's was the epitome of the worst of America: cheap frozen meat patties stuffed with grains and very little beef. It made me sad that the Russians could want that kind of crap, but I knew I could use the long line outside the chain in the video. We shot the footage in 8mm black and white. In editing, I spliced in some old Soviet footage of villagers dancing, guys doing gymnastics, and Young Pioneers saluting like Afrika and Timur used to do. We had also shot me on the beach in Leningrad dancing and pretending to drive a carcass of a car across the sand. Big Misha was squeezed in next to me, his forehead against the metal.

My favorite part of the video is when I'm walking on Tverskaya with a white mask on my face. It was eerie, and the strangers around me didn't know what was happening. I loved being hidden behind the mask. I could feel the truth in it – how we as people hide a part of our real selves in public. To this day it's actually one of my favorite videos and the closest manifestation of my artistic vision, how I saw the world through my own eyes.

I would fly to Leningrad on my down days to try to spend more time with Yuri if he was there. Ever since I moved to Moscow, Viktor and I would fly together between the two northern cities. We would curl up in the back of the plane and go through the bags of fan mail Viktor picked up from the Rock Club. He would read every letter.

"If people take the time to write them, I can take the time to read them," he told me.

"Boy, you are so loved, Viktor," I said, unfolding a letter filled with beautiful drawings. "It's amazing."

"The letters make me feel special," he would reply with a bashful smile. He deserved everything, and I loved getting to share those moments with him thirty-thousand feet in the air. We were flying high, heads in the clouds.

Viktor and I landed at Narita Airport in Tokyo on April 28, 1990, after a trippy experience leaving Moscow where all the passport control officers left their posts to get Viktor's autograph. This was a big change from the years of the mean, cold officers staring us down. We stepped off the plane, and Viktor was suddenly face to face with hundreds of people who looked so much like him, with expressive, Asian eyes that met his approvingly. He beamed.

Viktor had been invited by Yokichi Osato and his entertainment company Amuse, one of the biggest entertainment companies in Japan. He'd seen Viktor in *Igla* at the Sundance Film Festival, and his company wanted to release the film and Viktor's albums in Japan and have Kino tour there.

"Will you go with me?" Viktor had asked me when he found out. "I don't want to go by myself."

"Of course!" I said. I had been to Japan once before during my semester at sea in college, but I knew this would be extraordinarily different. Anything I did with Viktor was infused with more wonder, more laughs, and more magic.

The trip was very official. We were picked up from the airport in a limo, put up in a wonderfully lavish hotel, and all our food was complimentary. The first night, Amuse threw us a party with some of their performers and young staff members. They all adored Viktor, especially the girls. He looked like them but still stood out because of his height, something that mesmerized all the women as they craned their necks up to study his face, giggling if he caught them looking. Unlike the Russian women who would lay themselves at Boris' feet and stroke his sandals, these Japanese girls were shy and stared from a distance, as if Viktor were a statue they couldn't touch.

The next night we went to see Amuse's biggest pop star, Keisuke Kuwata, in concert. The crowd shouted his name over and over again, people falling over each other as they swelled towards the stage. To me the music was too syrupy, almost kitschy, but it was so much fun to be a part of something so different. We had dinner with Kuwata later that night, and he couldn't have been sweeter. As I sat and listened, he and Viktor spoke about their careers in their respective countries and in their halted, awkward English kept discovering they had so much in common.

"It is very... strange," Viktor mused. "To be a huge star in your own country but not be known anywhere else."

Kuwata nodded, the sparkle of kinship in his eyes. "There is a great tale in Japan about a frog born in a well. The frog was very proud of the fact that he was the biggest creature in the well. As a result, he believed he was invincible, and one day he left the well and ended up in the ocean, only to realize that he was much smaller than he thought."

Viktor listened, then cracked a smile. "I guess we are much wiser than the frog," he said. "We know how small we are!"

Kuwata laughed along with him, nodding and humble.

■ Viktor and me with his fans, Tokyo, April, 1990.   ■ A Tokyo punk band we saw playing in a park.

"Joanna, she is not a frog," Viktor added, his eyes meeting mine. He winked. "She is a Stingray."

The next day we had some free time, so Viktor and I roamed around the packed, bursting streets of Tokyo. People were everywhere, spilling in and out of shiny buildings and the numerous electronic shops that illuminated every street. Viktor loved how tech-savvy everyone was and pulled me up to many windows displaying video cameras and filming people to project on the monitors. We would make goofy faces and dance around.

Neither of us knew any Japanese, but their restaurants were full of fake food displays so we could point to what we wanted. Viktor had always been obsessed with soy sauce, his '*tsoi* sauce,' and it was everywhere we went. It was like the Japanese equivalent of American ketchup. I would laugh and cover my eyes as Viktor would tear open another packet and drown his plate in the sticky brown stuff.

In the evening we experienced Japanese Kabuki Theater for the first time. The performers wore elaborate, vivid makeup and every movement was dramatic, meaningful. We loved it.

Viktor and I got lucky enough to go backstage afterwards and meet some of the actors, who invited us out. The one thing the Japanese had in common with the Russians was that they enjoyed drinking and did it profusely. A couple of hours into the party the guys were rowdy and loud, and the girls giggled even louder than before, still standing and staring at Viktor. Viktor and I, besides a drink for a toast, drank very little. At many of the parties there, we would end up playing darts or pool together, surrounded by dazed, disheveled strangers.

Walking past street bands in bold colored suits and rainbows of hair, Viktor seemed happy that people didn't know him or ask for autographs. He loved blending into the city. In one of my favorite photos from the trip, it would have been impossible to find Viktor in the sea of Yokichi's party guests if it weren't for my bright hair standing next to him.

We took a night flight back to Moscow, staying up through the moon's fall and rise as we talked about the successful trip. I saw a new Viktor that night, one who in the comfort of Japan had been able to mature and consider his responsibilities in life.

"I have to take care of Marianna and Sasha, Natasha and her family, and the public all at the same time," he said to me. "I like that. It feels good to work to take care of everyone. I have everything I want in life. I am happy. Are you?"

I shook my head, staring adoringly into his twinkling eyes. "I'm not there yet," I admitted to him. "But it feels good knowing you are. It makes me think I'll get there someday too."

"Don't give up hope," he teased. "We can't all be frogs."

♦

If Russia was Wonderland for me, for Russians, Wonderland was New York City. The Big Apple was like a dream to them, springtime in Central Park and bright electricity in every building, a blinking, noisy Broadway, all kinds of people, limitless things to do and see. I was there briefly with Big Misha, and Timur Novikov was there for a couple months. It was both of their first times in the city that never slept.

Big Misha and I met with Bob Colacello, the witty editor of Warhol's *Interview* magazine.

"What's it like hanging around a genius?" Big Misha asked him, crossing his long legs and waving his hand around.

"The thing is, you can't hang around geniuses forever," Bob mused. "They end up taking everything you've got. That's why they're the genius, and you are not."

"Still, you're so lucky to be able to work here and create this stuff," I gushed.

He raised a teasing eyebrow at me. "Envy is a surefire party killer. Now, give me all the updates on the rockers and artists!"

The magazine had done a piece on me a few years back, followed later by a piece on Russian artists that included Afrika and his costumes and sets he designed for Merce Cunningham's Dance Company when he was in the city.

Big Misha and I also ran into the music video director Anton Corbijn, whom we had both met in Russia when he was with the UB40 tour. Big Misha was the one who

■ Timur, me, and Gustav, Leningrad, 1985. Artwork by Andrei Krisanov (top) and Oleg Kotelnikov (below).

recognized him. He always had a sharp eye for some of the biggest names and faces from the independent music world. I would have walked right past these people had it not been for him!

Timur was participating in two group art shows – one at the Paul Judelson Gallery called *The Friends of Mayakovsky Club Leningrad, U.S.S.R., and The Work of Art in the Age of Perestroika* at the Phyllis Kind Gallery. His work was so well received that the name Timur was becoming well known in the New York art scene. He hung out with many prominent figures in city circles to whom Afrika introduced him, including Paige Powell, one of Warhol's closest friends before he died; Jeffrey Schaire, the editor of *Art and Antiques* magazine; Rudolf Nureyev's boyfriend Robert Tracy, who introduced Timur to the visual art of ballet; DJ Dmitry, from the band Deee-Lite; and the Italian contemporary artist Francesco Clemente. It was a playground for Timur, and when Gustav visited him later the two lit up the town.

I'm not sure why it never dawned on me that Timur and Gustav were gay; that wasn't something that was considered or questioned in those days in Russia. Looking back, I remember Gustav wearing all his cut-off tees and the performance art he and Timur performed, but Russians always had a freedom to act crazy and be flamboyant behind closed doors and filled with alcohol. For me, too, I had had many gay friends in Los Angeles and West Hollywood before I ever went to Russia, and in Russia no one labeled anyone. Plus, homosexuality was illegal under Communism, so it stayed in the closet with the door locked while the Soviet public dutifully ignored everything around them that was out of the ordinary. Gustav and Timur were two stunning artists and remarkable friends, and that was all that mattered to me. We were all kind of crazy and out of the box, anyway, so they didn't seem any weirder or more colorful than the rest of us!

Unfortunately, after embracing the New York gay scene and going wild at the parties that lasted all night, both Gustav and Timur became ill in the years following their stateside trips. It broke my heart. Here were two of the sweetest, most angelic creatures – the brightest stars in the sky – getting sucked into the black hole of sickness and mortality. They had seemed invincible to me, unstoppable energy and magnetic smiles.

◆

In the middle of 1990, a new TV channel in Russia called the Commercheski 2x2, the third channel available in the country, was looking for content to air. I met with them and offered my music videos, as well as some Western music videos I could get as well. They immediately started playing my videos six, seven, up to eight times a day. Millions of people across Russia watched "Modern Age Rock 'n Roll" over and over again. I had never known anyone, especially in the West, who had ever gotten that much free exposure. It was a game-changer.

"Watch this!" I screamed to Yuri, flopping down with a bounce in front of the TV. I switched it on, and my face – jutted chin, eyes hidden behind sunglasses – stared back at me.

I didn't understand the magnitude of what was happening until one day in my apartment I heard some young voice singing. *Am I imagining this?* I thought to myself, struggling to hear the words. I went to the window and looked down, and there was a little girl dancing around outside singing my song "Modern Age Rock 'n Roll!" I got goosebumps up and down my arms. "My song," I told Big Misha, beaming. "She was singing and dancing to my song!"

Big Misha stared at me. "Joanna, I sing your songs all the time. You want me to dance too?"

◆

It was Friday night, June 22, 1990, and Yuri and I were staring at my album cover as the reporter held it up.

"These very minutes, as we speak, Joanna Stingray launches her album *Dumaiyu do ponedelnika* [Thinking Till Monday] at the Artists House on Kuznetsky Most in Moscow," I heard him say. "The record was recorded by Red Wave studio in Los Angeles and released by Melodiya."

Vzglad had become one of the most popular shows on TV, a symbol of *perestroika* and freedom of the press, and it had shaken up the Soviet public's notion of broadcasting and journalism. The program had young hosts wearing informal clothes – live streaming, not prerecorded – and popular music videos to break up the interviews. It was completely different from the rigidly rehearsed and censored programs overseen by the Old Guard. I was thrilled to be on it with my new album and my husband by my side, my "Keep on Traveling" video punctuating the breaks.

"You must have already seen this record – Joanna Stingray's *Dumaiyu do ponedelnika.* The record was released here, in our country, by Melodiya label." Later that night on another news program, I smiled at the same album cover as the reporter held it proudly. "Today, just a few hours ago, the record was launched at the Artists House. And you can see now how it was…"

The program switched to footage from my presentation party filled with many of my friends.[7]

"What is happening here?" The reporter asked me as we watched the footage.

"What is it?" I countered in Russian. "It's *tusofka* in general. It's a party – drinking, eating, with my friends here."

"This time she's in our country not as a producer but as a singer," the reporter continued over the silent video from the party. "She will perform in Leningrad, Moscow, Kiev, and a few other cities."

I sat there, stunned, unable to believe that all of this publicity was actually happening. To hear a reporter say it out loud and broadcast the news to so many Russians made it start to feel real.

I was beyond excited to have a full album released on Melodiya. My album cover was a landscape portrait that Boris painted, to which I had added five photographic figures of myself getting smaller and smaller across the canvas as if I was floating up into the clouds. Boris had been so instrumental in teaching me songwriting, and four of the ten songs on the album I'd written with him, so I loved getting to incorporate his art onto the cover. I was paid no money for the album – as loose as the regulations were getting, the artists still didn't have much of a say in that regard.

A couple of nights later was Kino's biggest concert yet at the Luzhniki Stadium in

---

7   Rashid Nugmanov, Andrei Medvedev, Oleg Kotelnikov, Andrei Krisanov, Sasha Lipnitsky, Inal Savchenko, Andrei Makarevich, Olga Slobodskaya, Yuri and many others were there. Kino's new manager, Yuri Aizenshpis, also showed up, a man who was always nice to me but whom I still never fully trusted with Kino's earnings.

Moscow, and also Yuri's birthday. The concert was sponsored by the newspaper *Moskovsky Komsomolets*, and despite the other bands scheduled to perform as well, the crowd of seventy-thousand fans were all screaming Kino's name. Viktor had asked me to play a few songs as he always did, never leaving me out.

"Viktor, I've got an idea for a video I want to make to my song 'City of Lenina,'" I told him. "Can I get the singing footage at this concert?"

"Of course," Viktor told me, squeezing an arm around my shoulder. "Whatever you want." No matter how big Kino got, Viktor was still the gracious, twinkling guy he'd always been.

I no longer played with the same musicians from the Center band, except for Sasha as my drummer. Pavel, from Zvuki Mu, played keyboards for me, Yuri Ivanov played bass, and Valery Sargsyan played guitar. Timur Gasonov was still my manager.

The day of the concert we filmed a little for the video of soldiers and fans doing an extended arm movement, and then got footage of me performing. It was almost dusk in Moscow, the time of day when the sky becomes fuzzy and indistinct so that everything below it becomes sharper in comparison. It was such a big event for me with so many people, and even though the sound system was making feedback, the rush was amazing. Above the crowd at the back of the stadium was my name on a large score board: STINGRAY.

In the *M.K.* newspaper the next day, Artur Gasparyan wrote that "the audience roared with ecstasy as the American singer alternated her English and Russian language songs, and in the end, hailed and cheered the proclaimed Russian-American friendship."

After I finished my set, I hung out backstage with the guys before they hit the stage. As I sat there on Yuri's lap, laughing and joking with them all, I suddenly felt all of my energy leave my body. The excitement of the last three days – my album release and interviews and performances – had finally caught up with me. To add to that, I was supposed to leave early the next morning to fly back to Los Angeles. When Viktor and Natasha arrived, I could barely keep my eyes open.

"I'm so exhausted I have to go home," I told Viktor, getting up and giving him a big hug. "I don't know how you guys do it."

"Joanna, please stay. Watch us play." He refused to let me out of the embrace until I agreed. "This concert will be special," he promised.

I never met anyone who could say no to Viktor.

When Kino took the stage, darkness had settled in Moscow like a black cat curled around the city. Guys were screaming and girls were sobbing as if the messiah had stepped onto the stage. Viktor represented change, a symbol of hope and freedom and magic and rock 'n roll.

Everyone was on their feet, dancing and singing every single word. Fireworks erupted over us, and the Olympic flame burned. It was only the fifth time in history that flame had been lit, and it was hard to tell if the torch was reigning over the scene or if Viktor was commanding over the torch. He was so powerful, becoming bigger than life as the flame reflected his shiny dark hair and clothes. After the last encore, Viktor went up to the mike like Hercules, his tasks completed and success in his eyes.

"Thank you all very much for being here," he said in a soft, sweet voice. "All the best to you. I think that in the course of the summer we will record a new album. In autumn we will be shooting a new film. Thank you all for coming." He bowed his head bashfully. "Thank you, and goodbye.

With that, he left the stage. I was so lucky that I stayed to see it. In Viktor I could see the line to walk between pride and humility, fame and reality. Later, every time I took the stage, I tried to channel Viktor and what I had seen that night.

"I'm so glad I saw it," I told Viktor before leaving. "The concert was incredible." We did a handshake to consummate our plan to go to Disney World in Florida in February.

"I'll be in Riga for the summer, but if you need to reach me for any emergency you can call Natasha's mother in Moscow and she will give me the message," he said as he walked me to the exit. "If not, I will see you in September."

I wrapped my arms around his lean, sweaty shoulders, and he gave me a kiss.

"Don't forget me while I'm gone," I teased. I pulled away, watching his tall frame lean against the wall and watch me walk away.

"I'll wait for you here, Stingray, as always," he promised.

◆

As the Russians fled south to avoid the heat and humidity of July and August, I headed home. I was always amazed that all these people with very little money still found a way to go relax beside the Black Sea or recline in their countryside *dachas*. Even though I was pretty much living full time in Russia now, I was still a typical American who didn't know how to slow down. If I was leaving for the summer, it wasn't to go chill, but to go record new songs and work on editing my "City of Lenina" video.

The only issue was that Yuri and I would be apart again for a couple months. We had never again spoken about his cheating, and I knew I was too scared to bring it up again.

Somehow, I thought that if I hid it away in the dark, dusty corners of my mind, it

■ "City of Lenina" music video featuring concert footage of my performance from Luzhniki Stadium, where Kino was headlining. I spliced the footage into scenes from *The Truth About Communism*.

couldn't hurt me. I knew that he really did love me, and I tried to convince myself that I was enough for him. Viktor had asked Yuri to come spend some time with him at Natasha's *dacha* in Riga so they could work on the new album together. Yuri and I rarely spoke when we were in different countries, but this summer I knew there wasn't any chance at all. There was no phone at the *dacha*, and I hoped no other women.

Before I left, I made sure to give Yuri a huge hug, pressing our hearts against each other's, and a kiss. I felt strange, anticipatory of something, and I assumed it had something to do with Yuri and his cheating. *It will be fine*, I tried to tell myself as I walked away, but I couldn't shake it.

In Los Angeles, most of my time was eaten up in the editing room. I wanted to make a poignant music video that referenced the change in Russia since I'd arrived there seven years ago. The Games' song that I recorded with English lyrics had abstract references to Soviet life, Leningrad, and Lenin.

"On the frozen shore, the Winter Palace sleeps quietly on," I sang under my breath as I spliced archival footage of Lenin, the storming of the winter palace, and early days of Communism, together with red drawings made by my artist friends and shots from the concert at Luzhniki as soldiers stared down at a flood of people and rock hand signs. I had the rights to my dad's film *The Truth About Communism* and used a lot of the videos from there. "The sun rises up on the city of Lenina… Lenin rises upon the city like the sun."

"City of Lenina" is very fast-moving and jumps from archival footage to modern day. There's one part where Lenin unbends his arm forward from the elbow, and then we had shot a bunch of people and musicians doing the same motion. Sometimes we edited the film backward, so Lenin is walking in reverse or repeating a movement he just did. The manipulation of the editing was a bold choice, but one I felt inspired to make. After the last frame, we put up the word *WARNING!* in big red letters, with smaller white letters underneath saying *please remember to not take life too seriously.* There was no question that some would find the video controversial and offensive, but *glasnost* had been around for a few years now, and I wanted to take advantage of it.

I somehow got the video to a few stations in Russia at which I had contacts. While I was waiting to see if it would get aired, I got word that my album was selling, and the channel 2x2 was airing more of my other videos every day. Allegedly there were even some Stingray lookalikes popping up around Moscow – black clothes, platinum and dark layered hair, Ray Ban style sunglasses. It felt so funny to run around Los Angeles as an unknown, while halfway around the world there were people copying my image. Yet despite this increasing popularity, my "City of Lenina" video was not getting aired. Even the people in charge of my beloved *Vzglad* with whom I felt I had a great relationship were resistant. Every station to which I'd sent it came back saying they loved it and wanted to schedule an air date. Each time that day rolled around, though, the video didn't air. It wasn't unexpected, but I wasn't giving up without a fight.

"Ask the hosts of the programs what the problem is." I told Big Misha over the phone.

"Yes, I understand," he replied, speaking in his quick, considerate way. "But, you see, most are scared to give any reasons. Except one guy, he confided that a big boss from Gosteleradio[8] came to see the video and said no way."

"This is *glasnost!*" I argued. "What could be more emblematic of that than Lenin in a rock video!"

The video wasn't aired for the first time until two years after we originally wanted to release it. There was something satisfying in producing something that got censored, about being a rebel. It reminded me of the early days, skulking around underground. It was part of my image, and I was so proud to be pushing boundaries.

Still at home, I received a Western Union mailgram from Yuri on my birthday. It was the first telex I'd ever received from him. *Happy birthday,* it read, *miss you kiss you, husband.*

Even when I go back and read it today, it puts the same goofy, genuine smile on my face as it did back on July 3, 1990. It was so sweet and thoughtful, and assuaged all my fears I'd had right before I left. Everything felt good, and I was looking forward to going back to Russia in September. In the meantime, though, all I could hope for was another telex from Yuri. It made me giddy. If only I'd known that you should be careful what you wish for.

---

8 The Soviet State Committee for Television and Radio.

◆ I Had a Friend Named Viktor Tsoi

Sometimes things happen from which you will never, ever recover.

I was fast asleep on August 15, 1990. It was the middle of the night, the starless kind where clouds obscure the rest of the universe, when a loud sound jolted me awake. For the first couple of telephone rings, I thought it was happening in my dream. By the third time, I opened my eyes, forcing my tired body to move my arm and pick up the receiver.

"Hello?" I managed to croak out, still only half awake.

"This is the Western Union. I have a telegram for you." The man's voice was sharp, cold, too stark against the dreamy contrast of my dark room and soft bed.

"What?" I mumbled.

"I have a telegram for you that I need to read."

I fumbled for my analog clock, trying to make out the time.

"Okay," I said, accidentally knocking the clock off the table all together.

"Baby (stop) Viktor Tsoi is dead (stop) tragically perished in car crush at fifteen August (stop) kiss you Yuri."

I blinked. In my mind I couldn't process what I'd just heard so clearly. *It must be a nightmare*, I thought to myself. *Thank goodness I'll wake up soon.*

"I'm sorry," the man on the phone added.

"What?" I sat up suddenly, realizing it wasn't a dream or a nightmare. It was real.

"I'm sorry," he repeated. He hung up as I started to cry.

I remember nothing after this. Somehow, my brain knows it's not an experience I can ever revisit. Ever since I decided to tell my story and publish these memoirs, I dreaded coming to this point. I didn't want to try and remember, and I didn't want to be reminded, because the truth is that nothing can ever make it better.

Ernest Hemingway once wrote that "the best people possess a feeling for beauty, the courage to take risks, the discipline to tell the truth, the capacity for sacrifice. Ironically, their virtues make them vulnerable, and they are often wounded, sometimes destroyed." Viktor had been the best of the best, a man who treasured small things even when he became so big. He never feared but fought his way forward with music, appreciating the pain and willing to suffer through it for the things and people he loved. What Hemingway got wrong, though, is that even though Viktor had been fatally wounded, nothing could destroy him. It was the rest of us, the friends and fans left behind to cling with white knuckles to the virtues on which we depended so much, without which we didn't know how to hold ourselves up. We were the ones left vulnerable, alone, hearts broken, and thoughts demolished. To this day Viktor is still virtuous, still beautiful and courageous in our memories. He is an angel, and we're the ones with scars.

I couldn't call Yuri or anyone to get the details of what happened, so I figure the only thought in my mind would have been that I had to get to Russia immediately. Alex Kan recently reminded me that he was in New York when Viktor died, and I called him crying to tell him the news. Neither of us have any recollection of how I got back to Leningrad. I have photos of myself at the Bogoslovskoe Cemetery, but no memory leads to or from the gravesite. It was as if all life had stopped, staccato and senseless. Yuri, Natasha, Gustav, Rashid, Kino manager Yuri Aizenshpis, Igor Tikhomirov and his wife, and Irina my mother-in-law are standing in the photo, but from the looks on our faces none of us were really there. We were somewhere else, retreated into our bodies, unwilling to exist in this place without Viktor.

Around us were hundreds of people, everyone facing Viktor's photo, an acoustic guitar, and piles of flower bouquets. People left gifts of scarves, ribbons, letters, drawings, and crosses. The cemetery had become an enchanted forest of sorts, the colors of honor mixed with darkness and despair.

After the funeral I somehow made it back to Los Angeles, though again I remember nothing of this. I wrote a letter dated August 24, 1990, that I titled "I had a friend named Viktor Tsoi."

I woke up this morning and saw Viktor Tsoi standing in front of me, I wrote. *I could hardly breathe as I asked what he was doing here. He said it was all just a joke and didn't really happen. Tears started rolling down my face as I sat up to hug him, but instead, my eyes*

■ Viktor's funeral. I'm standing with Yuri, Viktor's widow Natasha, Gustav, Igor and Manya Tikhomirov. Yuri's mother is behind me along with hundreds of Viktor's fans.

opened, and I realized that I was dreaming. Viktor was not back, and as I looked around my room, filled with his paintings and photos from our many escapades, I felt empty without him. Viktor was a great star to many, but to me he was a great friend.

◆

To this day there is a void in my heart. I buried something in that grave with Viktor, a piece of myself and my life that I will never get back. When I returned to Moscow again, I drowned myself in work, refusing to go north to Leningrad for many years. It reminded me too much of him.

In the year after his death, Viktor visited me four or five times in my dreams, each experience so real that I would wake up and feel the sadness slightly lifted, because I was so sure he'd been there.

"Don't be sad, Jo. I am fine. It is all okay. Don't worry," he would say. Sometimes I would cry and tell him I was so happy he was there.

"I know, I am happy too," he'd smile. We'd have conversations about life and death, and I remember him always telling me, "It is okay. It is okay."

These meetings, though fleeting, feel as real now as I write this as they did back then. The tears and the sadness and the relief of feeling his presence again is just as convincing in memory as it was in reality. Somehow, at almost exactly a year after his death, he stopped visiting me. It had been long enough that I knew I had to accept he was never coming back to this seemingly empty earth. Like the lyrics in his song, *the star high in the sky was calling him on his way*, all I could do was angle my face up and hope he was looking down.

◆

"Tsoi means more to the young people of our nation than any politician, celebrity, or writer. This is because Tsoi never lied and never sold out. He was and remains himself. It's impossible not to believe him… Tsoi is the only rocker who has no difference between his image and his real life, he lived the way he sang… Tsoi is the last hero of rock." – *Komsomolskaya Pravda* newspaper, August 17, 1990.

There were no truer words. Tsoi had become the stuff of legends, the hero of modern Russia. Even the *New York Times* reported on his death.

"Viktor is an absolute genius of simplicity, clarity and sincerity," Boris had once said. "No other person in Russia composed like Tsoi did."

I was shocked by everything going on around Viktor's death. People were talking about conspiracies; fans were committing suicide. It was a tragic time in history. The only solace I had was that I knew Viktor must have been blissfully happy when he died. He had been in a small village by the sea with the love of his life. He loved to have space and peace, and he had been able to relax that summer out of the spotlight and away from the big cities and crowds of people. I knew that Viktor had gone fishing by himself and died in a car crash on his way home, but I never asked Natasha or Yuri for any details. I was so heartbroken that Viktor was gone I couldn't speak about it. It took almost thirty years for me to talk to Natasha and Yuri about it for this book.

"Viktor and I finished the new album on August fourteenth." Yuri's forehead was creased as he tried to remember, a mix of pain and stoic acceptance painting his dark eyes. "We were both exhausted, but I packed my bags and headed to Leningrad, arriving the next morning at seven. I went right to sleep."

On August fifteenth, Viktor got up quietly between five and six in the morning and slipped out to fish. Natasha spent the morning at the beach with her eleven-year-old son, Zhenya, and Viktor's son Sasha, who was five. They returned to the *dacha* around noon, sandy and red, hoping that Viktor was already there. He usually returned between eleven-thirty and noon from his fishing trips, but he wasn't there. There were no mobile phones, but Natasha knew cars frequently broke down and knew an hour or two delay could be explained.

By two in the afternoon, Natasha was pacing the small space. Now she was afraid that something happened. She left Sasha with her friend and took her son with her on a motorbike to all the lakes where Viktor could be, passing a bus that had driven off the road nearby the village. There was no trace of him – he had already become a ghost.

She and Zhenya came back with the last hope that maybe Viktor had returned while they were gone. He hadn't. Holding Zhenya to her chest, Natasha knew something horrible had happened. She asked a neighbor with a car to take her and her friend Alexei back to the bus she'd seen. It was about four in the afternoon when they reached the damaged vehicle, an unpredictable and overturned image against the soft blue of the horizon.

"I can't go," Natasha said, unable to move her body from the car. "Ask someone if there was another car," she told Alexei.

All she remembers is Alexei's shocked face on the way back to their car. He opened the door and stood on the road, one hand on the roof of the car.

"There was a black car. The collision was horrible."

In that moment Natasha was absolutely sure that there was no hope. They raced to the nearby hospital in Tukums. Natasha sat in the parking lot, staring at the sterile building and weighed down in the seat with the crushing realization that from this moment on, the love of her life would never share a smile with her again. She was speechless. Alexei went into the hospital alone, and he was the one who confirmed it was Viktor in the coffin.

"I woke up around noon on August fifteenth and headed to a friend's house. In the afternoon, I got a call from Marianna telling me the horrific news," Yuri remembered. Natasha had finally been the one to call Marianna. Exhausted and in shock, Yuri had found Igor Tikhomirov and told him. The two of them took their cars to the gas station to try to fill their tanks for the drive to Riga.

"That time was gasoline outages, and we couldn't get any." Yuri's lips curled in as he spoke, as if after decades the anger was still fresh. "So, we had to tell our tragic story, and then we were allowed to get gas."

Yuri and Marianna, and Igor and his wife Manya, drove the two cars that evening to Riga. They went into the morgue and saw Viktor in a coffin. Natasha told me that his skull was crushed like a broken vase, but the face was still untouched and serene.

"When I saw him, I understood the death was instant. The most horrible thought was that he suffered alone, but he didn't," Natasha wrote to me about it recently. As she stood over the wooden box, she stared at the body and realized it had nothing to do with Viktor anymore. He had gone away, somewhere that freedom and peace reigned supreme over the smiles and souls of spirits. The body had been nothing more than a vessel for his enchanted soul.

The next day, they all drove back to Leningrad, following the bus with Viktor's body and Natasha.

"Yuri, that story is awful," I told him, trying to choke back tears. To this day, I'm convinced God blinked the minute of the accident. Not even He could have let that happen.

"Yeah," was the only thing Yuri could say.

♦

Back in Moscow, in the fall of 1990, I couldn't figure out how to go on and return to regular life. I couldn't shake the sadness – I was like a dog drenched in tears who couldn't shake herself dry. I had heard that the day Viktor died someone had written a message on a big wall on Arbat that said *Viktor Tsoi has died today*. Others had followed, writing *Tsoi is alive* and *Viktor did not die, he just went for a cigarette*. I guess cigarettes burned better at altitude, way up in the clouds. It became known as the Tsoi Wall, a graffiti expression of love, admiration, sadness, and remembrance dedicated to Viktor. I decided to go see the wall early one morning. Under the glow of a rising sun through the city smog, I stood under the messages, lyrics, and drawings painted along the wall and was amazed. This monument to my dear friend gave me hope that he would never be forgotten. Every time I return to Moscow, I pay a visit to the site, and every time my eyes traverse the expanding, colorful art I can sense that Viktor knows how much he is still loved on this earth. When I stare at it, I feel Viktor's essence, can almost hear his whimsical, goofy laugh.

It has been thirty years since the last time I was with Viktor. I still miss him every day as if just yesterday we were together backstage, whispering and joking around. There has never been anyone like him, and all I can do is hope his image might be able to inspire people to be more like him in the future. Heroes don't all wear capes – some of them wear black boots, eyeliner, and a bashful smile on their perfect, handsome face.

◆ **Choose Hope**

Gone were the days of red and yellow – green was the new color! Not long ago, Greenpeace had officially opened an office in Moscow, and I had become determined after Viktor's death to help them in some way. I needed more of a purpose than just my own career, something I could do for other people. Not only was I more aware of how fragile life was and how much I wanted to do for others, but Viktor loved nature and I felt like I could honor him by pairing with Greenpeace.

One thing I had always noticed living in Moscow were the smokestacks that choked the city. Dirty clouds dragged themselves along the tops of buildings all day. I went to Greenpeace to start getting information about how air pollution and other forms of anthropogenic contamination were affecting the world. After talking with them I had an idea for a music video I wanted to shoot to one of Viktor's songs that I had rewritten in English. It was called "War," and while my updated lyrics were about soldiers heading off to battle, I had a vision to shoot the video as symbolic of war on the environment.

Greenpeace graciously gave me footage that I could incorporate into the video. I remember filming at night on Arbat Street as I and two musicians who usually played with me walked through crowds with our gas masks on. Most people just ignored us, their nervous eyes avoiding our covered faces, but some stopped and stared outright. As I walked, my vision blurry through the goggles and my breath echoing inside the mask, I remember suddenly feeling terrified that this was how life would be one day in the future. As I edited the video, watching footage of bloody white seals, gasping whales, and smokestacks, it was so hard for me to not become depressed about the state of the world. This video became an outlet for my anger, and every time I cringed at a shot, I extended it, repeated it, determined to force others to come to terms with what was happening. At the end of filming, as I stood in a studio with the band consumed by tails of dry ice and cigarette smoke, I was struck by what we were all doing not just for art but for the message we were trying to send.

Ultimately the video came from a place of hope – hope that if people understood what was happening, they would be compelled to change. If I hadn't had hope, I wouldn't have seen the point of making the video.

Greenpeace had been struggling to get their ads and information out to the Soviets, and they seemed thrilled that my video was being played quite often on the television. It was like a PSA disguised as a music video, something that people would actually listen to and let into their homes.

While the image I created in my videos was colder, more enigmatic, and less friendly or inviting, I think people started to understand that I was something nicer and cleaner. In interviews, despite my dark and standoffish sunglasses, I would talk about how I didn't drink, smoke, or do drugs, and how I was a vegetarian. My harder image was softened with my consideration for my health and for animals, and the way I was constantly laughing at people's reaction to my disclosures made me seem more engaging and fun.

"Why do you wear sunglasses?" An interviewer finally asked one day as they watched, baffled, as I smiled broadly at them.

"It protects me," I said honestly. "It puts a little space between me and the world."

Sunglasses inside made everything darker, the shapes fuzzier, so that big crowds or interview hosts weren't as noticeable or scary. It was also because I had no idea how to do makeup, and instead of wandering the streets with a plain face between faces filled with eye liner and shadow, it was easier to just put on my Ray Bans.

So, there I was, hidden eyes behind sunglasses staring at myself on a postcard. I had been meeting with a lot of creative people in Moscow, and one guy had designed this portrait to use for promotion. *Glory, Rock 'n Roll, Peace* was arched around my head like a halo, blue and red stripes like a curtain down the card, all flanked by my name in Russian at the top and English at the bottom. It was punk and patriotic, and I suddenly felt like a warrior. My career was moving forward despite my heavy heart, and even though Viktor popped into my mind constantly, it wasn't demoralizing or heartbreaking anymore – instead, it gave me inspiration, it gave me motivation, it gave me laughs.

"You like?" The man asked, holding the postcard higher.

■ "Glory, Rock 'n Roll, Peace" Stingray promotional postcard.

■ Stills from the music video for "War," 1990.

All I could do was stare at the huge, perky nipple he had clearly articulated in his art. In my head I could picture Viktor's reaction to it, his surprised eyes and then his deep laugh as he would crack up. I covered my mouth with my hand, trying not to offend the guy as I burst out laughing too.

Viktor was a hero, immortalized and empowered. When I climbed onstage or walked down the street, I always tried to channel his energy. There were very few other women in the Russian rock scene, and I wanted to make young girls feel capable and strong when they watched my videos and saw me on motorcycles, dancing, being silly, and taking charge. I strove to be like Viktor for my own demographic.

◆

Sasha Vasilyev started staying at my place some nights because he didn't have a place to live. He had a wry and witty sense of humor that lit up the sad mornings or dark evenings. During that hard time in my life all I really needed was a little laughter. For some reason, my connection to Yuri felt distant without Viktor there.

I hadn't seen Yuri since Viktor's death. We had always been 'the three musketeers,' and my marriage had been sewn into that friendship. Now, with one part ripped away, it felt like the whole thing was fraying, about to unravel.

I still loved Yuri, but I realized the disloyalty of his cheating had been constantly chipping away at me, and I was no longer in love with him. Somehow it went unspoken that we were no longer really together. We were untethered and floating away from each other. Viktor's death had been the storm that unmoored us both.

By the end of 1991, everyone knew Sasha was living with me, and I heard bits and pieces about someone with whom Yuri was living.

"Joanna, I'm sorry, but can I come to Moscow?" I wasn't surprised at all on the day I finally received Yuri's phone call. "For you to sign a paper for divorce."

Yuri sounded sad, and I realized so was I. It was the end to a dynamic, a way of life, that still held memories of Viktor.

A couple of days later, Yuri and his girlfriend Natasha came to my apartment. I signed the paper and slid it across the table to Yuri.

"Okay Joanna," he said. Then he left. It was almost too easy – just a signature in Russia and you could be born again, or buried. I didn't see Yuri for a very long time after that – he stayed in Leningrad, and I stayed in Moscow – but he has had and will always have such a big space in my heart. I've come to learn that in life there are two things we don't get to decide – love and death. With regards to those, all we can choose is to be hopeful.

♦

On March 1, 1991, my manager Timur Gasonov helped me find a new apartment to rent at 2 Krasnosilsky Pereoolik, House 2, Apartment 5. It was one hundred and seventy-five dollars per month, and I paid up front for the first two years. It was a bigger and nicer apartment than my other one, in an attractive residential area of Moscow with light brown trees and streetlamps. Sasha, my unofficial companion and occasional lover, moved in with me full time. But my faith in love had been so crushed by the failure of my marriage with Yuri, getting into a committed relationship with Sasha was the farthest thing from my mind.

I had a driver by this time and loved jumping from my building to the warm car on those freezing winter days. There were more cars on the roads than during the early communist days, but we could still move around fairly quickly down the wide streets.

One of the big things I noticed as we would drive along, a change that came with the looser regulations, was the littering. Russians seemed to be littering everywhere! I would

■ Stills from the music video for "War," 1990. Sasha Vasilyev is on drums.

watch cigarette butts fly out of open windows or gloved hands, trash stuffing the gutters and creating patterns on the sidewalks. Sometimes I would even see cars pull up to a red light, open their car door, and lay a bunch of trash on the ground before driving off.

"That's disgusting!" I shouted at my driver as the car beside us dumped what looked to be an entire week's-worth of trash on the pavement before turning right. "How is everyone okay with this? Animals instinctively don't poop where they live, so why are we piling trash under our feet!"

When I got home, I stormed up the steps and threw myself miserably into a chair. I suddenly had a vivid memory of when I was very young, watching a commercial over and over that showed a crying American Indian demoralized by all the littering. It had been the early 1970s, and the Public Service Announcement (PSA) was called "Keep America Beautiful." "Iron Eyes Cody," dressed in colorful traditional clothing and paddling a birch bark canoe down a tranquil and glassy river flanked by trees, was suddenly confronted with a river clogged by trash as he turned into a port with huge cargo ships and smokestacks spewing black clouds from the refineries on shore. He could barely land his canoe amidst the plastic cups, bags, and vile pieces of reject.

"Some people have a deep, abiding respect for the natural beauty that was once this country," a voice narrated as Iron Eyes Cody walked from the water to a bustling freeway choked with cars. "Some people don't." I'll never forget the next image of a bag of garbage flying from a car and landing at his feet, splitting open and spilling fast food onto his beaded moccasins. It was at this moment that he began to cry.

"People start pollution, so people can stop it," I said out loud, quoting the last line of the commercial.

The ad had been on billboards and print ads as well as on television, and I remember it had won awards and affected many, many people. For me and many other Americans at that time, such an ad became the quintessential symbol of environmental idealism and inspired a movement towards cleaner living.

An energy-efficient lightbulb went off in my head. I needed to do a PSA for Russians to create awareness about the harm of littering! I had never seen or heard anything like this on Russian TV, but I wasn't deterred. I sat there in my room for hours, wheels turning in my head.

Finally, I jumped up, grabbed my coat, and ran out the door.

♦

I knew that if I wanted to get the public's attention, I had to get some of my famous friends to be in the commercial. Boris, Kinchev, and my new friend Garik Sukachev from the Moscow band Brigada S all agreed right away. I also decided to ask Andrei Makarevich, one of the most famous Russian rockers, even though I didn't know him very well. He didn't hesitate to agree. With such a strong cast, I then had to set up short scenarios for each of them to film.

We started with a yellow taxi driving down an empty street. From the window came some trash that landed on the ground. Andrei Makarevich drove up in his blue BMW, stopped the car, and retrieved the trash. With a disappointed look on his face, he removed it to a proper trash can before driving off. Next, we filmed Garik Sukachev with one of his bandmates, who throws his burning cigarette onto the ground. Disgusted, we had Garik put the butt out with his foot, then pick it up and put it in the ash bin. With a glance at the camera, he shook his head sternly. For Boris, we shot a drunk guy ambling down the street and tossing his empty bottle across the way. As Boris passes him, he goes and picks up the bottle to put in the trash. Lastly, we had Kinchev walk out of a building past someone who spits on the ground. Seeing this, Kinchev grabbed the man's arm and pulled him to a small trash container where he demonstrated how one should spit into the container. For the closing shot, I recorded a closeup of myself.

"*Zemla eta nasha dom, ne nada musorit!*" – The earth is our home, don't litter!

The camera pulled back to reveal a group of people around me proudly putting trash into a garbage can.

"*Da?*" I asked.

"*Da!*" everyone shouted.

I was so impressed with how actively my friends wanted to help out with this. I

■ Clockwise from upper left: Garik Sukachev (with bandmate, smoking), Andrei Makarevich, Kostya
Kinchev (with extra), and Boris Grebenshchikov in our anti-littering campaign, 1991.

edited it all together and had Sasha compose music to go with it on a keyboard I'd given
him. He came up with funny noises to accentuate the actions and added such a kick to
the short video. I couldn't have been luckier with the people who collaborated with me.

The ad aired on TV and was a huge hit! It played numerous times over many weeks.
It was the most fulfilled I'd felt since the *Red Wave* production, to be able to use my
friends and our fame for something meaningful, something much bigger than any one
of us. Most Russians were probably just amused by the "Don't Litter" campaign, but in
the end, I'd be willing to bet at least one thousand teenage girls stopped littering just
like their idols. They may have still been itching to dress trashy, but all their garbage
went into the right place!

♦

"Stingray is an unusual presence in the Soviet rock world," I read in the *Moscow
Guardian*. It suddenly seemed that regardless of the work I'd done with *Red Wave*, the
songs I'd cowritten with Boris and Sergey, and the concerts in which I'd participated, I
was somehow becoming famous in Russia for being "the clean girl."

"*Smotri, eta Stingray, ne nada musorit,*" I heard from a group of people standing right across from me on the metro. ("Look, there's Stingray, she never litters.") I glanced over at them and they blinked, staring unabashedly as I tried to squeeze myself to the other end of the car.

I guess hardcore rock fans knew me for my music, but the rest of the public seemed only to recognize me from my ad. As time went on and people recognized me walking through Red Square and down Tverskaya Street every day with my Sony Walkman for exercise, I became known not just for my clean ad but my clean living. Soviet life never made time for exercise because so much of it was consumed by people schlepping themselves and their groceries to and from metro stations, offices, and houses. Without elevators, people trudged up numerous flights of stairs every day, so exhausted by the time they were done with work or errands that none of them in their right mind would elect to go back out and move some more. I'd come from the land of cars, where nobody would walk even a block or two to the corner store! There was even a famous song by Missing Persons in the eighties called "Walking in L.A.," where the chorus goes: *Walkin' in L.A., nobody walks in L.A.* That had been the culture of my youth, so exercise had to be consciously scheduled into my daily activities.

As I powered down the street, I noticed more and more people would be staring and pointing at me. Some even would stop me and ask for autographs. It was the first time I began to feel famous by myself, not just by association with my friends. I loved it, almost as much as I loved walking.

As I walked, I would think about ideas for my next video. I had gotten super into the new wave of videos screened on MTV that had been shot on film instead of video. The new stuff had a more surreal, authentic quality that made me feel drawn and invested into the depicted worlds. There was one Dutch photographer and music video director, Anton Corbijn, whom I had met briefly when he was in Russia with UB40, and who was the mastermind of many Depeche Mode and U2 videos. He shot on film with an artistic eye and produced these mini films that captured a story arc of real life. I wanted something like that for my song "Turn Away."

Somehow, I had gotten introduced to a young filmmaker named Misha Khleborodov, a burly and sweet beast of a guy with an impish face and easy smile. After all the thinking and stressing about the best way to approach my next video, I decided to just let Misha take control and do what he wanted to do. I loved being able to just show up for once and perform without any extraneous responsibility.

Misha made it a huge production, meticulously thought out and grandly executed. He had a set built to look like an archaic courtroom scene and cast Mario Samolea, a

■ Stills from my "Turn Away" music video directed by Misha Khleborodov.

producer with Brigada S, as a judge dressed in period clothing with a white wig, small spectacles, and velvet coat with lace. There was scaffolding raised to look like stands in a trial, where people stood with flashlights that they would move inconspicuously to cause the room to flicker with light and shadows. When I walked onto the set, I met lawyers, a prosecutor, a stenographer, and a huge man bulging with muscles, wearing only briefs, who was set to guard the defendant. Misha had gotten a very famous Russian actor, Igor Vernik, to play the accused.

I wore black clothes, black gloves, and had tucked my hair up in a black chauffeur's hat. I covered my face with my black Ray Bans and completed the outfit with blood red lips. For one part, Misha wanted to shoot some slow-motion footage with snow falling. I'll never forget what a pain the fake snow was, thousands of small plastic pieces flying into my mouth while I was trying to sing. It took me hours after the shoot to get all the tiny white pieces out of my hair.

By the end of the shoot, the courtroom had become a circus. Actors were ripping papers and brawling, shouting and tearing hats off of their heads. I tore off my own hat and let my blonde hair tumble in front of my face. Through the whole thing Misha kept his vision, maneuvering around everyone and capturing all the action. I was so impressed with everything, and so thrilled with the video and the story it told. It was written about in the newspaper as a hit and even won awards for best director, cameraman, set designers, and video at one of the first video award shows in Russia, presented by the director Sergey Soloviev.

♦

My fans were primarily young people, teenagers who were for the most part, girls. They were so cute, young and innocent while they dressed all in black and made sassy faces. One of my first fans was a fourteen-year-old name Lyuda Novosadova, who eventually became a dear friend.

"The first time I heard your song 'Feeling,' it was on the TV channel 2x2 sometimes in 1990. My sister said, look – it's a really nice song, and Viktor Tsoi is in the video. I watched it and loved it so much! Everyone did. I was watching and listening again and again," Lyuda told me recently. "I was so looking forward to go to your concert on June 23, 1991, at MDM (Moskovsky Dvorets Molodezhi). I bought my ticket the first day they went on sale. I couldn't wait to see you, to listen to your songs live. I remember I prepared my clothing, my favorite clothes, two weeks in advance. But then unexpectedly I met you on Arbat Street by Viktor Tsoi's wall. That was unreal! I remember I was next

■ Surrounded by Stingray fans with Lyuda Novosadova (without sunglasses) on my right, 1990.

to you, and my knees were shaking. People were pushing me, and I was constantly falling on the prickly roses you brought for Viktor's birthday."

My concert that Lyuda was coming to see was my first solo concert in Moscow. I stood backstage in the dim shadows and wished that Viktor could see it all. I was so nervous, but the smiling faces of fans I could see from the stage made it easy. I sang for them, and for my best friend.

After the concert, Lyuda was determined to find out where I lived.

"I heard some gossip that you lived in the same building as Dmitry Malikov, a famous Russian pop star. I probably knew it was Krasnoselskaya area. One day me and my friend Olga went to the inquiry office in Moscow to find Dmitry's registered address. We were lucky! His grandmother opened the front door. She was so kind to us – she told us the entrance of your building and the floor. There were only two apartments, and you opened the door of the first one!"

I remember when these two girls with big eyes and shy smiles knocked on my door. "Jaaa-na!" They screamed nervously.

I had been shocked they'd found me, but very impressed. They reminded me of myself and my best friend Diana, when we used to talk our way backstage at numerous rock concerts in Los Angeles. We spoke for a little bit, and they asked if they could come back.

■ My first solo concert in Moscow, MDM (Moscow Palace of Youth) , June 23, 1991. Photo by Anatoly Azanov.

"Yes, but please don't tell anyone else where I live," I told them. I loved my downtime, and my home was a sacred place after the rush of the stage and the streets. As I watched them giggle and whisper as they walked away, I realized my life had totally changed.

More and more frequently I was approached by people. What had been exhilarating at first started to become overwhelming. I suddenly realized how much strength Viktor had had, and how resilient my friends like Boris and Sergey and Kinchev all were. Sometimes, as I was walking through Red Square, I'd see a group of people rumbling towards me like a parade of little dragons, and I couldn't imagine what I'd say to them.

"Joanna Stingray! Are you Joanna Stingray?" One of them would call out as he approached me.

"Nope," I'd say, hurrying past them. There were enough look-a-likes that I assumed I could pass as one of them. It wasn't that I didn't love my fans – I was so appreciated and continually humbled by all of them. But what people don't tell you about fame is that it hits quickly, like a thunderstorm, and gives you no time to get ready. You could either stand there getting wet or put your head down and hurry through.

◆

"Energetic Joanna's fantasies have no limits," I read aloud from the *Moskovsky*

Komsomolets newspaper. I flipped to another article. "Joanna Stingray is the first American singer in history who builds her career in Russian rock, and, looking at the numerous phone calls to our paper, has succeeded in getting popular. Only girls are calling – they've found a new heroine!"

They say America is the land of dreams, but Russia had become my very own land of realities. In my Wonderland, I had endless opportunities to crank out all the ideas that came into my head. The entertainment industry of the country seemed to be in its own bubble, unattached to the bureaucracies that tried to make life more difficult.

I had this crazy idea to make a short film/cartoon called "Adventures of Stingray," a comedy of do's and don'ts about important issues like smoking, drinking, littering, or pushing. Reading what had been written about me gave all the more reason to try to broadcast important messages. Viktor had shown me that heroes didn't come out of fame, they came out of what you did with your fame. If people were watching me and listening to me, then I wanted to be standing for things that mattered.

I thought if I made my message funny, maybe some of them would sink in more or be more accepted. Living in Moscow was so different than the peaceful, hospitable spirit of Leningrad. Here, people were rude and absorbed in their own lives to a much greater extent, and it was starting to wear on me. Humor was the only weapon I had left to brandish.

Somehow, I partnered with TV director Misha Zhitko, who had a connection to a great animator. We wrote the script together, and he directed it, a mixture of live action and animation. What started as a cartoon gnome casting a spell on my gold record with me in an American flag shirt morphed into me leaving my apartment amidst hooligans and graffiti artists who were painting the stairwell walls and setting mailboxes on fire. The premise of the video was that flashing my gold record suddenly made everyone nicer, politer, more civilized. The music was motivation to be better and more aware of the world and the people in it, at least that was what I hoped. Different songs – "Steel Wheels," "Something Here's Not Right," "Love Is More Than Enough" – inspired different things. My favorite part is the animated Stingray fairy with my two-tone hair and, of course, huge boobs that the male animator couldn't resist including. She flies around the screen in a state of joy as the gnome smiles with his thumbs up.

One of the last shots is of me in my U.S. flag shirt with my Kramer guitar in a large grassy field. There are two other guitarists with me; I remember we had a helicopter hovering above us to shoot it, and that's why it looks so ridiculously windy. To prevent myself from being thrown backwards by the force of the air, I started leaning forward

■ Stills from the music video for "Walking Through Windows," directed by Misha Khleborodov with Sasha on guitar.

and hung in space against the wind. At one point in the video it's obviously we all were getting spooked by how close the helicopter was flying.

The film was aired on Russia's Channel One right before the 9 p.m. evening news. It was so easy to make it and send it to the television company – in America there would have been a year's worth of red tape and hoops to jump through in order to get anything aired. They would have had to approve the script, pick the production team, and would have controlled funding. As an artist, all I wanted was to get my ideas out of my head as quickly as possible, to realize a vision so as to make room for another one. With just a little money and a great director, in Russia the light was always green to go. One day I looked up and realized I was spending less and less time back home. When was the last time I'd actually been in Los Angeles?

I planned another video shoot with Misha Khleborodov because I loved the "Turn Away" music video so much. Once I found someone like him, he was my first choice for another project. We decided to work with the song Yuri and I had written called "Walking Through Windows."

"Just tell me your vision, and I'm ready for it," I told Misha excitedly. "I loved that shot in 'Turn Away' with the big fan, maybe we could incorporate something like that again?"

He raised an amused eyebrow at me. *"Just tell me your vision, and I'm ready for it?"*

The finished video was very simple. Yuri was supposed to be in it on guitar, but at the last minute he couldn't make it. I asked Sasha if he would step in. Even though we filmed in the same dark, dusty room, with sun spilling through the blinds and casting shadows through a fan, we're never in the video together.

◆ Fifteen Minutes of Forever

Briefly I ended up back in America in the summer of 1991. Big Misha, Sasha, and I went to New York and Los Angeles. It was Sasha's first time in the land of the brave, but before we could even land over the Hudson River, he got absurdly drunk on the plane and could hardly move.

"Sasha, New York is a crazy airport," I told him nervously, tugging on his shoulder to keep him upright as the plane taxied. "The passport control lines get totally out of control! Misha and I are gonna run ahead, and we'll save you a spot, okay? You'll join us there?"

As hundreds of us stood uncomfortably in the narrow, winding lanes, Sasha finally came stumbling towards us. One elderly man started screaming at him in Russian.

"You are drunk like a swine!" The man protested. "You are discrediting the Soviet people in front of Americans!"

I had never seen this side of Sasha, this uncoordinated and sloppy walk. Big Misha and I quickly propped him up and dragged ourselves through customs.

"What is this?" I hissed at Big Misha over Sasha's hanging head. "What happened to him?"

"Well, Joanna," Big Misha said slowly as he considered it. "It appears that he is drunk." In Los Angeles, the head of Sire Records, Howie Klein, agreed to meet me and the two guys. He was a friend who had given me lots of music videos from Sire and Warner Brothers artists to air back in Russia. I also took Big Misha and Sasha to see the sights all over town and out with my friends. Sasha would be so fun at the beginning of

■ Me and Sasha, Moscow, 1993. Photo by Leonid Sharapov.

everything, but soon enough he was as drunk as the day on the airplane.

On one of the days I had planned a party at my house for my birthday. A couple hours before the guests were supposed to arrive, I found Sasha sprawled out on the sofa absolutely plastered.

"Misha, what do I do!" I shrieked. "I have no idea how he's going to act!"

Always calm and collected, Big Misha helped me take Sasha to a motel room nearby where we left him with two packs of beer.

"We are going to be back in the evening," Misha told him with an air of dignity. "You leave us no choice."

I had already known that Sasha had a drinking problem. I never drank at all, so it was a strange life living with an alcoholic. Sometimes I questioned my choice to be so close with him, but when he sobered up, he was so funny and creative that he was irresistible. He was a brilliant composer and producer, a self-taught musician who mastered many instruments. I was in awe of him. He was also a fabulous cartoonist, and he made caricature drawings of the two of us that made me think and laugh at the same time.

"I love this one!" I would shout, grabbing a sketch of us being held by our pants by Santa Claus' outstretched hands as he asks, "Are these yours?" In another one, Sasha drew us in the middle of a long remodeling process, both with wings and halos looking down from the clouds as his portrait asked, "Have the workers finished remodeling yet?" In the most trying circumstances, his witty jokes and silly drawings were exactly what I needed.

◆

When I got back to Russia, *glasnost* was gone and suddenly *capitalism* was the new agenda. Everything from the West was suddenly being sold everywhere, and it seemed like some Russians suddenly had the money, even the U.S. dollars, to buy those things. Friends and neighbors began competing to see who could spend the most.

"How much did you pay for this new stereo?" A guest asked the host at an apartment party I was attending.

"Nine hundred dollars," the host boasted.

"Well, I've got one I bought for one thousand!" The guest bragged, his cheeks flushed with pride.

It was one of the most bizarre things I'd seen, until I was walking down the street and saw people wearing new Ray Ban sunglasses with the price tag still attached for everyone to read. It was like a bad episode of the *Twilight Zone*, where everyone is entranced and becomes consumed with the pursuit of material goods. As guys passed me on the sidewalk, they would flip open one side of the jacket to show the designer label.

This cultural phenomenon began incentivizing people to get money at whatever cost. I, like most people in Moscow, depended on open markets for fresh fruits and vegetables that were brought up from the southern parts of the country. I started hearing crazy rumors that unripe tomatoes were being injected with urine to make them red. I had no idea what to make of it!

Russia had become the Wild West. There were stories that Westerners were being beat up for their belongings, and allegedly one guy got hit in the back of his head with a baseball bat just so someone could steal his NY cap. I suddenly realized with a shock that as much as I had complained over the years about being followed by the KGB, they had been like my own private security guards. No one would even think about touching me if they knew I was being watched. Without them, all Western foreigners in the Soviet Union were left to the hungry wolves. The thing about wolves was that, despite their smaller size, they were much more outwardly aggressive than the former Soviet bears.

But the thing about, bears, however, is that you think they're gone, and then suddenly they appear out of hibernation. I was in Los Angeles in August when I saw a news story about a coup happening in Moscow. The hardliners who had consistently been against reform were trying one more time to take control and turn back the clock. As I frantically tried to call Yuri and my friends, I realized all the lines were busy or wouldn't work. It was, for a moment, just like old times.

I returned to Russia not long after the short-lived coup. The wolves were back, drooling over dollars and trying to drag huge boomboxes and designer furniture out of stores and down the streets.

"Watch it!" Someone scolded me in Russian as I dodged the huge silver platter extending from their arms.

"Easy cowboy," I muttered, ducking down a side street. Against the horizon I could see the light dipping towards the west, and with my arms wrapped around my body I ran off into the sunset.

♦

"What would you say to Joanna if you met her?"

A journalist stood in the crowd on Arbat Street, right outside the Melodiya store where my new record *Walking Through Windows* was being presented. It had been released by one of the new independent record labels that had popped up with the new *capitalism* called Sintez Records, started by the bassist and singer from the Time Machine group, Alexander Kutikov. It was September 14, 1991, and hundreds of mostly young fans stood outside the store waiting to make a purchase and get an autograph.

"We love you!" A fan cried in response to the journalist. "We wish you success in your music! More concerts! In Peter, in Moscow, everywhere!"

As the crowd started to get a little unruly, the store decided to let some people in to buy the album and poster earlier than was planned. As a thin stream of fans went inside, somehow the group outside continued to grow, filled with Stingray look-a-likes. The Soviet police were called to control it. They parked their boxy yellow cars on the sidewalk and formed a line of police to push the people back.

A video journalist kept sliding through the mass of people asking questions.

"You look exactly like Joanna Stingray," he said, stopping at one woman I would come to know as Anya. She had my exact hair, black chauffeur's hat, sunglasses, and hanging earring. "It's not a coincidence?"

"No!" She responded proudly. "But it's not a fanaticism. It's a bit more than fanaticism. I discovered Joanna for myself, nobody guided me to her."

"Is it a problem for you that she sings in English?" The reporter pressed. "Do you understand everything she sings about?"

"You know, I have her two records, and I have had them for a long time. I can easily understand everything there."

"And what about you?" The reporter moved on to another look-a-like. "You can ask

■ Outside the Melodiya record store before the release of my album *Walking Through Windows*.

her any question, and we will relay it to her."

"Will you really?"The woman looked directly into the camera. "Joanna, honey! What do you make of your Russian fans? I would want to ask about her plans for the future and ask her to make more concerts in Moscow. And not only in Moscow but throughout the U.S.S.R." She paused, struggling to find the next words she wanted to say in English. "Joanna, I love you very much!"

I was at my apartment getting ready for the signing. I had no idea such a big crowd had gathered, and in my mind, I was worrying that not enough people would show up. How embarrassing that would be! I finished getting dressed and sat on the corner of my bed, eyeing the clock as my nerves built.

The crowd was getting larger by the minute.

"Just send her a huge hello, we love her very much," another fan shouted to the camera.

"What do you love her for?"The journalist asked.

"She is a wonderful singer and a wonderful person!"

"How do you know what kind of person she is?"

"It's obvious!"

If only I could have heard what they were saying as I bounced my knees nervously in my apartment, chewing my nails and anticipating a quiet, sad event.

■ They closed the doors to control the crowds. Photos by Alexander Nemenov.

"We wish her happiness in her personal life, in music, health, all the best in every-thing," fans shouted. "And we wish she comes to the Soviet Union more often!"

Finally, a grey Lada pulled up to the store. From the front seat stepped Big Misha, and from the backseat came Yuri Aizenshpis and me in a yellow and black stripped shirt and leather jacket. I couldn't believe how many people there were.

Some of the kids near us realized it was me and started running up.

"*Privyet*," I said kindly as Big Misha tried to hold them back, but more started running towards us.

"We need to go to the back entrance," Yuri said quickly, surveying the crowd as it rushed towards us.

The next thing I knew, we were running up the sidewalk with a tail of fans pounding the pavement behind us. It was the first time I felt really famous, and as I ran, I flashed back to me and Viktor running from his fans outside the Leningrad bread shop. It felt so good but so strange, like being in someone else's body as you sit back to watch and giggle at the absurdity of it all.

I went into the store from the back stairwell. I could hear people whistling and cheering. The girls who worked in the store took me to a side where all my albums lined the wall and were stacked between Vysotsky albums for sale. I couldn't believe my record was right next to such legendary stuff!

"Oh wow," I breathed. It was crazy to see.

Timur Gasonov was there trying to help organize everything, and so was Mario Samolea, the judge from my "Turn Away" video with whom I'd become friends. I gave them both big hugs before I sat down and started signing. People's arms reached over one another as they waved my old and new albums, photos, postcards, and posters. It was crazy to see a bunch of Joanna Stingrays crowding around me – same crazy hair style and dark clothes. It was the biggest compliment I could have ever gotten.

Two police guarded the door, letting in small amounts of people at a time. I could see everyone else pressed against the glass windows trying to worm their way to the front. Many girls were holding red roses against their black jackets. When they would finally reach me, the girls would giggle or tear up, and the few boys would smile broadly as I signed their album.

Lyuda, the fan who had come to my home, showed up. I was so happy to see her familiar face! Later, she came through again, and later, once again. I was so amused by her determination, and happily signed whatever she had.

"Maybe you can sign faster?" Timur whispered to me, trying to get the people moving faster. "I'll asked the manager why we can't let more people inside."

"Please keep away from the door!" We heard her shout before Timur could approach her. "We're not going to let anybody in before you step away from the door!"

"We came from all over Russia!" A fan screamed back. They surged forward.

"Help me!" A girl screamed outside as she became compressed between the thick swarm of bodies.

The doors to the store closed until everyone stopped pushing, but it only made the crowd more impatient and rowdier. The glass in the front cracked, and suddenly the signing was stopped. I watched anxiously as Timur ran forward to help sort it out.

As I sat there waiting for them to let people back in, I was amazed that people would wait that long just to get an autograph from me. It was insane! They started playing my album over the speakers as Timur started pulling in person after person, moving the line quickly and efficiently.

"Tell me, please, you haven't just happened to be here?" I heard the journalist ask a young guy.

"No, not at all. I was here a year ago when her first record came out, and I met her then. Joanna as much as Viktor Tsoi is someone very dear to me, especially after Viktor's death. Her music helps us live at this difficult time."

It was surreal. I felt like my heart was going to explode I was so grateful and happy.

So, this is what it's like, I thought to myself, remembering all the times I'd watch as fans flooded around Boris and Kinchev and Viktor. I never imagined it would happen to me.

Andy Warhol had coined the term 'fifteen minutes of fame,' but this was the type of feeling that I knew I'd remember forever.

♦

Just to confirm that Communism was on the way out, Metallica, AC/DC, Pantera, and Black Crows flew to Moscow as the Monsters of Rock to put on a free concert for their fans in the U.S.S.R. It was sponsored by Time Warner, who promoted the concert as a "celebration of democracy and freedom" in a place that for so long had condemned both confetti and liberty.

Time Warner was even allowed to film the event for a documentary.

Instead of a conventional venue, the whole thing was going to be set up right at the Tushino Airfield outside of Moscow. I was invited to attend the concert and given a backstage pass, but because I didn't know many of the bands' songs, I was considering skipping it. In the end, I decided to go and see what I'd been missing in the American heavy metal scene all these years.

Thank goodness I showed up, because it ended up being one of the most incredible experiences of my life.

The little-used military airfield was transformed with a spectacular stage that was shiny with equipment. There were a couple of dozen camera operators on or near the stage at any given time during the concert, and automated cameras on booms that dipped and swung like aerial dancers. Hundreds of uniformed police stood around the stage, their eyes continuously drawn to their comrades hidden in trucks parked outside the scene.

I was taken from behind the stage to the side of it for the best viewing. I was shocked at the ocean of people in front of me, everything breathing and pulsing like white-capped waves. I knew some Russians enjoyed heavy metal, but I'd had no idea it was so many! At least three hundred thousand people groped towards the stage, cheering.

"Stingray! Stingray!" I heard a few people scream when they caught sight of me in my sunglasses and black leather. I smiled and waved, then walked back into the obscurity of the curtains.

The first band was Pantera, a collection of bare-chested and tattooed men I could see the girls loved and the guys wanted to be. There was lots of guitar distortion under the singer Phil Anselmo's low, devilish voice, and the cacophony overwhelmed me in a

■ Monsters of Rock concert at Tushino Airfield, September 28, 1991. There was no official count, but according to the *New York Times*, Times Warner estimated possibly over half a million people were in attendance. Image unattributed.

jarring and almost scary way. But as the crowd jammed their fists in the air and jumped up and down with the heavy bass beat, I couldn't help but get caught up in their excitement. The next band was Black Crows, a unique kind of hippie version of the Rolling Stones with prolific lyrics that made my jaw brush the floor.

"I can't believe it," I whispered to myself as my eyes drifted from the grungy band to the innumerable people screaming, singing, and holding up their hands in rock signs.

Metallica absolutely blew the crowd to pieces. James Hetfield's flowing hair and iconic mustache vibrated with his high pitches and the long guitar solos. There were a few incidences with the police during their set, dealing with drunk and rowdy fans, but even the police seemed thrilled to be there in the thick of things. I kept thinking how disgusted the old KGB would think it all was – the long, dirty hair, the eyeliner, the screams and the gravel in their voices. Just a few years ago AC/DC and their music had been banned from the Soviet Union. It almost made me laugh to imagine the old guard's twitching, traumatized eyes and frowning muzzles if they were to witness this.

AC/DC climbed the stage to the sound of shrieks and catcalls. I couldn't take my eyes off the guitarist Angus Young in his black shorts and tie. He was hysterical and hypnotic, performing against the lead singer in his black newsboy cap. Their first song, "Back in

■ Some of the strongest performers I saw in concert in the Soviet Union channeled that unmistakable masculine rock energy of their Western male peers. Left to right: Misha Barzukin of Televisor, Yuri Shevchuk of DDT, Andrei Panov ("Pig") of Automatic Satisfiers. Photos from various concerts in 1988.

Black," was one I realized I knew! Sasha loved that song, but I'd never known who the artists were. The singer, Brian Johnson had a voice like a bird plummeting from the sky, moving around the stage with an animated face. The whole crowd sang "Highway to Hell" in unison, and unlike the staccato songs of the previous bands, I could get swept up in a melody and a story. Out of the corner of my eyes, I could see even the police and guards had their hands up in reverence. Somewhere in the set, Angus Young lost his shirt, tie, and jacket, writhing on the ground with his fingers crawling around his guitar and sweat pooling around his body. As I watched a naked blow up doll with huge boobs float over the stage, I couldn't believe I was in the Soviet Union. I kept shaking my head, expecting it to all vanish and then settle like dust.

At the end of the last song, a stunning show of pyrotechnics and fireworks exploded around the stage. As the crowd began to pour out from the airfield, the military men formed two straight lines to make a path for the people. I watched bright and fiery eyes disappear calmly into the night. It was iconic. I stood there knowing the Soviet Union had reached a point from which there was no going back.

◆ **A New World**

"STINGRAY BEHIND BARS!!"

The headline in the newspaper *Moskovsky Komsomolets* caught my attention immediately.

"At 1 p.m. today, workers at the MosFilm studios were shocked by a whole mob of girls in black glasses and long-haired youth in fashionable clothes. Thirty young types of both genders sacrificed their day of studies to take part in a new video clip of Joanna Stingray," I read aloud. "The action takes place in the years of stagnation, which were symbolized with bars put all around the pavilion by the director, Misha Khleborodov. Some of the musicians who participated in the clip, which will be shown on the new TV program *Video Peak*, were musicians from Brigada S, Mega Police, and Message."

The end of 1991 wasn't slowing down as it raced towards the next year, and now that I could see such a growing fan base I tried to incorporate them in some of my plans. My third music video with the director Khleborodov was to the song "Rock Club," which was written with Games. The song was a celebration of the Leningrad Rock Club. Khleborodov got Misha Mukasey as the cameraman, a young and lanky guy whose father was a famous cinematographer in the U.S.S.R.

The video was simple, a stage behind a fence in an empty warehouse. A neon light spelling out *Rok 'n' Roll* hung above us. They'd tried to do the sign in English but had misspelled the first word. I loved it.

■ On the stage set for my "Rock Club" music video directed by Misha Khleborodov, January 30, 1992.

A bunch of the best guitarists and drummers[9] joined me for the shoot. I always loved when it was me and the boys. It made me feel strong and tough but still feminine in comparison. It was just the best.

Mario Samolea was working on the production team. He was the one who had found all the rocker musicians in it. As I walked up to the group, they all smiled at me, a cigarette hanging from each one of their mouths.

Behind the stage is where we put all the fans and look-a-likes. I stood above them playing my Kramer guitar embossed with two flags and singing into a red mic stand. We shot so many takes at so many different angles. For the bridge we had the fans holding up their lighters and a *Save the World* banner.

The thing I remember most from the shoot was this one punk guitarist with blond hair, dark glasses, black leather, and skull rings licking all his fingers. I thought he was so cute and edgy.

My fan Lyuda was, of course, part of the shoot, and remembers not washing her face for a week after I kissed her cheek with my black lips. She seemed to be everywhere I was and had even stopped by my apartment on her fifteenth birthday. I'd given her a

9 Sergey Galanin, Kirill Trusov, Oleg Nesterov, Viktor Zinchuk, Artem Pavlenko, Igor Yartsev and Pavel Kuzin

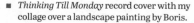

■ *Thinking Till Monday* record cover with my collage over a landscape painting by Boris.

■ Signing *Walking Through Windows* for a fan, Moscow, September 14, 1991. Photo by Alexander Nemenov.

signed photograph and a Soviet and American flag on a stand. I loved seeing her glowing, beaming face, which gave me an idea to put together a contest to spend a day with a few of my fans in Moscow. I edited a video promo for the contest and begged my manager Timur to do the voiceover.

"And you! Are you a fan of Joanna Stingray? If you are, you can be one of the three lucky winners of the 'One Day with Stingray' competition! To mark the release of Joanna's new album *Walking Through Windows* we're giving three lucky winners of the competition a chance to meet Joanna in Moscow, have a meal with her at a Pizza Hut restaurant and play bowling with her and her friends. Isn't it cool? Each of the three lucky winners will also receive an official t-shirt, a baseball cap, a badge, an autographed poster, a tour billboard, photographs, three albums released in the U.S.S.R. – *Joanna Stingray, Thinking Till Monday, Walking Through Windows* – and her American 1983 record. And finally, they will receive a backstage pass to any of Joanna's concerts. So, how can you have One Day with Stingray? First, you should be a Joanna Stingray fan. You may or may not look like Joanna. You may be large or small, but you have to be a Joanna fan. Second, you should send a postcard with your name, age, address and telephone number to the address: Joanna Stingray Fan Club, Post Restante, K-9, Moscow, 103009. All letters and postcards should be posted before December first this year. They all will be placed in a bag and on Friday the twentieth of December, three winning postcards will be revealed on the *OBOZ* TV program. And if you are lucky, you will spend One Day with Stingray! One Day with Stingray! It's fantastic!"

■ In concert, Leningrad, 1988. Photo by Dimitri Konradt.

I had to keep my hand over my mouth while he recorded to keep from laughing at his animated face and energetic voice.

During the editing, we added effects to his voice that made the phrase "One Day with Stingray" booming and dramatic. The video behind the sound included crowd footage and shots of what the three winners would get. We filmed me, Timur, Mario, and Khleborodov eating pizza and then shot Big Misha wearing the shirt, hat, pin, and everything else. I'll never forget the image of him standing in full Stingray regalia with his arms full of Stingray stuff as stoic as a Victorian model. We were laughing so much during the whole thing. The last shot was Timur next to a life-size cut out of me with his arm around it.

"It looks real," I whispered to Big Misha just as Timur picked up the cutout and wandered out of the frame. We added a loud crash to the end.

The ad got aired a few times on the new hit TV program on Channel One, *MuzOBOZ*, which was run by a youthful blond named Ivan Demidov. He was one of the founders of VID Television Company. On December twentieth I went in to announce the three winners.

"Svetlana Ershova from Moscow, Maria Kotomueva from Perm, and Michael Rotov from Yurga!" They were fifteen, nineteen, and fifteen, respectively.

Not long after, we were all together. They were so polite and sweet, and after a long day of fun were gracious and thankful. I loved being with them and seeing the world and myself through their bright eyes. I would have loved to do that every week if I could.

On December twenty-third, I had my second concert at the MDM in Moscow. I was getting comfortable performing a solo show in front of a large crowd. Sasha was always right behind me on a riser in a leather vest and headband, and I trusted him with the music. In between each song, ten to twenty fans would run up on stage to hand me flowers and give me kisses.

Timur was always there to try to rush them off so I could go on to the next song.

"JO-AN-NA, JO-AN-NA," the crowd chanted. It felt amazing. Every time we'd start a new song, the crowd would roar with recognition. I felt like a floating, impermeable balloon.

It was going to be my first Christmas in the Soviet Union, and that concert was the best gift of all. Most Russians still celebrated it on the old calendar, but I was so excited to celebrate in Moscow. That morning I turned on my TV to an unexpected surprise. Gorbachev was on Central Television announcing his resignation as President of the U.S.S.R. He would be the final leader of Communist Russia.

"I want to thank from the bottom of my heart those who during these years stood with me for a right and good cause."

Looking back now, I realize I could never have done what I did without Gorbachev in power. I would have been thrown in jail or out of the country. I was proud to be there witnessing this historic moment, my face glowing in reflected light from the television against the twinkling Christmas lights.

The next day, the red flag of the Soviet Union was lowered in front of a few onlookers and replaced by the tricolor of the Russian Federation flag. For all the years I didn't believe in Santa Claus, I had believed in the Russian people and a peaceful surrender of the past.

◆

"What do you mean the mafia would like to meet with me?!" I stared at Timur, my mouth immediately dry.

Russia at this time was written and talked about as being like The Wild West, and it was becoming wilder by the day. Suddenly the streets of Moscow were filled with swollen, blacked-out Mercedes cars and rumors that many criminals who had run some of the former Soviet Union's industries were taking advantage of the chaos and embezzling lots of money. While the average Russian was still struggling to understand what this new capitalist existence was, the masterminds were taking advantage of it. I'd also heard about the mafia starting to control some aspects of society and fighting with each other for authority, but it had all seemed far away, like a dark and twisted fairy tale. I was so wrong.

"One of your former bodyguards is now part of the mafia," Timur explained to me. "They want to set up a meeting to speak."

"Speak about *what*?" I asked. I couldn't imagine what we could possibly have to offer each other. I did respect that they reached out to ask me, instead of just grabbing me at a concert and dragging me into a basement. We decided the meeting would take place at my apartment, because my old bodyguard Misha had been there many times.

"We have seen many of your videos all over the TV that you pay to get aired," Misha said bluntly as he sat down. "We would like some of the money."

"What do you mean I pay to get them aired?" I asked.

"All artists pay to have their clips aired," he replied.

I shook my head. "I have never paid anyone to air my clips." It was the truth. "Some TV stations just asked for my clips and started airing them. Others air mine in exchange for Western videos I give them to play. I haven't gotten money from any of my albums, and I pay very little to get my own videos made!"

He studied me, his dark eyes unmoving. "Okay. We'll let it go for now, but we might have to meet again in the future."

"Okay," I said uncertainly, showing him the door. It was nerve-wracking, but at least they ran it like a business, and I knew exactly what their motives were. It was a lot less scary than being attacked by a random hooligan in the street. It rattled me anyway, but I tried to ignore it and to keep being creative.

♦

I was meeting and hanging out with more of the Moscow musicians and starting to feel that amazing energy of community I'd felt in Leningrad. I missed those guys, but I loved being part of a posse again. There was the guitarist from Brigada S, Sergey Galanin, Alexander "Sasha" Sklyar from the punk metal band Va-bank, Valodia Shakhrin from the Sverdlovsk band Chaif, the blues guitarist Sergey Voronov from Crossroads, and the consummate front man of Brigada S, Garik Sukachev. They were all badass and creative, a band of pirates led by Garik. He was the type of person who made me want to follow him on adventures and search for treasure. He was the son of a World War II military man and Nazi concentration camp survivor. Garik was one of the best showmen I'd ever seen, whether or not he was onstage. The world was his audience, and he reveled in constantly trying to surprise it. His voice, actions, and energy were all freebooter – lawless and dangerous but considered and strategic. He could just stand there, exuding a force of nature like wind through sails. When he got drunk, he became a time traveler from the seventeenth century, cursing and stalking about like a buccaneer with stains on his shirt. I considered him a piece of art, and of course asked him to make a cameo in my next video.

The cameraman Misha Mukasey had introduced me to the young director Fedor Bondarchuk, son of the famous Soviet director Sergey Bondarchuk who had directed *War and Peace* and won an Oscar for Best Foreign Film. There was a trend I was noticing that was starting in Moscow, where the children of famous parents were coming up in the same business. It reminded me of my classmates back at Beverly Hills High School who had followed in their famous parents' footsteps as well. I liked Fedor's vibe right away. He was young and charismatic but almost manic in his creativity. Fedor's partner, Styopa Mikhalkov, was the son of a renown Russian filmmaker Nikita Mikhalkov. Fedor and Styopa had a company on the MosFilm lot called "Art Pictures," and they used their entitlement to make the most of everything they had. We discussed having Fedor produce and direct one of my videos with all of his resources.

"'Dancing in the Sky,'" he decided, a song I'd written with Sergey Kuryokhin.

The set was its own miniature version of a rabbit hole. We had a blood-red backdrop behind a naked girl painted like a zebra and a guy painted in red and white. It was unpretentious but dramatic, with a lot of closeup shots. Superimpositions of white birds flew around my big red lips and dark sunglasses, my hair hidden in a leather cap. I felt intense, angry almost, and in the editing Fedor used effects to make the video pulse to the beat. For the bridge we had Garik, the flamboyant leader of Brigada S, in all black, his white face stark behind his brown mustache, sitting at a black upright piano that was patterned by live birds sitting on top. I remember watching him play the notes with his right hand while he twisted his whole body and stared into the camera.

Fedor was born to be a director. He was Zeus over our set of misfit deities. Growing up I'd always heard stories about actresses falling for their director and it had always seemed so silly to me, but I fell hard for Fedor. It wasn't that he was a gorgeous man, but he had power and vision that made him indelibly attractive. Very often on the shoot he would stand behind the camera in silence, just staring at me. He would roll his hand up and stare through it, walking closer and closer until we were just a fist away from each other. He'd reach out and move a piece of hair from my face, and I felt like I was melting. I kept it to myself the entire time we were filming, but after the wrap he walked up to me and I couldn't resist.

"Don't you want to kiss me?" I asked. And he did.

It was the beginning of both a professional and sometimes personal collaboration.

■ Stills from the music video for "Dancing in the Sky," directed by Fedor Bondarchuk, with Garik Sukachev on piano.

♦

Now that the Iron Curtain had finally dropped, Westerners were heading to Russia. The first to come from America were missionaries, hellbent on saving the people they had never met. One day I opened my door to four young fans, the kind I was used to asking me for an autograph or leaving me cards or fresh fruit. Instead, they all bowed their heads.

"We love you so much," they spoke over each other. "We just want to make sure you believe in Jesus, so you don't go to hell."

It took everything to keep my composure and not burst out laughing at the strangeness of it all. "Religion is a very personal thing," I told them. "It's not something you have to share with others."

This happened a couple more times, baffling me to no end, until I realized that a religious group from the States was proselytizing through them.

"Don't worry about me," I sighed when I opened the door to them yet again. "I believe in God. I'm very spiritual." I closed the door before they could say anything.

I had been raised by a Jewish father and a Catholic mother, and I'd had more TV-dinners growing up than conversations about religion. I think the only time I'd heard mention of Jesus Christ was when my older sister Rebecca would get mad at me.

"Jesus, Joanna!" She'd scream, her tall and lean frame casting a shadow over me. "What is wrong with you?"

I'd always believed in God, but not in the institutional way. For me, it wasn't about a church or a temple, but just about a feeling inside me or a twinkle in the universal night sky.

It was slightly disconcerting to see these young, impressionable women huddled around my door telling me to believe in Jesus because they loved me. They looked so stressed, even a little fearful, at the prospect of what would happen if a person didn't agree to the principles of Christianity. I never thought religion should be about fear or anxiety. Spirituality, like music, should inspire and instill hope.

Another American group that came, AESOP (AIDS Evaluation of Street Outreach Projects), was dedicated to spreading awareness about HIV/AIDS. Since I had already lost many of my gay friends back in Los Angeles to that horrific disease, I decided I wanted to help tackle this taboo subject. Homosexuality was still in the closet in Russia, and intravenous drug use was on the rise, so AESOP was angling their information to emphasize that HIV/AIDS was happening to straight people too. I went to a few gatherings of girls to talk. I'd start off discussing the environment and giving out Greenpeace pamphlets, something familiar to ease them into the positive propaganda, and then transitioned to talking about sexual transmission of HIV/AIDS.

"The best way to stay safe is to always use a condom," I said again and again. From what I knew, very few Russians ever used a condom, and they were hard to find. I had even learned that some of the upper-class Russians used abortion as a kind of birth control. It seemed reckless and destructive, and I wanted to help these girls avoid that.

After a specialist explained about sexual transmission of HIV/AIDS, I had the girls follow me in a hands-on demonstration. We handed each individual a cucumber and had them practice putting condoms on. It was absolutely hysterical.

The girls giggled, trying to make it fit, cucumbers and condoms jumping over tables and across the room. We sent each of them home with a rainbow of colorful condoms.

♦

I was still trying to do my daily walks, but more and more people were stopping me in my tracks. They were very sweet, asking for autographs or to talk to me, but walking was my meditation, and without it I was crazed and frazzled all day long.

I started tucking my hair up in a hat and trying different ways to disguise myself. I loved being recognized in certain places, like at a restaurant where I could get seating right away or brought a special dessert, or at a concert where I could get backstage passes and invitations to the after parties, and written about in the newspaper. There were moments, though, when it made me uncomfortable. When I was in the market, people would literally come up and try to see what I was buying, or comment on me as if I wasn't even there.

"Why do you care what I eat?" I wanted to ask them. "Why do you care how I'm dressed?" I understood it came with the territory, but sometimes I couldn't help but wish I was invisible. What I would give to run through the grocery store with my hair down and my cart full, unencumbered by scrutinizing eyes.

I didn't know how David Bowie dealt with being such an iconic superstar not just in his home country but around the world. I sat and interviewed him with his new group Tin Machine and couldn't believe how normal and nice he seemed. It was as if the pressures of fame hadn't sharpened his edges at all, just turned him into a diamond.

"Nice to see you again, Joanna," he'd said with a huge smile cracking his sweet face. I could tell he was just having so much fun with his life and his new band. He was passionate about the music and getting it out there, so I put together a record deal with one of the new independent labels in Moscow, SNC Records, to get his stuff released in Russia. Bowie was thrilled, especially because I got their cover of four naked males approved as well.

"'Atta girl!" Bowie cheered when I told him.

I had started interviewing different Western bands with the help of my friend Howie, who ran Sire Records and had numerous connections. I wanted to make all the interviews into a program somehow. I had many of my own connections to important people at the

Russian TV stations. It wasn't like the old days when meetings with executives would just be me and these older men, throwing back shots of vodka every ten minutes to toast to business. Now, with the young rising execs, I didn't have to force my face into a smile as I cringed at the bitter burn of alcohol. These new guys were hip and capable of talking to me about more Western visions. One of the most impressive young guys I met was Kostya Ernst, who had been one of the *Vzglad* team and now had his own program he'd named *Matador*. He was refined for his age, good looking with a sharp mind and a special *it* in his personality my stepfather always told me some people are just born with. I knew Kostya would be very important one day – and he is – currently as CEO of Russia's Channel One. He aired some of my stuff on his show and gave me guidance in other endeavors I was doing. With his encouragement I took the interviews I'd done with Western bands and edited them with some video footage.

The program *MuzOBOZ* aired segments on their weekly shows.

◆

At this time, I was also invited to take part in Garik Sukachev's remake of Kinchev's song "Fsyo Eta Rock'n Roll" – "Everything Is Rock'n Roll." I was thrilled to be included in the group! I showed up to see almost every important current Russian rocker there. We all recorded our parts at the SNC studio, and even though I only had three lines besides joining in at the chorus, I had one of the more controversial lyrics.

"Well, we, well we are homosexuals," I sang, since none of the guys would sing that line with Kostya. What I didn't understand was that, in Russian, the word I sang for homosexuals was mean and slang jargon. It makes me cringe today, thinking about how I'd sung it. If I'd have known the impact behind that language, I would have passed.

We all got to shoot a video for the song together, a band of rascals having the time of our lives – Garik, Kinchev, Shevchuk, Butuzov, Galanin, Shakhrin, Sklyar, Voronov, Alisa guitarist Igor "Chuma" Chumychkin, and a Brigada S guitarist and drummer. We all stood in front of an orange and red brick wall and did our own thing, free to move, sway, and dance in any way that expressed the rhythm of our souls. I danced and sang a line together with Shakhrin, leaning into his serene disposition. The chemistry between all of us could have rocked the cosmos. You could tell these musicians adored one another and respected everyone in the group immensely. I was swept up in it and never wanted that day to end.

And the fun continued – on May 16, 1992, Brigada S put on a concert named after Kinchev's song we remade, and the whole clan from the video got to be a part of it. There

■ Video shoot for "Fsyo Eta Rock 'n Roll," Moscow, Spring 1992. Left: Garik Sukachev, Sasha Skylar, Valodia Shakhrin, and me; right: me doing make up with Kostya Kinchev.

was even a shirt made featuring all of our faces that I still have.

The concert was at the Soviet Wings Universal Sports Palace in Moscow, which had fifty-six hundred seats. I was part of two songs, some of my all-time favorite performances I have ever given. First, I sang Creedence Clearwater Revival's "Have You Ever Seen the Rain" with Garik Sukachev. Garik's voice cut through the stadium like a sword, right through everyone's skin and down to their bones. I got to wear a great shirt I had bought in England with big white skulls and *FUCK CENSORSHIP*. I felt so empowered to know I was being filmed in it and would be seen on Channel Two's *Programma A*. This type of shirt would never be approved for American TV, so I felt like a real rebel. In that moment, kicking my legs and leaning on Garik, I felt I was right where I was supposed to be.

The last song of the concert was, of course, "Fsyo Eta Rock 'n Roll." The minute the crowd heard the first bars they leapt towards us screaming, pumping their arms and waving sparklers. Watching the video now still makes my blood roar with the energy shooting off the stage that night.

"It might as well be the last at least in terms of that genuine brotherhood atmosphere that reigned at the concert," Sergey Antipov, a presenter from *Programma A*, stated about the concert. It was such a special performance. For all of us on stage that night, *fsyo eta rock 'n roll* – everything really was rock 'n roll!

✦

"A clean life is a good life," I promised in my interview after the Clean Water Concert, but Russians were beginning to realize a clean life was an expensive life now too.

After the initial excitement during *glasnost* and the introduction of capitalism, Russians got a rude awakening to learn that they were suddenly being charged for energy and water use in their apartments. Up until this point they had only paid *kopeks* for this, but freedom never came without a price. Now the cost was adding up quickly in many Russians' lives.

I had grown up with a father who constantly badgered me to turn off the light whenever I left the room to save money, so I was already in an energy-conserving mindset. For everyone else, the change was painful and confusing, and it was taking time to adjust. I wondered if Yuri still took hot baths with the water running continuously like he used to.

Speaking of distant memories, my *tusofka* lifestyle had become a thing of the past. Life had become fast-paced, and I was on a train of imagination plowing full speed ahead. I put together a fan club with Lyuda Novosadova, who ran it. I'd opened a post office box on Tverskaya Street for the "One Day with Stingray" contest, but even months afterwards I was getting fan mail and drawings from people all over Russia. I made a whole collage across my wall of these images. Yuri Shevchuk came back from the polar port city of Murmansk and told me there were even many fans over there and girls copying my hair and style. The fan newsletters that Lyuda sent out every few months gave me the opportunity to update all these people on my upcoming activities and answer some questions that people sent in. We had an official J Stingray Fan Club stamp made for the newsletters and added photos from fans or sketches that Sasha would create.

Meanwhile, Fedor would show up on occasion to my apartment and even once at Big Misha's. I would go insane waiting around for him, until I opened up the door and saw his charming, coquettish grin. He was passionate and irresistible. He agreed to shoot my next video if I told him what song. I chose a composition of Viktor's he had allowed me to rewrite lyrics to in English that I titled "Danger." It had an apropos chorus to the situation Fedor and I had put ourselves in.

"Danger," I recited to him in the darkness of the early, early morning. "Evil love will burn in the fire."

Fedor became fully focused on the video. When he committed to a project nothing could take his attention away, not even lust. He shot it beautifully, in black and white. A big part of it was actually shot without me, at a cold and wet Russian prison. It followed the story of a new prisoner, a gorgeous and brawny man with a hard jaw and sad eyes. Fedor created intense moments with close ups of slamming a cell door or scrubbing the floor. When I watched it the first time, I was hypnotized by the action.

For my part, Fedor filmed me on a sound stage. I wore a black wig with bangs and

■ Me and director Fedor Bondarchuk during the filming of my music video for "Steel Wheels."

my new favorite round and mirrored sunglasses. He lit my head from behind so that you couldn't see my face unless I brought my hands up and let the light bounce off my pale fingers onto my face.

"Play with it!" Fedor encouraged me as we shot. He would take my hand in his and move it slowly, showing me how I could control the light and the shadows. I felt powerful in that song, punk and poignant and enigmatic. If only we could control ourselves this way in everyday life, allowing ourselves to fade into momentary darkness. I was so honored that Fedor allowed me a chance to experience that.

After "Danger," Fedor made another video for me with "Steel Wheels." Each video he did had a totally different feel and vision. He was a well of imagination and fantastical realities. It was an all-night shoot in the basement of an old apartment building. The set looked like the remnants of an armageddon, pipe water dripping into a forgotten, ghostly world filled with plastic igloos. That shoot had a lot of waiting for everything to be ready – extras, make up, set design. I stood around with Fedor and the cameraman Misha Mukasey. We were kidding around, taking some photos, but I was so obsessed with Fedor in the nightly light. Every time he brushed up against me or his eyes darted to mine, I wanted to send everyone home and just have sex with him right then, at the end of the world.

When the filming finally started it was easy to embrace the vibe of the video surrounded by total, despairing darkness. It's a string of dramatic shots, people out-of-place, barren

■ Stills from the music videos for "Danger" (top, middle) and "Steel Wheels" (below), directed by Fedor Bondarchuk.

space filled with candlelight, a large iron wheel on fire rolling towards the camera, a half-naked girl working on an old-fashioned typewriter, and a muscular dog with punk spikes on his collar and frosty breath.

The bare lighting that was used against the gloom made the skin of my face and hands ivory white and almost sparkle. My two favorite shots of the video are where I unfold my hands and there is bright red blood in the middle of them like crucifixion wounds, and where it's just my saturated red lips singing against my icy teeth. It reminds me of the iconic opening shot in *Rocky Horror Picture Show*, a movie that always fascinated me.

The video ends with a slow pan of a fire burning that fades to black. We all stood in the darkness, imperceptibly touching as the ash settled, and began to cheer.

◆

Summer of 1992 was coming up, and I was headed to participate in an environmental Volga river trip for a festival called Clear Water Rock. A bunch of musicians, some from the West, would go down the Volga on a boat and stop at about six cities to perform and raise awareness about water contamination. I agreed to join Brigada S, Chaif, Alexander Sklyar, and Voronov for part of the tour. There were also bands from Ireland, Italy, and Canada.

As I floated down the Volga between Sklyar in his skull bandanna and Voronov in his black fedora, I saw churches pass by on the shore. It was so peaceful. Everyone was relaxed in the warm weather, wearing shirts and shorts and guzzling beer from the moment we left dry land. At one point, a bunch of the guys tried to play music by blowing into their bottles. There's a great photo of Sukachev and the others around a table full of bottles and burnt cigarette butts.

When we stopped in the little towns, it was as if we'd been transported back in time at least forty years. In one town, residents were protesting. Their signs read *Don't spit into the Volga, you may have use of it*, which is a paraphrase of a Russian proverb that says, "Cast no dirt into the well that hath given you water." The Volga had fed Russia for centuries but had lost nearly all of its fish stock. The local people were understandably angry. It was so eye opening to travel to places that, unlike cities, didn't have every type of produce and merchandise available to them. It made me so aware of everything in Moscow when I got back – the full markets, the constant beam of streetlamps and illuminated windows, the crowds of people packing into the dirty streets.

On the eleventh and twelfth of June, I got to play a live show in the concert hall Rossia. It was a prestigious space that could seat twenty-five hundred right near the

■ Getting pulled off the stage by fans until my bodyguards intervened, Moscow, 1992.

Kremlin, and one of my favorite venues. The whole place was packed, and as I sang, I could hear everyone singing along with me, our voices echoing against the high, flat ceiling. The sound system was better quality than I had played on before, and the sound engineer was incredibly professional and skilled. The lighting guy, too, was really good. As I danced around the stage, I'd see the stage turn different colors and see smoke blow through, which added such a fun vibe to the show. The backdrop was a life-size image of myself with my signature at the bottom, hanging over the stage.

The first night, the kids all left their seats and crowded up around the stage. Some even sat on the edge, their legs dangling and their torsos angled towards me. I loved having them so close and watching their lips move with my lyrics. A few times I got physically pulled into the audience. I could tell it scared Timur and the other guards as they frantically would run over and pull me out.

For "Tsoi Song," I voluntarily headed down into the crowd and had them sing the "ye mans" with me. They roared like beasts every time I sang the part "Tsoi, Tsoi," and it echoed through the room.

At the second show I was surprised to climb onto the stage and see a barrier between the stage and seats. Lyuda remembered this.

"The second day everything was changed – there was a big gap between us and the stage. I thought you didn't like us to be that close to you."

I had had no idea they were going to change the set up. I was more energized with the fans right up against me, feeling their movements around my ankles.

"Timur, why would they change it?" I complained to him backstage.

He handed me a copy of *The Evening Club*, which had written that my "grateful fans, probably because of their great admiration, almost killed the singer on stage. The security guards were sweating while trying to push back her fans to the seats that they paid for."

"Well if I'm going to die," I muttered, "that's the way I'd want to go."

After the concert there were pools of fans waiting for me to exit and sign autographs. I made sure I stayed until I signed every single one.

♦

I didn't think anything could get better than the high of playing a concert, but what happened next put me on cloud nine.

Dima Litvinov, the head of the Russian branch of Greenpeace, asked if I would participate in Greenpeace's first peaceful protest in Russia. I immediately said yes.

"Just tell me when and where I have to be!" I said excitedly.

"The action will take place on June fifteenth, but we will have a practice the day before to go over everything," Dima said. He was a warm and passionate guy with a bushy beard and dark round glasses. "You cannot tell anyone about the act or that you will be a part of it. The success of the protest depends on it being a surprise, with nobody forewarned."

I learned from Dima that there had been an injunction in England to stop a peaceful protest against a plutonium processing plant. We would be protesting that violation of free speech. I felt my body fill with energy as we talked, realizing that this was going to be something incredibly important to participate in.

I showed up at Greenpeace's office the day before the action. Greenpeace was so meticulous and detailed when orchestrating their protests, and between bouts of intense excitement I was deeply impressed.

"We are going to chain ourselves to the British Embassy here in Moscow," Dima said to the group. Each of us received a chain and lock and had to practice quickly locking ourselves to a fence. I remember being so focused on the task that my whole world reduced to the metal pieces in my hands. I didn't want to be the weakest link in the chain, for sure.

We were instructed it would all have to move very quickly. We would pull up to the British Embassy in a white van, and when the door to the van was opened, we would have to pile out and chain ourselves to the Embassy fence while Dima, with his hands

■ Greenpeace action at the British Embassy, Moscow, Summer 1992.

up, would walk towards the Russian guards and explain that what we were doing was a peaceful activity. Once chained, we were all supposed to tie Union Jack gags over our mouths and hold up a large banner reading *U.K.: PROLIFERATE FREE SPEECH, NOT PLUTONIUM! GREENPEACE.*

We rehearsed the plan in the courtyard at Greenpeace numerous times. No running, no screaming or laughing – focus. It felt to me as if we were in a movie. The day of the event, I felt the same type of nervous, tingling energy I would feel before a concert. I stared into the mirror, realizing I was part of a pivotal group fighting for basic decency in the world and that the shirt, the word *Greenpeace*, held so much power and meaning.

We all huddled in the van, making our way to the Embassy in silence. The dark space felt charged with determination and spirit. The biggest risk we faced were the armed Russian soldiers, because Russians were not accustomed to Greenpeace or any type of peaceful protest. If it had been British soldiers, they would have understood what was happening, but with these soldiers, it was much more of a wild card.

"Please don't let them shoot us," I whispered as I felt the van slow to a stop. The door opened unbelievably fast. "Go, go, go!" I heard someone say.

I stepped out and was laser focused on the gate in front of me. I walked quickly, chained myself mechanically, and handed the key to the Greenpeace organizer collecting them. I heard a frantic disruption between the Russian guards and Dima but couldn't understand what was being said. I almost felt as if I was underwater, submerged by the

■ "Proliferate Free Speech, Not Plutonium! Greenpeace."

gravity of what we were doing. Thank goodness the altercation didn't last long.

We stood there, calmly waiting and hoping that we'd get results for our action before we'd get arrested. Thomas Schultz and Shaun Burnie from Greenpeace International were inside the Embassy speaking to the new British Ambassador Sir Brian Fall, and as we craned our necks outside to try and see through the imposing windows, I heard another car pull up, then another. The press had shown up and began shouting questions at Dima. He commented on the irony of being able to demonstrate in the former Evil Empire but not in the mother of democracies, the United Kingdom.

I was interviewed by the *Moscow Guardian*. "I'd worked with Greenpeace in the U.S.," I explained to them. "Having lived in Moscow during pre-*glasnost* days, the concept of freedom of speech is especially important to me."

An hour or so after we had arrived, the British Ambassador promised to communicate Greenpeace's concerns to the British Government. At that, the protest was ended. I felt relief flood my body. The whole experience had made me feel acutely human and aware of the solidarity of being on this earth together. We had to fight for each other and what we had.

In addition to sending a message to England, the success of the peaceful protest showed the Russian people that they had a right to speak up in their own evolving nation. I will never forget the feeling I had walking around the rest of the day, an intense satisfaction and pride in this country that had become my second home.

■ Viktor Tsoi memorial concert, Luzhniki Stadium, Moscow, June 21, 1992.

I could have almost devoted my entire life to working with Greenpeace, but two days later I found myself back on stage at the Luzhniki Stadium for the Tsoi memorial concert.

"Today is a hard day for me," I told the packed stadium. I looked out over the sea of Kino banners and raised fists. "Last time I played here was two years ago with Kino. It was the last time I saw and spoke to Viktor. Simply, I really loved Viktor."

I sang Viktor's song "Gosti" to honor him, and I thought he'd be proud that I sang it in Russian.

"Hey there, who will be my guest," I sang as loudly as I could, my face turned to the sky in the hopes he could hear me. I wondered if free speech was loud enough to reach heaven. I wanted to let my favorite guest know how much I missed him.

✦ On Camera

After touring around Russia and participating in the "Women in Rock" festival in Kiev, Ukraine, as a special guest, it was suddenly my birthday. July 3, 1992, was one of the few birthdays I spent in Russia, bowling at the Moskva Hotel with Brigada S.

"Happy fuckin' birthday to yoooou," Sergey and Garik sang in unison. They were two of the most exuberant party animals.

There was food, alcohol, and a packed room filled with friends. I was running around giving hugs and getting gifts. I got home that night exhausted, ready to collapse into bed, when I got a phone call. It was Roman Kachanov, a young movie director.

"I would like you to star in a movie I am making," he told me when I answered. "It's a fairy tale for adults."

A movie? I had never before considered acting in films, but like most things that had happened in my life this far, the opportunity fell in my lap. I couldn't say no.

Roman and I met to discuss the film and try on some dresses to see how I'd look in character.

"My only request is that I can keep my hair the way it is," I told him. I don't know why this felt so important to me, but Roman agreed.

Despite the fact that I could converse in Russian by this point, I still didn't read Cyrillic well enough to understand the script. I had some friends read me the general descriptions that were being printed.

"*Efir* [Aether] magazine says that in terms of its genre, the movie will be a fantastic fairy tale with some comedy elements, or, if you like, a comedy with some fantasy elements," Big Misha read. "Inna Tkachenko from *Kommersant* newspaper said that 'Freak' is an excellent example of Russian comedy mystification, proving that there is nothing funnier than scary. A freak is born in a provincial maternity hospital at the age of thirty years and begins his journey through life. He has the unique gift to assimilate the image of anyone who draws his interest, from the Count of Monte Cristo to Arnold Schwarzenegger and Jesus Christ. Naturally, he is hunted by a KGB maniac. The freak, as expected, falls in love, but not before reading the revelations of the *Kama Sutra*. There is nothing more fun than the struggle between good and evil."

"Wow," I said after a silence. "That sounds pretty crazy."

"Yes, should be easy for you," Big Misha mused. "Since you are, in fact, pretty crazy."

I had the part of the Freak's girlfriend, an American named Jane. Nikita Vysotsky was cast as the Freak. He was the son of the most famous bard singer in Russia, Vladimir Vysotsky, who had died in 1980 and was still selling the most albums of any artist over a decade later. The maniacal KGB Colonel was played by the amazing Aleksey Zolotnitsky. When I watched the film once it was completed, I thought Zolotnitsky was one of the best actors I'd ever seen from any country. He was funny and scary at the same time, a caricature that was as relatable as the people next to me. It was incredible.

We filmed in Sochi and Moscow. Sochi was such a beautiful place, where I could imagine all the tourists crowding the Black Sea during the summer months, but back in Moscow it was an unusually cold, frigid winter for us. The freezing temperatures made the memories I have of shooting all the more vivid and memorable. We shot outside in Moscow so many days, and they would have me run between the scene and a warm van after every shot. After five minutes exposed to the air, I literally wouldn't be able to feel my body, kind of galloping and stumbling to the heated van on feet that felt like blocks of ice. As I threw myself in the van like a Hail Mary pass, people would cover me with warm blankets and warm my hands and feet before shoving me outside again for another take.

The biggest joke on the set came from a shot where the Freak and I are running up a large staircase and we stop in the middle to kiss. Everyone on set knew that cigarettes made me nauseous, and Nikita, like everyone else, was constantly smoking. He tasted like an ashtray, and everyone on the crew kept calling for another take because they thought it was hysterical to see me try not to grimace with each kiss. When I finished cringing, I couldn't help but laugh.

During a scene at a bar, the Freak transformed into Schwarzenegger and had to carry me down some steps. He looked completely pumped, but it was just padding shoved

■ Shots from the film *Freak* with Nikita Vysotsky, Moscow, 1992.

under his clothes to disguise his skinny frame. I was so nervous the whole time, digging my fingernails into him as I prayed that he wouldn't trip and send us both flying to the ground.

There were so many Russian words I didn't understand that I had to say, but Roman told me to just forget about it and do it in my slang Russian. He promised they could fix it in overdubbing.

"Great," I said, nodding. "I'm ready."

"Great," Roman responded, wandering over to a camera. "Give me an hour."

What I learned about making a film is that most of an actor's time is spent sitting and waiting. They would put a ton of makeup on my face every morning, so thick it was like a mask, and then I would sit with it drying on my face for up to six or seven hours! I knew from my videos that there is always constant waiting for one thing or another to be set up and checked, but films took so much longer. The hardest part was that with all the makeup coating my cheeks and lips I was afraid to eat and mess it up. Once in a while, when I felt like I was about to faint, I'd try to eat a hard-boiled egg. I ended up losing five pounds by the end of the whole thing!

My scenes with Aleksey felt way too real, and there were moments when I would get freaked out and wonder if he was a genuine KGB agent pretending to be an actor pretending to be an agent. His face would contort into these expressions that were peculiar, almost otherworldly.

The most dramatic scene of the film was the last one, where the Freak leaves and walks out across the ocean. There was a stone wall out in the ocean just under the churning water, and they drove Nikita out to it. He was really walking on water. I was supposed to cry during this scene, but since I wasn't a trained actor, I had no idea how to get the tears going. Everyone just kept telling me to think of something sad or painful. I stood on the shore desperately flipping through my childhood memories of dead pets and gymnastic injuries, but nothing was working. I was getting so nervous, wracking my brain for a way to make this happen, when I heard the director's voice drift along the water.

"Go!" Roman shouted.

I looked out desperately at Nikita's figure over the sea, but suddenly it wasn't him I saw walking on water but Viktor. I gasped, feeling the salty tears rolling down my cheeks. He was really there, I could feel it, and it made me so sad I couldn't reach him.

♦

Recording all the voiceovers for the movie in Moscow, the director and sound people seemed so excited by my ability to match up my words to my lips in the film, even though I was saying a slang version of the words during filming. All of my time spent making music videos had made me the queen of lip syncing. When I had been editing my own stuff, there had been nothing more upsetting to me than watching a take that wasn't perfectly matched.

The last vocal I had to do is the part in the movie where the Freak and I have wild sex after he reads the *Kama Sutra*. The director was very timid in explaining what he wanted.

"Roman," I cut him off. "I know exactly what you want." I had seen Meg Ryan in the film *When Harry Met Sally*, and I tried to copy that. My voice over only took one take, and as I walked out everyone was still sitting on their stools, speechless.

Two of my songs that I'd written with Boris were edited into the film – "Baby Baby Bala Bala" and "Modern World."

The premiere was on April 4, 1993, at the Oktyabr Theater on New Arbat in central Moscow. I hadn't seen the film yet, so when the lights went down, I snuck in the back and crawled into a seat Timur had saved for me. As my name came on during the opening credits, I heard the crowd roar around me with delight. They cheered again the first time I appeared on the screen, and in another scene where I enter in a long, strapless red dress hugging my body, they whistled and hooted as if the building were on fire. No one in Russia had ever seen me dressed like that, and they loved it.

There's a scene in the movie where I get a young black man drunk until he tips over and falls on the floor. I was surprised by how many people erupted into laughter in the theater.

"Why are they laughing like that?" I whispered to Timur. "Is it really *that* funny?"

■ On the *Freak* film set, Sochi, 1992.   ■ At the film release, Moscow, April 4, 1993.

It was only later that I understood what a novelty a black person was in Russia at that time. People were fascinated by them.

Making this quirky film was a different experience than anything else I'd ever done. I was so grateful to be a part of it, and honored that *Moskovsky Pravda* confirmed I wasn't such a bad actress. The film had also made me realize, though, that if I were going to be on camera, I would prefer it to be in one of my music videos.

♦

Back in Moscow, I was working with different musicians from various bands every performance. The only constant was Sasha. The guitarist we had been using was great, but he drank way too much, and I only had the energy to deal with Sasha on occasion, not two of them. I had recently started playing with band members from Brigada S – Sergey Galanin on guitar and vocals, and smiley keyboardist Rushan Ayopov – as well as guitarist Igor Kozhin from League Blues. Igor was a straightforward, dependable guitarist who was always prepared and who never seemed to get nervous or strung out. Sergey was one of the most prolific bassists and singers around. He reminded me of those famous Western sidekicks, like Pete Townshend in The Who, Richie Sambora in Bon Jovi, or Jimmy Page in Led Zeppelin – guys who sat at the back of the boat with the tiller in their hands and a cigarette in their teeth, making sure everything went in the right direction. Galanin was an amazing addition to my group. I had never had someone do backups with me on stage before, and I loved standing right beside his full head of long black curls and singing into a mike together during concerts. He had the most powerful voice and could screech like a falcon.

For the past few years, my life had been non-stop with concerts and filming. It didn't really give me a lot of time to reflect on everything or consider how everything was going. Then one morning I woke up and realized if a person is living with an alcoholic, a person is living *like* an alcoholic. Even though Sasha's binges only happened three or four times a year, it turned everything upside down when they happened. Sometimes, when he ran out of booze, he would stumble out into the night at one or two in the morning like a scavenging animal. Once, I woke after sunrise and couldn't find him anywhere. I was convinced something horrible had happened to him in a dark alley or long street. I opened the door and found him lying on the concrete with our house keys on the floor next to him. I got chills thinking of what kind of stranger could have come along, grabbed the keys, and let themselves into our home.

"Sasha," I said to his slack face. "I don't want to live like this anymore."

It was such a difficult decision. There was so much I adored about him, and in many ways, he made my life better. But I was starting to realize that I couldn't save him or fight his demons for him, because deep down he didn't want me to. I'd been fighting fire so long, and I should have known fire would win.

It took me a couple of days to figure out what to say to him. He was a great guy with a bad problem. Finally, I approached him on our sofa.

"I've decided not to drink anymore," he said casually before I could confront him. I stood there, shocked. "Well, will you get help?" I managed to stammer out. "No, I don't need help," Sasha replied. "I am just going to stop."

I studied him skeptically. I didn't think it was possible, but I knew how stubborn he could be and knew that such a quality could prove useful. His lips didn't touch alcohol for the next three years.

The two of us moved into an apartment on Leninsky Prospekt. Timur had charmed someone into letting me buy an apartment in Moscow. Foreigners weren't allowed to own property yet in Russia, but Timur had found some of my fans in the district office who would sign off on it.

"You could run the country if you wanted to," I told him, giving him a huge hug. "You get everything done!"

A few months later, after a complete remodel, I was relaxing in my high-rise apartment. It had two bedrooms and a bathroom, plus a European-style kitchen. I'd heard it was suddenly possible to do European remodels on apartments if someone had the money. There were so many things in Russia that I still didn't like – factory pollution, pushing crowds, traffic, cigarette smoke – but from my new apartment I could hear church bells chime every day. The sound touched me in a spiritual way, found its way under my skin and to my bones. I felt humble, inspired, safe. It's one of my fondest memories of living in Moscow. At my house in Los Angeles, I now have a wind chime that is ever reminding me of the bells back in Moscow.

Sasha and I each took a bedroom for ourselves. We had such different schedules that I don't think we could have functioned any other way. Sasha was up most of the night composing music for my next album, and because of this, he slept through most of the day. I would fall asleep around midnight or one after I'd watched CNN, which I was so excited was now available in Russia. I would wake up around ten in the morning and my driver would pick me up at eleven to go to meetings, the heat blasting in his car because he knew I'd be freezing. In the winter it would be dark by the time I got home at three or four in the afternoon. It was such a strange experience to me to have it dark that early, even after so many years. I'd walk across the packed snow that was glowing under the streetlamps and feel like I was walking across the moon, then run upstairs, hoping Sasha had the apartment warm.

♦

Chastnaya Vecherinka, or "Private Party," was one of the hippest shows around. They would ask a star to invite some of their friends to perform, do some parodies, and make fun of themselves. I was so excited to be asked to have my private party! It was a huge show where I could push my "Don't Litter" campaign and Greenpeace agenda, but it also gave me the chance to invite some of my old band of pirates from Leningrad.

The hour-long program was filmed in a dark club with a small stage, interspliced with my music videos and PSA as well as shots of me on the street asking people if they littered. Towards the end there's footage of me walking up to two street cleaners lounging against a wall.

"Why aren't you working?" I asked them.

"Hey girl, don't even ask such a question! After your social ads the streets became perfectly clear, almost sterile," one said with big eyes.

"If it goes like this any further, we would lose our jobs!" The second one said. The shot was staged, but I like to think it could have been real.

Throughout the show I interviewed some of my friends, and they each played a song.

■ On the show *Chastnaya Vecherinka* ("Private Party") April 13, 1993, with the leader of Nautilus Pompilius, Slava Butuzov, who later formed the group U-Piter.

Lyosha Cherry reminisced about recording my song "Feeling" in his home studio. Misha Barzukhin spoke about his new album and the ease of selling music today versus underground in 1984. Vitia Sologub harped on the fact that I had been in Russia a decade. Slava Butuzov mused about reading books in his bathroom. I also got to sing a duet with Galanin, his song "Mama."

Chaif couldn't make it to Moscow, so Shakhrin in a Greenpeace shirt sent a taped message wishing me the best and saying that on April twenty-second, he would join the Earth Day activities and clean the dirty streets in my honor.

"Goodbye from Sverdlovsk!" he concluded.

"What are you doing talking into the camera to me?" I asked, walking into the room. "I'm right here."

It was a prerecorded bit we had filmed together before he left Moscow to return home, but I thought it was hilarious.

My favorite part of the day was seeing Sergey Kuryokhin again. He walked into the room, and it was flooded with his radiance and energy. I'd forgotten how much I'd missed him.

"Thank you, Joanna, for inviting us to this great party," Sergey said, wrapping his arms around me. "It's so wonderful here, everything's illuminated, lots of beautiful girls, tons of champagne." He pulled back, his crooked smile filling his beautiful face. "It's so rare that I go out to parties, so I'm really enjoying myself. Thank you so much! And also,

Vitia Sologub's here."

Vitia nodded and walked up to the two of us. We stood in a little circle, toes towards each other.

◆

"What was the first Russian word that you learned?" Vitia asked me.

"You know, Kuryokhin was my teacher," I said.

Sergey laughed. "Yes, we loved teaching foreigners Russian, and naturally it all started with swear words."

"About ninety percent of my vocabulary comes from you!" I told him. "Sometimes you do need those words."

"We give thanks to these words!" he announced. "You finally made it, became famous. I want to drink to Joanna, for your health."

Watching the video of this exchange makes my heart ache. It reminds me of how Sergey lit up my eyes and my life. He was a force of nature.

The skits made up for the program were the best part. I think being able to make fun of myself when I was famous was a very important part of staying normal. Behind my steely looks and big sunglasses, I never felt worthy of the adulation. These skits gave me a chance to be my silly self.

I did one with my friend, the entertainment journalist Artur Gasparyan of *Moskovsky Komsomolets*. He was very important for all of us in show business, and he had been the one to start the infamous parade called "Soundtrack" – "Zyukavaya Dorozhka." If Artur liked you, then life in the public eye was good. I got so lucky.

For my private party, Artur and I are standing outside, and he is raving about me in front of a camera. "You brought an unusual streak to the Russian rock scene, and you enriched it with your music. Without you it would be depleted of your originality. You are a great singer, Joanna," he gushed stoically. After we checked that the camera had stopped filming, even though in real life it was still recording, I handed Artur a wad of dollars.

"This is all you are giving me?" Artur deflated like a balloon. "I said wonderful things. This isn't enough."

"I'm sorry," I told him. "That is all I have."

"You gave me so little money that I can't even afford to eat at McDonald's!" He swiveled and stared directly at the camera. "No, Joanna is not such a great singer. She should get back home."

In another skit, I tried explaining to a young boy how important it was not to litter.

■ Fedor Bondarchuk on my "Private Party."   ■ Sergey Galanin, me, and Garik Suchakev at the Brigada S concert, Moscow, May 16, 1992.

I point to a man emptying his trash, only to have him turn around and recognize Kolya, the singer from the band League Blues. Back in the club, I pretended to interview Mario about his great role in a commercial where he gets doused with red paint, and as he answered that it was the worst day of his life a vat of milk dumped down on him. One of the best, I think, was a staged interview with me and Fedor Bondarchuk. We're both wearing sunglasses, and when asked why it became my trademark, I revealed I was actually cross-eyed!

"You know, Joanna and I have a lot in common," Bondarchuk interjected. "Including our eyes." He lifted his glasses to show his own crossed eyes.

As the credits rolled on the program, you heard some of us talking as if we thought the sound had been turned off.

"Is the filming over, finally? I so want to smoke, does someone have a cigarette?"

"Vodka!" Mario boomed.

"Yes please! Mario, let's drink," I say.

"I have some old Kolbasi from the train last night. Would you like some?" Galanin asked.

"Hey, Joanna, where do I throw my litter?" Timur's voice cut in.

"Just throw it on the floor," I sang.

At the end, my face comes back on camera and fills the screen. "*Eta buela shutka, eta buela shutka!*" It was a joke, it was a joke.

✦ Music for Peace

When Greenpeace initially opened their office in Moscow, they released a compilation album called *Breakthrough* of twenty-five of the coolest bands in the world. It included Peter Gabriel, INXS, R.E.M., and Dire Straits, and was launched to raise money for Greenpeace efforts around the globe and celebrate their Russian opening.

Flash forward a couple years later, and I got an idea that we should do a compilation of Russian bands to benefit Greenpeace. Viktor had told me how important it was that Russian youth had their own Russian heroes to emulate, and I wanted to continue honoring that.

"We can donate the royalties from our songs to benefit Greenpeace," I said and tried to explain to the musicians why it was worth it to participate in what Greenpeace did. They were unaccustomed to non-profit organizations but got on board quickly. I was thrilled! Kinchev, Sukachev, Makarevich, Grebenshchikov, Butuzov, Shakhrin, and Yuri Shevchuk. I didn't know Shevchuk well, but he was the burly and sweet singer of DDT and I had fallen in love with his song "Actress Spring," a song about his late wife that broke my soul and put it back together again. He agreed right away to join our campaign.

Each artist donated one song for the album, and I had recorded a new song I'd written with Boris and Kuryokhin called "Boom Boom." The guys from the band Moral Codex did the backing vocals. Since all the other songs on the album were already well-known,

■ Shooting the "Come Together" video with Boris for *Greenpeace Rocks*.

■ *Greenpeace Rocks* album cover with Shevchuk, Kinchev, Sukachev, Stingray, Makarevich, Grebenshchikov, Butuzov, and Shakhrin.

I thought it would be fun to include a new one of mine to grab attention. Sasha had produced the track, and it was so clean and powerful that I asked him to arrange a version of The Beatles' "Come Together" for Boris and me to sing too. He absolutely killed it. From the first chord, our alternative was addictive, and I thought it was better than the original. There was a seductive cello and violin part in between the verses, and a piano solo at the bridge that to this day is my favorite piano part of a song. It was genius. It had to be on the record.

Part of the process of Russia becoming more westernized was that the record company was now concerned with whether or not I had permission to release The Beatles song. I knew that Michael Jackson owned all the publishing rights to The Beatles' catalog, so I reached out to my dermatologist back in Beverly Hills, Dr. Arnold Klein, whom I knew was Michael Jackson's doctor and close friend. Dr. Klein's nurse, Debbie, was the woman who eventually gave birth to Michael Jackson's two older children.

"Could you ask Michael about the rights?" I begged the doctor.

Word came back that if it was for release exclusively in Russia to benefit Greenpeace, Michael Jackson was fine with that.

As I was sitting in the studio and listening to the final cut of "Come Together," I knew we had to make a video for it. Bondarchuk and I had become good friends, so I called him and asked if he could quickly shoot a video for the song to release at the same time as the Greenpeace album.

■ "Come Together" music video shoot with Bondarchuk, Sukachev, and me, Moscow, 1993.

"For you," he said. "Absolutely." He offered to do it for free.

I also asked Garik Sukachev to be a part of it too. He played the guitar with a mask over his face that gave him these intense cat eyes, morphing into an animal curling over his instrument as he rocked it. He also played the cello, his true pirate self in an embroidered long jacket, stripped shirt, and pirate hat.

"You're so feisty!" I told him when I saw him.

"Brutish," he growled with a wink.

Sasha would also be in the piano bridge part, and we hired two young violinists, dressed in all black.

Only a day or two later, we all met up at the soundstage with Bondarchuk. Boris showed up in black with a leather vest and my round aviator sunglasses. We shot on black and white film into the night, singing the song to each other in different ways and positions. Bondarchuk had the camera on a dolly so it rolled back and forth, making it look like Boris and I were the ones in motion.

The last shot of the video is Garik, Boris, and I all sitting in Greenpeace shirts.

It was a long, long night, but none of us noticed the time flying by. Fedor managed to edit the video by the next evening. He somehow made it so that each one of us stole the show. He was a master of storytelling, even in an abstract way.

Handing the video to *Programma A* to premier it was one of my proudest moments. It was such a dynamic, rich, and bold video, and to pair it with a chyron with Greenpeace's information at the end was a powerful match.

On June 11, *Moskovsky Komsomolets* wrote that we "delivered with a bang, and there are all the chances that the masterpiece will break the tops of the charts."

I couldn't stop smiling the whole day. It felt like everything was finally coming together, right now, over me.

◆

Are you happy? It's the million-dollar question. For the first time, I really liked who I was and everything I was doing. The *Greenpeace Rocks* album was released with a stunning cover and a lot of fanfare. Photographers George Molitvan and Alexander Shishkin took simple black and white photos of each band leader, and Yuri Boxer designed the album cover. On the back was information about Greenpeace and its uncompromising but peaceful fight to preserve the environment.

Ksiusha, who had her own show on TV, let me talk about how the water and air in the country was contaminated by pollution.

"We want people to ask Greenpeace for information about what is happening," I said. "Knowledge is power. I want to motivate the people to get the facts and decide what it means to them."

Ksiusha also showed the ad "One Day with Rockers" promoting the upcoming concert.

On June 19, 1993, a group of rockers made the Dom Kultura Gorbunova shake. The place was filled to capacity, the two balconies brimming over, the main floor packed like a tightly sliced loaf of hot bread. All the proceeds from the ticket sales benefited Greenpeace Moscow. It was being filmed to air on *Programma A*, as well as broadcast live on Radio 101 Stereo. There was a *Greenpeace Rocks* banner over Brigada S, who was the backing band for most of the performers.

"For me, it's not just another *tusofka*," said the punk Sasha Sklyar backstage to a reporter. "It's an important action. Yes, I'm aware that it probably won't change much, but is there anything we can change in our life?"

"Yes, of course we doubt the purity of some of our foodstuffs," Voronov responded to another. "But we are going to fight to prevent them from being poisoned!"

I stood, listening to both of them and beaming.

The fans were on their feet for the entire concert, singing and cheering. They waved flags and *Greenpeace Rocks* albums, and even some of my black and white press photos. We all sang back up for each other, and it reminded me of the Leningrad Rock Club days in the mid-eighties when we all shared a stage and played for the love of it.

"I am so very happy you are all here tonight!" I shouted out after my first song. "Do you guys love Greenpeace?" Everyone cheered.

"*Davai, vmeste sa mnoi, Greenpeace!*" I yelled. "Come on, with me, Greenpeace!" I pumped my arms and the audience followed, all of us sending our energy into the electric air. It felt amazing.

"*Zemla eta nasha dom, ne nada musorit!*" I said after Galanin, and I sang "Turn Away." "Earth is our home, don't litter!" I felt my face flush and my head spin as I heard a chorus of every voice in the building repeating it back to me over and over.

Sergey Voronov, the bluesy hippie, came out after me in a white jacket, hobo cap, and a hoop earring. He sang an English song called "Walking in the Diamond Rain" with his slide guitar. Sklyar sang a poignant, stripped down and acoustic version of his song "Drunk Song." I had never seen him like I did that night – beautiful, a bard from some far away castle telling stories through his music. Time Machine's Andrei Makarevich, who was known as one of the godfathers of Russian rock, sang some of his hits like "Marionetki" along with the whole audience, a smile on his boyish face. Garik Sukachev sang a cool version of Tsoi's "Beatnik," and Yuri Shevchuk from DDT, in his big, gravelly voice, sang a resonant ballad on acoustic guitar that gave everyone in the place chills.

To close out the concert, Brigada S with Sasha on drums started "Come Together." I remember striding forward in a turquoise shirt and whimsical flowered hat and feeling like I was floating.

"I want the whole Earth to be covered by the same flowers as on my hat!" I told everyone after we all sang the last lines of "Come Together" together. Everyone roared, lions and tigers in a wilderness of song.

Programma A was a huge part of the success of the project. They let me use their program as a forum to explain environmentalism and make it a familiar concept for the Russian people. What I and the rockers were doing with Greenpeace was so new, and I knew that if the public didn't understand how it was put together it wouldn't get through. I went on *Programma A* and gave a statement about the donation of time and energy, the creative collaboration, and the reasons it was important. During the program, they even allowed us to air a Greenpeace ad. It was strong and terrifying, a mother sending her son out to play in a spacesuit to protect him from pollution, but it was so important. Rock music had always been about transformation, about motivating and inspiring some type of emotion and action. An iron fist was no longer holding the Russian people down, but now we had to take the pressure off the planet.

■ Me with Reeves Gabrels and David Bowie from the band Tin Machine in rehearsal studio. Photo taken during our shoot for my *Red Wave Presents* program, 1993.

◆

As much as I loved the concerts I was doing, my biggest dream had become to have my own show on Russian TV. I pitched a thirty-minute program called *Red Wave Presents*, where I would interview Western bands and intersplice it with their video clips. This time I got positive feedback from the TV company, except for the issue of payment. No one had any way to fund the idea. Instead, they offered me three minutes of advertising that I could fill.

The next day I tracked down a number of Western companies that had recently opened offices in Moscow to pitch them my idea.

"What?" I would ask when each one agreed. "Really?"

I was shocked at how easy it all was – these companies were offering me money left and right.

Mr. Fumihiko Kanagawa from Sony seemed especially interested when we spoke. "Let me get back to you," he said with a promising nod.

What I didn't know was that after I left, he met with his Russian staff and asked about me. After learning that I was a famous rocker in Russia known for not drinking, smoking, or littering, he was sold. Sony actually became my long-term sponsor and was part of everything else I ended up doing in Russia. It was such a prominent and respected company, and I knew their reputation was everything, so I was beyond honored and grateful for their support. Finally, I had validation that being the "clean girl" wasn't just a silly dream, but a solid identity.

Kodak, Mars, and British Airways also offered me deals, as did Nike and Coke later

■ Me in Moscow with David Byrne, who also was part of my *Red Wave Presents* program, 1995.

on. I also always saved a thirty-second spot out of my three-minute advertisements to air a Greenpeace ad. Greenpeace always had a tough time getting their stuff on television, and it made me feel so empowered that I kept finding ways to help them.

For the first time in my life I was making a living and had money to help me do more things. Sasha, armed with new equipment from Sony, also became my cameraman and flew with me to the States and England to interview any bands we could get to meet with us. Howie Klein gave me access to many of the Sire and Warner Brothers bands, and somehow each connection we made led us to another.

◆

"Hey, Joanna," I heard as I answered the phone. "It's Dave Weiderman. What are you doing right now?"

"Nothing," I said. "What's up?"

"Want to run over to Guitar Center and interview Bo Diddley?"

"Are you kidding me?" I said, grabbing Sasha by the shirt collar and dragging him to the door. "I'm on my way!"

I knew Bo Diddley was one of the most important musicians in American history, but more than that, I knew a lot of my Russian friends had been influenced by his music. They would think it was so *krutoi* ("cool") that I got to speak with the icon himself! He had a sublime character – laid back with a big smile and expressive eyes.

"I would like to say to everyone in Russia and to all the people in the world wherever they are, Bo Diddley is yours forever! I love you all!" He spoke into the camera at the end.

Over the next two years, we filmed over twenty-five groups. The list included Graham Nash, Julian Lennon, Ozzy Osbourne, Green Day, David Byrne, David Bowie, Chrissie Hynde, Alice Cooper, KISS, David Gilmour, Little Steven Van Zandt, and Roger Daltry.

For the interviews, Sasha would set up two cameras at different angles.

"Are you sure that's how we normally have it?" I'd ask every time in Russian as the artists sat and waited for us. They always seemed intrigued by the foreign, poetic language.

"It's better than we normally have it," Sasha would always reply.

Bowie, Chrissie Hynde, and Alice Cooper were the most earthy, humble, and easy-going interviews. I felt like I was talking to friends when I was with them. We even got Alice Cooper to look into the camera and say, "Hey stupid, *ne nada musorit!*" Billie Joe Armstrong from Green Day and Chris Robinson from the Black Crowes were among the most intelligent and considerate, much more so than I ever expected.

"If you weren't doing music, what would you be doing?" I asked Billie Joe.

He laughed. "If I wasn't doing music, I'd be doing music," he then said with a shrug and a smile.

"And what about the heavy metal concert you were at in Russia?" I asked Chris Robinson. "What did you think?"

"I didn't expect to see so many cops," he said thoughtfully. "And that they were beating people up. The violence surprised me, and I live in Los Angeles."

Little Steven was just overwhelmingly passionate about his activism. David Gilmour was more standoffish, especially when I asked about Roger Waters. At that time in the early '90s, there was a growing sentiment that songwriters were the only real artists, and I felt that both Gilmour and Roger Daltry became defensive around this topic. The funniest interview was with Paul Stanley and Gene Simmons of KISS. They sat side by side but never once acknowledged each other, the animosity between them was so thick. While one spoke, the other would roll his eyes.

The hardest interview was with Ozzy Osbourne. He was so authentic and sweet, with tattoos, blue-tinted sunglasses, and gold bangles on his wrists, but he couldn't ever finish a complete thought. It was like trying to catch a fish in a tube of toothpaste. Transcribing the interview took us forever. Ozzy would start talking about one thing, and then right in the middle of a sentence switch to an entirely new idea. I remember having a really hard time trying to understand what he was trying to convey. At the end, he let me interview his eight-year-old son Jack. It was so funny to go from slang jargon and curse words to the King's English, but I got a better understanding of who Ozzy was, not from him but from his little boy.

"Many people who see your dad on stage say that he's really crazy. I'm sure he's not like that at home?" I asked tentatively.

"No, not at all." Jack shook his head honestly. "Sometimes he just rides his stationary white bicycle or watches TV."

"Really?" I couldn't resist casting a glance over at his father.

Ozzy shrugged with a conspiratorial grin as if we shared a secret. "If you read C.S. Lewis, he says what you see and hear depends a good deal on where you are standing."

◆

The last quarter of 1993 was not slowing down. I was voted one of the Hot 5 Rock Artists from the Ovatsia national music awards (the Russian version of the Grammys) and asked to sing two songs at the presentation. I also set up a video shoot with Fedor for my song "More Than Enough." I had come up with the idea and promised to edit it if he could take the time out of another project to just shoot it with me. He gave me a young, talented director of photography, Maksim Osadchy, and brought in a set designer who helped manifest the most magic parts for me of Russia. Some days I just wish I could live inside that video. They made a large, colorful, papier-mâché airplane hoisted onto a pole in which I could sit, with a working propeller and balloons bouncing off the back.

Fedor filmed it so it looked like I was actually flying.

I got to wear so many fantastical outfits on that shoot. There was an orange jumpsuit, a black and white checkerboard jacket, flowered shoes… Sasha, not on drums for this shoot, wore a long fuchsia wig under a tall striped hat that danced around his guitar as he moved. I edited the middle section of the song with a kaleidoscope effect, and the whole thing had a hippie vibe. Of course, Fedor was wonderful, always just off camera standing on ladders and blowing bubbles.

Suddenly, an unexpected constitutional crisis started to unfold at the Russian White House. Demonstrators ended up removing police cordons around the parliament and taking over the mayor's office. They also tried to storm the Ostankino radio and television tower. On October 4, the army descended in tanks on the Supreme Soviet building. By Yeltsin's orders, they shelled the White House and arrested the leaders of the resistance. The ten-day conflict became the deadliest single event of street fighting in Moscow's history since the Russian Revolution.

This tragedy was incredibly powerful not just because of political repercussions but because it made me realize how distorted the news reported on events. Every single person I knew in America called me telling me I had to leave Russia, that their televisions were broadcasting a war that was happening in Moscow. As I stood with the receiver in my hand, I glanced out of my ninth-floor window, a little over three and a half miles from the White House, and saw everyone going on with their daily routines. Some entered bread shops, others lined up for the bus. In fact, right in the middle of the whole thing, on October 2, 1993, I participated in an outdoor concert with Sergey Galanin on Old Arbat. It was a little under two miles from the White House, and we were having a celebration for Arbat's five-hundredth birthday. People packed around us, smiling and unconcerned.

Back home I turned on CNN to see hours of footage of the demonstrators fighting in front of the White House and tanks shelling everything. It looked so real and oppressive that I kept glancing out of my window to check if anything had changed, but everything looked completely normal. From then on, I understood how press focus on crises to get more views and attention. I decided to dedicate the rest of my career to playing a kind of media antagonist, only producing content that was inspiring and unfeigned.

I started expanding *Red Wave Presents* to include the concerts of Western bands. I would license these concerts from the U.S. and England and then broadcast them along with the advertising I'd acquired. I aired some of the most important bands of the music world – Depeche Mode, Erasure, Pink Floyd, Dire Straits, Bob Marley, Genesis, KISS, Roxy Music, Diana Ross, Status Quo, David Bowie & the Tin Machine, Willie Nelson, Frank Zappa, Lou Reed, Seal, David Byrne, Morrissey, and even a six-part episode of Woodstock.

I started recording my fourth album, *For A Moment*. This would be the first record that I recorded almost entirely in Russia, and the first to come out on CD. It was mixed in Los Angeles by the famed engineer Ed Thacker, who I paid in artwork because his fee was much more than I could afford. It would be released by the independent Russian label Moroz Records. Sasha, under the new pseudonym Sniper, was the producer of the whole album. It actually took him over a year to finish because he was such a perfectionist. He played the keyboards, bass, and percussions, as well as programmed all the drums. We used four different guitarists, Igor Kozhin and Artem Pavlenko in Russia and Tim Torrance and Rick Blair from America. For almost all the songs on the album, Sasha had written the music and I had written the lyrics, except for a few of my earlier songs he redid as well. It was a huge production, and looking back, I think my lyrics had reached their most prolific, complex expression as well. I was still searching for the meaning of life that we all struggle to understand, and after my clarity about the distortion of reality on TV, I was determined to share my questions and search for the answers.

◆ One Week with Stingray

On January 17, 1994, there was a devastating 6.7 magnitude earthquake in my hometown of Los Angeles. Fifty-seven people lost their lives, and eight-thousand seven hundred were injured. It was one of the costliest natural disasters in U.S. history.

My phone started screaming with Russian friends frantic that Los Angeles was completely gone. From my Moscow apartment I turned on CNN and saw what looked like the whole city in ruins.

"Mom," I choked on the phone, tears in my eyes when I heard her voice. "I thought the worst!"

"Yes, there's destruction, but it's mostly isolated in the Valley. There's very little damage in most of Los Angeles," she said calmly.

Once again, I was so upset that the news would exaggerate something that was already so bad and horrific. Thank goodness the feature film in which I'd been cast, *Urod*, at least had the decency to make up freaky stuff and promote it as such. It was aired on Russian TV while Chaif, Alisa, Va-bank, and I headed out to Volgograd for another *Greenpeace Rocks* concert. I also released the latest B-52's album through SNC, and all their royalties were donated to Greenpeace Russia.

"I trust Greenpeace, because I'm sure the money goes towards the cause and not towards the purchase of a Mercedes for some official," I told the *Moscow Tribune*.

My action with Greenpeace had been so motivated by Viktor and his belief in people being their own heroes instead of depending on others. I wanted to celebrate Viktor as my muse and the nation's hero, and decided to put together a color photo book on him. The issue was that I wanted it to be good quality and the good paper from Finland would cost twenty-five million rubles. The publisher told me they couldn't cover that cost. Lucky for me, Fumihiko Kanagawa at Sony came to my rescue yet again and paid for the paper. Talk about heroes. With additional help from Kodak, the book with about two hundred color photos of Viktor's life and his artwork was underway. His legacy has always been very important to me.

While I wasn't concerned with my own legacy, Moroz Records was proactive enough to release a CD called *Joanna Stingray* containing eighteen songs from my first two vinyl releases. They also put out a video cassette called *Joanna Stingray – Ten Years of Video* with all my twenty-two video clips and some commentary on my career, life, and videos.

My weekly *Red Wave Presents* program continued, and finally the album *Red Wave – Four Underground Bands from the U.S.S.R.* was released in Russia, eight whole years after it first debuted in the U.S.!

The band Mess Age had broken up because the guitarist Artem Pavlenko was trying to emigrate to England, but I ended up with their bassist Robert Lenz. He had bushy hair, blue jeans and a black hoodie, and an indie vibe that emanated out of him when we performed together. He spoke great English too, mellow and sweet.

"I remember that you were a cool, open, and sincere person and I was very happy and proud that we knew each other and that I was able to play with you," he told me recently. "Now, looking back, I understand that you were one of the symbols of the era when a lot was new, sincere, and creative." I told him how much I loved having him on stage with me. So much of my creativity and sincerity came from being around amazing, inspiring people who made me feel comfortable and empowered.

Robert played with me on October 13, 1994, for my gala we called *Ten Years in Russia*. The concert was at DK Gorbunova, put on by Feelee Management and Europa Plus Radio. *Programma A*, still one of the most popular programs on Russian TV, was scheduled to film and air it, and I was always so grateful to them and Sergey Antipov.

The only problem was that it was becoming harder and harder to get my friends to commit to showing up to a group concert. They all had their own stuff going on. We billed the concert as my performance with "special friends," so I was beyond appreciative that many participated despite their busy lives.

The fans were waving American flags and tossing black balloons. Games sang "City of Lenina" with me and Shevchuk and Sukachev with his new band Neprikasaemye (The Untouchables) each did a song as well. The surprise of the night was the appearance

■ Boris, me, and Robert Lenz, with Sasha Vasilyev on drums, perform Sasha's arrangement of "Come Together," Moscow, 1994.

of Andrei Makarevich, who with his long sideburns and bright eyes sang a ballad on acoustic guitar.

I had Sasha on drums, Robert Lenz on bass, and Igor Kozhin on guitar. Around this time my style had become less black and more hippie, with a flowered short dress over black capris and combat boots. I sang songs off my upcoming album – "Clouds of My Mind" and "Off the Rails" – and I remember how good the sound was in that place, so driven and dynamic. When I performed Tsoi's "Gosti" the whole room was swallowed with his music.

"And now on the stage... Boris Grebenshchikov!" The crowd erupted like fireworks as Boris sauntered onstage in his black top hat from the "Come Together" video. It was the only time Boris and I performed this song together live, and somehow the audience seemed to know how historic this moment was. It wasn't his thing to be part of group concerts, which made it even more special to have him show up for me. He stood like a mod poser, facing out from the stage, but for a moment it felt like we were back on his roof like the old days. As we sang the words, "Come Together" in unison, he looked at me and smiled. How blessed was I that this enlightened soul had brought me into his magic and gave me the universe. At the end of the song, I introduced the friend who originally brought Boris and me together, Andrei Falalayev. As I stood up there with the two of them, my ticket master and my guide in Wonderland, I felt like everything had finally come full circle.

The closing song "Feeling" was another I had never sang live before. Vitia Sologub was the only one there for his part, so Robert and Garik filled in for Viktor, Yuri, Boris, and Sergey.

Garik, drunk by now, danced across the stage as he shouted out the lyrics to a song that was an essential reminder of my Leningrad days.

"Rock me!" We all sang at the chorus.

"Fuck me!" Garik kept chiming in.

◆

After my big celebratory concert, I had an event at the Pilot Club to air my new ten-year video release and auction off many of my well-known outfits. The point was to raise money for Greenpeace and AESOPS, because I always wanted to remind myself that being famous wasn't just about me. It was so easy to get swept up in the attention, so I tried to fight that tendency when I could. The famous actor Igor Vernik graciously agreed to run the auction. We made over four million rubles. There was also a Stingray look-a-like contest, and the prize was what we called a *Stingroshka* – a wooden *matroshka* doll that an artist painted in my image. Every guest of the auction left with something, though: posters, brochures, and condoms of course! I never talked about my own private life in public, but I did advocate for safe sex every chance I got.

In my Leningrad days, the boys had called me the Tractor, but looking back on my Moscow days I feel like I should have renamed myself the Bullet Train. I was speeding from one project to another, performing while pushing for environmental awareness.

"Unfortunately, we are governed by the kind of people who are deaf to all protests, and eventually our entire environment will be destroyed," I remembered Sklyar saying at the *Greenpeace Rocks* press conference.

"I'm happy to be a part of this project," Yuri Shevchuk also said. "I sing rock 'n roll in Russian, that is, I irrigate and sanctify this tree that we call the Russian language with holy water."

As I thought about Yuri's words, I decided I needed to do even more to raise awareness through rock 'n roll. I called my most ambitious project yet "One Week with Stingray in Los Angeles." It was a contest to bring four Russian teenagers to L.A. for a week of fun and environmental exploration. The contestants had to be between sixteen and twenty years old, not smoke, drink, or litter, and write in one hundred words or less how they could help me clean up the world. The response was insane! In the end, we picked Ludmilla Novosadova, Marina Semenova, Yuri Barsuk, and Olga Yurevich.

■ "One Week With Stingray in Los Angeles." My translator friend Alex Kan is on the right-hand side of the photo, Universal Studios Hollywood, December 1994. Photo by Deb Watson.

Before we even left Russia, our winners met with the heads of all our sponsor companies. They received informational pamphlets and diagrams about environmental procedures each company implemented to help keep the world clean, like recycling or using organic materials. The kids also received armfuls of gifts including Nike tennis shoes and backpacks, Kodak cameras and rolls of film, bags of Coca Cola merchandise, and prized Sony Walkmans with headphones.

On December 11, 1994, the four winners boarded a British Airways plane with me, Sasha, Alex Kan as a translator, and a Russian film crew with producer Sergey Suponev and cameraman Yuri Rossiski.

The week was like riding one of California's ocean waves. We went to a recycling plant, walked around Disneyland, where there were so many trashcans not a piece of litter could be found, met an artist who worked with materials from the trash, planted trees at Tree People, and spoke with lower-income African-American students from Crenshaw High School who had started their own vegetable program called Food from the Hood. The coolest place we went was the home of actor Ed Begley Jr., one of the most devoted environmentalists around who was known for riding his bike through the canyons from his house to the studios instead of a car. He had a large compost, grew his own vegetables, had solar panels and an electric car. The power company paid him every month for energy he fed to them with his stationary bike that fed power into a transformer to collect energy when he pedaled. He was off the grid and onto something.

■ Clean Week in Los Angeles,
December 1994.

■ Paul Delph and I recording in his converted bus studio,
Malibu, 1986.

One of the last things we did was meet my good friend and producer/engineer of many of my songs, Paul Delph. He was dying of AIDS, and I could see meeting him made this disease a reality for these young adults.

"The whole trip was something I couldn't even have dreamed of," Lyuda told me years later. It was such an incredible trip. It was more than just a frivolous adventure, but an impactful experience that made us realize how human, real and similar we all are. We made all the footage into a one-hour film that aired on Channel One, and then released a longer version on video with all the proceeds benefiting Greenpeace Russia. I also made a montage of the footage to my song "Save The World" that I'd written with Sergey Kuryokhin. I was determined to show that despite the Kermit the Frog's children song, it *was* that easy being green!

◆

It was 1995, and the streets of Moscow were overrun with big, blacked out window Mercedes cars. The only thing more foreboding than that was when their drivers checked for bombs under the cars with mirrors on long poles. I spent most of the winter working on my programs at Ostankino, which I had nicknamed Brazil after the science fiction movie. I would drag myself through an endless maze of a building every evening after sitting in a dark room with an editor. All I wanted was to get into my waiting car and go relax at home. One day as I was heading to the exit, a soldier refused to let me out the door.

"Go the way you came in," he grumbled, looking at my papers. The way I'd come in was the complete other side of the building, probably a couple miles away!

"Please, can you just let me out here? Come on, you know who I am, Joanna Stingray. Please let me out."

"Sorry." He shook his head sternly.

"*Mudak!*" I cried out as I turned to take the long road back to the other exit. Tired and out of patience, it was the first time I'd seen myself act like a spoiled, entitled brat. It disturbed me so much that ego had gotten the best of my attitude, and I was so disappointed in my behavior. If I could find that soldier today, I'd apologize. It was a really humbling experience.

They say karma is a bitch if you are, and not long after I found myself with blue hands and chattering teeth as I stood outside the city in an unforgiving, icy cold. I had hired Andrei Stankevich to do a music video for my song "Sanctuary," and we couldn't have picked a colder day. The whole time I tried to ignore my burning fingers and toes, but it was so painful. Even Robert reminisced not long ago that all he remembers from that shoot was how cold it was, and that's saying something coming from a Russian!

At this time, I also met a young, doe-eyed Canadian photographer named Heidi Hollinger. She had moved to Russia to take photos of politicians and interesting people, and she reminded me so much of how passionate and fearless I had been in the '80s. Through her, I met and interviewed David Byrne from the Talking Heads when he was visiting the country. Talking Heads was one of my favorite bands, and David Byrne was considered one of the trendiest characters around. In our interview he was so open and mused about how nothing can be art and art can be nothing.

"And what about racism?"

He kicked one ankle up on his knee. "It's inbred into each of us by society, and the only way to overcome it is to accept that it's there."

I loved doing these interviews so much. I felt like I could go on doing it for years until I exhausted all the musicians I could find around the world. What I'd forgotten was that, as it had happened so often, the only thing guaranteed in life is that change will come and smack you across the face.

On March 2, 1995, Channel One was turned off for twenty-four hours. I had heard it was because they had realized they were losing millions of dollars to producers who controlled their advertising. Someone told me recently that a minute of ad time back then could go for twenty-thousand to sixty-five thousand dollars! No wonder I got so many sponsorships, since I didn't ask for anything near that. What I found out later, though, was that the real reason the TV was shut down was to honor the CEO of the channel, Vladislav Listyev, who was shot and killed, likely assassinated, the day before.

■ "Sanctuary" video shoot with Sasha on drums and Robert Lenz on bass.

He had made an initiative to take back control of the advertising, and someone hadn't wanted him to do so. Days later the channel was reorganized, and after a number of incarnations came back as the government-controlled Channel One.

"So, what does this mean for my program?" I started asking around. Would I be able to continue?

A week later I had a concert at the Pilot Club to present my new album *For A Moment* along with my video for "Sanctuary." I was playing in a few new clubs around Moscow, and although I loved singing some of my new songs, the atmosphere in the clubs with drunk people falling towards the low stage made it a different experience than a concert hall. I found it harder to transform into my performing persona in a club, but also difficult to be stripped down and intimate with anyone.

As I looked out at the crowd and sang "Lost Souls" I felt so unsure of myself, despite what people might have assumed when they watched me. I glanced back at Sasha, with his flowing long hair, and realized how proud I was of the new songs and how happy I was to be singing them live. Lucky for me the *Moscow Tribune* gave me the best album review I'd gotten to date!

Joanna Stingray has improved a lot in her career lately, her band lineup, her recording facility, her lyrics and Joanna's own voice has finally graduated to the level of such stars as Bob Seeger (Night Moves) and Shakespears Sister. I predict a great future for her "Demons Dancing" track. In the time when Russian themes and lyrics are in big demand, the American singer Joanna Stingray has become known as Russia's own.

Lost Souls

I hear your voice
I feel your desperation
I hurt for you
Suffering in isolation

The chosen ones
Drowning in anticipation
The golden ones
Black skies of desolation

Lost souls lost souls
Lost in this perfect world
Lost souls lost souls
Lost in the perfect world

I hear your voice in anger
I feel your body pulse
I want to offer solace
My strength has wavered false

From the darkest, darkest direction
Now shines a glow of light
Meet you down at the resurrection
Can you follow me into the night

Lost souls lost souls
Lost in this perfect world
Lost souls lost souls
Lost in the perfect world

There's a beauty on the horizon
There's a star in the distant sky
There's an angel, there must be an angel
There's a twinkle in the savior's eye

From the darkest, darkest direction
Now shines a glow of light
Meet you down at the resurrection
Can you follow me into the night

Lost souls lost souls
Lost in this perfect world
Lost souls lost souls
Lost in the perfect world

◆ Growing Pains

"Oh my god," I gasped. "You're almost an old man!"

I hadn't seen Sasha Tsoi since he was two years old and hadn't spoken to Marianna since Viktor's funeral. They came to support the release of my Viktor Tsoi photo book at the event Lipnitsky helped put together at the Manhattan Express nightclub. The space used to be the Rossia Concert Hall where I had performed. When I hugged Sasha, it made me feel so good to know that a piece of Viktor was still on this earth. Marianna's face, though smiling, looked a little different to me, but at the time I had no idea she was sick. The next time I would see her would be almost a decade from this point, when I spent half a day in St. Petersburg and ran by to say hello and found out how ill she'd been.

"This sucks, right?" She'd said as a way of greeting me that last time. "Fuck life!" No matter what had happened to her, she was still the rough and bold woman I adored. It made me laugh and cry.

The Tsoi book looked so great with all the color images showing his life and art.

Unfortunately, the publisher had put a price of seventy-three thousand rubles, which most people didn't have. If I could, I would have just given them away.

Then, a little while after, the unthinkable happened! My Communist-hating, Soviet Union-fearing father stepped off a plane in Moscow. It was a historic event. The program "Fan Club" filmed him meeting all my fans on Old Arbat, and as each one went up and shook his hand, he was beaming. The interviewer asked him in Russian if he liked Russia. Before anyone could translate for him, he turned and looked right in the camera.

"*Zdrasvewti, Rossia. Kak vew pazheviate?*" – "Hello, Russia. How are you doing?"

My fans started laughing and cheering. I could tell my father must have practiced those lines for weeks. I was so proud of him – living proof that you could teach an old dog new tricks.

◆

As April melted away the last of the snow, I kept busy. Sasha and I wrote new songs, and I went on a TV show called *Rok Yrok* to answer questions. I also had performances for M Radio at the Russian Army Theater and on *Live* with Max at Ostankino.

"Today we have someone who is possibly the most famous immigrant from America, and who is, as a matter of fact, probably the only one of her kind!" Max introduced me. I got to perform songs and get questions and compliments from the viewers. I had really started channeling my emotions into my lyrics and it felt euphoric to belt them out. *I'm lost in your hatred but found by the light of day… I resist to your thunder but am soiled by the greed you play… I'm cleansed by the rays of light that shine on demons dancing.* It was one of those times where everything came together, and I loved it.

On April 28, 1994, I was back at Ostankino to perform two songs on *Rok Yrok* with my new guitar player, Gleb. As I was walking into the studio I unexpectedly ran right into Sergey Kuryokhin.

"Zhoanna," he said with a big smile.

I hadn't seen him in a long time. As I wrapped my arms around him it felt like a piece of my soul grew back, right beside my heart. Sergey was such a big part of who I had become. I showed him my new CD, and he just beamed like a proud parent. He had just performed on the show, and he gave me one more huge hug for luck before I did the same. It was a wonderful moment.

As I performed my two songs, I couldn't stop replaying the reunion in my mind. Even though I loved the stripped-down sound on the stage, the only thing I could think about was finishing quickly and catching Sergey before he left. Right after the song, I bolted to the dressing room to see if he was still there. He wasn't.

I went out of the room, standing in the dim light of a long and lonely hallway. I had no way of knowing that the reason I felt so sad was because I would never see him again. Just over a year later, the maestro, our Capitán, would be gone. I can still imagine him in heaven, orchestrating all the angels into crazy, twisted song.

◆

The funny thing about time is if you don't pay attention to it or are having too much fun to notice, it will tap you on the shoulder and run the other way.

For the first time in a long time, I finally took a deep breath and sat down to take a break.

I had a flashback to my first year in Russia, when people would get so surprised that I was twenty-four years old and hadn't had a child. I always knew I wanted children, but I had been in no hurry. In America, people waited until their thirties! But I had blinked, and suddenly my thirty-fifth birthday was coming up.

"I want to have a baby," I said out loud to myself. "Now."

It became all I could think about. I told Sasha about it, and at five years younger than I was it hadn't crossed his mind. It was always hard to say no to me though, and he agreed.

On June 30, 1995, Sasha and I performed at the MK Zvukavaya Dorozhka concert at Luzhniki Stadium with Artur Gasparyan, five days before Sasha and I left for America. We then continued writing songs for our new album, *Shades of Yellow*, from the West Coast. Sasha would play me the melody, and I would conjure up the lyrics.

Give it all that you got, don't live by the things you have not, I'd sing to him. *Try to seek and you will find, a place hiding deep inside your mind*. It was so easy with someone as talented as him. Together the music felt meaningful, evolved. I was so proud of those songs.

In the middle of all this, I met with my doctor, and he said that it would be wise to use an ovulation kit to help pinpoint the best timing to get pregnant because of my age. Sasha would be in the middle of programming drums for the new album when I would run into the studio waving a white stick.

"Hey, Sash, I need you now!"

"Now?" He would ask.

"Yes, now!"

◆

As part of the Los Angeles International Festival, I set up a dual photography exhibit at Bergamot Station in Santa Monica. I displayed photojournalist Heidi Hollinger's series "Faces of the Opposition" in addition to work by one of the New Artists' group, Vladik Monroe, born Vladislav Mamyshev. I had met him through Afrika and Gustav, and he was probably the most outrageous character of all my Russian friends. He was the Russian Marilyn Monroe, and very often dressed as her in drag. Growing up next to boys' town in West Hollywood, I had seen many drag queens in my life, but Vladik was by far the winner. He was stunning.

■ Me (pregnant) and Sasha, Los Angeles, Spring 1996.

Vladik's photography series for the show was called "Tragic Love," a fifteen install-ment fotonovella chronicling Ms. Monroe's love affair with a manager that came to a terminal end. To me, Vladik's photos had a beautiful shine that masked a sadness underneath. He continued to be an enigmatic force, dying mysteriously almost two decades later.

Then, sometime after the art show, I learned I was pregnant. I felt like a different person, freer than ever before. My focus, which had been on myself and my career my whole life, was suddenly entirely on this child inside me. To care, to love another above everything, is what it means to be a social creature like a human.

At three months, we found out that the baby was going to be a girl. I was over the moon. I suddenly decided that I wanted Sasha to marry me so we wouldn't have this angel out of wedlock. A couple of days later, we were standing in a Beverly Hills courtroom with my parents, a judge marrying us during his lunch hour. It was so different from the complications and formalities of my Russian wedding but felt right.

Over the next few months, singing in the studio became harder and harder. With all the extra weight on my body I had a hard time reaching some of the high notes. Frank, our engineer for the album, remembers Sasha making me sing the highest section of "Up All Night" over and over again.

"Sasha," I gasped as he told me to do it again. "This baby is going to pay me back and keep *me* up all night!"

I got word from Moscow that since my next *Red Wave Presents* series was already under contract with a number of companies, they would allow me to air twelve final segments. After being cleared by my doctor, I flew to Moscow, leaving Sasha in Los Angeles where by now he preferred to be. I arrived on a chilly January day and spent the next three weeks or so editing in a ground floor apartment in the center of the city. I had always planned to give birth in the States and then return with Sasha and the baby to continue living in Russia, until one day when I inhaled a puff of diesel in the studio that made me so sick. I asked the editor to go see what it was, and he reported that a diesel truck was in the courtyard idling the vehicle so he could use the heat.

"Can he turn it off?" I coughed.

"That's just the way it is here," the editor shrugged.

"Yes, it is," I said to myself. "Yes, it is."

For the first time I started thinking that maybe the smartest choice was to raise my little girl somewhere other than Russia.

I went back to my apartment, exhausted, and spent the next day packing to go back to Los Angeles. As I looked out my window at the dimming sky over this vast country I called home, I realized I had finally found what I had come here in the '80s searching for. I had found friends, I had found purpose, and I was about to have a family, but more than that I had met myself in this crazy, complicated world. And I loved the woman I had become.

◆

On Tuesday, February 20, 1996, I woke up. I really woke up. I felt more awake than I'd ever felt in my life. I stood up and felt like I had been shot out of the rabbit hole and back to reality from my dozen-year-long daydream. In that very moment, I knew I was not coming back to Russia.

Sitting on the plane hours later, I felt drunk as the memories of my time in Russia passed through my mind like a movie. In some ways, it had happened so fast, and in another it seemed like multiple lifetimes. There had been so many thrills, colors, and fantasies, and so much heartache too. I couldn't figure out if I was leaving it behind or taking it with me.

"What do I do?" I muttered to myself as the plane caught the wind and soared away. Do I look out the window to say goodbye, or just let it go? "Who am I?" I asked aloud, "without this place?"

■ "More Than Enough" video shoot with me and Sasha.

As I finally glanced out to see the tail end of the city disappear into the clouds, I put a hand on my pregnant stomach. I became flooded with happiness and love and gratefulness, the pure joy I had felt in the early days of Leningrad. You can't search for or try to get to Wonderland. It is something that just arrives on its own, and you find yourself immersed – all the memories, all the faces of the people I loved who were here and there and gone, were all going to be written on this little girl's face. She would remind me of everything that had gotten me to this point.

On that flight I finished the lyrics to my new song I would record when I got back to L.A., "Wonderland."

Wonderland

She strolled by the corner
And she glanced up at the crowd
Faces shiny faces
How they lit up all the town

Spins round
Like she lost her head up high
Going down
Down to Wonderland

She stopped at a café
And she flipped back her hair
And faces shiny faces
How she felt them everywhere

Says aloud
My head is up so high
Going down
Down to Wonderland

In your hands,
In your eyes,
In your mind
The days last forever

She took, took a long break
As she focused inside
Feeling, funny feeling
It could not be denied

Stands proud,
Like she knows her head is high
Going down
Down to Wonderland

In your hands,
In your eyes,
In your mind
The days last forever

◆ 1996—2020 ◆

◆ Epilogue

In the spring of 1996, when a person left a place they really left. There was no Internet, no easy way to stay in touch, and Russia was an entirely other slice of the world. Footprints faded quickly, and my connection to that beastly wonderland was already becoming a faint fairy tale once I made the decision to leave and boarded a plane back to Los Angeles.

I had a new purpose. My daughter, Madison Alexandra Stingray, was taking all my energy and focus, and this transfer of love was profound. I had no regrets giving up my old life to be a mother. My life in Russia had been fueled by my emotions, but having a child flipped a switch in my brain that made me more logical and aware of responsibility. A child needs consistency, and not even a record deal could distract me from trying to recreate a new, mini wonderland for this tiny creature.

"Hi, I just heard the album you sent Mr. Ertegun a few months back. *Shades of Yellow?*" The voice on the other end of the phone was deep and methodical. "This is really cool. We are interested in signing you."

"Sorry, who is this?" I balked, stepping over a ball that dominated the center of the living room.

"I'm from Atlantic Records," was the response.

I blinked. "I don't know what to say."

"I'd love to discuss the writing and production of this album. It would be great to get a band together and tour a little by bus," he continued.

I shook my head, trying to clear the soft buzz in my ears. This had always been my dream, something to which I'd fall asleep, and now I was wide awake watching it unfold. But the thought of miles of road and nights in cheap hotels was suddenly incompatible with the idealistic life I decided I wanted to try to give my child.

"I'm so sorry, but no," I told the A&R guy. It was a surprisingly easy decision.

I had purchased a house just off Benedict Canyon, and by Madison's first birthday I was basically running a one-child preschool out of it. The tiled floors were covered with colored foam mats, and a slide dominated the entryway.

"Are you running a daycare?" A Chinese-food delivery man asked one day at the door.

"No," responded Teresa, the guardian angel who had become Madison's nanny.

"How many kids do you have?" he asked quizzically.

"Oh, just one," she said, closing the door.

Sasha had made the room over our garage into a home studio where he spent hours and hours writing new music. As a perfectionist, his work was never really done, and so the childhood kingdom into which the main house had been transformed was often without his big smile or curious eyes. When he did come down, it was magical for Madison. She and he always had the most fun. He was silly and playful, and Madison adored him, but he was almost more like a visitor than a parent. His creative work would always come first, and by the time Madison was three years old, I asked Sasha for a divorce. We were like two boats passing but never exchanging goods, each running low on supplies.

Sasha moved to an apartment in the steaming valley north of Beverly Hills, and Teresa and I kept Madison busy going to museums, aquariums, pony rides, hikes, and parks. She loved fairy tales and would play by herself for hours too. Sometimes I would tell her about the colorful stories from Leningrad, but I'm pretty sure she thought it was all made up.

As time wore on, there were moments where even I questioned the reality of my experiences in Russia. I barely had any interactions with my old friends. A couple of times a year I'd get contacted by the Russian press wanting to send a camera crew to my house to talk about my Russian career and Viktor Tsoi, or the phone would ring and Seva Gakkel or Sasha Lipnitsky would be calling to tell me that another one of our friends had died. Kuryokhin, The Pig, Dusha from Aquarium, and Timur Novikov. Whenever I picked up the phone and could hear the static of a long-distance call, I would start shaking.

"Who is it?" I would whisper. "What special soul have we lost now?"

I never imagined that by the time I would write this book, over twenty of my close friends would be gone. There is a sadness that saturates my heart and will never dry.

◆

In 2004, eight years after I'd left Russia on the horizon where the sun rose, I decided to visit in honor of the twentieth anniversary of my first time there. I also wanted Madison to see her *dyeda* and *baba* whom she had only met once when she was a baby in California, and to see the land that made up half of her heart. I had recorded a new album with a few of the songs Sasha and I had written years before and a number of acoustic versions of my old hits. Matt Roberts, a guitar player with shaggy hair and sweet eyes, helped with production and came along for the ride. Sasha Lipnitsky had set up a concert at a Moscow club called B2. When I stepped into the time capsule masquerading as an airplane, I had no idea what to expect.

We arrived in Moscow on a cold winter night as the snow hung almost frozen in the air. Two of my fans, Lyuda and Olga, surprised us at the airport with a hired limo. Madison's *baba* was there as well – she had walked, taken the bus, and traveled on the underground to get there, standing proudly in her black hat, fur coat, and sparkling earrings. To this day, I find it uncanny how similar she and Madison look. They have the same nose, soft blue eyes, and curled mouth. Eight-year-old Madison was fussed over like a princess, and I could see in her eyes how overwhelmed she was. This was just the beginning.

Over the next couple of days, I melted back into my Russian life that I thought had been lost to the pages of a history book. Madison didn't even recognize me. She wrapped a scarf around her head like the *babushkas* on the street and hid behind her imagination, pretending the entire thing was some modernized, freakish story from a Grimm's fairy tale. *Tusofka* at Lipnitsky's became a tea party with the mad hatter, the Kremlin Armory became a fortress stolen from her, Red Square was a foreign land filled with ghosts and spirits, and the titanium sculpture of cosmonaut Yuri Gagarin was a living guardian she felt was a long-lost lover. When we went to visit her grandparents' apartment, the room of her *dyeda* was pretty much a shrine to her, his little angel. There were photos of her all over the room, and drawings he'd done of her from the images. Unable to communicate in Russian with someone she barely knew, Madison was completely freaked out, trapped in a matrix in which she had existed without ever living there.

My old tried-and-true friend, Sergey Galanin gathered a couple of musicians who worked with Matt to get together a set of my songs. As we rehearsed, I saw Madison

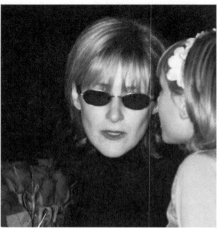

■ Me and my daughter Madison at my twentieth anniversary concert at B2, Moscow, 2004.

fidgeting by the side of the stage.

"*Idi syuda!*" I called to her. "Come here!"

She crawled up on the stage with her scarf and unblinking eyes.

"Sing the Russian ditty you know so well," I told her. "*Pust vsigda budyet solntse*" – "May there always be sunshine."

That evening at the concert, Sasha Lipnitsky introduced Little Stingray. She stood there in my dark, circular sunglasses as the crowd cheered her on. A cappella, she sang the four lines in Russian and then in English, her thin, angelic voice smoothing out every line. In that moment, I knew she was damned to the twisted, whimsical world of music and performing that I loved so much.

At the end of my set, the blues guitarist Sergey Voronov joined me on stage for a version of "Come Together." Madison also joined in on the choruses. I'd forgotten how much I loved to perform, how much I missed the shine of the lights against the stage and the faint thumping of a thousand hearts beating together.

There are two photos from the concert hanging up in my home today. In one, I'm sitting on the edge of the stage with Madison with fans handing me flowers, touching my clothes, and asking for autographs. Madison's face is a painting of confusion and shock. In the second photo, Madison is tugging my arm in the middle of my set, stretching on her tiptoes to whisper a question in my ear and ignoring the crowd leaning in against the stage. Both of these remind me of the lives I was straddling, this rockstar history and this maternal responsibility. I'm so lucky I had a chance to have both.

■ Tea at Sasha Lipnitsky's with Madison during an interview with Russian TV, Moscow, 2004.

■ Madison and her *baba*, Tatiana Vasilyeva, Moscow, 2004.

Since my set wasn't long enough for an entire concert, I asked my favorite pirate Garik Sukachev if he would play after me. He tumbled onto the stage in a mess of wild hair and a gravelly voice. Madison had never seen anything like it, and she was scared and thrilled by this powerful creature. Later, as we all stood downstairs contemplating the snowstorm that blocked our exit, Garik came over to Madison and knelt beside her.

"Is this your first Russian winter, little one?" he asked her.

"It's my first time in Russia," she whispered.

"Have you ever seen Moscow snow and such big flakes as these?" he asked.

"No, never." Madison shook her head.

He put his arm around her, and she immediately softened into his warmth. "Watch," he told her. It was a beautiful sight, this crazy, burly rocker and an eight-year-old American girl staring out into an indistinct world.

◆

After Viktor died, I had rarely returned to Leningrad. On that 2004 trip, I planned an overnight train to the Venice of the North, a stopover of only a few hours before my flight back home. I asked Seva to see if anyone was around, and decided to take it from there.

A few hours before the train, I was asked if *Rolling Stone* Russia could interview me for a profile piece. The next thing I knew, it was midnight on a roaring train and Madison, Matt, Lyuda, two drunk reporters, and I were jammed into a single private car. Madison sat tucked under the blankets, fixated on these drunk people and unable to understand why they were acting so strange. We ended up sleeping maybe two hours that night, crawling off the train and into the brutal black cold at six in the morning. It brought back so many memories, and inside my blood, I felt an energy I had forgotten I had. For the first time in a long time, I felt like I was home. Even to this day, that happens every time I step foot into that lavish city built on a swamp.

Vitia Sologub and Seva met us at the station. We all went to Seva's for tea and then to the Platforma Club, where I saw a sea of many of my old friends and musicians.[10] Yuri and his wife Natasha also showed up, and I was so thrilled to see him. We hadn't seen each other or even spoken for years. He looked older, but still had the same sweet smile, mischievous eyes, and broad shoulders. He was enamored with Madison, and I remembered his desire for a baby after we were married.

We didn't have much time before going to visit an ill Marianna and then to our flight, but when Yuri said Gustav wanted to see me, I had to jump at the chance. Madison and I followed Yuri to Gustav's. I remember feeling nervous as I stood at the door – with Gustav I had never known what I was going to get. His eyes lit up when he saw me, and the love I felt for him washed away the difficult parts of his character that irritated some memories. He was gaunt and unstable, and I was deeply saddened to recognize the look that I had seen in many of my friends who eventually died of AIDS.

"Jo," Gustav said in his low voice. He opened his arms for a hug.

We only stayed briefly in that wonderful room filled with his paintings. We somehow both knew that this would be the last time we would meet in the physical world, and we grabbed each other to signal we would never forget all we'd been through. As I looked back at his crooked parting smile, I knew Viktor would be glad to get his combative, feisty friend back.

On the plane ride home, it felt so bittersweet. The memories that I thought had faded from the surface were tattooed deep inside my soul. It was a power switch and a sharp itch at the same time. It would take another thirteen years until I put my feet on Russian soil again after that trip, but I'm so lucky that the iconic memories of the '80s Leningrad rock period have never left me.

♦

---

10 Among these: Kolya Vasin (The Beatles Guy), Oleg Garkusha (front man for Auction), Nastia Kuryokhin and her son Fedor (wife and son of Sergey), Kolya Mikhailov (director of the Rock Club), Olga Slobodskaya (secretary of the Rock Club) and her daughter Polina, the music engineer Fearsoff, Alexander Lyapin and Misha Feinstein from Aquarium, photographer Dima Konrad, and music journalist Andrei Burlaka from the former underground magazine *RIO.*

In 2014, I was interviewed for a documentary called *Free to Rock* that tracked rock 'n roll's influence on the downfall of the Iron Curtain. The producers asked for some of my photos and footage, which triggered my memory and compelled me to go through the boxes and boxes of photos I had kept. There were easily thousands I had stored away from my Russia days. I started scanning all the photos and then hiring someone to make me an archival website. Some local friends advised me against putting all the photos online, but I felt that these images could be a gift to the Russian people as a thank you for all they gave to me.

I knew that Russians would like the website, but I had no idea how much it would blow up. I had press contacting me left and right about stories they wanted to do on it. I gave everyone permission to use what they wanted for free, hoping the gift could be spread. A half a million people were on the site in the first couple of weeks. I realized that things never really end, they just progress and evolve with the people that we become.

One day I was sitting at my computer, looking at Facebook and wondered if any of my Russian friends had joined the ubiquitous platform. I had originally joined to post travel photos for my local friends, but I hadn't had any idea how many Russians were on it as well. I reconnected with Boris, Kostya, Garik, Galanin, Alex Kan, and a number of others. It was a gateway to my past and a lens to the present. To be able to watch videos of Boris still playing music to crowds on the side of a highway or street renewed my faith in mankind. It was the purest form of my friend, and the fact that his heart and his footsteps had sustained throughout the decades was unbelievably beautiful.

A year or two later, Yuri asked if he and his wife Natasha could come spend the day with me. He was playing a concert with the group U-Piter in San Francisco, and they would be flying back to Russia through Los Angeles. I could tell Yuri was so nervous around me, but Natasha just sat calmly and let Yuri and I reminisce and catch up. She was the coolest, most confident woman I'd ever met. Yuri was more mature and nostalgic than I had ever seen him. There was such warmth and happiness in his gaze.

"It's you and me now. Viktor and Gustav are gone, and we need to stay in contact," he said. It was so sad but so beautiful. In this moment I saw that the chain had never been broken and that the bond that forms between humans of the same experiences never relinquishes its hold on the heart or the mind. The distance didn't matter – it was all about the chronicle, the saga. Our love hadn't just been young love – it was enormous and everlasting.

✦

I always wanted to write a book about my time in Russia, but I was too busy working a job in real estate, managing an estate, and coordinating publications for my high school alumni association. There wasn't even enough time to find a writer! There was a film script written about my adventures, but it was only a sliver of the cosmic story. A book could tell it all, and it was always in the back of my mind. At a *Free to Rock* screening in Washington D.C., I met a writer whom I ended up hiring to write the book with me. I would write my story and send it to him to 're-write' into a more appropriate novel format. When he sent it back, I could see it was formatted more like a formal book, but it somehow felt flat, monochromatic and listless. It didn't capture the essence of what had changed my life. He didn't seem to get it, and the whole introduction about the rabbit hole was something I could feel he didn't understand. I asked my daughter, a brilliant yet bashful writer, if she would read the few chapters and give me her feedback. She had zero interest.

Then, right before we were heading out on one of our obsessive jaunts to visit a number of countries, Madison asked if we could go to Russia.

"Why?" I asked. "We've been there already."

"I want to go," she said, shaking her head adamantly. "We *have* to go."

I didn't understand it at the time, but she had a transcendental connection pulling her to Russia. I am convinced Viktor and Sergey had something to do with it.

Normally I wouldn't change a planned trip, but when I read there was a new high-speed train from Helsinki to St. Petersburg, I couldn't resist. I hadn't been to Russia in over a decade. I thought we could sneak in for three nights, and I could show Madison one of my favorite cities in the world now that she was old enough to really have it resonate. I decided to keep the trip a secret from my Russian friends so it could be about myself, Madison, and the sites. The universe had other plans.

After making a comment on one of Afrika's Facebook posts, he jokingly replied asking when I was coming to Russia. I messaged him back that I'd be there in a few weeks. He posted it, and suddenly people started reaching out to make plans.

Between our tours with an incredible, bubbly guide name Olga Bycheck from Be Happy Russia, Madison and I scheduled many social encounters. We were staying at the Belmond Grand Hotel Europe (Hotel Evropeiskaya), my old stomping ground where Boris had gotten arrested and my KGB meeting had happened in the '80s. Everything worked out so well it truly felt like the two of us were meant to be there at that time. The weather was fifty degrees and sunny, and because of protests, Nevsky Prospekt was closed to vehicles so we could walk through the crowds in the middle of the pavement. For the

■ Inside the Church of the Savior on Spilled Blood, St. Petersburg, May 2018.

first time ever, people were allowed to tour the Church of the Savior on Spilled Blood, the very place I had spent days admiring from Boris' roof. It had been an insurmountable amount of time, but here I was, almost as if I'd never left.

◆

"He just kissed me on the mouth!"

Before I could respond to Madison, Fearsoff leaned over and gave me a bear-hug and kiss on the lips too. All I could do was laugh.

We were sitting with Seva Gakkel and Vitia Sologub at a great vegetarian café in St. Petersburg. Vitia and Seva were the perfect compliments to each other, Vitia's intense energy and Seva's balanced spirit wrapping the table in a safe warmth. The restaurant was right next to the Neva River, and the next day I decided I wanted to do something I'd never been able to do in all my days in Leningrad: go out on it.

I rented a beautiful small speed boat with wooden panels to take me, Madison, Yuri and his wife Natasha, and Alexander "Sasha" Tsoi, an accomplished musician and video producer, out on the water. We wove through the canals and looked up at all different angles. The city of my heart had never looked so beautiful. I hadn't seen Sasha since he was a boy, and he was now so tall and powerful, with his metal jewelry and tattoos. Olga, our favorite guide, brought snacks and tea. It was hysterical – on the way to the

■ Natasha Kasparyan, Sasha Tsoi, Madison, me, and Yuri, Neva River, May 2018.

■ Sasha Tsoi and Madison on the Neva River, St. Petersburg, May 2018.

boat we all walked together from the hotel, and Olga handed her rolling bag of treats to Sasha. I almost pointed out to her that she shouldn't make the son of Viktor Tsoi drag this bag, but Sasha was so gracious and happy to do it. He really was his father's son, an unpretentious and chivalrous man attuned to those around him.

It was so surreal to see Madison and Sasha sitting and talking, occasionally bursting out into quiet fits of laughter as we bobbed over the windy water. It made my heart ache for Viktor.

"I want to tell you funny stories about your dad," I told Sasha excitedly. "How he would roll the *rrr* sound in words right in front of my face, and how he would kung fu kick me like he was Bruce Lee."

Sasha was such a warm and open soul. He talked about how hard his twenties were as he coped with being the son of Viktor and the pressure to fill his father's shoes. Now he was in a better place, and it showed.

"After Viktor died, people were interested in me because I was so close with him," I told Sasha. "Try to embrace your connection with him. It's a good thing. It may open doors or create interest, and then after that people will see that you have something uniquely worth hearing, and continue to like you for *you*."

We got off the boat near Yuri's apartment with Natasha. They had bought two units, side by side and made it into one large flat. Yuri had converted one room into a studio with a large computer and electronic equipment.

"I want to see it," Madison said immediately.

Yuri was working on something called Symphonic Kino, his project of Kino songs played by a full symphony orchestra, and it blew both Madison and me away. It was

■ Me and Yuri on my hotel balcony looking over Arts Square toward the Church of the Savior on Spilled Blood, St. Petersburg, May 2018.

amazing, overwhelming, but the music held you like a cradle.

"I am so proud of you," I told Yuri. I knew Viktor would be too.

Yuri pulled out his guitar and started improvising on it.

"Remember when you and Viktor and Gustav used to sing The Cult's song 'Nirvana' and change the words?" I asked, laughing and remembering it fondly.

The next thing I know Yuri started strumming the chords and belting out, "Every day, JOANNA, yeah, yeah, yeah!" I was speechless. Suddenly I was back in the shadows of an apartment with Kino as their teasing voices filled my ears. It was so emotional, so profound. I did the only thing I could do and burst out into tears.

"Stop!" Madison cried from where she was filming on her phone. "We need to make you laugh! Where the hell is Fearsoff when you need him?"

◆

There in technicolor, with his tinted sunglasses, was Boris standing on my hotel terrace. I had heard he was in town recording at a studio and invited him and his wife, Irina, to come to dinner. Madison had headed off with Olga to the famous ballet.

Boris looked the same. He was a little older and a little thicker, but he had his same charismatic smile and winking eyes. Irina still had all her beauty, and the way she looked lovingly at Boris was just as powerful as when they were both married to different people decades ago. It was clear how much she adored him and loved to dote on him. They seemed like the perfect match.

"Wow," Boris said, stepping outside and seeing the Church of the Savior on Spilled Blood sparkling in the sunset.

■ Boris and Madison, St. Petersburg, May 2018.   ■ Me and Madison with Boris.

"It's like we're hanging out on your old roof, right?" I asked him.

"Yes." He smiled.

"You're so lucky you caught him here," Irina told me over the breadbasket. "He's hardly ever in St. Petersburg. We're only here because he had a major health problem on the road and ended up in a coma, you see. The doctor said he had to stay put for a few months."

"Did you see the light?" I asked Boris curiously. "So many people say it is calming when you're close to death."

"No," Boris shook his head. "It was horrible. Scary. Dark."

We talked about all his recordings and concerts and projects. Boris was one of the few of our old gang that had no interest in reminiscing about the past. He was moving forward, a train going one way to the horizon piled with light and gold.

"Madison will be so sad to miss you!" I told him as we moved inside for desserts and he pulled out some gin and tonic from the mini bar to mix.

"Come over and visit in the morning," he invited. "I am just off Nevsky Prospekt."

The next morning, Madison and I took a brisk walk down the wide, packed street to see him. Madison walked quickly, almost frantic, and I could tell she felt that same magnetic pull I'd always felt towards Boris. He'd just woken up when we arrived. He and Irina lived in a large apartment with an art studio, the walls filled with Boris' beautiful landscapes.

"This is a big step up from the communal flat," I teased him.

We sat for tea, Madison and I crunched in a sofa pushed all the way up against Boris' desk. Somehow, Madison started talking about how mean and vindictive people can be, a race of inherently selfish souls.

"Madison, your life is like a play, and you are the director," Boris leaned forward, looking her in the eyes. "If you don't like some people, just kick them out. Tell them to go fuck themselves."

As I watched, the two of them dissolved into a philosophical conversation. I could see myself sitting exactly where Madison was, lapping up Boris' wisdom thirty-five years before. The world can be such a spiritual, inexplicable place.

Before we left, Boris reached into a cup and pulled out a skull ring that he gave to Madison. She slipped it on her middle finger, the face pointing down.

"No, Madison, have it facing out," Boris instructed. "Always have it facing out, towards the world."

Madison was quiet, almost transformed, as we made our way back to the hotel.

"Let me read the chapters that guy wrote," she finally blurted out in the lobby.

"Sure," I said. "I'll get the book upstairs."

I opened the door to the room, and there were Afrika and Big Misha waiting to order room service.

"When did you get here?" I asked.

"Just before I did," Seva said, stepping in from behind.

We sat in a circle in the room, Afrika speed-talking as always. He was the same skinny, mischievous eighteen-year-old I had met in 1984, coming up with crazy ideas and wild stories. Big Misha hadn't changed either, a Greek statue of a man who considered all his words and never wasted a breath.

"Kostya Kinchev is out in the country," Seva told me as he ran through his list of updates.

"Can we call him?" I interrupted excitedly. I hadn't had any communication with him since probably 1993. I knew he was still a huge deal in Russia, and his legions of fans known as the Alisa Army were everywhere, but I also knew he had suffered a heart attack the year before, and I didn't want to miss the chance to reconnect with that crazy cat. I wanted to hear his voice.

"*Privyet*, Jo," I heard from Seva's phone.

"*Privyet*, Kostya, *kak dyla*?" I was shocked how easy it was to communicate with him in Russian, almost as if we'd never missed a beat. "I want you to know that you were very important in my life, and you will always be close to me."

"Me too," he replied warmly.

"Please be well, I love you," I finally said.

"I love you too," he answered before the line clicked off.

■ Afrika Bugaev, me, Seva Gakkel, and Big Misha Kucherenko, St. Petersburg, May 2018.

■ With Boris (above) and Yuri (below), May 2018.

That same day, I also said goodbye to all my friends. Madison and I had a train to catch. I gave Afrika, Seva, and Misha huge hugs, and closed the door behind them. Immediately, there was a knock on the door.

"What did someone forget?" I laughed. I opened the door to see Yuri standing there.

"I will see you off," he told me ceremoniously.

He stood by the entryway as Madison and I ran around the hotel room and rushed to throw our bags together.

"Where's my charger?" Madison screamed from the bathroom.

"Have you seen my wallet?" I yelled back. "Oh my god, I forgot to put this bulky jacket in the bag!"

"I need you to fit my jacket!" Madison cried out. "I can't even make my computer fit."

"What do you mean? I can't fit it!"

"Girls!" Yuri's strong voice overpowered both of ours. He stepped forward and pointed to the bed. "Sit!"

Immediately, Madison and I sat.

"Now, breathe. Wait for a moment," Yuri directed.

Madison and I each inhaled deeply.

"Okay." Yuri nodded. "Now get your things. We go downstairs."

It was such a flashback to the Yuri I'd fallen in love with, this calm and collected spirit who tempered me. Madison was absolutely enamored with his sweetness.

As our van left the hotel, we stared out the back window and watched Yuri walk away and down the street. He kept looking back over his shoulder, just as he had when I was leaving before my visa got declined.

"This is so sweet, but so sad!" Madison cried, giving him a final wave.

I try to live my life without regretting, but one of my biggest regrets was not seeking out more old friends while I was in St. Petersburg. A couple of months after this trip, I lost Andrei Krisanov and Kolya Vasin, the first to illness and the second to an apparent suicide. I will never forget the tangibility of Andrei's young, vibrant spirit, and Kolya's mantra of *all you need is love*. He will forever be the walrus.

◆

That trip changed everything. I was even more devoted now to doing my friends justice in a book. There was only one problem.

"These first three chapters that guy wrote suck," Madison told me. "I could do much better."

"Go for it," I told her.

A couple of days later, I sat down to read what she had written. The story had been transformed, from a flat and watery swampland to a colorfully textured landscape. She had brought my history and my friends back to life. I let go the original writer and hired Madison on the spot.

I got a book deal with the biggest publisher in Russia – AST Publishing. We decided to make the book into two parts, my early days in Leningrad under the transition from Communism to *glasnost*, and my career in Moscow as capitalism moved in. I would write down my memories and hand them off to Madison, who would weave them into chapters with an articulation and way of storytelling that was poetic and pulsating. She spent hours looking at photos and watching my old videos, capturing the nuances of how people spoke and moved. My friends became as important to her as they were to me, and she became obsessed with cementing their legacies in print.

Out of all the people she studied, she watched the most videos of Tsoi and Kuryokhin. One day she came to me in tears.

"I am so sad I'll never meet the two of them," she told me. "It's not fair."

The next morning, she came downstairs later than normal.

■ Madison and me just off Arbat Street in Moscow at the wildly colorful and spraypainted memorial wall for Viktor Tsoi, 2004. The wall is over ten feet high, with lyrics and all the messages from fans stretching its length. People regularly leave fresh flowers and cigarettes.

"What's wrong?" I asked her immediately.

"I had a dream about Viktor," she said solemnly. "And I've written a song about him."

"A song? What's it called?"

"Muse."

Listening as she played me the song on the piano, I knew immediately that Viktor had visited her like he had visited me after he died. I felt tears roll down my cheeks as Madison sang her haunting vocals.

◆

In March and September of 2019, I had my books released in Russia. My good friend Alex Kan translated both and traveled with me to do all the press and signings. The books were a huge hit.

I had originally thought I wanted to publish these books as a gift for the Russian people, then I thought I was telling the stories for myself, but what I learned was that I did it for my guys. It is the best feeling in the world to know they are living forever.

During that first book tour I had an epiphany I'd never allowed myself to have. I realized I had made a difference. I was an ordinary person who had the chance to do extraordinary things, by luck of fate and connection to some of the most magical people in the world.

As I had learned throughout my years in Russia, though, everything in the universe has to be balanced out. After leaving Russia on high for the first book, I landed at LAX to the news that my mother had died. It was totally unexpected, and absolutely devastated me. During my second book trip, I got the news that Sasha, my second husband and the father of my daughter, had taken his own life in Los Angeles. The sound of Madison wailing over the phone was the most painful sound I had ever heard in my life.

There are moments when life feels like something happening to someone else, as if I'm just an observer who lived in St. Petersburg in a past life. But the emotions of sadness, hope, beauty, tragedy, and wisdom are too overpowering to ignore. I feel everything in my bones, from then until now. Life is about figuring out who we are as humans and why we end up where we do. Loss is a misconception, because everything we had has made up who we are and is something we carry with us every day. I look at my daughter as she concentrates on signing these books, and I recognize in her face everything I thought I'd lost. Years go quickly, but history is unchanging, infallible, and forever part of us. An average person like myself can be part of a magnificent adventure, and nothing can take that away. My guys, my music, my home – not even death can render these things irrelevant.

"I wish I had been able to see Wonderland," Madison told me.

"You have," I replied. "You dipped your toe in the water and your pen in the ink, and you'll never be the same."

◆ SPECIAL ACKNOWLEDGMENTS ◆

Madison Stingray, the biggest piece of my heart, for taking my life and placing it beautifully on the page. You infused the book with your thoughtful and imaginative understanding and appreciation for Russia and my friends, and your talent for writing has transformed what was history into a palpable, colorful, and contemporary story.

Joan and Fred Nicholas, the lighthouses that cleared a path for me through my darkest days and helped me navigate my life across an ocean and two continents. There would be no story without them.

Judy Fields, who documented the life I led in Russia and whose videos and photos captured the memories and marvels that we saw and can now share. Your dedication and encouragement through the long winters and humid summers gave me strength to dare what we dared and now makes it possible to return to those stories and those days.

Alex Kan, the only person I could have trusted to translate my story and all of its colorful, moving pieces and parts for my three Russian releases. You have honored our incredible friends in the characters you conveyed.

◆ THANK YOU ◆

Carrie Paterson, I love that you publish and bring to life stories from around the world, and I am eternally grateful for your endless energy and passion in bringing mine to light.

Debby Klein, for your amazing friendship as well as all your hard work and hours making this book happen.

Jeffrey Thal, for being such a champion of my story.

And Thank You...

BORIS GREBENSHCHIKOV

MIKHAIL GORBACHEV

PAVEL PALAZHENKO

GEORGE AND LEA ITZHAK

SARA DONNELLY

LYUDA NOVOSADOVA

YURI KASPARYAN

ALOSHA IPATOVSTEV

BIG MISHA KUCHERENKO

SASHA LIPNITSKY

SEVA GAKKEL

NATASHA RAZLOGOVA

KOSTYA ERNST

FEDOR BONDARCHUK

GARIK SUKACHEV

ARTEM TROITSKY

RASHID NUGMANOV

AFRIKA BUGAEV

ANYA KAN

RICHARD BEST

CLAY FROHMAN

SHIRLEY HAHN

TOBEY COTSEN

MICHAEL J. LIBOW

JIM ARKEDIS

ANDREI FALALAYEV

MARK ROSENTHAL

IRINA KHLOPOVA

NATALYA SERGEEVA

GREENPEACE

AND MY FAVORITE HOTEL IN THE WORLD:

BELMOND GRAND HOTEL EUROPE, ST. PETERSBURG

◆ ALSO TO THE PHOTOGRAPHERS ◆

My sister Judy Fields and I took most of the photos in this book. Because there are a few unknown ones, I would like to acknowledge the following photographers that worked with me during my Russia days.

DMITRY KONRADT

NATASHA VASILIEVA-HULL

VALENTIN BARANOVSKY

ANDREI WILLY USOV

ANATOLY SIAGIN

GEORGY MOLITVAN

SERGEI BORISOV

LYUDA NOVOSADOVA

VICTOR TIKHOMIROV

ALEXANDER NEMENOV

MIKHAIL MAKARENKO

OLEG BELIKOV

ALEXANDER SHISHKIN

ELENA PEKINA

IGOR PETRUCHENKO

VALERY POTAPOV

VLADIMIR BYSTROV

ALEXANDER PETROV

LEONID SHARAPOV

OLEG ZOTOVA

VICTOR NEMTINOV

ANATOLY AZANOV

ALEXANDER ASTAFIEV

ANDREI PARSHUTKIN

IGOR MUNCHIN

MARIA INKOVA

◆ ETERNAL MEMORY ◆
to those who left our world too early
and whose life and work
enriched my years in Russia

VIKTOR TSOI
SERGEY KURYOKHIN
GEORGY "GUSTAV" GURYANOV
TIMUR NOVIKOV
SASHA VASILYEV
ANDREI KRISANOV
KOLYA VASIN
ALEXANDER BASHLACHEV
GRYSHA SOLOGUB
MARIANNA TSOI
MIKE NAUMENKO
ANDREY "DIUSHA" ROMANOV
MIKHAIL FEINSTEIN
SLAVA ZADERI
ALEXANDER AKSENOV "RIKOSHET"
SASHA KONDRASHKIN
ANDREY PANOV "SVINYA"
VLADISLAV MAMYSHEV "MONRO"
VLADIMIR LIPNITSKY
OLEG KOLOMEICHUK "GARIK ASSA"
ARKADY DRAGOMOSHCHENKO
IGOR CHUMECHKIN
SERGEY SAVELYEV
KSENIA SAVELIEVA-NOVIKOVA
IRINA GOSLITZ KASPARYAN
TAMARA VICTOROVNA FALALAYEVA
NINA VICTOROVNA PLANSON
LIZA KURYOKHIN
EGOR LETOV
PAUL DELPH
ANDY WARHOL
DAVID BOWIE

AND MY WONDERFUL MOTHER
JOAN NICHOLAS

■ Madison and Joanna Stingray, St. Basil's Cathedral in Red Square, Moscow, April 2019.

To listen to Joanna Stingray's songs written with her Russian friends, go to:

◆ JOANNASTINGRAY.COM ◆

Joanna's daughter, who goes by Stingray and co-wrote Joanna's memoirs is also a singer/songwriter and wrote a song inspired by 1980s Leningrad rock 'n roll called, "Granite Soul" as well as one for Viktor Tsoi called "Muse."

To hear these and others, go to:

◆ IAMSTINGRAY.COM ◆